Adair

History and Genealogy

Compiled, Edited
and Published

By

James Barnett Adair, M. D.
Los Angeles, U. S. A.
1924

Copyright 1924:

By

James Barnett Adair, M. D.

Printed by Boylan and Boylan, Los Angeles

Copyright 2025:

By

James Barnett Adair, M. D.

Published by TotalRecall Publications, Inc.
Friendswood Texas 77546

General John Adair
The Eight Governor of Kentucky

TABLE OF CONTENTS

Preface x
Chapter I 1
   Introductory 1
   Anglo-Saxon Invasion 2
   Beginning of the Modern English Period 4
Chapter II 5
   Galloway—The Cradle 5
   Geography 5
   Forts 7
   History 7
   Strath-Clyde 7
   Religion 7
   The Reformation 9
   Education 11
   Ownership of Land 11
Chapter III 12
   Armorial Bearings or Heraldry 12
   Adairs of Genoch 12
Chapter IV 13
   Antecedents of the Adairs 13
   The Founder of the Geraldine Family 15
   Foreword on Surnames in General 17
Chapter V 18
   Origin of the Adair Name 18
Chapter VI 20
   British Adairs, Main Line 20
   Sir Robert Adair 22
   British Adairs—First Branch Line 28
   Adairs of Queens County, Ireland 30
   British Adairs – Second Branch Line 31
Chapter VII 33
   Biography of British Adairs James Adair, Lawyer 33
   John Adair 34
   Rev. Patrick Adair 37
   Rev. Patrick Adair, Jr. 39
   Professor John Ruskin 40
   Doctor Robert Adair 43
   Sir Robert Adair The British Diplomat 44
Chapter VII A 46
Chapter VIII 47
   William Adair, The Pioneer 47
   23 *Irvine James Adair* 52
Chapter IX 57
   Alexander Adair 57
Chapter X 60
   Betsy and Mary Adair 60

Chapter XI 62
   Biography of General John Adair 62
   Govenor Adair's Monument at Frankfort 76
   Record Taken from Family Bible of John Adair and His Wife, Catherine Palmer Adair 77
Chapter XII 79
   Hon. John L. Bridges 79
Chapter XIII 83
   Mrs. Florida White 83
   "Florida White" 86
Chapter XIV 97
   Monroe Branch of the Adair Family 97
   John Adair Monroe 98
   Judge Thomas B. Monroe and Eliza P. Adair 98
   Jude Frank Adair Monroe 99
   Judge Frank Adair Monroe 101
   The Leovys 103
Chapter XV 115
   Adair-Hardin Genealogy. 115
Chapter XVI 118
   Col. Wm. Preston Anderson 118
Chapter XVII 119
   Major General James Patton Anderson 119
   General Anderson Genealogy 127
Chapter XVIII 129
   Genealogy of Bybee and Bulkley 129
Chapter XIX 131
   Butler P. Anderson 131
Chapter XX 137
   Genealogy of Isabella Mccalla Dair Pleasants 137
Chapter XXI 144
   Sketch of Mrs. Annetta Scott Fox 144
   Hon. Andrew Fuller Fox 144
Chapter XXII 147
   Doctor William Henry Moore Adair 147
   Robert Scott, M.D. 147
   William Henry Palmer Moore Adair, M.D. 148
Chapter XXIII 152
Chapter XXIV 153
   General John Adair of Astoria 153
Chapter XXV 160
   LINE B 160
   Thomas Adair, with his family 160
   Joseph Adair, Sr. 162
   Joseph Adair, Jr. 163
   John Adair 164
   19 Joseph Alexander Adair 167
Chapter XXVI 169

Genealogy of James Adair, Sr. 169
Chapter XXVII 182
    Sarah E. Adair 182
Chapter XXVIII 184
    Robert Presse Adair Of Clinton, South Carolina 184
Chapter XXIX 187
    Line B—The Weyman Adair Line 187
    First American Ancestor, Thomas Adair 187
Chapter XXX 196
    Doctor William W. Adair's Branch 196
    Descended from Benjamin Adair 196
Chapter XXXI 207
    Elisha Adair 207
    And His Genealogical Line 207
Chapter XXXII 212
    Hughston-Walker Genealogy and Walker Biography 212
Chapter XXXIII 217
    Genealogy of Charity Adair Little 217
Chapter XXXIV 231
    Jane Adair Holland 231
Chapter XXXV 234
    Col. George W. Adair of Atlanta 234
    Forrest Adair The Noted Financier 240
Chapter XXXVI 246
    Jones Adair 246
    Joseph Benjamin Adair 247
    James William Adair 249
    Patrick l. Adair 250
Chapter XXXVII 251
    Augustus Dixon Adair 251
Chapter XXXVIII 257
    Jane j. Adair-Mccord 257
    Genealogy of Louisa Mccord Mcmillan 258
    James Washington McCord 262
    Columbus Howard McCord 271
Chapter XXXIX 275
    James McCord Adair and His Descendants 275
    Julius Oscar Adair 279
    885. Minerva Cornelia Adair 283
    Doctor Robert Benjamin Adair of Atlanta 285
    Herbert Spencer Adair, D.D.S. 295
    892. Doctor Eugene Franklin Adair 298
Chapter XL 301
    S.C. Hays, M.D. 301
Chapter XLI 303
    Mrs. Dillard 303
    An Incident Showing the Heroism of a Heroine of the Revolution 303
Chapter XLII 306

    James Adair...306
    Line D..310
Chapter XLIII 310
    Hon. John Adair of Knoxville 310
    Honorable John Adair of Knoxville 323
Chapter XLIV: 328
    General Daviess Lafayette Adair 328
Chapter XLV..332
    Sir James Adair, Bart 332
Chapter XLVI 335
    George Bancroft Adair of Seattle...335
Chapter XLVII:..338
    Hings for Future Investigation 338
    George Ade 340
    Lineage of Mary Moore Adair 345
    Acknowledgment..346

LIST OF ILLUSTRATIONS

General John Adair *The Eight Governor of Kentucky* iii
Galloway Scotland Map 6
ARMS OF ADAIRS 12
Flixton Hall 14
Lord Waveney (Adair) as a Grand Master, Free Mason 25
Judge Irvine Adair, from Portrait. 50
Ms. Irvine Adair, from Portrait Painted 1824 51
William Arthur Adair 54
Mrs. Hattie Colmary Adair 55
Kate Adair, A Southern Beauty of Her day. 58
Mrs. Florida White, Noted for Brilliance and Beauty. --Courtesy of Mrs. Kate Adair Hines of Athens. Alabama 87
Hon. Frank Adair Monroe, Late Chief Justice of Supreme Court of Louisiana. 100
Major Gen. J. Patton Anderson 120
Mrs. Etta Adair Anderson, Wife of Gen. Anderson. 123
Miss Margaret B. Anderson 128
Butler P. Anderson, Yellow Fever Martyr. Courtesy of Mrs. Kate Adair Hines of Athens, Alabama 132
Doctor Wm. Washington Adair 195
Wm. Franklin and Wife of Dallas 203
Mrs. Emma Little Glenn. 228
Col. Geo. W. Adair, Father of Atlanta 233
Forrest Adair, Financier of Atlanta 238
Augustus Dixon Adair, Late Merchant Prince of Atlanta 252
Guyte P. McCord, Mayor of Tallahassee. 268
James McCord Adair 276
Doctor James Barnett Adair, age of 60. 291
Virginia Hare Adair and Capt. Herbert S. Adair. 293
Doctor Herbert S. Adair. 296
Unveiling of Monument of Knoxville 311

PREFACE

On the last day of December, 1914, the Editor was badly injured by being run down by an automobile driven wild by a reckless boy; he was badly injured and confined to bed for many weeks; when convalescence was advanced, the son of the editor (who was just out of his teens, now a prominent Dentist of Los Angeles,) asked his father to tell him all about hi kin and put it on paper. When the father undertook it he found that he knew but little to tell; so, he promised his son to ascertain the facts of the history for him. And began to write letters to persons supposed to know, for information; His cousin, A.D. Adair of Atlanta (the princely Merchant), answered with a copy of his Autobiography and tradition; and advised the following it up. Well, the Editor has been following the investigation ever since and the results are embraced in this book.

The sources of information embraced in these researches include all kinds of authentic history. Court House Records, marriages, deeds, and probate records, church records and military history, family bible records and tradition. And in Galloway Scotland, the land records were kept in Latin and embraced some sketches of their owners. In Great Britain the Peerages kept up the genealogy of the titled Adairs, but they do not take the trouble to start very far back.

Much of the history is meager and conflicting. Our task has been to collect this data, sift out the truth, correlate it and make a straight, harmonious story of it. We make no pretense of giving all the Adairs complete. In many families we found no member of the family that would answer a letter; and a few expressed themselves as indifferent. Most of the cities in America contain a few scattering Adairs, and we soon found it was useless to try to include them in the genealogy. We did include most of the principle families and made them as complete as available data would permit.

Integrity and Intelligence are common characteristics of the Adairs, and members of the family are universally proud of the name. They cherish a legitimate pride of pedigree and country.

The extraordinary stimulus given to researches in the genealogical field by the various patriotic societies is one of the happy signs of the times.

We hereby acknowledge our obligations to various cousins in the different Adair centers, for their assistance in collecting data, for without their assistance we could not have succeeded. We mention the following as among our valued assistants: Mr. W.W. Adair of Dallas, probably leads in enthusiasm; Rev. Charles Noble of Washington, D.C.; Mrs. Emma Little Glenn, of Spartanburg, S.C.; and Mrs. Margaret Adair Hay, of Clinton, S.C.; Mrs. Laura P. Barker of Portland, Ore.; Miss Annie Fall Monroe of Paris, Texas. Miss Margaret Bybee Anderson of Palatka, Fla., and Mrs. Kate Adair Hine, of Ala., have both furnished, not only important data, but valuable pictures of historic importance. Mrs. Annetta Scott Fox of West Point, Miss.; Mr. Harvey B. Broome, of Knoxville; Mrs. I.B. McFarland of Houston; Mr. James Franklin Adair, of Morgan Co., Ga.; Mr. J.A. Sarrett of Cairo, Ga., and Rev. J.D. McCord of Bartow, Ga.; Mrs. Helen Mary Hall of Portland, Indiana, and many others. These people have all worked for the love of the cause and none of them have received or expected any fee or favors. It is the same with the Editor. His work has been purely a labor of love, and if he realizes enough from the sale of copies to pay Printers for getting it out, he will feel gratified. This is the usual experience with publishing genealogies. They do not pay for three reasons. 1st, the sales are confined to the kin and therefore limited. 2nd, it is an expensive kind of printing. 3rd, such a large number are careless and do not buy copies, who ought to do so.

  A Genealogy is an index of the character and intelligence of the family it represents; our ancestors are reflected in their biographies; and the ideals and sentiments of living members are shown in the kind of Book they demand and support.

  We hope this Book will be found worthy of the honorable family it represents.

  We tender our thanks to the California Society Sons of the Revolution for courtesies.

  And especially to the Los Angeles Public Library, we tender our thanks for courtesies and service, and to Miss Clara M. Rowell of the Genealogical Department of the Library for numerous courtesies and advice.

CHAPTER I

INTRODUCTORY
A Brief History if the British Isles,
Their Early Inhabitants and Language.

The British Islands were formerly a Peninsula attached to the Continent of Europe, and the earth movements which opened the English Channel, and thus made Islands of it, took place long after the Human-period i.e. after the advent of man on the earth.

Archaeology teaches that the cave man existed on these islands before the English Channel was made, and before the art of navigation was understood; which accounts for the appearance of man as early here as on the Continent.

When the great Celtic Aryan race invaded Europe from the heart of Asia, they carried their settlements clear through Europe and into Britain, the art of navigation having been discovered or acquired by them.

It is probable that these Celts had been preceded by at least two previous races of man on these islands, before the historic period.

The historic period begins about 60 years B.C. when Julius Ceasar invaded Britain with a Roman Army.

The Romans found these islands inhabited by the Celtic race, the same as inhabited France, Belgium and other western European countries; and the Romans called these people Galli; and they called these islands Britannica.

The Celts were the earliest Aryan settlers in Europe, according to common theory. They appear to have been driven westward by succeeding waves of Teutons, Slavonians and others.

Herodotus mentions them as mixing with the Iberians who dwelt around the river Ebo in Spain.

They appear to have reached the zenith of their power about the 3d and 2d centuries B.C. Some tribes of them settled in Asia Minor to which the name Galatia was given. They finally went down before the power of Rome.

At an early date the Celts divided into great branches speaking dialects widely differing from each other but belonging to the same stock.

One of these branches was the Gadhelic or Gaelic, represented by the Hylanders of Scotland, the Celtic Irish and Manx; the other was the Cymric, represented by the Welsh, inhabitants of Cornwall and those of Brittany.

The Sun seems to have been the principal object of worship among the Celts. Their Temples of worship were composed of a remarkable circle of stones called a Druidical circle, was located in a grove of Oaks.

The worship of the Sun seems to be a more sensible religion than that of any of the savage races.

Many of the early Celts had black hair, remnants of these persisted and were absorbed into the succeeding races. The succeeding race was another branch of the Celtic race who were mostly blonds, Gaelic Celts. These were the foundation stock of the British People.

As stated above, the historic period began with the invasion of Britain by the Roman army under the personal command of Julius Caesar. And Britain became a part of the Roman Empire and so remained for five hundred years.

Rome trained the militia, built forts, military roads and bridges and taught the people a civilized language, Latin.

Notwithstanding the long control of the British Islands by Rome, five hundred years, the greater part of Scotland was never conquered, nor brought into the Roman Empire. And in order to prevent the barbarous tribes of northern Scotland from over running this part of the Roman Empire, the Romans built a great wall across Scotland from the Firth of Forth on the east to the Solway on the west, after the manner of China. This first wall was built of turf and was a failure, so they constructed a new one a few years later and used stone this time as a building material, and much of the wall is still standing after 2000 years. This second wall was located far enough north to take into the whole Province of Galloway. The object of this wall was to prevent the invasion of the more civilized country by the barbarous tribes of the north and save the expense of a military establishment for defense.

ANGLO-SAXON INVASION

We have been taught that the Germans, under the name of Anglo-Saxons, had considerable to do in conquering, civilizing and grading up the early Britains, and the early language was called the Anglo-Saxon language. The Roman writers have caused this and much confusion by the erroneous and indiscriminate use of the Saxon name; these writers confused the nationality of these pirates and invaders; they thought them German, and subsequent historians have followed their dictum without investigation for these fifteen hundred years.

But late investigation proves that the so-called Angles and Saxons were really Scandinavian; they hailed from the Scandinavian countries and some of the smaller Baltic states but few were German.

(See Bosworth. Also McKerlie in History of Galloway Lands and Their Owners. Shore's History of the Origin of the Anglo-Saxon Race and Language.)

We quote from the last-named author as follows:

"One of the conclusions to which the evidence that has been brought forward leads us is that the old English, or Anglo-Saxon race was formed on English soil out of many tribal elements, and that the settlers who came here were known among themselves by tribal names, many of which still survive in those of some of the oldest settlements, where they lived under customary family and kindred law.

Under the general names Jutes, Angles, Saxons, Danes and Northmen came numerous allies. It appears certain that Frisians of various tribes were, in regard to numbers, as important as any settlers; and that they came among the Angles as well as the Jutes and Saxons. Under the Saxon name there can be very little doubt that colonists were settled on the east coast of England before the withdrawal of the Romans.

In reference to Danes and other Scandinavians it appears from the evidence adduced that they brought with them many allies from various countries on the Baltic Coast on which they had previously formed settlements, or which they had brought under subjection.

The old English race grew by the absorption into it of tribal people descended from various ancient races. It assimilated to a great extent their dialects and the Old English as it prevailed in various parts of England, was formed by this process.

No example of an Anglo=Saxon language has ever been found outside of Britain itself. It arose here, like the race itself, by the blending of tribal dialects, of which those of northern or Scandinavian origin are important.

In the Old English speech, as it has come down to us, there are as many as ten words, more or less synonymous, for the word man, and as many for woman. The language abounds in synonymous words, thus showing a commingling of elements from many sources. Its obscure etymology, its confused and imperfect inflections, and its anomalous and irregular syntax point to the same conclusion and indicate a diversity of origin.

It is probably largely owing to this absorption within itself of people of other descent that the race owes much of its vigor. In all ages of the world and in all countries, it is and has been the ablest and strongest of a tribe or nation that has been selected by natural circumstances or political considerations for conquest and colonization. Those who have gone to the wars, or have been successful colonists, have been among the ablest of the race."

Thus, we have given a brief abstract of the conclusions of Shores in his history of the English race during that formative period called the Old English or Anglo-Saxon period, which lasted about six hundred years, i.e. from the withdrawal of the Romans to the Norman conquest.

BEGINNING OF THE MODERN ENGLISH PERIOD

In the year 1060 William the Conqueror from Normandy, in France, invaded Britain with an Army and conquered it and ruled it; modified the language, the laws, customs and civilization.

Surnames were not in use before this period, and it took several centuries for the use of surnames to become general.

On the existing English elements, the "Anglo-Norman Gentlemen" now poured in. This last accession was for all of the upper classes. With their introduction the racial element became complete, and as such practically persists to the present day.

The Normans tried to establish the French language but the result of the admixture with the Old English was the modern English. The evolution of the modern English language was a slow and gradual process. It has been a complete language for less than 800 years, but it now requires a larger Dictionary to define it than any other language, and more educated people use it than any other; there are over 200,000,000 people using it and the language is still growing.

We are all proud of our race as well as our language.

CHAPTER II
GALLOWAY—THE CRADLE

In as much as Galloway was the cradle of the ADAIR Family for the first two hundred and fifty years, we deem it proper to review the geography and history of this province in this introduction:

GEOGRAPHY

The ancient province of Galloway occupies the peninsula in the southwest corner of Scotland. It is bounded on the south by Solway Firth; on the west by Saint Patrick's Channel; on the north by the old Roman Wall or Rampart; and on the east by the river Nith. The old Roman rampart separates Galloway from Ayshire. It embraces a little over two modern counties, (or Shires as they are called in Scotland) to wit: Wigtonshire, Kirkcudbrightshire, and the part of Dumfrieshire west of the river Nith. It is 35 to 40 miles from north to south, and 50 miles from east to west; and contains less than 900,000 acres. The rivers beside the Nith are the Cree, the Bladenoch, the Luce, the Ken and the Dee. The northern portion of Kirkcudbrightshire is mountainous, the hills ranging from 1142 feet to 2764 feet high. This being mainly a grazing region, while the southern and western parts are agricultural. The land was formerly covered with a dense forest.

The harbors are Stranraer, Wigton, Garlieston, Port Patrick, Isle of Whithorn, Dromore and Port Williams; Loch Ryan is the only land locked saltwater harbor. Kirkcudbright, (named for Saint Cuthbert) is the only one to the east.

The old Religious Houses were the Abbeys of Glenluce, Saulseat, Wigton, and the Priory of Whithorn; while the remains of ancient Chappells still stand or can be traced; of the latter the most ancient and interesting is at Cruggleton near Garlieston, a portion of which still exists, it was built when the Irish-Scottish Church was in existence, the Church of Iona, and of the same denomination represented by Saint Ninian and Saint Patrick.

In Kirkcudbrightshire are also remains of the religious establishments which existed before the Reformation, viz; Dundrennan, Tungland, Balmacross, New Abbey, Lincluden; also, the Priory of St. Mary's Isle. Also, the remains or sites of various small Chappells can still be seen or traced.

Galloway Scotland Map

FORTS

One of the features in Galloway, from which more or less is to be learned, are the circular earthworks or forts, with ramparts and ditches. They are on the tops of hills and are numerous.

HISTORY

GALLOWAY means mixed or hybrid race.

Practically the same races who peopled Great Britain also peopled Galloway; for most of these races were connected more or less with the history of Galloway.

There are three distinct races to be dealt with:

1st, the Aborigines of whom nothing is known.

2d, the Goidels or Gaels who were the first Celtic invaders.

3d, the Cymri or Brythons, who followed.

The first or Aborigines were called Picts because they painted and tattooed their skins. They inhabited both England and Scotland and their history or any knowledge of them is shrouded in darkness, and may be treated as prehistoric.

Tacitus relates that what sort of men did at first inhabit Great Britian, whether bred and born in that land or whether they came thither from foreign parts, among such barbarous people, could not be discovered.

STRATH-CLYDE

Strath-Cldye as a kingdom had its own Kings from CAW, A.D. 520, to EOCHAID the BALD in 1018; and Galloway formed part, as it is to be expected from its Geographic position.

Its population then was largely composed of Irish Scots, who had been crossing the channel during the whole existence of Strath-Clyde as a Kingdom. The Kingdom of Strath-Clyde is now little heard of, and therefore known to few, but it is believed to have been the first constituted kingdom within the present limits of Scotland after the departure of the Romans.

RELIGION

The religion of the Aborigines of the British Isles was that of Druidism or worshippers of the SUN. The druids were priests or philosophers among the Cymri (Celts); but among the Gaels the name generally applied to a magician.

In Christian times it was about A.D. 397, (when Rome was relaxing her grip on Britain,) that the celebrated NINIAN was at Whithorn to preach Christianity to the inhabitants of Valentia, which under Roman rule was so named, and comprised the lowlands of Scotland and Northumberland. Saint NINIAN devoted his life to Missionary and Scholastic work, and was called the Apostle of Scotland, as Saint PATRICK was called the Apostle of Ireland.

Ninian was of the Cymric race and had traveled as far as Rome. Patrick, who went to Ireland, is now generally allowed to have been also of the Cymric race. He was, however, a Strath-Clyde Britain. It is mentioned that his father was a deacon and his grandfather a priest. It is believed that St. Patrick converted Ireland from heathenism to Christianity, (however there is some dispute about this.)

St Columba was a native of Ulster, Ireland, and devoted his life work to preaching in Scotland.

St. Ninian, as already mentioned, was the first Churchman of any note in Scotland, who, although a native of Galloway and of the Cymric race, was educated in Rome. He died A.D. 432.

The greatest of St. Ninian's works was not the little Church built of stone, but the Conventual establishment. Here a Seminary known variously as Candida Casa, Magnum Monasterium, Futerna. The House of Martin, Alba and Rosnot; attracted youths of high birth from far and beyond the bounds of the province; and during the following two centuries it was the resort of those leaders of thought, of almost of European reputation, known as "Secondary Saints."

St. Patrick, a brief account of whom we have already given, is understood to have visited Gaul and Italy before his mission to Ireland.

These first churches were of the Ionian type of Christian Churches and flourished for five hundred years.

It was during the reign of King Malcolm III of Scotland, who died A.D. 1093, the ruin of this Irish Scottish Church was commenced by Margaret, his Queen. It was by royal decree that the Roman Catholic Church superseded the Ionian, Irish-Scotch Church. This Ionian Church was monastic, but did not acknowledge the Pope.

Galloway was badly priest-ridden, and Church-ridden after the advent of the Roman Catholic Church. But Galloway always suffered to a great extent from this cause. With the advent of the Church of Rome, abbeys, priories, churches and chapels were erected everywhere, until the district became studded with them. The church ruled. In addition to their clerical duties, the clergy became the best agriculturists of the time and were also found as commercial men of much note. The profession of arms, or at all events the assuming command of armies, was another characteristic. As truly said by McKenzie in his "History of Galloway," "The Clergy were the great depositories of learning; without being very profound, but with few exceptions they could read and write. Latin was understood by most of them. Among the Monks and Secular Clergy there were some of the most skillful mechanics. In fact, Churchmen, or rather the clergy did everything; and believed to possess the keys of entrance to the next world; brave men as well as weak ones trembled under the rebuke of the Church.

This power was made use of not for good purpose for others, for prior to the Reformation, the Church of Rome held one-third of the land with the best soil in Scotland.

THE REFORMATION

The collapse of the Church of Rome need not be entered on here.

After the collapse of the Roman Catholic Church in Britain, two other Churches sprang up in its stead. The Anglican or Episcopal Church in England and the Presbyterian Church in Scotland.

The Presbyterians were in the majority in Scotland, but the Sovereign Government of Great Britain undertook to force uniformity in Churches by requiring the Presbyterians to accept the liturgy and prelacy of the Episcopal Church, and there was cruel persecution in consequence.

On the other hand, when the Presbyterians had their way with the Government they were cruel and intolerant; they advocated murder of prisoners of war and indulged in the past-time of burning witches.

From the earlies times within the range of history, Galloway was essentially an ecclesiastic district; ruled by one after another until we come to the seventeenth century, with the cruel persecutions and misery that attended it.

The stern attitude which Galloway held had much to do with the Presbyterian being at last acknowledged and settled by law in Scotland.

The Presbyterians and Episcopalians were intolerant of each other and both sides became very bitter.

Prompted by the Episcopalians, the High Commission Court, the creation of which was one of King CHARLES' mistakes, was established by warrant, given at our honor of Hampton Court 21st of Oct. 1634.

Its powers were very wide, and were as follows: "To call before them or any seven of them, at whatever time or place they shall please to appoint, all that are scandalous in life, doctrine, or religion; resetters of Seminary priests, hearers of mass, adulterers, contemners of Church discipline, blasphemers, cursers or swearers." The composition of the court was, from the first, too clerical; Episcopalians being in power, Presbyterians might easily be made amenable to the charge of being contemners of Church discipline.

And so early was this bias shown, that soon after, we find Lords Galloway and Kirkcudbright declining to mix up with such arbitrary proceedings. But their abstention had the effect of giving the bishop and the clergy at his back their own way; which meant, that all avowed Presbyterians were liable to be dragged before the court and dealt with as recusants.

This Court could and did convict for religious or political opinion; without evidence or with flimsy evidence; and penalties ranged from death to banishment. The records who many cases of such outrageous proceedings. Some of the Adairs were heavily fined for not having their children baptized in the Episcopal Church, they being Presbyterians.

The unexpected result of the Hight Commission was to swell the ranks of the Solemn League and Covenant by scores of men otherwise of moderate opinions.

This LEAGUE was composed of men taking an oath to stick together in opposition to the prelacy of the Episcopalians, and it led to civil war, especially in Ulster, Ireland.

By and by the Presbyterians gained control of the Governmental policy and they were just as bitter and intolerant.

Before dismissing the Religious history of Galloway, we will relate an amusing incident which occurred in the General Assembly of the Presbyterians about 1949. In this my Lords Cassalis and Argyle sat as lay elders. One Mr. Naysmith argued much that the "haill teinds" should be recovered to the Church. Cassalis, who had the lion's share of the great tithes of Galloway, did not at all relish the proposal, and he and Argyle tried to put it down with a high hand as a proposition "Much scandalizing the profession and their often promises." Mr. Naysmith was irrepressible, affirming "That the whole were the actual property of the Church, and that by Divine Law." To this Cassalis retorted, "The more ye get the worse contended ye are, but in this ye have neither Divinity under the gospel for the same, nor reason nor any point of human law." To this Argyle added, "the Church has already the tenth of all the rent on the land, and yet it seems they are no content. They are not the thirtieth part of the inhabitants, I may say not the hundredth part. It is not good to awaken sleeping dogs."

The Moderator getting alarmed, as Cassalis and Argyle were great pillars of the Church interposed. "Our brother, Mr. Naysmith, spoke more nor he was aware of, and he admired he was so impertinent, and therefore willed him to be quyet." Naysmith, notwithstanding, had the last word, interjecting that "he only spoke out that which many of his profession thought." Upon this, "some lay Elders that were Barons desired him to deny that, otherwise they would make the sword decide that question, and let him and such covetous persons see the teinds were not under the Gospel, juris divini, but juris humani."

(Balfour III, 417. Sir James Balfore here writes as an eyewitness.)

Besides being amusing, the above shows a sample of the early language.

EDUCATION

In 1636, KING CHARLES II summoned a Parliament to meet in Edinburgh.

The most memorable act of this Parliament was the ratification of the Statute of 1616 for the establishment of Schools, decreeing the erection of schools in every parish, the basis of a system which long proved a boon to Scotland.

The first school of any note was established by St. Ninian just before the departure of the Romans from Galloway.

The diffusion of knowledge began with the introduction of printing early in the sixteenth century. It was in 1494 that a law was enacted for the compulsory education of the eldest son.

OWNERSHIP OF LAND

Prior to the eleventh century, Galloway lived under the patriarchal system of land titles, i.e. absolute free titles. But after the eleventh century the feudal system was introduced with the incoming of foreigners from England. Under this, charters were granted subject to a superior, generally the Crown, Church or some newly exalted individual, such as the Lords of Galloway. The Superior had great power over the owner, if desirous of exercising it. It worked great hardships on the owners in many cases.

The ownership of land was confined to the NOBILITY.

CHAPTER III
ARMORIAL BEARINGS OR HERALDRY

From ANCIENT Armorial Bearings much that is historical can be gathered.

HERALDRY is the Short=Hand of history. In its figures, properly interpreted, we read the Chronicles of Centuries.

ARMS OF ADAIRS

ADAIRS of Kinhilt and Lord Waveny.

ARMS—Perbend, or an Argent, three dexter hands couped and erect. Gules, quartering Shafto.

Crest—A man's head affronte, couped at the neck and distilling drops of blood.

Motto—Loyal a la Mort (Faithful Unto Death).

Manibus Victoria Dextris.

ADAIRS OF GENOCH
And Adair of Loughanmore
Have mottos as follows: Arte et Marte. Fortitudine.

CHAPTER IV
ANTECEDENTS OF THE ADAIRS

The ADAIRS sprung from the Noble House of FITZ-GER-ALD, Anglo-Norman Viceroys of Ireland, and Earls of Desmond and of Kildare in Ireland. The Fitz-Geralds trace their lineage back to the Dukes of Tuscany, and the Tuscans claim their origin in the plains of Troy.

We know nothing beyond the Trojans. But according to these claims, we trace the ancestry of our Antecedents back to sometime in the ninth century.

One of the Dukes of Tuscany migrated to Normandy in France and Settled. By and by when Prince William was making up his army of invasion these Tuscans took a prominent part. After the Conquest of Britain in 1060 A.D. these Tuscans were honored by the King with Cabinet positions and other prominent places. About a century later or about three generations, they were sent to Ireland by King Henry, the 2d.

The following Allegory fairly describes this illustrious family.

"In the land of Hetruria there flourished once a mighty vine thither translated from the desolated plains of Troy. Florence claimed his beauteous plant her own; and well might she glory in it, for its branches stretched forth unto the sea, and its boughs unto the river. From the banks of the Arno and the shores of the blue Tyrrhene Sea the branches of that great tree extend themselves to the far-off land of Erin.

That tree was the noble race of the Geraldines, who, under the shadow of the Tuscan banners, penetrated regions whither Roman legions never dared to venture."

The history of this Florentine family has been my special study; for it is intimately associated with that of my religion and country; and proudly does it cherish the memory of the Geraldines."

So wrote Father Dominic O'Daley to their Eminences Anthony and Francis Barberini, Cardinals of the Holy Roman Church. To them he dedicated his history of the Geraldines.

When did the Geraldines come to England? When did they settle in Ireland? Father O'Daley was perfectly clear in his answers to both questions: They came to England with WILLIAM at the Conquest; and they went to Ireland under Henry II. He had moreover a dim conception of the true facts of the case. He said that WILLIAM gave them the Castle and the Lordship of Windsor.

Flixton Hall

Florence has produced more celebrated men than any other place in Italy, or, perhaps in Europe.

Lineage of the Geraldines from Normans of the King's Official Household.

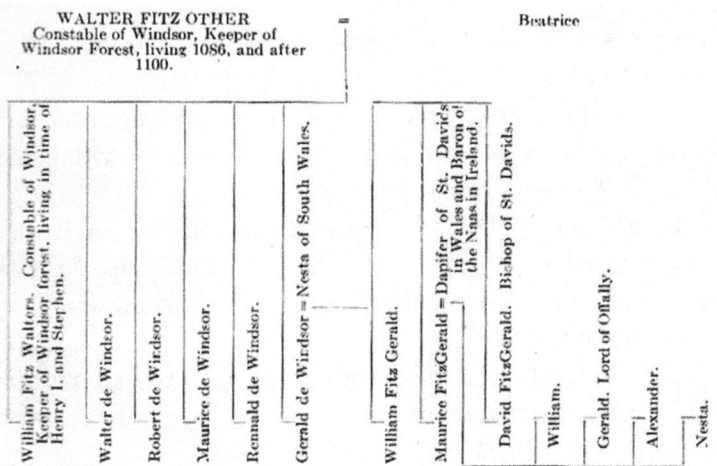

THE FOUNDER OF THE GERALDINE FAMILY

MAURICE FITZ-GERALD, the founder of the house of Geraldine, came to Ireland with Robert Fitz-Stephen, and other Anglo-Norman Chiefs in 1169, and assisted STRONGBOW in the reduction of Ireland.

He is thus described by Cambrensis and Holingshead:

"A man he was, both honest and wise; and as for truth and valor, very noble and famous, a man of his word, of constant mind, and a certain bashfulness, well colored, and of good countenance, of middle stature, and compact at all points; courteous, gentle, and moderate; a patron of sobriety and good behavior; a man of few words; his speeches more full of wit and reason than of words; more wisdom he had than of eloquence; in martial affairs bold, stout and valiant, and yet not hasty to run headlong into any venture, but when an attempt was once taken in hand, he would pursue and follow the same."

He was appointed Chief Governor of Ireland, A.D. 1173, by HENRY II, and he and his descendants got large grants of lands in Leinster and Munster, chiefly in the counties of Kildare, Wicklow, Wexford, Cork, Kerry. He died in 1177 and was buried in the Abbey of Grey Friars at Wexford. From him descended the Noble family of FITZGERALDS, one of the most distinguished in Ireland.

A branch of them were Earls of Desmond, down to the reign of

Elizabeth; and had immense possessions in the Counties of Cork and Kerry.

Another branch became Barons of OFFALY, Earls of Kildare and Dukes of Leinster.

There have been so many other eminent families of the name in Ireland.

The Earls of Desmond and Kildare were frequently Lords Deputy and Chief Governors of Ireland.

The Noble FitzGeralds frequently joined the Irish against the English Government; hence they were charged by English writers with being more Irish than the Irish themselves.

The territory of Desmond, (the word signifies in Irish, south Munster,) embraced a vast area, including the whole part of the present county of Cork, the greater part of Kerry, a part of Waterford, and small parts of Tipperary and Limerick.

These Earls had vast numbers of vassals under them as peasants and laborers, mostly trained to military service, so that they were a power in the land, with whom even the King mush reckon.

The following is the Genealogy of these Earls:

1st. Maurice FitzGerald, the founder of the family. (Died 1177.)

2nd. Thomas Fitzmaurice FitzGerald, a younger son.

3rd. John Fitzthomas FitzGerald.

4th. Maurice Fitzjohn FitzGerald.

5th. Thomas Fitzmaurice FitzGerald, Court of Appeals Justice of Ireland in 1295. His wife was Margaret the King's cousin. He died in 1298.

The following were some of the Earls of Desmond:

1st. Maurice Fitzthomas FitzGerald, first Earl of Desmond, Justiciar of Ireland, and Viceroy of Ireland during the last year of his life. (Succeeding Rokesky) died in 1336.

Maurice's father died while Maurice was still a child, and left his vast estates in Munster, second only to those of the DeBurghs, among the Anglo-Irish Nobility, to be protected by royal nominees.

In 1329 Maurice was created first Earl of Desmond, and received a grant of the Couny Palatine of Kerry, with royal liberties therein to be held of the English crown.

At the same time, he received the grant of the advowson of Dungarvan.

Desmond was married three times. His first wife was Catherine DeBurgh; she was the mother of Maurice and John the 2d and 3d Earls of Desmond, respectively. She died in 1331. His second wife was Evelina, daughter of the Lord of Kerry. She was the mother of Gerald FitzGerald, the 4th Earl of Desmond, called Gerald the poet. His third wife was Margaret O'Brien, daughter of the Prince of Thomond.

(No issue is mentioned.)

Gerald FitzGerald was the 4th Earl of Desmond, and Justiciar of Ireland. He was a son of the 1st Earl by his second wife, Evelina. He had several wars with neighboring tribes, but the Irish Analists are enthusiastic in his praise as a man of peace. The Four Masters describe him as a cheerful and courteous man, who excelled all the English and many of the Irish in the knowledge of the Irish language, poetry and history.

He was a man of culture and refinement, wrote poetry and was called Gerald the Poet. (Some of his verses survived, which is evidence of merit.) His wife was Elinor Butler, daughter of James Butler, Earl of Ormond. She is described as a beautiful and charitable woman, (died 1395.)

They had several sons; the eldest son John, the 5th Earl of Desmond, according to the ordinary reckoning, was drowned in a river a few months after his father's death. The next son Maurice, died without male issue, 1410.

Thomas, the 6th Earl of Desmond was the son of John the 5th Earl; but James, the O'Brien foster-son, usurped the Earldom from Thomas.

(References: Irish Annals by the "Four Masters." Dictionary of National Biography.)

FOREWORD ON SURNAMES IN GENERAL

Names did not become hereditary until about the end of the first thousand years of the Christian era.

The use of fixed surnames arose in France about the year one thousand; came to England about sixty years later with the Norman Conquest, and reached Scotland about eleven hundred A.D.

During the 11th and 12th centuries hereditary names were uncommon. A man's familiors designated him by allusion to some personal peculiarities, or occupation, rather than the name of his father.

It was not until the 14th and 15th centuries that the masses of people assumed the dignity of surnames as such.

CHAPTER V

ORIGIN OF THE ADAIR NAME

ADAIR was a place name in the County of Limerick in Ireland. It is derived from the Celtic and Gaelic, Ath a ford, and Dair, or Dara, the Oak tree; so, it literally means the FORD of the OAK tree and is Anglicised ADAIR.

Dair (dar) the common Irish word for oak, is found in many of the Indo-European languages.

Adare in the County of Limerick in Ireland was always called in Irish documents, Ath-dara; the ford of the Oak tree; a name which shows that a great Oak must have for many generations shaded the ford which in ancient times crossed the Maigue River.

(See Irish Place Names by Joice)

At one time this town of Athdara became an important place with its Abbeys, Churches and Castles; but now mostly in ruins; and at present a local railroad station.

Henry Harrison, in his "Dictionary of Surnames of the United Kingdon" defines the name thus –"Adair, a dweller at the Ford of the Oaks."

Mark Anthony Lower, in Patronimic Britannica, A Dictionary of Family names of the United Kingdom, thus defines the name—Adair: A branch of the Great Anglo-Hibernian Family of FitzGeralds, settled at Adare in County Limerick, and thus acquired the local surname.

In the XIV century Robert FitzGerald de Adair in consequence of family feuds, removed to Galloway, Scotland, and dropping his patronimical designation, wrote himself ADAIR.

In the time of King Charles I, the senior branch of the family transferred themselves to County Antrim, Ireland.

There are several versions of a tradition in different branches of the Adair family, attempting to explain the origin of the family and name. The facts of the origin, we have just quoted from the best authorities, but the circumstances and details of the origin, we have to cull and sift out from traditions, i.e., oral history handed down by word of mouth from parents to children, which thereby suffers variations and admixture of fiction. Tradition contains an element of truth mixed with fiction and differs from authentic history in degree only, as it, i.e., authentic history is part truth embellished with fiction by the author, or compiler.

The most plausible tradition we have seen is contained in a book on the "Derivation of Names," by the Rev. Wm. Arthur, the father of our late

President, Gen. Chester A. Arthur.

It runs as follows: "Thomas, the 6th Earl of Desmond, while on a hunting excursion, was benighted and lost his way, between Farlee and Newcastle, in the county of Limerick in Ireland, where he was hospitably received and entertained, by one William McCormick, whose daughter, Catherine, he subsequently married. At this alliance his family and clan took umbrage. Resigning his title and estate to his younger brother, (history says his Uncle James, the O'Brien foster son usurped the title and estate,) he fled to France, in 1418, and died of grief at Ruen two years afterwards. The King of England attended his funeral.

"He had issue, Maurice and John. Robert, the son of Maurice returned to Ireland with the hope of regaining the title and estate of Thomas, his grandfather. He slew Gerald, the White Knight in single combat, at Athdara, (the ford of the Oaks,) hence he received the name Anglicised Adair. He embarked for Scotland, where he married Arabella Campbell, daughter of the Lord of Argyle."

Now let us analyze this tradition and determine what is truth and what is fiction in it.

1st. Robert was a FitzGerald. As all the traditions, and all the authorities agree on that.

2nd. Robert was not a grandson of Thomas, the 6th Earl of Desmond. He, the 6th Earl's grandson, was born a hundred years too late for that; it was 1418 that Thomas, the 6th Earl married, resigned and went to France; and it must have been 1450 or 60, that his grandson was born, and could not have been a mature man before 1475 or 80. Now Robert Adair was married and settled in Galloway, Scotland, about 1388, and had grown sons in 1426. (See "History of the Lands and Their Owners in Galloway," by McKerlie.)

All that we know is that Robert was a younger son.

3rd. Robert fought a duel with a kinsman at Athdara, according to the authorities, and slew his antagonist according to Heraldry; The Adair Coat of Arms proves it, (see another chapter on Armor.)

The Adair Coat of Arms has for its crest, a man's head, couped and distilling drops of blood. It supports the claim that Adair was the victor. It was on account of this duel and feud that Robert migrated to Scotland. This was during the eighties of the XIV century.

4th. The circumstances corroborate Robert Adair's marriage to a daughter of the noble house of Argyle; Arabella the bride, is an Argyle name, and so is Neigello, his oldest son's name.

CHAPTER VI

BRITISH ADAIRS, MAIN LINE

Robert Adair, the first of the name, and founder of the family was a scion, or younger son of the Noble House of Desmond and Kildare in Ireland. According to tradition, (which is mainly confirmed by history and heraldry,) he fought a duel with the White Knight at the town of Adair, which was located on the Desmond Estate, in Limerick Country, Ireland. Robert slew his antagonist in single combat; he then sailed for Scotland under the name of Robert FitzGerald de Adair; but after landing in Galloway, he discarded his patronymic designation and wrote himself ADAIR. Robert Adair married a daughter of the most noble house in Scotland, to wit: the House of Argyle. This was during the eighties of the XIV century.

1. ROBERT ADAIR = ARABELLA CAMPBELL

Progeny

2.   I   Niegello, Who settled in Portre
3.   II Robert, settled in Kildonen.

Niegello Adair signed as witness, a document for the Hereditary Sheriff of Galloway in 1426, being a mature man.

NIEGELLO ADAIR = (Wife's Name Not Stated)

Progeny

4.   I   William
5.   II Thomas

And Others.

William, Neigel or (Niegello,) Robert.

William Adair was born about 1418, married Miss Vans, daughter of Robert Vans of Barnberoch.

William Adair = Miss Vans

Progeny

6.   I   Alexander.
7.   II   Name not known. He became a Bishop.
8.   III Madena,
       IV And Two other Daughters

Many marvelous legends are told of the miraculous things and doings of the Bishop and his sisters.

Alexander (William, Niegel, Robert Adair,) was born about 1445. Married Miss Euphemia Stewart, one of the many daughters of Sir Alexander Stewart of Garlies.

BRITISH ADAIRS

(6) Alexander Adair = Euphemia Stewart
Progeny

9.   I   Ninian. And others.

Ninian Adair, (Alexander, William, Niegel, Robert Adair,) was born 1470, and was married to Miss Katherine Agnew, daughter of Sir Patrick Agnew, Hereditary Sherriff of Galloway.

Ninian Adair = Katherine Agnew
Progeny

10.   I   William

And others.

William Adair was born about 1500, (Ninian, Alexander, William, Neigel, Robert Adair,). He married Miss Helen Kennedy, daughter of Gilbert Kennedy, second Earl of Cassalis, and nineth in lineal descent from Robert Bruce, King of Scotland.

William Adair = Helen Kennedy
Progeny

11.   I   Ninian.
12.   II   John, married his cousin, Christine Adair.

Ninian Adair, born 1531, died 1608. (William, Ninian, Alexander, William, Neigel, Robert Adair.).

Ninian Adair's Seat was Kinhilt, as it had been for many generations before. He married Elizabeth, daughter of Sir James Gordan of Lochinvah.

Ninian Adair = Elizabeth Gordan
Progeny

They are stated to have had a large family and a prosperous one. We only find the following.

13.   I   William, his heir.
14.   II   Patrick, who appears in the record as Patricio Adair Fratri Willielmo Adair de Kinhilt. He had a charter to the lands of Altoune in 1614.
15.   III   John, who married Christine Dunbar, one of the heirs portioners of Loch. He acquired the lands of Mary port.
16.   IV   Alexander, acquired the lands of Corgie and married one of the Stewarts of Garlies.
17.   V   Archibald, b. 158-, d. 1647, was a bishop of the Episcopal Church, and married one of the McDowells of Garthland.
18.   VI   Gilbert, had the lands of Cardryne.

William Adair was born 1565. Seats Kinhilt in Galloway and Bellamena, Antrim Co., Ireland. Lineage: (Ninian, William, Ninian, Alexander, William, Niegel, Robert Adair.) He was married three times.

William Adair = Rosena McLelland of Gelston, Mother of
19. Sir Robert Adair, his heir.
= 2d. Miss Houston, daughter of Houston
20. Rev. John Adair, of Genoch.
=3d. Miss Cathcart, daughter of Cathcart of Carlston. She was the mother of
21. Rev. William Adair of Ayr. And one daughter, Anna, married Thomas Kennedy.

SIR ROBERT ADAIR

19. Robert Adair was Knighted by King Charles I, which gave him the title of "Sir." He was well balanced mentally and physically, and he took a prominent part in public affairs.

Civil War in Ireland and the Causes which Led to it

During the reigns of Queen Mary and Elizabeth, the Civil History of Ireland presents a succession of rebellions and ferocious internal feuds. Exhaustion brought peace. And King James I took advantage of the desolation in Ulster to introduce Scotch settlers. These settlers were strongly opposed to prelacy and formed a basis for the Presbyterian Church in Ireland.

King Charles I, tried to ruinous policy of using Ireland as a power against his parliament. The Protestants were systematically disarmed, and the frightful outbreak of 1641 was the result. The Parliament sent Scotch troops to Carrickfurgus, attended by Chaplains; and among them, in 1642, was organized the first Presbytery of the Presbyterian Church in Ireland.

It was this movement of Scotch settlers then of Scotch troops into Ireland, that brought Adairs among the others into Ireland. Sir Robert Adair was a Colonel; then he was elected to the Scotch Parliament in 1638. Before this Parliament adjourned, they appointed a committee to act for them in vacation, or when not sitting. This committee was called the committee on governing the Kingdon, and Col. Sir Robert Adair was a member of that committee.

In 1647 Col. Sir Robert Adair was elected a member of the Scotch Parliament again and served almost continuously for four years. He was one of the Barons who rode to the Capitol at Edinburgh from the west on horseback; an anti-type of Gen. John Adair, Governor of Kentucky, when he rode to Washington.

Sir Robert Adair was born 1583, died 1655.

Sir Robert Adair's seats were Kinhilt in Galloway, Scotland, and Ballamene, in Antrim Co., Ireland. He married Jean Edmondstone, daughter of Sir William Edmondstone, of Duntrieth; a lineal descendent of William the Conqueror, King of England.

Sir Robert Adair took a leading part in all public questions of his time; and was an exemplary man and citizen.

Lineage – Sir Robert (William, Ninian, William, Ninian, Alexander, William, Neigel, Robert Adair.)

Sir Robert Adair = Jean Edmondstone

Progeny

22.	I	William, his heir.
23.	II	Alexander
24.	III	---------------- a daughter.
25.	IV	Jean, married her cousin, Rev. Patrick Adair, the Apostle of Presbyterianism in Ireland.

William Adair = Anne Hellena, daughter of Col. Walter Scott. Seats, Bellamena, Kinhilt, Hardwoodburn. (She remarried Archibald Edmondstone of Duntrieth.) Died Nov. 1661.

Progeny

26. Roberth Adair.

Lineage – Williamm, (Sir Robert, William, Ninian, William, Ninian, Alexander, William, Neigel, Robert Adair.)

26. Sir Robert Adair II, of Kinhilt and Bellamena, was born 1659, being two years old at his father's death.

He took part in the battle of the Boyne, having raised a regiment of horse soldiers for King William III, and commanded with such effect that he was Knighted by the Stodholder on the field of battle; hence he was Sir Robert Adair II.

Shortly before this he disposed of what remained of his Galloway Estates to Lord Stair, reserving for her life interest in her jointure to Margaret Agnew Adair, his uncle's widow, over that of Kinhilt and Dromore.

His home was at Bellamena, where a local distich runs thus:

"Sir Robert Adair, Laird of Kinhilt,

murdered his wife and married a jilt."

Which was his lineal descendant, the late Lord Waveney, explained, thus:

Sir Robert Adair II, was married four times: 1st,. Penelope, daughter of Sir Robert Colville; 2nd. Martha, whose family name has not been preserved, but who died at the end of a certain August; 3d. Anne McCauly, married on the 3d of October following; 4th Arabella Ricketts.

Much scandal was occasioned by his third marriage within a few weeks of the death of his second wife; the more so that the lady was engaged to a neighboring gentleman before Lady Adair died, but jilted her suitor when courted by Sir Robert; openly keeping company with him before his wife was buried.

A tradition as to this unseemly wooing is very amusing. One morning taking this damsel by the hand, he led her from the town of Bellamena, pointing by the way that the whole district was his property, over which he proposed that she should rule as mistress. The offer was a tempting one. The couple strolled on till they reached a wooded dingle through which a stream murmured pleasantly and here the enamored Knight broke out with "only be mine and all you see will be your dower;" the old love was discarded, the maiden sighed consent, well pleased with the settlement proposed, and a few days later the marriage contract was signed, couched in the identical terms used in the bethothal.

But inconstancy met its due reward. The honeymoon over, the lady found that the old bluebeard had only "kept the word of promise to the ear, to break it to the hope."

His engagement was fulfilled to the letter, but the life interest had been secured to her over such lands only as could be seen— from the deep dell where the proposal had been made; the range of smiling fields they had gazed on before they had reached it was there invisible; her domain was confined to a few acres of rocky ground in the deep hollow – her dowery was a dream.

A bridge adjacent to the spot is called the Dowery bridge to the present day, and Bellamena itself is often called Kinhilt's town in Antrim.

Lineage: Sir Robert II (William, Sir Robert, William, Ninian, William, Ninian, Alexander, William, Niegel, Robert Adair.)

His heir was a son by his first wife, William Robert Adair, of Bellamena, a Captain of horse. Lineage:

(27) William Robert (Sir Robert II, William, Sir Robert, William, Ninian, William, Ninian, Alexander, William, Niegel, Robert Adair.) Married Catherine Smallman, of Ludlow Co., Salop. Died 19th April, 1762, leaving Robert (28) his heir and William (29) in holy orders.

1753
William Robert Adair = Anne McAuley

Robert Adair, Bellamena, Married 25th March, 1753, Anne dau. Of Alexander McAuley of the city of Dublin, and died January, 1798, leaving William (30) and his heir and Robert (31) of Acton, Middlesex, born, 176-; married Elizabeth Payne, daughter of a London merchant, and left issue.

William Adair of Bellamena. Co., Antrim; Flixen Hall, Co., Suffolk, and Colehouse in Devonshire. Born 1754 married December, 1784, Camilla, daughter and heir of Robert Shafto, of Benwell, Northumberland, and by her (who d. 18, Nov., 1827) had issue.

Lord Waveney (Adair) as a Grand Master, Free Mason

Progeny

32. I Robert Shafto (sir) Created a Baronet.
33. II William Robert, d. at Harrow School.
34. III Alexander of Heather Park, Summerset, and Colehouse, Devon; b. 15th Sept., 1791. M. 17th June 1828, Harland; and d. 22d, Nov., 1863, leaving issue by her (who died Aug. 1878 Camilla. M. Rev. Robert Park Carrington, of Bridgeford. William Adair, died May 7th 1844, and was succeeded by his eldest son.

Sir Robert Shafto Adair, 1st Baronet, b. June 26, 1786; was created a Baronet Aug. 2, 1838

35. Robert.

He succeeded to Bellamena on the death of his father in 1762. He married Anne, daughter of Alexander McAuley, of Dublin, and had issue, but only eldest is mentioned:

36. William. He was born in 1754.

His father died in 1798, when his son succeeded to Bellamena, Flixton hall, and Cole House, Devonshire. He married Camilla, daughter and heir of Robert Shafto of Benwell, Northumberland. She died in 1787, and left two surviving sons.

37. Robert Shafto, born 1786.
38. Alexander Adair of Heatherton Park, Somersetshire, married and had issue.

William Adair, as stated died in 1844, which would make his age ninety years. He was succeeded by his son.

39. Robert Shafto Adair. He was created a baronet in 1838.

He was twice married, first to Elizabeth Maria, daughter of Rev. James Strode, of Burkhamstead, Burks., and had issue—

40. Robert Alexander Shafto, born in 1811.
41. Hugh Edward born in 1815, Barrister-at-law, M. P., for Ipswich.

He married his cousin, Harriet C., eldest daughter of Alexander Adair, of Heatherton.

40. Robert Shafto Adair, married secondly 1854, Jane Anne, eldest daughter of Rev. T. Clarkson, vicar of Hixton. Issue, if any, not given.

Sir Robert Shafto died in 1869. He was succeeded by his son.

42. Robert Alexander Shafto Adair, was second baronet.

He was M.P. for Cambridge 1847-1852. He married Theodosia, daughter of General, the Honorable Robert Meade. No issue.

He was raised to the peerage in 1873 as Baron Waveney. He died in 1886, when the peerage became extinct.

When Lord Waveney died, leaving no progeny, the Baronetcy devolved on his brother.

41. Sir Hugh Edward Adair, 3d Bart.; M.A. Oxford
Barrister-at-Law, J.P. and D.L. for counties of Suffolk and Antrim. Member Parliament for Ipswich, 1847 to 1874. Born 1815. Married July 10, 1856, Harriet Camilla Adair, eldest daughter of Alexander Adair, of Heatherton. She died 30 May, 1909, having had issue.

Progeny

43. I Hugh Alexander Adair, d. v. p. 4th May, 1868
44. II Frederic Edward Shafto Adair, (Sir) 4th Bart.
45. III Robert Shafto Adair, (Sir) 5th and present Bart.
46. IV Camilla Beatrice.

Sir H. E. Adair, died 2d March, 19-2, and was succeeded by his surviving son.

47. Sir Frederick Edward Shafto Adair, 4th Baronet, J.P. Norfolk and Suffolk, 1910. Sometime Capt. Rifle Brigade, born 15y Dec. 1860, died unm, April, 1915, and was succeeded by his brother, created Baronet (U.K.).

William Adair, a half brother of Sir Robert of Kinhilt; his mother a daughter of Catheart of Carlton; commenced life as a soldier, after wards entered the ministry of the Presbyterian Church, and was so much respected by all parties that, thought he refused to conform to Episcopacy at the Restoration he was among the few who were not deprived of their charges.

He was minister at Ayr for 44 years.

His first Church was pulled down by Cromwell, who required the site for a barrack; and a new one, now known as the old Church, was built under his superintendence.

He was married a Kennedy of the house of Kirkmichael, and survived until 1684.

A handsome monument was erected to his memory, which exists unharmed.

The inscription in Latin is as follows:

"Mr. Gaul. Adair antiquissiame familia de Kinhilt frater legitimus. Ecclesiae AErensis, per annos 44 pastor fidelissimus quod Caducum habuit hic depositum reliquit. Feb 12, 1684, act 70."

(He was the minister who administered the Solemn League and Covenant to the soldiers of the Scot's Parliamentary Army in Ireland in 1644.) (Rev. Patrick Adair's Mss.)

BRITISH ADAIRS—FIRST BRANCH LINE

2d Marriage: William Adair = Miss Houston, daughter of Houston of Castle Stewart

Progeny

20. John Adair, Minister at Genoch.

2d Marriage: William Adair = Miss Cathcart, daughter of Cathcart of Carlston.

Progeny

21. I William Adair, Minister at Ayre, Scotland.
22. II Anna Adair married Thomas Kennedy. In 1661 they owned the lands of Corpheine and other lands.

Sir Robert Adair (see special chapter on his biography)

Sir Robert Adair = Jean, daughter of Sir William Edmondstone, of Duntrieth, a lineal descendant of WILLIAM the Conqueror, King England

Progeny

22. I William, his heir.
23. II Alexander.
24. III ---, a daughter.
25. IV Jean, who married her 2d cousin, Rev. Parick Adair.

(For biographical of Rev. William Adair, see special Chapter)

(From this point to the present time, Burk's and other Perragers of Great Britian gives the genealogy of this first line of Adairs.)

20. Rev. John Adair= His wife's name is not given, of Genock, son of William, and half brother of Sir Robert, and Rev. William Adair.

Progeny

Three children, of which Patrick was third.

48. Rev. Patrick Adair was born in 1625.

He entered Divinity Classes at Glasgow College in 1644.

Lineage – Rev. Patrick Adair, (Rev. John, William, Ninian, Jr., William, Ninian Sr., Alexander, William, Niegello, Robert Adair.)

Rev. Patrick Adair was ordained at Cairncastle, Antrim, Ireland, and became the grate Apostle of Presbyterianism in Ireland.

Rev. Patrick Adair = Miss Jean Adair
Son of Rev. John Adair   Daughter of Sir Robert Adair

Which makes Patrick and his wife 2nd cousins, as their fathers were half brothers.

Progeny:
They had four sons and one daughter:
49.　I　Rev. William Adair, Pastor at Ballyeastern, Ordained, 1681; Died, 1698.
50.　II　Archibald Adair.
51.　III　Alexander Adair.
52.　IV　Rev. Patrick Adair, Jr., Pastor at Carrickfurgus, Died, June 1717.
53.　V　Helen Adair, the daughter.

Archibald and Alexander both married and raised families in County Antrim in Ireland, but a few years later, they dropped out of sight, and tradition says they migrated to America. McSkimmin's history of County Antrim, published in Carrickfurgus in 1750 makes no mention of them, which is circumstantial evidence that they had migrated and were soon forgotten; and it lends support to the tradition.

54. Our Thomas Adair, who migrated to Pennsylvania about 173-, and afterwards to South Carolina, was born 1680. He brought three sons with him, to-wit: James, Joseph and William; who became the fathers of the three principle families in America.

54. Hence Thomas Adair, the son of Alexander, and grandson of Rev. Patrick Adair is our American Line.

Rev. Patrick Adair Jr., son of Rev. Patrick Adair Sr., was a Presbyterian Minister; and Paster of Carrickfurgus Church until his death in 1717.

In 1711 there was a trial in Court in Carrickfurgus, of a half dozen women on charge of witchcraft; and Patrick Adair, among other ministers and laymen, appeared as witness. The women were convicted and sent to prison for one year.

About 1708 Carrickfurgus was distracted by the Whigs and Tories. Rev. Patrick Adair had a dispute with Rev. Matthews about the publication of a pamphlet. Adair proved his side correct, but the two subsequently met on the street and after how words, resorted to blows. Adair soundly thrashed his antagonist.

William Adair was a son of Rev. Patrick Adair, minister at Carrickfurgus. At an early age he was sent to Glasgow College. But his father dying, he left the University without taking a degree and in rather embarrassing circumstances. On leaving college he resided for a time with Willoughby Chaplin, Esq., by whom he was recommended to Robert Gardner, an eminent Army agent in London who took him into his counting room, where he conducted himself so well, that in a few years he was admitted to a share in the trade, and on the death of Mr. Gardner, he succeeded to the business. Adair was a mam of strict integrity, as he paid his debts at college with interest as soon he was able. Also some of his father's debts in like manner.

He was never married, and left in trust, two thousand pounds in consolidated 3 per cent annuities, to the Adair owners of the Ballemena estate, County of Antrim, to go annually for benefit of the poor freemen of Carrickfurgus, and to be divided as the proprietor of the Ballamena estate for the time being may direct.

At first it was difficult to get people to accept Adair charities; but later applications were numerous.

ADAIRS OF QUEENS COUNTY, IRELAND

George Adiar, Esq. of Bellegrove and Rathdair, Queens County, Ireland, b 13 Sept., 1784, m 16 May, 1822, Elizabeth, the 2nd daughter of the Very Rev. Thomas Trench, the Dean of Kildare and 2nd brother of the late Lord Ashtown, and by her, who died 23 March, 1823, had an only son; John George Adair, Esq., b 3rd March, 1823 at Rathdair, Queens County. J. P. and D. L. counties Donegal and Queens. J.P. for Counties Tipperary and Kildare, High Sherrif 1874 Donegal, m 29 May 1867, Cornelia, daughter of Gen. J. S. Wadsworth of Genesio, New York State, and widow of Col. Richie of the U. S. army, and d. s. p., 14th May, 1885. Progeny none.

The lineage runs back through John, Archibald, and Thomas, then becomes obscure. But they were of Galloway and Antrim Co., stock.

One authority states that the family were wealthy at one time, but a Sovereign of Great Britian confiscated part of their wealth on account of Adair's antagonism to the Catholic Church.

John George Adair acquired part of the land grant in the Pan Handle of Texas, obtained from the state by a Syndicate for building the Texas State Capitol. Adair made a model Ranch out of this fast body of land and he and his wife spent part of every year on this ranch and made it profitable.

After his death in 1885, his wife kept up the plans and enterprises inaugurated by her husband. They raised thoroughbred cattle, employed the best cowboys, and treated them well. They built a fine hospital, up-to-date in all its arrangements and a fine Y.M.C.A. Building, all in Clarenden, Texas, the nearest town to their ranch. The hospital is called Adair Hospital and is conducted on a liberal plan.

Mrs. Cornelia Adair died on her Irish Estate in Queens County in 1922, leaving a son by her first husband, Mr. Richie.

According to the London Times, the estate was worth $200,000, in the United Kingdom. In her will, she provided well for the Adair Hospital.

Ms. Cornelia Adair was endowed the St. Matthew's Children's Home. Also $10,000 for the U.W.C.A. both in Dallas.

For many years she was prominent in English Society

BRITISH ADAIRS – SECOND BRANCH LINE
Genealogy of Judge James Adair of London
1604

16. Alexander Adair = Miss Stewart of Garlies. 4th son of Ninian Adair II, of Kinhilt.

54   I   William Adair, b 1605. Owned the lands of Corghie in 1634.

55. William Adair = Janet McCulloch.

Progeny

56.   I   William Adair, B 1635. Owned the lands of Corghie in 1670.

57. Williiam Adair = Jean McDowall.

Progeny

58.   I   James Adair, b about 1670, owned the lands of Corghie in 1724.

James Adair = Name unknown
Progeny

60.   I___Son — Adair, b about 1705
61. _____Adair — Not Known

Progeny.

63.   I   James Adair, b 1738.

His parents moved to London to educate their son. They were finally buried in Barnhill cemetery.

62. James Adair inherited the lands of Corghie from his ancestors which he sold before his death. Was a bachelor. He died 1798, leaving no progeny.

Gen. Sir William Thompson Adair's Genealogy

65. Captain James Adair, supposed to have come from Lochan in Galloway. Settled at Loughanmore, County Antrim, in Ireland, about 1640. His will was proved in 1686.

66. Bejamine Adair, born 1665.

67. Thomas Benjamin, born 1705.

Progeny: Three Sons

68.   I   Charles Adair.
69.   II   Benjamin Adair, Colonel in the Royal Marines.
70.   III   William Robert Adair, Som of his descendants went to America, but there is no trace of them, in Ireland.

68   Charles Adair =

Progeny: Two Children

71.   I   Thomas Benjamin Adair, Mayor of Carrickfurgus in 1832. High Sheriff of County Antrim, 18-1. M Lenora Adair, daughter of his uncle, Colonel Benjamin Adair.
72.   II   Henry Adair, Sheriff of Carrickfurgus in 1822, died without issue.

71   Thomas Benjamin Adair = Lenora Adair

Son of Charles Adair.

They had a number of children, all of whom died without issue, the las survivor (male) was high sheriff of County Antrim in 1871.

69   Benjamin Adair =

Colonel in the Royal Marines

Progeny: Two Sons

74. Charles William Adair, Captain in Marines, Killed on board H.M.S. Victory at the battle of Trafalgar.

76. Thomas Benjamin, General of Royal Marines.

74   Charles William Adair =

76.   II   Henry Adair, Colonel Royal Marines, April 1882.
          III   Other Sons and Daughters.

74   Charles William Adair =

General in Royal Marines and K.C.B. Nov. 24., 1882.

Progeny: Four Sons

77.   I   William Thompson Adair, General Royal Marines and K.C.B.
78.   II   Charles Henry Adair, Admiral Royal Navy.
79.   III   Thomas Benjamin Adair, Admiral Royal Navy.
80.   IV   Hugh Robert Adair, Colonel in Royal Artillery.

77. General Sir William Thomas Adair Succeeded to the estate of Lochanmore in 1911 on the death of last of elder branch. Was High Sheriff of Co. Antrim, 1916.

CHAPTER VII
BIOGRAPHY OF BRITISH ADAIRS
JAMES ADAIR, LAWYER

James Adair, Sargeant-at-law, and Recorder of London, was educated at Peterhouse, Cambridge, where he graduated B.A. in 1764, and M.A. in 1767. He was subsequently called to the bar at Lincoln's Inn.

In the quarrel between Wilks and Horn Tooke in 1770, he intervened on the side of Wilks, who publicly replied in Adair's behalf to the attacks made upon him by Tooke, and the notoriety that he thereby acquired was material service to him in his professional career.

In 1771 he took a prominent part as one of the council for the defense in certain legal proceedings that followed the great trial of the printers and publishers of the "Junius Letters." Eight years later, his support of the popular cause secured for him the office of Recorder of London, a position which he held until 1789. His resignation in that year was due partly to his many professional engagements in the Court of Common Pleas, which left him little time to attend to the affairs of the city, and partly to his political views. The managers of the London corporation had transferred their political allegiance between 1779 and 1789 from the Whigs to the Tories under the younger Pitt, and with the latter, Adair had nothing in common.

From 1789 until his death, he sat in Parliament as a Whig representative, first of Cokermouth, and afterwards of Hiham Ferrars. His temporary connection with Wilks gained him for a time the reputation of being a "Wilkite," but in truth he was rather a timid Whig.

He was for some years a member of the famous Whip Club; but on the outbreak of the French Revolution, he parted company with Fox, with whom he had previously been connected.

As King's Sergeant, he was associated in 1794 with the Attorney-General, Sir John Scott, afterwards Lord Eldon, in the prosecution of Thomas Hardy and his old enemy Horn Took Chancellor, was assigned by the Court as council for the defense of William Stone, charged with high treason as champion of the French Revolution, and the prisoner's acquittal was doubtless in some measure due to Adair's energetic conduct of his case. (See state trials IIV, 1320 et seq.)

Adair's horror of the French Revolution did not, however, diminish with his years: At an advanced age, he joined a force of London volunteers, raised in 1798, when England was menaced with invasion. The fatiguing discipline to which he subjected himself, shortened his life. He died suddenly while returning from shooting exercises on July 21, 1798, and was buried in the Barnhill Field burying ground, near his parents' graves.

At the time of his death, he was the King's prime Sergeant-at-Law; member of Parliament for Hiham Ferrars, and Chief Justice of Chester.

Adair is the reputed author of the following books:

1st. "Thoughts on the Dismission of Officers, Civil and Military, for their Conduct in Parliament." Octavo, 1764.

2nd. "Observations on the Power of Alienation in the Crown, Before the First of Queen Ann, Supported by Precedents and the opinion of many learned Judges; together with some remarks on the conduct of Administration respecting the case of the Duke of Portland." 8vo 1786.

3rd. "Discussions of the Law of Libels," 1786, 8vo.

Almon in his "Anecdotes" fully summarizes the two first of these pamphlets, and applauds the learned Sergeant's regard for the Constitution, his ability as a lawyer, and his honesty as a man. (Wee Gentleman's Magazine LXVIII, Part II 720;)

Chalmer's Biographic Dictionary; Almon's Anecdotes, 1797. 182-92; Junius, printed by Woodfall (1872) III, 38- et seq.)

JOHN ADAIR
The Great Civil Engineer

Was of the family of Adairs of Galloway, (d. 1722.) an eminent Scottish surveyor and map maker, lived during the close of the 17th century and the first quarter of the 18th century. The earliest known mention of his name is by Sir Robert Sibbald, his patron, from whom Adair received his first public employment. In "An account of the Scottish Atlas," a kind of prospectus published in Edinburgh in 1683, we read: "The Lords of His Majesty's Privy Council in Scotland gave, commission to John Adair, Mathematician and, skillful mechanic, to survey they shires.

And the said John Adair, by taking the distances of the several angels from the adjacent hills, had designed most exact maps, and hath lately an hydrographical map of the river Fourth geometrically surveyed; wherein, after a new and exact way, are set all down all the isles, blind rocks, shelves and sands, with and exact draught of the coast, with all its bays, headlands, ports, havens, town, and other things remarkable, the depths of the water through the whole Forth, with the courses from each point (of the compass,) the prospect and the view of the remarkable islands, headlands, and other considerable landmarks. And he is next to survey the shire of Perth, and to make two maps thereof, one of the south side and another of the north. He will likewise be ready to design the maps of other shires that were not done before, providing he may have sufficient allowance thereof. And those who are concerned may be the better persuaded thereto, there is joined with this account the map of Clackmanan Shire taken off the copper plate done for it, where different face of the grounds, which are arable, and which Moorish; and by convenient marks you may know the houses of the nobility and the gentry, the churches, the mills, woods, and parks." (p. 4.)

For the better enabling Adair to carry on the design an act of tunnage was passed by Parliament June 14th, 1686, "In favor of John Adair, geographer, for surveying the Kingdom of Scotland and navigating the coasts and isles thereof" (Is Parl Ja, VII cap. 21.) At this period it would appear that his connection with Sir R. Sibbold had ceased. While engaged in this work he was elected a Fellow of the Royal Society, Nov. 30, 1688. In the report of the Committee of privy council, Aug., 1694, "The committee appointed to examine the progress made by John Adair in the maps of Scotland doe find that there are elleuen maps made by him relating to the land, and none relating to the sea," (note the English spelling in the 17th century, Ed.) The money raised in favor of Adair by the act of 1666 being found insufficient to cover his expenses, a new act of tunnage was passed July 16th, 1695.

In 1703 was published his "Description of the Sea Coasts and Islands of Scotland, with Large and Exact MAPS FOR THE USE OF Seamen, By John Adair, Geographer for the Kingdom. Edinburgh, fol." Of this work, the first part only was printed; it is now rare. The second part was never published.

The committee on public accounts, in their report laid before Parliament July 21st, 1704, state that four of our number did visit Mr. Adair's work, who told us it was far advanced and deserved encouragement," (acta Parl. Vol. XI App. P.49) Another act of tunnage was then passed in his favor, Aug. 8th, 1705, but the second part never appeared and his papers are not known to have been preserved.

Adair probably died in London towards the end of 1722, for we find that in 1723 his window obtained from government some remuneration, for her husband's labors and losses, which last must have been considerable, as Adair, as early as July, 1794, stated in a memorial to the lords of the privy council "that these losses were three times more than was ever gotten from collectors on account of tunnage."

Among the records of the court of Exchequer is an Inventory of the Maps and Papers delivered by Jean Adair, relict of Mr. John Adair, Geographer, F. R. S., to the Right Honorable the Barons of Exchequer in pursuance of a Warrant from the Lords Justices, dated 21st of June, 1723."

As is also a minute of the Barons of Exchequer, Martis 19, Nov. 1723, to the following effect: "Mrs. Adair, Relict of John Adair, late Geographer, having given upon oath an inventory of the Maps and Papers belonging to her late Husband, in pursuance of the Lord Justices Sign Manual, dated 21st June past, ordered that the same be lodge in the Rem'rs Office, and the receipt for payment of her allowance of I. 40 per annum be delivered to her."

Some of Adair's surveys are preserved in the Advocates Library, Edinburg, and others, MS. Maps, probably copies, are preserved in the King's library, British Museum. According to Gough, other sketches remained in the hands of his daughter, Mrs. Douglas. Gough also mentions that "Mr. Brian Shewed the Society of Antiquaries, in 1724, two drawings of the whole coast of Scotland, upon the Frith of Forth as high as Stirlang, and the Clyd to Glasgow, and of the Solway Frith to Carlisle," by the late John Adair. (British Topography, Vol. II p. 577.)

One of the charts found in "Description of the Sea Coasts and Islands of Scotland" is of peculiar interest; it bears the following title: "A true and exact hydrographical Description of the Sea Coast and the Islands of Scotland made in a Voyage around the same by the great and might prince, James V Published at Paris by Nicholay D. Aulphinois, Cosmographer to the French King; and at Adenburg by John Adair, Felloe of the Royal Society." The remaining documents of Adair that call for notice in the Inventory are as follows:

Principle Manuscripts not printed: "A Journal of the Voyage to the North and West Islands of Scotland by John Adair, Geographer in the year, 1698, consisting of fifteen full sheets, and seems to be the original by his own hand." A list of nine maps relative to the original by his own hand." A list of nine maps relative to the said Journal: -- 1. Channel between Hoy and Pomona; 2. West Coast of Ross; 3. Island and Port of Cana; 4. Scalpa, with the coast of Harris; 5. East Coast of Uist; 6 and 7. Views of the aforesaid Islands; 8. South Coast of Sky; 9. South Islands of Orkney.

Dictionary of National Biography pp 70-71-2.

REV. PATRICK ADAIR
The Great Apostle of Presbyterianism in Ireland.

Patrick Adair was born in 1625. His father was Rev. John Adair of Genoch. His grandfather was William Adair of Kinhilt, who was married three times and had only one son by each wife. By his first wife, Sir Robert Adair was born. By his second wife, Rev. John was born, and by his third wife, Rev. Williamm Adair, pastor at Ayre for forty-four years, and whose lot it was to administer the solemn oath of the "League and Covenant" to the Scotch Soldiers in Ulster in 1644.

Patrick Adair was the third son of Rev. John Adair of Genoch, but the names of Genoch's other children ae not mentioned in our history. Patrick Adair entered Divinity Classes at Glasgow College in Dec. 1644, and was ordained at Cairncastle, Antrim County, Ireland, 7th of May, 1646, by the Army Presbytery, which was constituted in Carrickfurgus June 10th, 1642, by the Chaplins of the Scottish regiments in Ulster.

We will follow the career of Patrick Adair somewhat in detail because of the importance of his work in establishing Presbyterianism in Ireland, and because it was some of his Progeny that established the first Adair Families in America.

In 1648 Adair and his patron, James Shaw of Ballegally, were appointed a committee to treat with General Monk and Sir Charles Coote the Parliament and held a meeting in Belfast, Feb. 1649, at which they protested against the King's death as an act of horror without precedent in history, divine or human, and agree to pray for Charles II who for his part, promised to establish Presbyterianism in Ulster.

The Parliamentary Generals replaced the Presbyterian by independent and Baptist ministers, and Adair had to hide among the rocks near Cairncastle.

In March, 1752 he took part in a public discussion on church government between Presbyterian and independent ministers at Antrim Castle. He was the mouthpiece of the ministers who declined (October and November) to take the engagement to be true to the Commonwealth against any King, and was one of the ministers appointed to wait on General Flweetwood and the council (January, 1753) to see relief therefrom.

Being told that papists might please conscience as well as they, Adair drew a famous distinction between the conscience of parties, "for papists consciences could digest to kill Protestant Kings." No relief was obtained; and commissioners were sent from Dublin in April to search the houses of such ministers as had not sought safety in flight. Adair's papers were seized but were restored to him through the daring act of a servant maid at Larne.

The Commissioners devised a plan for transporting the Ulster Presbyterian to Tipperary, but the scheme was abortive.

In April and May, 1654, we find Adair in Dublin pleading for the restoration of titles to the Presbyterian ministers and obtaining instead a maintenance by annual salary (the first donum to Irish Presbyterians). They got 100 L a year apiece till the restoration, but preserved their independence, and observing the Commonwealth fasts and Thanksgivings.

Adair was one of eight ministers summoned to the general convention at Dublin (February 1660) at a time when there was hopes of a Presbyterian establishment; soon dispelled by the restoration of Charles II.

Jeremy Taylor Consecrated Bishop of Down and Conner, on the 27th of January, 1661, summoned the Presbyterian ministers to his visitation; and on their not attending, declared their churches vacant. Thus, Adair was ejected from Cairdcastle parish church.

He went to Dublin to seek relief for his brethren from the Duke of Ormond, Lord Lieutenant of Ireland, but could obtain only permission to "Serve God in their own families."

In 1663 he was apprehended and sent to Dublin on a charge of complicity in Blood's plot but discharged after three months with a temporary indulgence on condition of living peaceably.

About 1668 a new meetinghouse was built for him at Cairncastle.

Adair was one of the negotiators in 1672 for the first REGIUM DONUM granted to Presbyterian by Charles II.

On Oct 13th, 1674, the Antrim meeting removed Adair to Belfast, in succession to Rev. William Keyes (an Englishman), not without opposition from the Donegal family who preferred the English rather than the Scottish type of Presbyterianism.

After the defeat of the Scottish Covenanters at Bothwell Brig in (June ?, 1679) fresh severities were inflicted on the Ulster Presbyterians; their meetinghouses were closed and their Presbytery meetings were held secretly by night.

The declaration of James II (1687) gave them renewed liberty, which was confirmed by the accession of William III, though there was no Irish toleration act until 1719.

Adair headed the deputation from the general committee of Ulster Presbyterian, who presented a congratulatory address to William III in London in 1689 and obtained from the King a letter (Nov. 9, 1689) recommending their case to Duke Schomberg.

King William, when in Ulster in 1690, appointed Adair and his son William Adair, two of the trustees for distributing his REGIUM DONUM.

There has been no minister at any period in the history of Irish Presbyterianism engaged in such continued series of important transactions as Patrick Adair.

(Armstrong).

Late in life he drew up a "True Narrative of the Rise and Progress of the Presbyterian Government in the North of Ireland."

Adair's Book covered the period from 1623 to 1670; but it is to be regretted he did not finish his book. Some years after his death the Presbyterian Assemble took up the manuscript and had it published under the supervision of Rev. William Adair, his oldest son.

For the religious history of the period, it is invaluable.

Patrick Adair married Miss Jean Adair, second daughter of Sir Robert Adair of Bellamena. Sir Robert Adair and Rev. John Adair were half-brothers and that makes Rev. Patrick Adair and his wife second cousins.

Their progeny was four sons and one daughter. As follows: Rev. William Adair, the oldest, was ordained at Ballyeastern in 1681, removed to Antrim in 1690, and died 1698; 2nd was Archibald; 3rd was Alexander; 4th was Rev. Patrick Adair Jr. Minister at Carrickfurgus; died June 1717; and the daughter, Helen.

Mrs. Jean Adair, the first wife died in 1675; and Adair married a second wife, Mrs. Elizabeth Anderson (nee Martin). A widow, but no progeny.

Adair died the latter part of 1694, and his will was proved July 6, 1695. Contemporary history seems to be silent on Archibald, Alexander and Helen; and that is strong circumstantial evidence that they left the country, and migrated to America, early in life; the home people soon lost sight of them, and they were forgotten by all except their parents.

REV. PATRICK ADAIR, JR.

Rev. Patrick Adair, Jr., was ordained in 1702 and served the Presbyterian Church at Carrickfurgus for fifteen years and then died in 1717. McSkimmin's History of Carrickfurgus gives the following items of biography; in 1711 there was a trial in court of half dozen women on charge of witchcraft, and Rev. Patrick Adair, among other ministers and laymen, appeared as witnesses against the accused, who were convicted and sentenced for one year. The Preachers and everybody believed in witches in those days.

About 1708 Carrickfurgus was distracted by the Whigs and Troies. Rev. Patrick Adair had a dispute about the publications of a pamphlet with Rev. Edward Matthews; Adair proved his side correct, but the two subsequently met on the street and after hot words, resorted to blows, and Adair thrashed his antagonist soundly.

Rev. Patrick Adair Jr. was married, but we do not know who, nor when. He had one son, William Adair, who was placed at an early age in Glasgow College. But his father dying, he left the University without taking a degree, and in rather embarrassed circumstances. On leaving college he resided for a time in Carrackfurgus with Wiloby Chaplin Esq., by whom he was recommended to Robert Gardner, an eminent army agent in London. Mr. Gardner took him into his Counting-house, where he conducted himself so well that in a few years he was admitted to a share in the trade. And on the death of Mr. Gardner, he succeeded him in the business.

Adair was a man of strict integrity, as he paid his college debts, principal and interest, as soon as he was able, and his father's debts likewise.

William Adair, Esq. was not married but died in 1782 in the parish of Westminster, where he lived, age about 80 years. He left in trust L 2000, in consolidated 3 per cent annuities, to the Adairs, owners of the Bellamena Estate in County Antrim, Ireland, to go annually for the benefit of the poor freemen of Carickfurgus, and to be divided at the proprietor of the Bellamena Estate for the time being may direct. At first it was difficult to find people to accept Adair charities, but later applications were numerous.

PROFESSOR JOHN RUSKIN
British Artist, Author, and Critic

Professor John Ruskin was born in London, Feb 8th, 1819. His memoirs published on authority of his family, trace their descent to the Adairs and Agnews of Galloway, Scotland. In this family tree are men famous in arms and in public service; Sir Andrew Agnew of Lochnaw, Admiral Sir John Ross, Field Marshal, sir Hew Dalrymple Ross, Doctor John Adair, in whose arms Wolfe died at Quebec, and the Rev. W. Tweddale of Glenluce, to whom the original covenant, now in Glasgow Museum, had been confided.

John Ruskin, the author's grandfather, ran away with and married Catherine Tweddale, daughter of the Covenanting Minister and of Catherine Adair, then a beautiful girl of sixteen. He settled in Edinburgh and became a wine merchant (which was an honorable calling in Great Britain).

The youth of John Ruskin, the boy, was largely passed in systematic traveling in search of everything beautiful in nature and in art. And to one so precocious, stimulated by a parent of much culture, and ample means and great ambition, this resulted in an almost unexampled aesthetic education. In childhood also he began a systematic practice of composition, both in prose and verse. His mother trained him in reading the Bible, of which he read through every chapter and every book year by year; and to this study he justly attributes his early command of language and his pure sense of style. His father read to him Shakespeare, Scot, Don Quixote, Pope and Byron, and most of the great English classics and his attention turned to the formation of sentences and the rhythm of prose. He began to compose both in prose and verse as soon as he had learned to read and write, both of which arts he taught himself by the eye.

His first letter was written at the age of four. His schooling was irregular and not very successful. At the age of eleven he was taught Latin and Greek by Doctor Andrews, a scholar of Glasgow University.

About the same time he had lessons in drawing and painting by Runciman. French and Euclid were taught him by Rowbotham. In painting he had lesson from Coyley Fielding and afterwards from J. D. Hardking. His training had been too much diversified for him to gain much knowledge of classics and mathematics to the time he matriculated at Oxford.

As a boy he was active, lively and docile, a good walker, but ignorant of all boyish games, as naive and as innocent as a child; and he never could learn to dance or to ride. He was only saved by his intellect and his fine nature from turning out an arrant prig. He was regarded by his parents and seems to have regarded himself, as a genius.

At the age of seventeen he had his first love affair, but was turned down by his sweetheart, and it nearly upset his health; he lost two years from college on account of ill health.

As the father was resolved that John should have everything that money and pains could give, and was one day to be a bishop at least, he entered at Christ Church, Oxford as Gentleman-Commoner—then an order reserved for men of wealth and rank.

John finally graduated from Oxford in 1842.

Long before Ruskin published books he appeared in print. In March, 1832 when he was but fifteen, Louden's Magazine of natural history published an article of his on the strata of the mountains, and an inquiry as to the color of the Rhine, and various articles on different subjects for various magazines.

Ruskin's literary life may be arranged in three divisions. From 1837 to 1860 he was occupied mainly with the Arts. From 1860 to 1871 he was principally occupied with social problems. From 1871 to 1885 he was again drawn back largely to Art by his lectures as professor of Art.

John Ruskin founded the Reformation in Art.

It was considered that many of his theories in Sociology were wild and impractical.

Ruskin was married, but that match was made by his parents and her parents. It was not based on love and affinity; consequently, it did not last long. The wife had the marriage annulled under Scots Law.

Ruskin spent his fortune of 200,000 pounds, partly for charity, but mainly in philanthropy. He wrote and published a great many books which had large sale on which he got a royalty; his income from royalties amounted to about 4,000 pounds per year, which was a comfortable living for him.

In mastery of prose language, Ruskin has never been surpassed, when he chose to curb his florid imagination and his discursive eagerness of soul. The beauty and gorgeous imagery of his Art works bore away the public from the first, in spite of the too frequent extravagance of rhetoric. His later economic and social pieces, such as "Unto The Last", "Time and Tide", "Sesame and Lilies", are composed in the purest and most lucid of English Style, and many of his technical pieces have the same quality.

Towards the close of his life, in "For", and "Practerita", will be found passages of tenderness, charm and subtlety which have never been surpassed in our language.

John Ruskin died in January, 1900, at 81 years.

The close of his life was one of peace and honor. He was loaded with the degrees of the Universities, and memberships of numerous Societies and Academics. His works were translated and read abroad and had no enormous circulation in Great Britian and the United States. He was author of Books, Pamphlets, and Magazine articles, all told to the total number of 1200.

Ruskin's life and writings have been the subject of many works composed by friends, disciples and admirers. The principle ones are the "Life" by Collingwood, his friend and secretary, 1900. His pupil, E. E. Cook, studies in Ruskin, 1890. J. A. Hobbs in 1899. An analysis of Ruskin's work by Mrs. Mynell, in 1900, and many other works.

DOCTOR ROBERT ADAIR
Surgeon to King George III

Doctor Robert Adair was born in Ulster, Ireland, of Galloway Adair stock, though there seems to be a gap in his lineage. The date of his birth was about 1715. He acquired a medical education and located to Dublin to practice medicine; but being involved in a scandalous affair, was compelled to quit the country, and he went to England.

Near Holyhead occurred the first of a series of incidents which finally gave him the giggle of the "Fortunate Irishman." The carriage of a wealthy lady was overturned, and Adair ran to her assistance. Being somewhat hurt, she requested him to travel with her to London, and on their arrival there she gave him a fee of one hundred guineas and a general invitation to her house. There he met Lady Caroline Keppel.

Lady Caroline is said to have fallen in love with Adair at first sight. Adair promptly followed his advantage, to the dismay of her family, who tried every possible expedient to break up the attachment. These include several journeys, on one of which, at Bath, she is said to have written the words of a beautiful song which follows and set them to a tune which she had heard him sing. The air is claimed by both the Irish and Scotch. The family finally gave up their opposition when they saw that her health was affected, and the lovers were married. After a few happy years, the lady died, leaving three children.

Adair (who never married again) was a favorite of King George III; was made, successively, Inspector-General of Military Hospitals, Surgeon-General, King's Sergeant Surgeon, and Surgeon to Chelsea Hospital. Doctor Robert Adair died in 1790, aged 75 years.

A Sketch of their son, the Right Honorable Sir Robert Adair, the great British Diplomatist in hereto attached.

ROBIN ADAIR
The Ballad

1   What's this dull town to me? Ro-bin's not near.
    What was't I wish'd to see, what wish'd to hear?
    Where's all the joy and mirth Made this town a heav'n on earth?
    Oh, they're all fled with thee, Rob-in A-dair.

2   What made th' assembly shine? Ro-bin A-dair.
    What made the ball so fine? Ro=bin was there.
    What, when the play was o'er, What made my heart so sore?
    Oh, it was par-ting with Ro-bin A-dair.

3   But now thou'rt cold to me, Ro-bin A-dair.
    But now thou'rt cold to me, Ro-bin A-dair.
    Yet I love so well Still in my heart;
    Oh, I can never forget Ro-bin A-dair!

SIR ROBERT ADAIR THE BRITISH DIPLOMAT

(b 1763, d 1855) was the son of Doctor Robert Adair and Lady Caroline Keppel Adair, of London. He was born May 24, 1763, and was sent to Westminster School, thence to the University of Gottingen.

His father was Sergeant-Surgeon to King George III, and his mother was the second daughter of the Earl of Albemarl, Royal Governor of Virginia for seventeen years without having visited the colony.

At the university Cannik satirized him as falling in love with "Sweet Matilda Pottingen." Before he was twenty, he was ranked among Fox's intimate friends, and, had the Whig minister gained the seals of the Foreign Office in 1788, Adair would have been his undersecretary.

When the French revolution broke out, he visited Berlin, Vienna and St. Petersburg to study its effects on foreign states, and to qualify himself for diplomatic office. Some of his political opponents believed that he had been dispatched by Fox to Russia to thwart the policy of Mr. Pitt, and the accusation was reproduced in 1821 in the Bish of Winchester's "Memoir of

Pitt," which brought about an angry correspondence in print between the Bishop and Adair.

He sat in Parliament for the Whig Boroughs of Appleby and Camelford.

During Fox's tenure of office in 1806 he was dispatched to Vienna on a mission to Warn Austia of the dangers to which she was exposed from the power of France, and on his return from Vienna was sent by his old antagonist, Canning, to Constantinople to open up a negotiation for peace with the Porte. Memoirs of these missions were published by Adair in 1844 and 1845. In 1828 his diplomatic services were recognized by his admission to the privy council. In 1831 to 1835 he was engaged on a special mission in the Low Countries, where his exertions prevented a general war between the Flemish and the Dutch troops.

He was appointed G.C.B. (civil) in 1831, and the success of his mission was further rewarded by the grant of the highest pension which could be awarded to him.

Among his other writings are a reprint in 1802 and 1853 of Fox's "Letters to the Electors of Westminster in 1793, with an application of its principles to subsequent events," and a sketch of the character of the late Duke of Devonshire (1811).

His wife was Mlle. Angelique Gabrielle, daughter of the Marquis D'Hazincourt. His stories of recollection of diplomatic and political life made him a frequent guest at the chief Whig houses in London until the end of his long life, and his name is often in the diary of Tom Moore. Full of years and honors, he died at Chesterfield Street, Mayfair, on October 3, 1855, aged 92 years.

(Gent. Mag., 1855, N. S. Sliv., p. 535; Lord Albemarl's Fifty Years of Life, I, 225; Lord John Russell's Memorials and Correspondence of C.J. Fox, Vol II, appendix.)

CHAPTER VII A
OUR ROYAL LINEAGE

WILLIAM The Conqueror, King of England
****

Gundred, dau. of William The Conqueror

William de Warren, Earl of Warren and Surrey

Adaline, dau. William, Earl of Surrey.

David, Earl of Huntington

Issabel, dau. of David, Earl of Huntington, and Co-heir.

Robert Bruce, King of Scotland

Princess Mary, dau. of Robert Bruce, King of Scotland.

Robert Bruce, II. King of Scotland. Crowned at &-one 1327.

Robert Bruce, III. King of Scotland Died in 1406.

Sir James Kennedy,

Cutherine, dau. of Herbert, Lord Maxwull.

ELIZABETH, dau. of Alexander, Lord Montgomery

AGNES, dau. of William, Lord Borthworth

ISSABEL, dau. of Archibald, Earl of Argyle.

Hellen, dau. of Gilbert Kennedy, 2d, Earl of Cassalis.

) Maud, daughter of Baldwin, Count of Flanders.

William de Warren, Earl of Surrey.

Elizabeth, dau. of Hugh the Great, Earl of Yermauclois.

Henry, Prince of Srotland.

Maud, dau. of Hugh de Kerlico Earl of Chester.

Robert de Bruce, Lord of Annandale, Called the Noble.

Issabel, dau. of Donald, Earl of Marr.

Walter, Lord High Steward of Scotland.

ELIZABETH, dau. of Sir Adam Mure, of Rowallen.

Annabella, dau. of Sir John Drumond, Knight of Slobhull.

Princess Mary, dau. of Robert Bruce, III. King of Scotland. Widow successively of George Douglas, Earl of Angus; of Sir James Kennedy; and of Sir William Graham. And wife of Sir William Edmondstone of Duntrieth.

Sir Gilbert Kennedy T<nt. Created Lord Kennedy in 1452.

John, 3d, Lord Kennedy, died in 1508.

DAVID, 3d, Lord Kennedy, Created Earl of Cassalis in 1502. Fell at Flodden.

Gilbert Kennedy, 2d, Earl of Cassalis, was slain 1527.

William **Adair**.

15th in lineal decent from WILLIAM. The Conqueror, King of England: and 0th from Robert Bruce, King of Scotland, to the Adairs.

CHAPTER VIII

WILLIAM ADAIR, THE PIONEER.

About 1730, Thomas Adair, with his family, migrated from County Antrim in Ireland, to Chester County, Pennsylvania. They spent about 20 years in Penn, then joined the Waxaw.

Colony of Scotch Irish settlers from Penn, who migrated to South Carolina and settled in the middle north Counties date about 1750-55.

McGrady's History of South Carolina says the Adairs were prominent members of this Colony, which produced so many noble men and women.

Thomas Adair brought three of his sons with him to S.C. (we do not know whether this was all of his family), these three most prominent families of Adairs in America. They were James, Joseph, and William. (ranked in the order named,) James was born 1709, was an Indian Trader and Author, and his progeny are in Arkansas and Oklahoma.

Joseph was born in 1711; his progeny are in S.C. and the Southern States to the west of S.C.

William Adair (whom we designate as William, the pioneer) the youngest son, was born in Antrim County, Ireland in 1719, and hence was eleven years old when his father brought him to America; they settled first in Pennsylvania, Chester County; where they remained twenty years, and where William Adair was educated.

The WAXAW Colony had lands in Chester and adjoining Counties in S.C., and the ADAIR Colony had lands in Laurens County, adjoining the WAXAW on the west; but the two Colonies were practically one, because they were established about the same time, and both composed of Scotch-Irish settlers from Pennsylvania and elsewhere.

William Adair married in 1754, secured land on Fishing Creek in Chester County, S.C., Cleared Land for a farm; built a house, locating it near the water, as did the other pioneer settlers, for the better protection against the Wild Indians.

It was as a family man that William Adair shone most. He educated his children to the best of his ability; sent them to Charlotte, N.C., for their high school training; he was altogether an enterprising and public-spirited citizen. His son John was a student in the Charlotte High School, where Doctor McWhorter was Principal, when he espoused the American Cause and went into the American Army, and William Adair's other two sons, Wiliam Adair, Jr., and James, both followed into the American Army; also Adairs' foster son, Edward Lacy, whom they had raised and treated like one of their own sons. Lacy became a Colonel and was in many of the important battles of the revolution, and he was elected County Judge of Chester Co., after the war was over; he was an honorable citizen and always appreciated his foster parents.

Some battles of the pending war were fought on Fishing Creek in Adair's neighborhood; Hauck's party stopped at Adair's on their way to Williamson's. After having taken the silver buckles from Mrs. Adair's shoes, the rings from her fingers and the handkerchief from her neck, they took her husband out and put a rope around his neck and were about to hand him because his sons were out with the rebels, when some of the stories pleaded in his behalf that the old man was not so much to blame, it was the mother who had encouraged her sons, and urged them to their rebellious course. The officer then drew Mrs. Adair apart; and remarking that he had understood her sons were fine young men, and that her influence over them was such that she could persuade, them to anything she pleased, promised, if she would swing them over to the King's service, he would obtain for each of them a commission in the British army.

The matron replied her sons had minds of their own, thought and acted for themselves.

The call made by the Whigs before daylight next morning, July 12 has been noticed. After they were gone, Mr. and Mrs. Adair left the house quietly, leaving the two officers in bed, who had quartered themselves upon them, for they know in a short time there would be warm work at their neighbors, had scarcely reached the shelter of a thicket when they heard the first gun fire, and for an hour or more while the firing continued they remained in agitating suspense. At length, venturing in sight of the road, they saw the red coats and Tories flying, and soon afterward, the gallant McClure in pursuit; no longer in fear, they returned to the house. When they went to the battle ground, Mrs. Adair helped to dress the wounds of Captain Anderson, who had insisted that she send sons to him, and reminded him of the order. His reply when she showed her son was ill, "a little too late."

The sons removed their aged parents with their movable property to Virginia, and then came back to the Camp, and all again took up arms, which were never laid down until the surrender of Cornwallis.

Then they returned home, and each took up bravely the work of once more replenishing the comforts of homes so often over-run during the war. After the middle of the year 1788, William Adair's whole family, after selling their home, moved off to Kentucky, and henceforth William Adair, the Pioneer, was known as the father of the Kentucky Adairs.

1754
2 William Adair=Mary Moore 2a

Son of (I) Thomas Adair   Daughter of (2b) James Moore and Eliza Newfville Moore (2c).

Progeny: Six Children

3.   I   Betsy Adair, b about 1756, m John Moore, and raised 15 children.
4.   II   John Adair, B 1757, m Catherine Palmer, and became Governor of Kentucky.
5.   III   William Adair, B 1759, m Mary Irvine, was Lieutenant in Revolution Army.
6.   IV   James Adair, b 1761, remained single, d, age 29 years, a Revolutionary soldier.
7.   V   Mary Adair, b 1763, was a Heroine of the Revolution, m 1st John Nixon; 2d marriage to David McCalla, raised two families.
7a.   VI   Alexander Adair, died at the age of 16 years.

(2) William Adair and his wife spent their old age in Mercer County, Ky., and were buried at Whitehall in that County.

4. WILLIAM ADAIR, The Soldier in the Revolution

William Adair Jr., son of William Adair, the pioneer, was the third child in the family of his parents. He was a soldier in the American Army, War of the Revolution, and took part in many important battles. He served part of the time in Col. Casey's regiment as Adjunct, and part of the time with Col. Lacy (his foster brother).

The following was copied from the records of South Carolina after the War was over;

"State of South Carolina in account with William Adair:

June 18, 1780; To 60 days as Adjutant	L 38-	11-	5
Feb. 12, 1781, To 30 days as Adjutant	L 9-	12-	11
Less	L 9-	12-	11
	L 28-	18-6 ¼	

Sworn to by Col. Casey."

State of South Carolina: In account with William Adair:
Sept. 19th, 1781.

Receipt of William Adair, 1070 wt of flour, 5 ½ bushels of wheat, 5 bushels of corn, for the use of widows and distressed Families in Col. Casey's Regiment.

Judge Irvine Adair, from Portrait

Ms. Irvine Adair, from Portrait Painted 1824

Per, Joseph Adair Sr., Commissary, D. Co.
Sworn to by Col. Casey.

(4) William Adair, Jr.   =   Mary Irvine. II

Progeny: 2 Sons

8	I	William Irvine Adair.
9	II	Alexander Adair.

William Irvine Adair was well educated, and a polished gentleman. He was a nephew of Governor Adair, which gave him prestige, was admitted to the Bar at Greensburg, Green County, Ky., in 1805; a few years later, in 1808 he was elected to the Kentucky State Legislature. In 1812, President Madison appointed him Capt. In the U.S. Army, with special duty as recruiting officer for Kentucky. After peace was made in the War of 1812-15; Wm. I. Adair settled in Madison Co.,, Alabama, in the northwest part of the State. Here he practiced law and became a judge of one of the higher Courts of Alabama, and held the office during the remainder of his life. Judge Adair took an active part in the State Militia Organization and was elected and served as General. He was married about 1820.

1820

(8) Judge William Irvine Adair = Miss Martha Jones 12

Progeny: 4 Children

13	I	William Arthur Adair, Father of the Marshall Editor.
14	II	Jones Baker Adair, father of the Bellingham Banker.
15	III	Mary Adair, m Mr. Brooks; she and her children all died early.
16	IV	Kate Adair; m, 1st, Capt. Cook; m, 2d, Doctor W.H. Dial, buried in Marshall.

(13) William Aruthur Adair =

Progeny

17	I	William Arthur Adair Jr.
18	II	Alexander Adair, m; his descendants live in Memphis and Jackson, Tenn. His other children died in infancy.

17 William Arthur Adair, Jr. = Hattie Colmary 8

Progeny: Two children

19	I	Munsell Lee Adair, m, is a Physician in Shreveport, Louisiana.
20	II	Octavia, daughter, m Doctor R. G. 21 Granbery of Marshall, Texas.

23 *IRVINE JAMES ADAIR*

Son of 24 Jones Baker Adair, and Mary Rebecca 25 (Cooke); Grandon of 8 William Irvine Adair of the Alabama Supreme Court; born Sept. 21, 1851, at LaGrange, Tenn. Lineage: Jones Baker Adair, William Irvine Adair, William Jr., William Sr., Thomas Adair.

1873

23 Irvine James Adair=Willie Anne Thompson 26

Progeny: Four Children

27 I   Irvine James Adair Jr. died in 1877.
28 II   Katherine Adair, married Hugh I. Burlingame 32.
29 III Mary Adair, m. Lamar W. Lidstone, 31
30 IV   Franklin Fagon Adair, Killed by an Automobile, July 27, son, Irvine James Adair 3d.

(28) Katherine Adair = Hugh I. Burlingame.

Progeny: Three Children

33 I   Annie Adair Burlingame.
34 II   Hugh Insley Burlingame.
35 III Aline Burlingame.

(29) Mary Adair = Lamar W. Lidstone.

Progeny

36I 3Irvine Leslie Lidstone.
37II 3Nicholas Adair Lidstone, (just appointed a cadet at Annapolis.)
38III 3Helen catherine Lidstone.

All now living in Bellingham, Washington.

(23) Irvine James Adair was a Civil Engineer until his marriage, when he entered the mercantile business in Lagrange, and cigar mfg. business in Memphis. The panic of 1873-4, and yellow fever epidemic in 1878, took his means, except enough to buy a small Orange Grove in Florida, which he sold in 1879, and moved to Dallas, Texas; becoming employed in the Exchange Bank of Dallas in 80s; in '83 went with the owners of this bank into the American National Bank of Dallas, now the American Exchange National Bank of Dallas, where he was employed until July 1887; leaving then to become assistant Cashier of Merchant's and Planter's Bank of Pine Bluff, Arkansas,, where he remained until June 1890, when he organized the Merchants and Planters bank of Warren, Arkansas, being its Cashier and General Manager, until Jan. 1905, when he moved to Bellingham, Washington, and organized the Northwestern State Bank of South Bellingham and Northwestern National Bank of Bellingham both Washington.

William Arthur Adair

Mrs. Hattie Colmary Adair

He was continuously president of both these banks until 1912 when he and his friends sold their interests in the National bank and he remained from then on as president and general manager of the State bank until its conversion into the American National bank of Bellingham in 1922, since which time and until the present date he was still holding that position 1919, just six months after being discharged by the army. He left a

Mr. Adair has never been a politician, and is independent in politics He is a member of Kulshan Club, Bellingham Golf and Country Clubs, a Scottish Rite Mason and a Shriner, and a Presbyterian.

CHAPTER IX
ALEXANDER ADAIR
The Marshal of Florida, and His Descendants

(9) Alexander Adair, son of William Adair, Revolutionary soldier and Nephew of the Governor; Was appointed Marshal of Florida, being a Territory at that time, Florida was largely ruled by the U.S. Marshal. Everything was moving along orderly when Marshal Adair was suddenly attacked with Yellow-Frever and died, leaving a family of little children. The God-Mother of these children put them in covered wagons and carried them overland back to Kentucky, where they were raised and most of them continued to live in Green County, Kentucky.

9 Alexander Adair=Eliabeth W. Monroe 39
Nephew of the Governor
Progeny: Six Children

40	I	William Adair, b
41	II	Mary Pawling Adair, b.
42	III	Anna Bell Adair b.
43	IV	Andrew Monroe Adair, b.
44	V	John Alexander Adair, b.
45	VI	Kate Adair, b.

40 Doctor William Adair=Elvira Bowling 46
Progeny of Doctor William Adair and Elvira Bowling:
Three Children

47	I	Alexander M. Adair.
48	II	William Bowling Adair.
49	III	Mary Eliza Adair.

41 Mary Pawling Adair=Thomas M. Wagoner 50
Progeny: Five Children

51	I	Betty Wagoner, m Thomas Edwards 51, one daughter, dead.
52	II	Adair Wagoner, died.
53	III	Arthur Wagoner.
54	IV	Cattie Wagoner, m Rev. Thomas M. Gunn, 56, have four children.
55	V	Thomas Wagoner, killed on Brush Creek, Green Co., Ky., during Civil war.

42 Anna Bell Adair=Doctor A. S. Lewis 57

Kate Adair, A Southern Beauty of Her day.

AMERICAN ADAIRS—Line A

Progeny: Six Children

58. I   Kaste Lewis.
59. II   Thomas Lewis.
60. III   Mary Lewis.
61. IV   Lilly Lewis.
62. V   William Lewis.
63. VI   Stuart Lewis.

58 Kate Mildred Lewis=Lucien Durham
Oldest daughter of Doctor A.S. Lewis and
Anna Bell Adair Lewis.

Progeny: Four Children

65. I   Henry Adair Durham.
66. II   Anna Bell Durham, m James Patten Strader, one son, Harry Adair Strader (died, Home Canadian, Texas.)
67. III   Vivian Elizabeth Durham.
68. IV   Archie Lucien Durham.

43 Andrew Monroe Adair, died single.

44 John Alexander Adair=Bird Stockton 69
Son of Alexander Adair

Progeny: Seven Children

70. I   Kate Laura Adair.
71. II   Willis Adair.
72. III   Anna Bell Adair.
73. IV   John Horsen Adair.
74. V   Jessie Adair.
75. VI   Shelly Adair.
76. VII   Chester Adair.

45 Kate Adair=Gen E.H. Hobson 81
Daughter of Alexander Adair.

Progeny: Six Children

77. I   William Hobson.
78. II   Anna Hobson.
79. III   Atwood Hobson.
82. IV   John Adair Hobson, m Hattie Hodges, 85, Progeny, none.
83. V   Edwena Hobson, Single.
84. VI   Betty Hobson, m 86 L.C. Alcorn.

CHAPTER X

BETSY AND MARY ADAIR
Sisters of the Governor
4 Betsy Adair=John Moore 95

Oldest child of William and Mary Moore Adair.
Progeny: Fifteen Children some of their names are 96 John, 97 Louise, 98 Anne, 99 Abigail, and so on to fifteen. Whose name as marriages we do not know.

Baylor University: the great Baptist Institution of Texas, was founded and established by the Burleson brothers of Waco, Texas. Their names were Rufus C. Burleson (101) and Richard B. Burleson. (100)

Their tradition was to the effect that their mother was one of the Adair stock, related to the Governor; she was noted for beauty, intelligence and piety; and it was from her that they inherited their noble qualities.

Her name was Abagail and it is probable that she was a daughter of Betsy Adair Moore, a sister of the Governor.

8 Mary Adair=John Nixon 86
Fifth Child of William and Mary Adair.
Progeny: Two Daughters

87	I	Margaret Nixon, McCown of S.C. no progeny.
88	II	Mary Nixon, married David Hemphill, progeny; One son, David Hemphill, Jr.

Second Marriage, (8) Mary Adair=David McCalla 89
Progeny: Five Children

90	I	James McCalla, m Miss Moore.
91	II	Polly McCalla, m Mr. Padion.
92	III	Betsy McCalla m another Mr. Padion.
93	IV	Thomas McCalla died young, unmarried.
94	V	Isabella married Mr. Armour.

Mary Nixon's second marriage was to Rev. Doctor John Hemphill, (the two Hemphills not being blood related.) She, Mary, died in 1854, leaving three sons: James, David and Robert Nixon. David died in 1842, leaving a widow and three children, (we presume these children are named Hemphill, but the copy does not say so.)

The two sons were killed in the war, and the girl's husband also.

Robert Nixon Hemphill is a planter and was living on the old homestead in 1882.

James Hemphilll is a lawyer of Chester, S.C., since 1836. He married a Miss Brawley of N.C. and has seven children, four sons and three daughters. Eldest son a banker, second son a lawyer, third a Presbyterian Minister, Pastor of the Second Presbyterian Church in Louisville, Ky. The fourth son graduated from Princeton, N. J., in 1882.

CHAPTER XI

BIOGRAPHY OF GENERAL JOHN ADAIR

Eight Governor of Kentucky
By THE EDITOR

John Adair, (John 3 Adair, William 2 Adair, Thomas Adair) was born in Chester District, South Carolina, on the 9th of January, 1757.

His father was William 1 Adair, who was a member of the noted Waxaw colony of Scotch-Irish emigrants from the north of Ireland, who settled first at Chester, Pennsylvania, but after a short time, moved to South Carolina and settled in Chester and neighboring districts.

This Conoly was noted for the intelligence and public spirit of its members and produced such noted Americans as the subject of this sketch, General Andrew Jackson, Hon. John C. Callhoun, Doctor J. Marion Sims, General Wade Hampton, Bishop alexander Gregg and many others. So, Adair not only came from good stock, but he also had a good environment. He attended the primary schools of his neighborhood and was sent to High school in Sharlotte, N.C. While he was at High school, the Revolutionary War broke out and John Adair, with a number of his fellow students, went into the American Army, first as a private, and was in many battles. Was with Sumpter when he was surprised in camp at Fishing Creek but escaped and made his way to Charlotte. In a few days he was sent out, with George Weir as a companion, probably to learn of the welfare of his companions; they went to the house of a friend to spend the night, and while there they were captured; they had a chance the next night to escape, but Adair had his heart et on two good horses that he needed, so lost his opportunity. They were taken to Camden Jail, and were brought before Lord Rawden, who had halters put around their necks to frighten them into giving information, but they would say nothing except they had no disclosures to make. Adair was kept a prisoner for nine months, suffering from hunger, needed clothes, and finally taking small pox; though only 18 years old he was brave and tried to keep his fellow prisoners cheered up. A few broke jail and tried to escape, Adair among the number, though he was covered with smallpox; and he was traced by the blood from his feet and legs.

Thomas Wade took Adair on his back to hasten with him before they would be overtaken. He begged to be laid down and for the others to leave him, but they did not and were all captured and taken back to Camden. When the guards came back with them, Lord Rawden had one ankle of each prisoner chained to the floor. I have heard that John Adair carried the scar to his grave.

Mrs. Sarah McCalla's husband was also a prisoner, suffering from smallpox, and she was always petitioning for a pardon for him. Taking John Adair's sister Mary with her, she went before Lord Rawden and procured the release of her husband, Thomas McCalla, and John Adair; these soldiers were too weak to walk, but the women had gone on horseback, and gave the horses to the sick men, alternately walking; they reached McCalla's home the next day.

After John Adair's recovery, he served the remainder of the war on the staff of Gen. Sumpter as aid-de-camp and ranked as Major.

On September 9th, 1984, Major Adair married Miss Catherine Palmer whose mother was a Huguenot, named Bennoist (pronounced Benny).

In April, spring of 1788, Major John Adair was a member of the South Carolina Convention that ratified the new Constitution of the United States.

The next thing we hear of Adair, he is in Kentucky. There seems to be some discrepancy about the date of this Migration; but it is certain that he was a citizen resident of South Carolina during the first half of the year of said Convention to wit; 1788 and served as a member thereof.

The Kentucky Militia were noted as brave soldiers, and it devolved on this State to defend the Northwest frontier, embracing Ohio, Indiana, and Illinois, against the Indians who were continually incited against, and led by the British and the French Canadians to make raids on the Americans.

General Adair took an active and prominent part in these defensive Wars and was in many battles with these Indians during the ten years following 1792. In this year of 1792, at the head of a body of mounted volunteers from Kentucky, he fought a desperate battle with the Indians near Eaton in Preble County, Ohio. In that battle George Madison, afterwards Governor of Kentucky; Col. Richard Taylor, the father of President Taylor, and many others were wounded.

On another occasion the Kentucky troops under command of Adair were surprised by Chief Little Turtle who band of Indians largely outnumbered the Kentuckians. Adair extricated his troops in good order after inflicting more losses on the enemy than they received. Adair was promoted again for bravery and military skill.

Our British Neighbors in Canada kept up their attacks through the Indians until General Wm. Henry Harrison, in command of Kentucky troops trashed them out and captured Tecumseh and his prophet at Tippecanoe.

The British had given the Americans so many causes for War during Jeferson's Administration, that the majority of the people wanted War with Britain, and they got it during Madison's Administration, in the War of 1812-1815. The United States was not prepared for it and the British go the best of it during the first year; they went up the Potomac River to Washington and burned the Capitol; and they whipped the Americans at Detroit and round the Great Lakes because the Americans were commanded in Michigan by mere politicians with no military skill.

Gen. Adair at Battle of New Orleans

But the turning point came for the Americans with the victory of Commodore Perry in a Naval engagement on Lake Erie, and especially with the American victory on the River Thames in Michigan, about the same time, just as King's Mountain was the turning battle in the Revolution.

It is a remarkable fact that Gen. Shelby was the commander in both, and Gen. Adair was in both battles. Adair was first aide to Gen. Shelby at the battle of the Tames and was promoted for bravery and generalship. Governor Shelby appointed him Adjutant General of the Kentucky troops and sent him to New Orleans with the brevet rank of Brigadier-General. When they reached New Orleans, General Thomas, the senior officer, was ill, and Gen. Adair, being next in rank, took command of the Kentucky troops.

Late in 1814, a treaty of peace was signed at Ghent between the Representatives of Great Britain and the United States which was intended to terminate the war; but his was before the day of Steam railroads and telegraphs, and the armies in the field had not heard about it until after the battle of New Orleans. But this w3s very fortunate, because it was the greatest battle of the war, and the greatest victory for the Americans. It gave the Americans confidence and self-respect. And it took the pride and haughtiness and conceit out of the British and made them respect us as nothing else could. In short, it secured PERMANENT PEACE between the two countries.

In December, 1814, General Andrew Jackson was in command of the department of the Southwest, and General Packenham, the British commander, had an army of thirty to forty thousand troops afloat on the Gulf of Mexico in forty odd transports, conveyed by numerous Naval vessels. They were the flower of the British army.

It seems that Gen. Packenham planned to capture New Orleans before he sailed from his home port. And Gen. Jackson was watching him and keeping tabs on his movements for several weeks before the battle occurred. The mouth of the Mississippi was too shallow for deep water vessels to enter from the Gulf which made it necessary for the British to land and march overland up to New Orleans. Gen. Packenham felt the need of spies to pilot his army; he tried to engage one of the noted Lafitt Brothers, the pirates who maintained a station not only on Galveston Island, but they had a regular colony or town near the mouth of the Great River. Well, Gen. Packenham tried to engage them for spies, but instead the Lafitts made haste to see Jackson who was then at Mobile, and he lost no time in getting back and getting ready for the great battle. Jackson promised Lafitt a pardon for their Piracy crimes. He had the whole colony enlisted and put them in front of the battle in the thickest of the fight.

Both the armies began to throw up breastworks and mount batteries. They had some skirmishes during the last days of December, 1814. It was early in January following that the troops from Tennessee in command of General Carrol, and the Kentuckians under Gen. Adair reached New Orleans. President Madison's Secretary of War neglected and refused to equip the Kentucky troops, furnish them with uniforms, arms or transportation, notwithstanding it was his power and duty to do it. Gen. Jackson scored him heavily and the President finally removed him, but not in time to save the situation.

The Quartermaster of Kentucky finally advanced money from his private resource and secured some old cast-off Flatboats and started them down the river; but the troops had to stop a week at the mouth of the Cumberland River, to get out into the timber, split out boards and rebuild their boats before they could proceed.

When the Kentuckians finally reached camp, they were in a pitiful condition; only one suit of clothes, which they had on their backs. It was raining and cold and the mud and water ankle deep, no tents and no arms. But the people of Louisiana, and of New Orleans appropriated money and the good women of New Orleans made clothes for them. They had only about six hundred arms to equip two thousand soldiers. On the seventh, anticipating the attack by the British the following day, Gen Adair went into New Orleans and pleaded with the Mayor and the committee of safety to lend him for temporary use, several hundred stands of arms stored in the city Armory, held for defense of the city. To this the Mayor and committee finally agreed on condition that the removal of the arms be kept secret from the public. Thus four hundred more of the Kentuckians were armed ready for tomorrow's battle.

In council with Gen. Jackson, Gen. Adair had suggested "that the British would most probably endeavor to break our lines by throwing heavy columns against it at some given point, and that such was the discipline of their veterans, they might succeed in the effort without great resistance was made. To be prepared for such a contingency, it would be well to place a strong reserve of troops centrally in the rear of the line, ready at a moment's notice to reinforce the line at the point of assault." Gen. Jackson approved the suggestion and ordered Gen. Adair to hold the Kentucky troops of his command in position for such a contingency. So, Gen. Adair with about a thousand troops under arms took a position just in the rear of Gen Carroll's Tennesseans, occupying the center of the breastworks. On the left bank of the river, Gen. Jackson had 4600 men on the day of battle, 4000 of whom were in battle line.

The British under Gen. Packenham had 8000 in their attacking line of the left bank, the very flower of the British army.

In topography, the land along the Mississippi is higher next to the river, and a level prairie extends back about a mile to a swamp covered with timber; so that Jackson's trenches and batteries extend across from the river to the wooded swamp.

Both the main Armies were on the left, or east side of the river. On Saturday the seventh of January, 1815, everybody was on the qui vive in expectation of the great decisive battle.

Sunday, January 8th: It was not yet daybreak on Sunday morning when an American outpost came hastily in, with the intelligence that the enemy was in motion and advancing in great force.

In a brief time, as the day began to dawn, the light discovered to our men what seemed to be the entire British army in moving columns, occupying two thirds of the space from the woods to the river.

Obedient to the commands of their officers, who gallantly led in front of their men, the massive columns of the enemy moved up with the measured and steady tread. Suddenly a Congreve rocket, set off at a point nearest the woods, blazed its way across the British front in the direction of the river. This was the signal of attack. Immediately the first shot from the American line was fired from the twelve-pounder of Battery 6. This was answered by three cheers from the enemy, who quickly formed in close column of more than two hundred men in front and many lines deep. These advanced in good order in the direction of batteries 7 and 8 and to the left of these.

It was now evident that the main assault would be made upon that part of the breastworks occupied by Gen. Carroll's Tennessean's, with the intent to break the line here and flank Jackson's Army on the right. (just as Gen Adair anticipated and suggested to Gen. Jackson the day previous). As soon in the morning as word came that the British wee in motion for an advance, Gen. Adair formed his Kentuckians in two lines in close order and marched them to within fifty paces of the breastworks in the rear of Gen. Carroll's Command. The enemy's heaviest columns moved forward in Carroll's front.

The lines of the Kentucky troops were moved up in order of close column to the Tennesseans, deepening the ranks to five or six men for several hundred yards. Batteries 6, 7 and 8 opened upon the enemy when within four or five hundred yards, killing and wounding many, but causing no disorder in his ranks, nor check to his advance. As the enemy approached in range, the terrible fire of the rifles and musketry opened upon him from the Tennessee and Kentucky infantry, each line firing and falling back to reload, giving place to the next like to advance and fire. The British attack was supported by artillery fire, while a cloud of rockets continued in showers throughout the contest.

The assaulting columns did little execution with their small arms as they came up, relying more on the use of the bayonets in case of effecting a breach in our line. Some of them carried facines and ladders in expectation of crossing the ditch and scaling the parapet. But all in vain. The musketry of the Tennessee and Kentucky militia, joining with the fire of the artillery, mowed whole files of men and so decimated their ranks as to throw them into a panic of disorder and force a retreat. This disastrous repulse was within twenty-five minutes after the opening fire of the battle. Writers present who have undertaken to describe the scene at the time say that the constant rolling fire of cannon and musketry resembled the rattling peal of thunder following the lightning flashes in a furious electric storm. The defeated column forced to fall back broken and disordered, was finally rallied by the heroic efforts of their officers, reinforced by fresh troops, and let to a second assault.

But the carnage and destruction were as great as in the first attempt, while almost no impression was made on the defensive line of the Americans. The British were again compelled to retreat in disorder, leaving great number of their comrades dead or wounded on the ground, or prisoners to the Americans.

The hope of victory had now become a forlorn one to the British. They were broken in numbers, broken in order and discipline, and broken in prestige. Yet their brave officers, led by their Commander-in-Chief, Gen Packenham, determined not to give up the contest without a last desperate effort.

A part of the troops had dispersed and retreated to shelter among the bushes on the right; the rest retired to the ditch where they were first perceived in the morning, about five hundred yards in our front. In vain did their officers call upon them to rally and form again for an advance, striking some with the flat of their swords, and appealing to them by every incentive. They felt that it was almost certain destruction to venture again into the storm of fire that awaited them and were insensible to everything but escape from impending death. They would not move from the ditch and here sheltered the rest of the day. The ground over which they had twice advanced and twice retreated was strewn thickly with their dead and wounded. Such slaughter of their own men with no apparent loss on our side, was enough to appall the bravest of mankind.

Nearly a hundred of the enemy reached the ditch in front of the American breastworks, half of whom were killed and the other half captured. A detachment of British troops had penetrated the wood on our extreme left, to divert attention by a feint attack. The troops under Gen. Coffee opened on these with their rifles and soon forced them to retire.

After the main attack on the American left and center had begun, another column of over twenty-five hundred British, under command of Gen. Keene, advanced along the road near the levee, and between the levee and the river, to attack the American line on the extreme right. They gained a temporary advantage. But Gen. Beale's rifles and the seventh Regiment from the city defending this extreme, poured fatal volleys into the head of the column, while batteries 1 and 2 mowed down the rank. By these the further advance of the enemy was made impossible, while the nearest ground they occupied was strewn with their dead and wounded, among whom was Gen. Keene, Colonel Rence and many other prominent officers.

The battle was now ended so far as the firing of musketry was concerned. The last of these ceased one hour after the British column first in motion attacked our line upon the left center at half past seven o'clock. In that brief time, one of the best equipped and best disciplined armies that Britian ever sent forth was defeated and shattered beyond hope by half its number of American soldiers, mostly militia.

Adjutant General Butler in his official report to Gen. Jackson, a few days after the battle on the eight, placed the loss of the British at seven hundred killed, fourteen hundred wounded, and five hundred prisoners; 2600 men, or almost one third of the entire number of the enemy admitted having taken part in the contest of the day.

The loss of the Americans was six killed and seven wounded, thirteen in all.

(See Filson Historical Club Publication, Vol. XIX; page 84 et seq.)

The foregoing account was of the main battle, by the main armies, and on the east or left bank of the river, where the British army of invasion met the American army of defense.

General Jackson had anticipated that part of the British army might cross the river and go up on the west side of the river, but he did not seem to attach much importance to that side. He did not go and select a proper place for fortifications, but sent Gen. Morgan, who selected a place more than a mile wide from the river to the swamp, instead of finding a narrow place; Morgan's troops, with the help of Negro Slaves from the neighboring Plantations dug a trench three hundred yards long on the side next to the river and got through with it Saturday night, the seventh.

Gen. Jackson promised Gen. Morgan reinforcements by daylight on the morning of the eighth. So, late Saturday night Gen. Jackson ordered 175 of the Unarmed Kentucky militia (because they had the greatest reputation), to march over to Gen. Morgan's camp; the distance being ten miles, 5 miles up, and across and 5 miles down on the other side. It was raining and the mud and water was ankle-deep. They arrived at daybreak and were placed in battle line with no chance to eat or rest. Gen. Jackson intended to arm them from the arms stored in the armory of the city of New Orleans, but Gen. Adair had already secured those arms to quip four hundred of his command or troops in the main Army, not knowing that Gen. Jackson contemplated using them for any purpose. This detachment of 175 Kentuckians had no Muskets or rifles. Gen. Jackson finally found a few hunting pieces and sent them, but enough to supply only a small percent of the need and still fewer of these were in working order; therefore, it is not misstating the case when we say that these 175 Kentucky troops were unarmed.

These Kentuckians were placed, not in Gen. Morgan's trench, nor in line with it, but some distance in front near an old mill race, and in that mile of open country on their right, where they were expected to hold this vast space with no breastworks nor trenches, and no arms, except a few squirrel pieces. It was wonderful, the exaggerated ideas that Gen. Morgan and Gen. Jackson had about what the Kentucky troops could do. Gen. Morgan had his troops safe in the trench.

When the British army came up, about 2000 strong their Commander saw the situation and went for the weakest point, which was this mile of undefended space. They flanked the Kentuckians on both sides; about this time one of Gen. Morgan's aids came up and seeing the situation, he ordered the Kentuckians to withdraw to the line of Morgan's trench, which they did in good order. Up to this time they were giving the enemy the best they could with their Squirrel pieces, i.e. they were doing the enemy as much harm as they were receiving.

When the British came up in line with Gen. Morgan's breastworks, this little bunch of Kentuckians and Maj. Arnaud's command of Louisiana Militia were scattered out thinly trying to hold this wide, unprotected space, with no breastworks and no artillery, these militia did the only sensible thing they could under the circumstances; they retreated. But they were not alone; Morgan's whole force of 500 men left the trench and fled too. Gen. Morgan could have held his works with 200 men. He had artillery too. But they spiked their guns and all fled.

Gen Morgan reported to Gen. Jackson the misfortune he had met, ad attributed it to the flight of these troops from Kentucky and Louisiana, who had drawn along with them the rest of his forces. True, they were the first to flee; and their example may have had some effect in alarming others.

But in situation the troops differed, the one was exposed and enfeebled by th4e manner of their arrangement; the other much superior in numbers, covered a less extent of ground, were defended by a splendid breastwork manned by several pieces of artillery; and with this difference— the loss of confidence of the former was not without cause. Of these facts Commodore Paterson was not appraised; General Morgan was.

Both reported to General Jackson that the disaster was owing to the flight of the Kentucky Militia.

Upon this information, General Jackson founded his report to the Sec'y. of War, by which these troops were exposed to censures they did not merit. Had all the circumstances as they existed been disclosed, reproach would have been prevented. At the millrace not troops could have behaved better; they bravely resisted the advance of the enemy. Until an order to that effect was given, they entertained no thought of retreating.

Folling is the language of General Jackson in his report to the Secretary of War:

"Simultaneously with his advance upon my lines, the enemy had thrown over in his boats a considerable force to the other side of the river. These having landed were hardly enough to advance against the works of

General Morgan; and what is strange and difficult to account for, at the very moment when their discomfiture was looked for with a confidence approaching to certainty, the Kentucky reinforcements, in whom so much reliance had been placed, INGLORIOUSLY FLED, drawing after them by their example the remainder of the forces, and thus yielding to the enemy that formidable position.

"The batteries which had rendered me, for many days, the most important service, though bravely defended, were of course now abandoned; not, however, until the guns had been spiked."

Thus, General Jackson attempts to take spite out on the Kentucky militia for the grievance he imagined he had against General Adair, who had been the unwitting offended, in securing ahead of him, the arms stored in the Armory in New Orleans. Jackson gave all the blame to the 175 Kentuckians, unarmed as they were, unprotected and without a leader, because they did not and could not restrain the British army of 2000 men. Jackson had no censure for General Morgan and the remainder of Morgan's troops who were well armed and protected with breastworks and artillery, who fled when this little bunch Kentuckians were pushed back. Neither did he give any credit to the main body of the Kentucky army in the main battle, under the command of General Adair. He left that to be gathered from other sources. Morgan wanted a scapegoat for his blunders and cowardice, and Jackson wanted to ventilate his fury against General Adair; but Morgan and Jackson leave a poor monument to posterity in this event.

General Adair demanded a retraction from General Jackson; but General Jackson was not a man to retract anything, especially to General Adair.

General Jackson did, however, appointment a court of inquiry, who rendered a compromise verdict. But this was not satisfactory to General Adair, nor the Kentuckians who felt very bitter over the way they had been treated. General Adair kept repeating his demand to General Jackson for a retraction. Even after the armies had disbanded and returned to civil life, General Adair gave General Jackson no rest on the subject and the controversy became very bitter and resulted in a resort to the field of honor, (as dueling was called in those days.)

At the appointed time they met on the line between Kentucky and Tennessee with their Seconds, Surgeons, etc. Both principles were ambitious and had many friends. Their Seconds were broad-minded, so the matter was amicably adjusted when General Jackson retracted.

GENERAL ADAIR AS A STATESMAN

This field-of-honor incident was not published in detail until 1911. It was published by the Filson Historical Club of Louisville.

It was a tradition in the Adair family. The late venerable General D.L. Adair, of Hawesville, Ky., related in detain before he died. He was a son of Doctor Adair, who was a cousin of General Adair, and acted as a Second and Surgeon to Gen. John Adair on this field of honor occasion.

General Adair maintained in a most creditable manner the reputation of the Kentucky troops.

"In 1816 the Legislature of Kentucky passed a vote of thanks to General John Adair for his Gallantry at the battle of NEW ORLEANS, and more particularly for the deep interest he took in vindicating a respectable portion of the Kentucky troops from the libelous imputation of cowardice most unjustly thrown upon them by General Anderw Jackson."

General Jackson and General Adair belonged to the same political party; and there was nothing political in their relations.

Some Historians, who have attempted to write a Biography of General John Adair, have stated that General Adair became unpopular at one time, about 1807, on account of his friendship for Col. Aaron Burr. (See articles in the Encyclopedias.) All of which makes it desirable for us to review the character of this man Burr, in brief, to show that it was very creditable to General Adair, or any other man in those days to have such a friend as Col. Aaron Burr. Colonel Burr came of good stock, had a good education, married a brilliant woman, was a brave and loyal colonel in the Revolution, was shrewd and brilliant Lawyer, a sharp politician and an able Stateman; he was the most eloquent speaker that American had produced up to that time.

Mr. Burr was one of the first Senators in Congress for New York; and in 1800 he ran for the Presidency and tied Jefferson, in the Electoral College. The election was thrown into the House of Representatives, where Jefferson won out by one vote, by desperate lobbying. That make Burr Vice-President. After his term was out, he quarreled with general Hamilton and then killed him in a duel. His noble wife died about that time, and he retired from politics. As a practical politician and statesman, Colonel Burr was more than a match for any of his contemporaries, and many of them were jealous and afraid of him.

Colonel Burr obtained a land grant in western Louisiana and thought to form a nucleus there from which to colonize Texas, which belonged to Spain at that time; his plan was to gather settlers in the country tributary to the Ohio river as he passed won in boats; at this time President Jefferson gave out the charge that Aaron Burr was guilty of treason against the United States because he contemplated a colony in Texas, which might ultimately become a Republic.

Jefferson had Col. Burr arrested by the federal authorities in Kentucky, where he was tried, defended by Henry Clay, and acquitted.

Col. Burr's boats sailed on down the river, but on reaching the line of Mississippi, the Governor of that Territory, (for it was not yet in the Union,) being an appointee of President Jefferson, had Col. Burr arrested again. He kept him in prison for many, many months without a trial, and finally when they could hold him no longer, the president ordered him to Richmond for trial by Chief Justice John Marchall. And Col. Burr was acquitted, there being no evidence4 against him.

If Mr. Jefferson had any evidence, he was too cowardly to bring it up in court. It was simply persecution on the part of Mr. Jefferson, prompted by jealousy.

General Adair was not a many to sympathize with jealous persecution, nor condone it. Of course, it made Gen. Adair unpopular with Mr. Jefferson's followers and henchmen who believed that Col. Burr was guilty of treason against the United States, simply because President Jefferson said so. The Encyclopedia writers on the Biography of Gen. Adair seemed to think that Gen. Adair needed an apology. And this is our excuse for this digression.

But we have been taught by our schoolbooks, for a hundred years, that Col. Aaron Burr was guilty of treason against the U.S. notwithstanding the fact that he was acquitted of the charge.

Mr. Stephen F. Austin followed up Col. Burr's enterprise and established a colony in Texas, a few years later, and it was esteemed quite an honor to him.

General Adair's first experience as a Statesman was as a member of the South Carolina Convention to ratify the Constitution of the United States in 1788. He favored the adoption of that Instrument, and also some amendments thereto.

He migrated to Kentucky in 1789 and established his home in Mercer County. He was a delegate to the first convention and helped to make the first Constitution of Kentucky. Then for the next ten years he was a member of the State Legislature of Kentucky, one or two terms in the Senate, but most of the time in the Lower House, where he was Speaker of the House a part of the time.

In 1803-04 General Adair was Register of the U.S. Land Office at the Capital of Kentucky, Frankfort.

In 1805, there was a vacancy in the U.S. Senate from Kentucky, an unexpired term. After he had served less than two years, it came time for his successor to be elected. Adair was a candidate for the new term, but he was defeated by Senator Pope. Therefore, he resigned and refused to serve out the senatorial term that he had, and Henry Clay was elected to succeed him.

In 1817 Adair was in the State Legislature again.

In 1820 General John Adair was elected Governor of Kentucky: the eighth Governor of the State in numerical order. His competitors were Judge Logan, Governor DeSha, and Col. Butler; three of the most popular men in the state, and he outdistanced them all.

Governor Adair served out his four-year term with great credit. Some of his achievements were the enactment of laws favoring public schools and establishing schools for higher education in the state. And for progress in general, Governor Adair had many difficult problems to deal with during his term; but he discharged the duties of his office with great ability, establishing himself in the confidence of the people; taking a position among the most worthy and patriotic Governors of the state.

Governor Adair had a term in the Lower House in Congress from his district in 1830-1.

The incidents in Governor Adair's life show him to have been a strong character. He was independent, with strong will, perseverance, dignity, honor and broad patriotism. He was brave and sagacious in war; broad and wide in statesmanship; true to his friends; and a most lovable man in his family and home.

Governor Adair never was known to flatter any man, so that when he passed compliments on a military man, it meant volumes in praise of that man. We have read incidents bearing this out.

Adair's independence is shown when he resigned his seat in the United States Senate because he was not re-elected to succeed himself.

Copy of a Resolution by the Legislature of Louisiana
Acts of 1815, Page 70

"Resolved by the Senate and House of Representatives of the state of Louisiana in General Assembly Convened:

"That the Tanks of the General Assembly shall be presented in the Name of the State to our brave brother soldiers from Tennessee, Kentucky and the Mississippi Territory, and their gallant Leaders, Generals Coffee, Carrol, Thomas, Adair and Colonel Hinds, for the brilliant share they have had in the defense of their Country, and the happy harmony they have maintained with the inhabitants and militia of this state.

Magloive Gurehard,
Speaker of the House of Representatives.
Fulmer Skipwith,
President of the Senate.

Approved: Feb. 2d, 1815

William C.C. Claiborne,
Governor of the State of Louisiana.

Another Resolution by the same Legislature adopted a special vote of thanks to General Adair for the part he took and the service he rendered in the defense of New Orleans. Authenticated by the same officers of the Legislature and Approved by William C.C. Claibourn, Governor of the State of Louisiana.

A former Chief Justice of Louisiana told this Editor that he had often seen this resolution in the Acts of the Legislature, but Resolutions not being indexed, he could not find it at the time.

Governor Adair's traits were well shown in his controversy with General Andrew Jackson. This incident shows Adair's strong will, perseverance and his sense of justice, in his defense of the troops under his command in Jackon's army. At first Gen. Jackson flatly refused to retract the slanders he uttered against the Kentucky troops. General Adair continued his demand for a retraction; then Gen. Jackson tried to evade it by having a pact court ease him down, but Adair would not agree to it. Then Jackson tried to bluff Adair with abusive language; but finally, a resort to the field of honor was the last resort. Adair was willing to put himself up as a target to vindicate the honor of innocent soldiers in his army. If General Jackson had not retracted, either one or both would have been planted in the cemetery. But fortunately, the seconds on both sides were broad-minded men, and after a consultation, they required Gen. Jackson to make a full retraction, which he did, and all was forgiven. The Kentucky Legislature, which was then in session (1816,) accepted the retraction and thanked Governor Adair for his full vindication of the Kentucky troops, and his worthy service in the battle of New Orleans.

Kentucky, Missouri and Iowa each have a county named in honor of Gen. John Adair, the eighth Governor of Kentucky.

General Adair and Mrs. Catherine Palmer Adair, his wife, raised a large and interesting family of nine daughters and two sons, all worthy children. Their home, called White Hall, in Mercer County, was noted far and wide for its hospitality.

When Governor Adair was in the Senate in 1805-6; and again in 1830-1 was in the House of Representatives, some of his daughters always accompanied him and spent the winters in Washington. They went overland on horseback and rode the finest horses. (We will have more to say about their children later.)

GOVENOR ADAIR'S MONUMENT AT FRANKFORT

Having attained the age of four score and three years, he passed away at his home at White Hall on May 19th, 1840, and was buried there; but in 1872 his remains were removed to the State Cemetery at Frankfort, where the State erected over his grave a monument with the following inscription:

On the North Side

"John Adair was born in Chester District, South Carolina, January 9th, 1757; died at White Hall, Mercer County, Kentucky, May 19th, 1840, age 83 years.

"This monument is erected by the people of Kentucky, in pursuance of a resolution by the General Assembly, approved March the 5th, 1872, as a mark of their appreciation of his services as a Soldier and Statesman."

West Side

"AS A STATESMAN—Previous to his removal from South Carolina, served as a member of the Convention which ratified the Constitution of the United States. Becoming a citizen of Kentucky, he represented the County of Mercer in the legislature in 1895-6, afterwards frequently a member of both House and Senate. In 1805 he was elected to the U.S. Senate to fill an unexpired term. In 1820 was elected Governor and served the four-year term. In 1830 served one term in the lower House in Congress."

Ease Side

AS a Soldier—He entered the Revolutionary Army at the age of seventeen, and served through the War, first as a private, afterwards as aide-de-camp to General Sumpter. Moved to Kentucky in (1789). Participated in Indian campaigns in 1791-2-4; and the war with Great Britian, 1812-15.

AMERICAN ADAIRS—Line A

South Side

Catherine Adair, wife of John Adair, born near Charleston, South Carolina, October 17th, 1768. Died at Montrose near Frankfort, Ky., September 24th, 1854, and was buried at White Hall by the side of her husband. Her remains have been removed to this spot and now rest in the same grave with his after a union in life of fifty years.

In death they are not divided.

RECORD TAKEN FROM FAMILY BIBLE OF JOHN ADAIR AND HIS WIFE, CATHERINE PALMER ADAIR

(2) William Adair, Sr. (Born 1719) Married 1749, Mary Moore, his wife, (Born 1729.) Had four sons and two daughters. John Adair, son of William and Mary Adair Born Jan. 9, 1757. Catherine Palmer, his wife, Born Oct. 17, 1768, Married 1784.

Catherine Palmer was the second daughter of Henry Palmer and Ann Benoist Palmer.

Children of John Adair and Catherine Palmer Adair

75. I **Anna P. Adair,** Born April 8, 1786. Died 1853. Married Judge John L. Bridges in 1803. Had six daughters and four sons.
76. II **Mary Adair,** Born April 17, 1788. Died May, 8, 1813. Married Mark Hardin (lawyer) in 1805. Had one daughter and two sons.
77. III **Eliza P. Adair,** Born August 10, 1790. Died 1871. Married Judge Thomas B. Monroe in 1812. Had five sons and four daughters.
78. IV **Catherine P. Adair,** Born July 17, 1792. Died Nov. 16, 1820. Married John M. Foster, (lawyer) in 1814. Had two daughters.
79. V **Margaret L. Adair,** Born May 28, 1794. Died --. Married Col. William P. Anderson in 1814. Had two daughters and five sons. She afterwards married (second husband) Doctor Joseph M. Bybee and had one daughter.
80. VI **Sarah B. Adair,** Born March 8th, 1797. Died October 1854. Married William Butler (lawyer) in 1815. Had no children.
81. VII **Isabella M. Adair.** Born May 3rd, 1799 Died --. Married Benjamin F. Pleasants (lawyer) in 1815. Had three sons and two daughters.
82. VIII **Eleanor K. Adair.** Born June 5th, 1801. Died --. Married Col. James M. White (lawyer) in 1820. Had no children. Married for second husband, Doctor T. Beatty, no children by this marriage.

AMERICAN ADAIRS—Line A

83. IX **Henry P. Adair,** (Afterwards changed to Henrietta.) Born Aug 12, 1805. Died Aug. 31, 1833. Married Charles Buford (lawyer) in 1821. Had two daughters and one son.
84. X **Doctor William H. Adair.** Born July 9th, 1805. Died 1959. Married Elizabeth A. Cromwell in 1830. Had three sons and three daughters. Two sons and one daughter died in infancy, living only an hour. (Doctor Adair's full name was William Henry Palmer Adair.)
85. XI **John Adair, jr.,** Born Aug. 8th, 1808. Died at Astoria, Oregon, In 1888. Married Mary Ann Dickerson in 1834. Had eight daughters and five sons (He also was a lawyer.)

Total 58 Grandchildren

CHAPTER XII
HON. JOHN L. BRIDGES
A Justice of the Supreme Court of Kentucky

75 Anna P. Adair, the oldest daughter of Governor and Mrs. Katherine Adair, was born in South Carolina, April 8, 1786. She married Hon. John L. Bridges, who was Chief Justice of the Supreme Court of Kentucky. Judge Bridges got considerable prestige by his decision in the celebrated case of Wilkersons and Taylor—in which case Sargeant of S.S. Prentiss, distinguished himself in his wonderful defense of Wilkerson. It was in this "Change of Venue Case," that Judge Bridges was crowned with glory and distinction. In honor of his brilliancy, a painting was made of him and hung over the Judges' Seat in the Court House at Herrodsburg, Kentucky.

Married 1803

75 Anna P. Adair = Judge John L. Bridges, 86
Daughter of Governor   Chief Justice, Supreme Court of Kentucky
And his wife of Kentucky

Progeny: Six Daughters and Four Sons

- 87. I Isabell Bridges, born about 1804.
- 88. II Benjamin F. Bridges, born about 1806.
- 89. III Another daughter, married Doctor Thayor.

87 Isabell Bridges = Doctor Robert L. Scruggs, 88
Daughter of Judge John L. and Anna P. Bridges.

Progeny: Three Children

- 89. I William Adair Scruggs, m Miss Bell Herndon.
- 90. II John Bridges Scruggs, m Virginia Wilbourn.
- 91. III Penelope Andrews Scruggs, who married McGuire.

91 Penelope Andrews Scruggs=Thomas Richard McGuire 92
Daughter of Isabell Bridges and   of Irish Stock
Doctor Robert L. Scruggs.

Progeny: Four Children

- 92. I An infant, died.
- 93. II Nellie McGuire, died in her teens.
- 94. III Robert Joseph McGuire, a Spanish War Veteran.
- 95. IV Rosa Bell McGuire.

95. Rosa Belle McGuire=William A. Shelby, 96
Daughter of Penelope and Thomas R. McGuire.

Progeny: One child.

97. I Richard Denny Shelby, who married Miss India Merchant, 98.

(97) Richard Denney Shelby, was the son of Rosa Belle McGuire Shelby and William A. Shelby. He was an Aviator in the World War, first with the 139th Squadron, then with the 141st. He drove a Spad Machine, was made Flight Commander, and Captain of the 141st Squadron, and was decorated with the Distinguished Service Cross, at Chaumont, France, by Lieut. Col. Ulio. Captain Shelby's citation as copied from "Heroes All," reads:

"Distinguished Cross Citation."

1st. Lieut. Richard Denney Shelby, A.S. 13th Aero Squadron, distinguished himself by extraordinary heroism, in connection with military operations against an army enemy of the United States at Verdun, France, on Oct. 10th, 1918. Lieut. Shelby encountered six enemy planes at a very low altitude strafing our trenches. He immediately attacked, and dispersed the planes, and by skillful maneuvering brought one of the planes down, just behind our own lines, and in recognition of his gallant conduct, he was awarded the Distinguished Service Cross.

1850

88 Benjamin F. Bridges=Edna Withers Miller, 99
A grandson of Governor Adair
Progeny: One Daughter

100. I Anna Adair Bridges.

Married 1874

100. I Anna Adair Bridges=William D. Rembert 101
Great granddaughter of Governor   Of French Huguenot
Adair of Kentucky   stock, was a Confederate soldier
and a Successful businessman

Progeny: Three Daughters and One Son

102. I Elizabeth B. Rembert.
103. II Edna M. Rembert.
104. III William Adair Rembert.
105. IV Jesse Lee Rembert.

1898

102. Elizabeth B. Rembert=Russell V. Rogers, 106
Great-great-granddaughter of Governor Adair of Kentucky

Progeny: Two Children

107. I Vivianne Rogers, B. March 3, 1899.
103. II Russell V. Rogers, Jr.

1898
103. Edna M. Rembert=Rhodes S. Baker, 109
Great, great-granddaughter of
A Prominent Lawyer of Dallas
Governor Adair of Kentucky.

Progeny: Three Children\

110. I Dorothy Adair Baker, b. June 14, 1901.
111. II Winnifred Baker, b. Nov. 1907.
112. III Rhodes S. Baker Jr., B. Nov. 1912.

104. William Adair Rembert=Sarah E. Stevenson
Great, great grandson of Governor Adair of Kentucky.

Progeny: Two Sons

113. I William Adair Rembert Jr., b. Dec. 1911.
114. II Russell Stevenson Rembert, b. March, 1917.

1912
105. Jessee Lee Rembert = James Hart Willis, 115
Great, great granddaughter of Governor Adair of Kentucky.

Progeny: One Child, a daughter

116. Anna Rembert Willis, b. March 28, 1923.

(99) Edna Withers Miller, wife of Benjamin F. Bridges, (82) was born at the home of her grandfather, General Thos. Kennedy, in Garrard Co., Kentucky. Her parents being:

117. John A. Miller=Elizabeth Kennedy 118
They both died young.

We now take up the other progeny of Benjamin F. Bridges and Edna Withers Bridges, his wife.

I Elizabeth Miller Bridges, b 1851, died in infancy.

1885
119. Thomas Miller Bridge=Margaret Green 120

Progeny: Two Daughters

121. I Anna Lee Bridges.
122. II Bernice Bridges.
123. Katherine Pauling bridges, b. 1858, married John McNees. No Progeny.
124. John Miller Bridges, b. 1861, Single.
125. Benjamin F. Bridges Jr., b. 1866. Married (see next paragraph).

1890
125. Benjamin F. Bridges, Jr.=Alice Craig 126

Progeny: Five Daughters and Two Sons

127. I Edna Alice Bridges.

128. II Anna Bridges.
129. III Doris Bridges.
130. IV Ruth Bridges.
131. V Losi bridges.
132. VI John Craig Bridges, enlisted in the U.S. Navy.
133. VII Alexander Bridges, in Aviation service, near Dallas.

All the Bridges family being decedents of Governor John Adair and Katherine Palmer Adair, his wife.

CHAPTER XIII
MRS. FLORIDA WHITE
The Most Brilliant Woman the Adairs Ever Produced
BY MRS. ANNETTA SCOTT FOX

Second to her illustrious father, Governor John Adair, probably the most notable and distinguished member of the American branch of the Adair Family was his daughter, Eleanor Katherine, who, because of her beauty, intellect, grace and charm, was full of most interesting incidents and experiences, a romance which lasted from youth to a well-preserved old age.

She was born on June 5th, 1801, at her father's home, "White Hall", near Harrodsburg, Kentucky, one of a large family-nine daughters and two sons-of John and Katherine Palmer Adair. She received her education from a private tutor in the home; or, rather, received the foundation for that education which came from many years of study, extending far beyond the influence of governess or tutor, and which made of her a woman of remarkable intelligence and attainments. She was married at the age of sixteen to Col. Joseph M. White, the young couple are going at once to the newly acquired territory of Florida and settling in Escambia County at Pensacola. Col. White, who was a man of splendid mentality and unusual ability, soon became a lawyer of prominence and later an author of books on legal subjects, which even at the present time are used as authorities. After a few years he was sent to Washington to represent Florida in Congress, where he made a special study of international law, particularly as applied to Spanish claims in Florida. At this time his wife, "Ellen Adair," came to know all the notables of America, and soon gained in the social life of the Capitol a prominence most remarkable. When the well-known picture, painted to decorate the walls of Faneuil Hall, and at great cost by contributions of the wealthy merchants of Boston, designed and executed by the most distinguished artists in this country and Europe, to represent the group of the beauties of Washington assembled in the Senate at the Great debate between Webster and Hayne, the most conspicuous of the group is the beautiful face and elegant figure of Mrs. "Florida White."

Col. White was later appointed by the President Minister to France, and afterwards to adjust matters still pending between the Federal Government and Spain, growing out of the purchase from the latter of the territory of Florida. This work necessitated a long residence in Europe, through many visits were made to the United States and to the beautiful winter home, "Casa Bianca," which they had built in Jefferson County, Florida, near the old town of Monticello. During these many years of residence abroad, Col. And Mrs. White made an extensive acquaintance and many warm friends. It has often been said that no other American woman had ever received the attentions, nor been accorded the privileges and honors that were given this remarkable young woman, her popularity being as pronounced on the continent as it was in Great Britain. With splendid introductions which have her entrée into the most exclusive circles, she was presented at every European court and numbered among her friends many of royal birth.

Col. White died before the completion of the work in Spain, leaving no children, and an estate which at that time was considered a fortune.

Ellen, who in her early Washington days became known as "Mrs. Florida White," because there was another member of Congress by the name of White, a name which clung to her as long as she lived, returned to America after the death of her husband, making her home at "Casa Bianca," though continuing to spend much time in travel. While visiting in New Orleans some years later, she met Doctor Theophilus Beatty, a physician, member of an English family belonging to the nobility, a very handsome, intellectual, cultured and attractive man, when she later married. This marriage was congenial and happy, but unfortunately Doctor Beatty lived only a few years, and again, while still a young woman, Mrs. "Florida White," was a widow. Her after life was spent in intellectual pursuits and in charitable and religious work, rather than in social activities, though she still graveled a great deal, both in America and Europe, enjoying frequent visits to the family of her British husband. She had heretofore been recognized as a brilliant conversationalist, and now Mrs. Beatty became known as a writer of no mean ability. Her book of travels, which was published sometime after the death of Doctor Beatty, was most interesting. A later book, "The souvenirs of Noted Men and Women I Have Known," was never published, and there has been much speculation as to what became of the manuscript.

To her religious and charitable work, Mrs. Beatty gave herself with the same devotion and enthusiasm which had characterized earlier work that interested her. She was a devoted Presbyterian, giving liberally of her time, thought and means to further the work of that denomination. She became especially interested in the education of young theological students and gave generously to this cause. One of her beneficiaries was a young man who afterwards was a noted Southern preacher, to whom Mrs. Beatty became greatly attached, and, though there was no legal adoption, she often spoke of him as her "son," presenting him with a watch which he greatly prized, inscribed, "To My Son."

The last important church work in which she took part was the organization and building of the Southern Presbyterian Church in the City of Washington.

This noble woman died in Oxford, Mississippi, November 22nd, 1884, 83 years of age.

Sketches of Mrs. "Florida White," with interesting incidents of her life, were often published in books, magazines and newspapers. The only available one at this time, telling much of her social achievement, and written by a well-known Southern newspaper woman, Mrs. Mary E. Bryan, is valuable as coming from the pen of one who had personal acquaintance with Mrs. White, and also because it was written at a time when many were will living who were familiar with the events recorded. Some may consider Mrs. Bryan's sketch exaggerated praise, but Ellen Adair seemed always to inspire in those who wrote or spoke of her this enthusiastic admiration. The writer of this sketch can vouch for the authenticity of the incidents related, having heard in her youth the same events and many other romantic stories told by those who had personal knowledge of them. It seems to her not amiss to attach to this article this sketch written by Mrs. Bryan.

"FLORIDA WHITE"
A sketch of Ellen Adair Beatty—one of the noblest, most beautiful and most honored women of America.

By Mary E. Bryan in "New York Fashion Bazaar"

I remember once-ah! Many years ago-that I sat on the broad high steps of the old castle-like home of my childhood, among the pine hills of Florida, watching my father's return. I had not seen him since he bent over my trundle bed and kissed me goodbye in the early morning. Now, the moon was rising over the far hills-the full, rich, yellow moon; and the bright blooming jasmines were opening all their pale green chalices and steeping the air with perfume. I heard the roll of wheels at last; I saw the barouche with its black horses coming up the drive, and presently I was in my father's arms. As we came up the steps, I noticed that he was in full dress.

"I have been dining at a grand house today and with a grand lady," he said. "I have been a guest of Mrs. Beatty at her home of Casabianca. Some day you shall see her. She has received more homage abroad and at home than any other American woman."

"Is she so beautiful, father, and does she dress so fine?"

"That is a true feminine question. Yes, Mrs. Beatty is the most beautiful woman I ever saw. As for her dress, it is like herself. It seems a part of her. But it is not alone her beauty or her grace and intelligence that makes her so admirable. It is her great heart, her gracious and noble manner."

She cannot be at all young," my mother said, feeling a little natural pique to hear another woman so extravagantly praised.

One does not think of age when looking at Mrs. Beatty," my father said, "or if one does, it is only to remember Shakespear's word:

"Age cannot wither her, nor custom stale

Her infinite variety."

The incident stayed in my memory; my father's description of the Lady of Casabianca impressed me deeply.

"She must look like Mary Stuart," I thought, and I pored over the picture of that fair, ill-fated kueen—one of my earliest idols—now, alas! Dethroned by iconoclastic biographers. "Stately,—sweet, with dark gray eyes under black lashes and fine black eyebrows," so looked the picture of the

Mrs. Florida White, Noted for Brilliance and Beauty.
--Courtesy of Mrs. Kate Adair Hines of Athens. Alabama

hapless Scottish queen in the gorgeous purple-bound "Keepsake," and so booked (as I had learned by cross-questioning) the grand lady with whom my father had dined. I looked forward eagerly to the fulfillment of his promise that I should see her.

It was not fulfilled in those days. And they were long ago. Beautiful Casabianca with its magnificent old live-oaks—the pride of Florida—has passed into alien hands. Its grandeur is a memory. The house was destroyed by fire some years ago. The two hundred and fifty slaves, whose neat cabins clustered like a pretty village about the big house, are scattered far and wide by "freedom," and the mistress they loved so well—the Lady of Casabianca, was homeless in her last days—she who had given homes to so many.

I met the lady of my childish dreams for the first time summer before last on Lookout Mountain, or rather in Chattanooga, for she was not strong enough for the mountain trip. I had come at a summons from her to assist her in compiling a book—her "Souvenirs of Noted Men and Women"—personal reminiscences of the celebrated wits and statesmen of America and Europe whose friendship she had enjoyed, and whose letters to her filled a large, quaint, brass-bound chest.

She was now an octogenarian, but her tall figure was still erect, her beautiful eyes were still bright with kindness and intelligence, and her manner retained its old charm and stately sweetness. Looking at her even then, you realize why it was that crowned heads and strawberry leaves, as well as bays and laurels bent to la belle American; that famous sculptors and painters begged to reproduce her form and face, and the poets and wits of the day left their tribute to "Florida White."

She was a native of Kentucky (do all beautiful American women come from Kentucky?), and her father was that Generals Adair who figured so gallantly at the battle of New Orleans as to throw even General Jackson into shadow, and to the proud distinction of a vote of thanks for "saving New Orleans" at the hands of the Louisiana Legislature. That vote of thanks was a thorn in the side of "old Hickory" all his life, though he bestowed the most glowing eulogies on General Adair in his report of the battle. Yet he challenged him to a duel. That challenge is a matter of history, and it is needless to speak of its cause; only, thereby hangs a tale of illustrative of the spirit and wit of the Kentucky officer's daughter—fair Ellen Adair. The challenge grew out of an injustice done by General Jackson in his report of the battle of New Orleans. He wrote:

"The Kentucky troops stationed on the other side of the river fled ingloriously on being attacked." He failed to state that they fled because they were unarmed and had been ordered to retreat in case of an attack. It was before the days of steamers. The "men and munitions" of war were laboriously poled up the river in flat boats. Consequently, arms were wanting. The small body of Kentucky troops, so harshly stigmatized, had not a dozen guns among them. They were stationed on the bank of the river opposite to the scene of the main fight—for show—like the ox-hide elephants in old classic days or the log cannon of our Revolution times. They were commanded to retreat if attacked, and they did so. General Adair was impressed by the injustice of his superior's report. It mattered not that his own courage and military ability had been extolled in that report—it had been unjust to others. He replied to it in the newspapers and set the Kentucky troops right in public opinion. General Jackson was wroth and sent a peremptory challenge. It was accepted. "Rifles at six paces" was the answer of General Adair, who, as the challenged party, had the right to name the weapons and conditions. The challenge was withdrawn

Afterward when the old hero was president, and General or Governor Adair (as he like best his title of Governor of Kentucky) w3as sleeping the calm sleep of the brave and good, the Louisiana Legislature through the Secretary of State, petitioned his daughter Ellen to write a sketch of her father's life. She was then the wife of the accomplished Senator White, and the belle par excellence of Washington. When her sketch appeared in a handsome little volume, it roused the wrath of the president. He sent a peremptory summons for the author to appear before him. This she chose to disregard, and he sent his secretary with a courteous request for a private interview—he himself was not well enough to call. She drove to the White House—her husband remaining in the carriage—and found the president walking the floor with knitted brows. He stopped and bowed stiffly. "Macam" he said when he was seated, "you have written a book I wish I could suppress." No doubt he felt it a grievance that he could not order the volumes to be burned—magnificent autocrat that he was. "Fortunately, general, this is a free country," said the beautiful daughter of Adair. "But I shall answer it, madam—I shall answer it, rest assured." "Do so, general. It will give me an opportunity to sense of my father's modesty and reticence as to his own deserts, I have forborne to mention some incidents that would have reflected honor upon his memory—for instance, the fact that the Legislature of Louisiana voted him thanks for saving New Orleans." The president started and changed color. That shot touched the weakest part of his steel armor. He always wished that vote of thanks to be forgotten. He took two or three buried turns about the room, stopped in front of Mrs. White, and held out his hand. "You are the daughter of a brave comrade-in-arms and the wife of a man I honor," he said. "This discussion is idle. Let by-gones be by-gones. Shake hands with me and let us join the ladies upstairs and have some tea." And with a little smile of a quiet triumph, fair Ellen touched with her gloved fingers the horny hand of the hero; but she declined his proffered hospitality for that time.

How peerless she was in those days! She was the wife of the most accomplished gentleman in the capital city. She had transcendent beauty, wit, grace and esprit. Her toilets were ravishingly picturesque with a touch of her own strong, but pure personality. Men of letters, politicians, poets, crowded around her. Washington Irving was her friend. His letters overflow with her praises. John Quency Adams declared she was the Tenth Muse. His verses to her are almost the pretti4s in her album filled with the brilliant gleams from the famous stars of the day. This album had a little history. It was given her on her birthday by some distinguished worshiper—Irving or Judge Story. As she turned the tint, richly polished pages, she said:

"What a pity to spoil all these fair leaves with silly sentiment! I have a mind to say that no one shall write in it who is not over fifty."

"Dull and didactic it will then be, to the last degree," replied her young interlocutor.

"No, for I shall dedicate it to Folly," cried fair Ellen, and forthwith she painted the cap and bells on the initial leaf. Taking the cue, John Quincy Adams wrote these graceful verses:

> "Come, bring the cap and bring the bells,
>   And banish sudden melancholy,
> For who shall seek for Wisdom's cells
>   When Ellen summons him to folly?
> And I 'tis folly to be wise,
>   As bards of might fame have changed,
> Whoever looked in Ellen's eyes,
>   And then for sage's treasures panted!
> Oh! Take the cap and bells away;
>   The very thought my soul confuses
> Like Jack between two stacks of hay,
>   Or Garrick's choice between the Muses."

Senator White had represented our Government at several of the important courts of Europe; but he was not ambitious of political honors. His inclinations were social and literary in their nature. He adorned his charming wife and delighted in her social success. He determined that she should enjoy the best society on the continent, so they set sail for Europe for a long sojourn in its chief capitals.

They were furnished with letters of introduction from foreign ministers and American men of eminence. "But we found the letter of Washington Irving the most cordial 'open sesame' to London society," said Mrs. White.

The most exclusive London circles threw open their doors to Senator White and his lovely wife. Ellen's beauty, her peculiar grace, artless yet imperial, and her sparkling vivacity, made her the ornament of courtly drawing rooms, while her gracious and kindly temper disarmed envy and won her many true friends.

Tom Moore was then the sere and yellow leaf, and he was suffering with gout, but he made a special pilgrimage to the city to see la belle American. For the first time in years, he sat down to the piano (stipulating that she should stand by him) and sang some of his own songs, "The Last Rose of Summer," and "There's Nothing Sweet but Heaven."

"His voice was a little cracked and tremulous," said Mrs. White, but he made a striking figure at the piano—a little silver-haired, bright-eyed man, dressed in the height of the fashion.

Mrs. White enjoyed several of those "literary breakfasts" given by the millionaire poet—Samuel Rogers, which the writers of that day have described for us. Here she met the lions of the world literature, art, and diplomacy. Here she first saw Talleyrand, for whom she had conceived a prejudice, that thawed into admiration of his keep wit and lightning intelligence. Afterward he became her friend and correspondent.

"But always," she said, "I stood in awe of those sharp little flashes of irony. His caustic humor lighted here and there, rapid as it was keen. It spared neither friends nor foe."

It was at Roger's house that she first saw Coleridge. "His eloquent monologue" she said "sometimes became monotonous and was incomprehensible. It owed its chief charm to his musical utterance. Here also, fair Ellen heard Lamb recite an impromptu verse and listened to Hazlitt's brilliant talk.

Beautiful Mrs. Norton was there in the first flush of her lyric fame. "She moved like a queen, always surrounded by her admirers." Said Mrs. White.

Sir Edward Lytton, the famous novelist, was then the plain Mr. Bulwer, and not so honored among the aristocracy as he was afterward. He was the center, however, of a brilliant coterie, and the head of a social club that eagerly besought Mrs. White to become one of its members. She consented, but soon after the club proposed as one of its by-laws that no member should accept an invitation to an entertainment to which the other members of the society had not been invited. This was done, no doubt in order to utilize the popularity if the fair American. At Mrs. White's protest this by-law was omitted. Afterward, while she was attending a court fete, the club met, and Bulwer read the following verses inscribed to "Florida White— our truant member."

> "You have gone from us, lady, to shine
>   In the throng of the gay and the fair,
> If you're happy, we will not repine,
>   But say, can you think of us there?
> Circled round by the glittering crowd,
>   Who flatter, gaze, sign and adore,
> I would ask, if I were not too proud,
>   Has your heart room for open image more?
> Forgive us, sweet lady, oh do,
>   We'll blot out these words from our song;
> Though absent, we know you are true,
>   Though jealous, we feel we are wrong.
> Some millions of insects might pass
>   In your rays as in those of the sun
> Then is it not folly to ask
>   Your glances should beam here alone?"

Mrs. White was often a guest at King William's court; and when Victoria ascended the throne at her uncle's death, she appeared at the young queen's first "Drawing room." All the court was, of course, in mourning. Ellen's splendid brunette beauty had always, at her husband's desire, been set off by bright colors. On this occasion she wore black for the first time as full dress. Crepe and bombazine was the regulation costume prescribed for all British subjects at court, but foreigners could wear other materials, always provided they were black. Ellen's dress was brocade satin and velvet, her ornaments diamonds.

"I shall look a fright in it, brown as I am," she said to her friends at one of her receptions.

"Put it on beforehand, and let us judge," they answered.

It was arranged she should put it on the next day, and they should see its effects. A number of other friends heard of the matter, and her parlor next day was quite full. There were at least fifty people present. In the midst of the compliments and wine, who should be announced but Louis Napoleon.

A chill fell upon the aristocratic company. The future emperor was but a poor young adventurer then, living in London in obscure lodgings. His mother, the brilliant Hortense, lived in Switzerland—an exile forms her adored Paris. Mrs. White had been hospitable entertained by the ex-queen in her Swiss chateau part of the summer before, and her friendship for Hortense had extended to her ill-fated son. When the American pair came to London, Louis Napoleon went at once to see his mother's lovely friend, and the Whites did what they could to brighten the exile-life of the prince.

But he was not admitted into society. He had never attended "Florida White's" receptions. He visited her only when he felt sure of meeting few, if any, guests in her parlors. He had come this time at an unfashionable hour. Ass the drawing-room door was brown open, he started back surprised—dismayed to see the brilliant company. He was in plain dress, and his pale somber face little accorded with the scene. But Ellen's kind heart and American independence saved him from slight. She came to meet him, smiling a welcome, her rich black robes trailing, the black plumes nodding above her radiant brown. She helped him to tide over his embarrassment by her graceful cordiality.

"I was not aware you had changed your days for receiving madame," murmured the prince.

"Nor had I. This reunion is wholly impromptu. My friends have come to see how hideous I look in black."

"Hideous! You would make an esquiman costume seem classic. You look like the Goddess of Night, madame," gallantly replied the young Louis.

After a short stay he withdrew, his embarrassment not removed by the haughty state of those British dames and lords. When the door closed upon him, the sharp-toned voice of Marchioness—somebody—said to Mrs. Whtie.

"This is one of my strongest objections to your republican country. Its principles oblige you to receive everybody as your equal. For instance, the adventurer who has just left."

"Your ladyship is mistaken," replied our American princess. "The democratic principles of our government in no wise effect our social laws. We do not admit everybody as our equals any more than you do. As for the gentleman who has just left, I know nothing against him but his misfortune and his poverty. This is no crime in my country."

The marchioness bowed, but her lip curled with a little smile of doubt and disdain.

Years afterwards, "Florida White" (As the London poets had christen4ed her, because her best loved home was in Florida, the American Italy) had her revenge on the supercilious marchioness.

The whirligig of fortune had tossed Louis Napoleon into the throne. He was emperor of France. The British Queen had paid her distinguished respects to the new monarch, and he and his fair Spanish bride had gone to London to return the royal courtesy. There Victoria had publicly decorated the French potentate with the order of knighthood. The Paris newspapers were full of this and illustrations of the Imperial visit and the queen's reception of the emperor. It was the topic of the evening at a large party in Paris where "Florida White" was the center of attraction. The marchioness, who had sneered at the "adventurer" in Mrs. White's London drawing-room, sat near her now. Ellen's sweetness was adverse from spite; but she could not resist throwing a little malice into her tones as she said to the marchioness:

"It seems, my lady, that others besides Americans sometimes received adventurers; but I did not kneel and tie the garter around this one's leg as your royal mistress has just done."

Among the souvenirs of Mrs. White is a beautiful hand in bronze— a copy of   —"The loveliest hand in all the land—"

The venerable mother of Napoleon had sent for Mrs. White to visit her. The room was filled with noble guests, but Ellen was given a place by the aged lady's couch, and at the leave-taking she drew the fair American into her arms and kissed her. The charming Queen of Naples pressed her hand, saying, "I shall never forget you. What shall I send you as a token of my regard?" Ellen looked at the famous hand that lay in her and said, archly, "Your hand." The queen smiled and bowed. When Ellen had returned to America, she received an affectionate letter from Caroline and an ebony-and-pearl-casket, enclosing a bronze copy of the queen's hand with a diamond ring on the third finger, had previously been sent to her, but the vessel on which it was sent was wrecked at sea. Its cargo was wholly destroyed, and many lives lost.

The most valuable and noted of the many gifts that "Florida White" received from royal and eminent persons was the diamond cross given her by the Pope. She was not of his religion, but he paid distinguished homage to the charms of mind and person that made her, as he said, a queen in her own right. The cross was very valuable. In the center was an exquisitely carved image of Christ in amethyst. The diamonds encircling it were large and perfect—the setting was unique. Mrs. White sold this cross and number of other costly relics to help build the Southern Presbyterian church in Wahington City of which Rev. Mr. Pitzer is now pastor. It is due to her zeal and generosity that his church is in existence.

"Florida White" was as much admired in Paris, Rome and Vienna as she had been in the English capital. But all this admiration did not spoil her. The gallantries and social license of these foreign courts left no taint upon her beautiful nature. She was still the same rare, radiant being—half child, half queen. Her native candor and purity and her single-hearted love for her husband, who always seemed to her "the grandest man in any assembly," saved her from the temptation that beset a surprisingly lovely woman in a dissipated court. "She is almost too perfect to be a heroine," I said to myself when I studied her personally, and through her correspondence and diaries, with a thought of putting her into a novel. I had always held that nature never bestowed all four of her royal gifts—beauty, grace, intellect and goodness—upon one mortal. But here was a woman who had worn this perfect diadem down to venerable age. Here was a perfect rose of womanhood. Lamartine described her, when he wrote of Delphine Gay, the first wife of Girardin: "She had beauty, wit, vivacity, poetic passion, womanly tenderness, sincerity, eloquence—she was even a Christian."

She returned to America, and after a long period of mourning for her first husband, she married the learned and good Doctor Beatty, and settled down for half of every year at least, in her beautiful home at Cas Bianca near Monticello, Florida. Here she became an elevating and beautifying influence in the community. She drew about her a number of cultured people, and she had many distinguished quests. She visited the sick and poor and gave help and counsel to the struggling.

Mrs. Beatty's fortune of nearly a million had diminished to a few thousands before her death, though loss of slave property, through bequests and charities, and injudicious investments by her agents. But she had sufficient for her wants. Her dress was always elegantly simple, and her habits involved no costly expenditure. Pure, sweet with the rare grace of majestic age and child-like gentleness, was the sunset of this most lovely life.

I never wearied of hearing her talk. She had too much noble modesty, regard for others and cultured tact to be egotistical; but I had come to write her reminiscences, and it was my business as well as pleasure to draw her out. She looked then, past eight, as she was. I never saw her in the flush of her glorious beauty, and I prefer the picture I saw of her at this time to others that show her as she looked when she charmed Talleyrand—her caustic critic—and one from the Pope the praise of being the most beautiful woman in the world. There are several full-length pictures of her by famous painters, and a sculptured bust of her at Rome by some Italian artist whose name does not come to my pen as I write.

CHAPTER XIV

MONROE BRANCH OF THE ADAIR FAMILY

(296) JUDGE THOMAS BELL MONROE—LAWYER, was born October 7, 1792, in Albemarle County, Virginia, and was the son of Andrew J. Monroe, a near relative of President James Monroe. His mother, Ann Bell, was of Irish Descent. His parents located in Scott County, Kentucky, as early as 1793.

Judge Monroe acquired some knowledge of books, and after reaching manhood; settled in Barren County. In 1816 he was elected to the Legislature; in 1819 began to study and practice law, never having read a law-book until he announced himself ready to practice; removed to Frankfort in 1821; in the winter of that year attended lectures, and graduated in the Law Department of Transylvania University; was Secretary of State one year, from September 1823, under Governor Adair became reporter of the decisions of the Court of Appeals, by appointment from Governor Desha in 1825, and published Monroe's Kentucky Reports, in seven volumes; from 1833 to 1834 was United States District Attorney; in March 1834 was appointed Judge of the United States District Court of Kentucky by Andrew Jackson, and held the office over twenty-seven years; and in 1861, he abandoned his office and home and fled to within Confederate lines.

As a judge his decisions were of the highest order, being seldom reversed, and his long term of office was characterized by learning, justice, fairness and great honor.

He became a professor in the University of Louisiana in 1848; spent several winters in New Orleans in discharge of his duties with that institution; afterwards filled the Chair of Civil, International and Criminal Law in Transylvania University; was also Professor of Rhetoric, Logic and History of Law at the Western Academy at Drennon Springs; taught a law class at his own home, near Frankfort; had conferred upon him the degree of L.L.D., by the University of Louisiana, Centre College and Harvard University.

He was early a supporter of the doctrine of Mr. Jefferson; but after becoming a judge ceased to take on an active interest in politics; after his sons had all taken a stand with the South, he followed them, and at Nashville, in 1861, took the oath of allegiance to the Confederacy; remained at Canton, Mississippi with his family until after the fall of Vicksburg; remained at Marietta, Georgia for a time, earnestly engaging in the care of the sick and such other duties as he could perform. In 1864 went to Richmond; was in the Confederate Congress till the fall of Richmond, and attempted to practice law; soon became weary of the strife, and returned to his family at Abbeville, South Carolina, and after the surrender of Gener Lee, went to Pass Christian, Mississippi, where he spent the remainder of his day, never having an opportunity again to see his beautiful home in Kentucky.

Judge Monroe died December 24, 1965, while an exile from home. His wife was Eliza Palmer Adair, daughter of Governor John Adair. His son. John A. Monroe, died at Frankfort in 1873.

JOHN ADAIR MONROE

(301) John Adair Monroe, born Feby. 22, 1823, Married Maria E. Bacon, Oct. 26, 1848. Died Feb. 12, 1873, Frankfort, Kentucky.

Second son of Judge T.B. Monroe and Elizabeth Palmer Adair Monroe, born at Whitehall, in Herrodsburg, Ky., home of Gov Adair. Was educated at Sayre Academy, Frankfort, Ky., and taught there several years to help pay his way through Transylvania University.

Graduated in law under his father, was chief clerk to the Judge of the U.S. District of Kentucky, until the resignation of his father, in 1861. Was professor in the Ky. Military Institute, teaching Latin, Greek and Hebrew, until he was appointed Chief Clerk to the Commissioner of Insurance Bureau, by Gen. G. Smith, until his death. He was always a student and considered one among the best scholars in Kentucky.

JUDGE THOMAS B. MONROE
AND
ELIZA P. ADAIR

His wife and their Descendants, of Ky., and other States

1812

77 Eliza P. Adair=Judge 296 Thomas B. Monroe
Daughter of Governor Adair and   b. Oct. 7, 1791, in Alber
Wife, Catherine Adair, of Ky.   Marle Co., Va.

(See Biography)

Progeny: 5 sons and 5 daughters

297. I   Victor Monroe, b 1813. M Mary Polk of Md.
298. II   Anna Bell Monroe, b 1815. M Richard Pindell
299. III   Catherine A. Monroe, b Dec. 10, 1817, never married
300. IV   Mary Hardin Monroe, b Aug. 25, 1820. Single.
301. V   John Adair Monroe, b Feb. 22, 1823, m Maria Elizabeth Bacon.
302. VI   Margaret Monroe, died in infancy.

303. VII   Andrew Monroe, b 1826, d 1849.
304. VIII Elizabeth A. Monroe, b Dec. 4, 1828. M Henry J. Leovy.
305. XI   Thomas B. Monroe, Jr., b July 3, 1833. M Elizabeth Grier, of Philadelphia.
306. X   Benjamin James Monroe, b Aug. 1836. D 1862.

1840
297. Victor Monroe=307 Mary Polk, of Md.
Son of Judge T. B. Monroe and Eliza P.
Adair Monroe. (See Biography of Victor Monroe.)

Progeny: Four Children
308. I   Williiam Winder Monroe, b Oct. 1841, m 1870
309. II   Frank Adair Monroe, b 1844, m 1878.
310. III Thomas B. Monroe, died in infancy.
311. IV   Mary E. Monroe, b Sept 9, 1849. M Vincent, 1871. M. 2nd. Judge J.G. Baker, 1912.

1870
308. William Winder Monroe=312 Louvinia Blackburn Berry of Ky.
Son of Victor and Mary Polk Monroe
(See Biography.)
Progeny: Four Children
313. I   Henry B. Monroe, died at 2 years.
314. II   Anna Pindell Monroe, m George Lyons of N.O. La., one Son, Winder Monroe Lyons.
315. III Katherine Monroe, m Lake Dudley of Flemingsburg, Ky., in 1904, 2 girls, Winder and Katherine Dudley of Flemingsburg, Ky.
316. IV   Mary Vincent Monroe, died in infancy.

JUDE FRANK ADAIR MONROE
Late Chief Justice of Louisiana

Judge Frank Adair Monroe was born in Annapolis, Md., Aug. 30, 1844; his parents were Victor Monroe and Mary Townsend (Polk.)

Educated in private schools and in 1860-61 entered Kentucky Military Institute, but left the latter at the beginning of sophomore year and entered the Confederate Army. He served four years, partly in Co. E. 4th Kentucky Infantry and the remaining time in Co. C, 1st Louisiana Cavalry. He was wounded and captured near Summerset, Kentucky, March 1863; exchanged Oct., 1863; and was finally paroled at Abbeyville, S.C. in 1865.

He married Alice, daughter of Jules A. Blane of New Orleans, January 3, 1878. Mr. Monroe was admitted to the bar in 1867 and practiced in New Orleans. Was elected Judge of the Third District Court, Parish of New Orleans in No., 1872; was dispossessed of office after a few months. Took Part with White League in action of Sept. 14. 1874, which overturned "Packard" Government. He was re-elected Judge in Nov., 1876; was appointed Judge of the Civil District Court, Parish of New Orleans, 1880; reappointed in 1884 and 1892. Mr. Monroe took part in the anti-lottery campaign in 1892.

Hon. Frank Adair Monroe,
Late Chief Justice of Supreme Court of Louisiana.

He was Supreme Court of Louisiana in March, 1899; was elected without opposition for terms 1908-1920 and 1920-1932; became Chief Justice, April, 1914. He retired January 2, 1922, after forty-five years' service on the bench.

elected a member of the Louisiana Convention and helped to make a new Constitution for the State, 1898. He was appointed Associate Justice of the Judge Adair Monroe was a member of the Law Faculty of the Tulane University of Louisiana for twenty years. Was president of Association Army of Tennessee (Camp No. 2 U.V.C.) For many years he was a member of the board of governors (Confederate) Memorial Hall at New Orleans. Judge Monroe is a member of the American Bar Association, of which he is vice-President for Louisiana. Home: 1331 Phillip Street, New Orleans, Louisiana.

JUDGE FRANK ADAIR MONROE
Late Chief Justice of Louisiana
And his descendants
1878

309. Judge Frank Adair Monroe=Alice Blane
Son of Judge Victor and Mary Polk   of N.O., La.
Monroe. (See Biography.)

Progeny: Ten Children

318. I   Frank Adair Monroe, Jr., b about Nov., 1879; m Elizabeth McNary; 3 children, Elizabeth Monroe, Allan Adair Monroe, Willis Lathrop Monroe, Lawyer in N. O., La.
319. II Jules Blane Monroe, also a prominent lawyer in N.O., m May Logan; 3 children, Raeburn Monroe, Malcolm Monroe.
320. III Alice Monroe, m Sam S. LaBouisse; 3 sons: Sam S. LaBouisse Jr., Monroe LaBouisse, David LaBouisse.
321. IV Kitty Monroe, m Gus Westfeldt; no children
322. V   Gertrude Monroe, m Muldrop Logan, of N.Y.C. 3 daughters: Alice B. Logan, Virginia King Logan, Gerturde Logan.
323. VI Adele Monroe, m 1911 Geo. Williams: 3 daughters, Katherine Williams, Geo. E. Williams, Jr., Adele Williams, b 1919.
324. VII Winder Polk Monroe, Killed by a train, in Greenville, S.C., 1915. Was riding a tricycle.
236. VIII Marion Monroe, m 1922, John T. Chambers: One son, John T. Chambers, Jr., Baton Rouge and New Orleans, La.
326. IX   William B. Monroe, m Artie Vassin, 2 children: Wm. B. Monroe, Jr., Artie Monroe.

327. X James Hill Monroe, b 1899; Businessman, Single.

1871

311. Mary E. Monroe=328 Geo. A. Vincent
A Businessman.
Two children

1912

(2d marriage) Mary E. Monroe=Judge 329 J.G. Baker
No Children

Daughter of Judge Victor and Mary Polk Monroe. She was born Sept 9, 1949.

Progeny: Two Sons

- 330.   I   Winder Monroe Vincent, b in N.O., La., 1872. M 331 Ruth Robinson, of Corsicana, Texas, in 1905. 3 Children; 332 Mary Adlaid Vincent, 333 Monroe Vincent (a girl), 335 George A. Vincent, Jr.
- 330   Winder Monroe Vincent married 2d, Jenny McElroy, no children.
- 330   Winder Monroe Vincent, died 1919 at Houston, was with the Gulf Refining Co.
- 336.   II William Germain Vincent, b 1882 in N. O., La., A businessman; m 337 Lucy Gyern Coleman of Ky., in 1907. 2 daughters, 388 Luida Monroe Vincent and 339 Clotilda Germain Vincent, living in San Francisco.
- 310.   Thomas B. Monroe 3d, a son of Victor and Mary P. Monroe, died in infancy. Buried in cemetery at Fankfort, Ky.

1838

298. Anna B. Monroe=293 Richard Pindell

Daughter of Judge T.B. and   Lawyer at Montrose, practiced
Eliza P. Adair Monroe.   Law in Lexington, Ky.

Progeny: One Child, Died in Infancy

340. Katherine Adair Monroe, b Dec. 19, 1871. D Dec. 13, 1901. Single. Was called "Kitty." She was noted for piety and amiability.

341. Mary Hardin Monroe, called "Polly." Born Aug. 25, 1820, at Glasgow, Ky. She remained single, and died in 1913, at Pass Christian, Miss., a remarkable woman, very affable and affectionate.

1847

301. John Adair Monroe=292 Maria Elizabeth Bacon Son of Judge T.B. and Eliza P. Adair Monroe.

Progeny: Eight Children

- 342.   I   Thomas B. Monroe, Jr., b 1843, m 1872, 349 Blandina Broadhead Hord.

343. II   Annie Fall Monroe, b 1850.
344. III   Eliza Adair Monroe, b 1852, m, Oct. 1, 1878 in Louisville, Ky., to Gen. 346 Thomas H. Taylor. She died in Paris, Texas, 1902. Buried in Frankfort by the side of her husband. They had five children.
347. IV   John Adair Monroe, Jr., b Frankfort, 1853, d 1909 at Paris, Tex. Buried There.
348. V   Alice Bacon Monroe, B Jan. 18, 1855, died, June, 1855.
349. VI   Mary Temple Monroe, b Jan. 18, 1855 (twins) n Rev. W.S. Clark in 1878. One son and four daughters.
351. VII   Victor Monroe, Jr., b March 8, 1859. D June, 1875, just 16 years old.
352. VIII Willie Monroe, b daughter and eighth child of John Adair, and M.E. Bacon Monroe, b Dec. 29, 1863. D Feb. 1875.

(343) Annie Fall Monroe, b Dec. 22, 1850, at Frankfort, Ky., (north side,) daughter of John Adair Monroe, and Maria Elizabeth Bacon Monroe. Miss Monroe devoted her life to a business career. After getting an education, she started as a teacher; later on she took up post office work and became Registry Clerk in the Post Office at Louisville, Ky. Next, she was transferred to the Post Office Department in Washington, D.C., where she served continuously until she was entitled to retire. Then she was retired on a pension. She owns a farm in Lamar Co., near Paris, Texas.

Miss Monroe is sociable and popular in the family. Enterprising and honorable, she deserves the credit for the accuracy and completeness of the Genealogy of the Monroe branch of the Adair Family.

THE LEOVYS

Elizabeth Monroe married Henry J. Loevy who had studied law under her father, Judge Thomas B. Monroe. Mr. Loevy's father and grandfather had been lawyers. He himself later became one of the best-known lawyers in the South. He was one of the organizers of the Morgan Steamship Company and the Morgan Louisiana and Texas Railway, the forerunner of the Southern Pacific Railway.

At the time of his death, Col. Loevy was attorney for the Southern Pacific Railway, the Wells-Fargo Express Company and the Western Union Telegraph Company. He served in the Confederate Army during the War between the States, attaining the rank of Colonel.

1853
Elizabeth Adair Monroe=Henry Jefferson Loevy

Eighth child of Judge Thomas B. A Lawyer of New Orleans, b May 2, 1826; and Eliza Adair Monroe; b Dec. 2, 1826; d 1905. 4, 1828: d in New Orleans, 1905.

Progeny: One Daughter, Five Sons

I   Eliza Adair Leovy, m Alfred Lovell Hall, a Lieutenant in the U.S. Navy, just before the Hispano-American War; their romance was short-lived, as he died a few months later from fever contracted in China. Mrs. Hall was very active for many years in the Daughters of the Confederacy, having charge of their Museum for a time.
II George Julien Leovy, b March 25, 1859, in New Orleans.
III Victor P. Leovy.
IV Frank Adair Leovy.
V   Henry Hurley Leovy, d in 1888.
VI Thomas Monroe Leovy, who died while still a boy.

George Julien, the eldest son, was born in New Orleans on March 25, 1858. He attended the Virginia Military Institute and later the University of Virginia, where he got his degree. He was admitted to the bar in Louisiana in 1880, and commenced law practice the same year. He also married that year.

Moved by considerations for his health, he went with his family to San Diego, Cal., in 1887. He was admitted to the California bar on April 11, 1887. His law office was in San Diego, but sometimes he was in Los Angeles. He was part of the time alone in practice, but most of the time in copartnership, first with George Puterbaugh, firm name of Puterbaugh and Leovy; afterward with Mr. Charles F. Humes, firm name of Puterbaugh, Leovy and Humes. Subsequently Mr. Puterbaugh was appointed judge and Mr. Humes died; then Mr. Leovy practiced alone until his death, which occurred on August 27, 1921, at his home in San Diego.

During the World War, when our Government was looking around for efficient men to help run the Navy, Mr. George Julien Leovy was selected and appointed. His qualifications were: First, his general intelligence and aptitude for matters marine; his training in the Virginia Military Institute; his experience as a sporting yachtsman; his knowledge of naval and marine law were all favorable to his appointment. So, he was commissioned outright as a Lieutenant in the U.S. Navy, and he served faithfully and efficiently at San Diego, Los Angeles Port, and San Francisco, until the occasion which called him Into service had passed, and he received his honorable discharge in August, 191.

Lieut. James T. Leovy and

Presse Adair of Clinton, S.C.

Mr. Leovy was appointed by the judges of the District Court of the United States for the Southern District of California, Southern Division, to the responsible office of commissioner of that court at San Diego, a position which he was admirably qualified to fill.

Mr. Leovy died in San Diego in September, 1921, and the Bar Association of San Diego adopted resolutions both eulogistic and sympathetic.

1880
George Julien Leovy=Lucy Gilmore, of New Orleans

Son of Henry J. Leovy and Eliza Adair Leovy.

Progeny: Ten Children

I	Thomas Monroe Leovy.
II	Died in infancy.
III	Also died in infancy.
IV	Edith Leovy, an artist.
V	Lucile Elizabeth Leovy, m Waddell.
VII	James Gillmore Leovy.
VIII	Louis Leovy.
IX	Catherine Leovy.
X	George Julien Leovy, Jr.

Victor Leovy succeeded his father in the law practice in New Orleans and became very prominent.

Victor Leovy=Alice Sessions

Son of Henry j. Elizabeth Adair Monroe Leovy.   Daughter of the Episcopal Bishop of New Orleans

Progeny: One Daughter

I   Barbara Leovy.

Frank Adair Leovy was for a time attorney for the Southern Pacific Railroad. Later upon the discovery of oil in Texas, he went over to the Gulf Oil Corporation, now the largest independent oil company in the United States. He is now its first vice-president.

Frank Adair Leovy=Augusta Glenny

Son of Henry J. and Elizabeth A. M. Leovy.   Of New Orleans

Progeny: Three Children

I	Augusta Leovy.
II	Elizabeth Leovy.
III	Helen Leovy.

Edith Leovy, daughter of George Julien and Lucy Leovy, had great talent for art, and hastened her death in 1921 by overwork in teaching it.

Lucile Elizabeth Leovy, one of the daughters of Julien and Lucy, was born in New Orleans in 1906.

Lucile Elizabeth Leovy=William Waddell
A Lieutenant in the Navy, now lieutenant Commander.
Progeny: Two Children

I   Ward William Waddell, Jr., b 1920, at Long Beach, Cal.

II George Waddell, b 1922, at Long Beach, Cal.

Thomas Monroe Leovy, the oldest son of Julien and Lucy Loevy. for a time, practiced law with his father in San Diego, but during the World War h served in the Navy as Lieutenant, Senior Grade, for more than a year, having charge of the officers' training camp at Great Lakes Station. After the war he remained in the service.

1915
Thomas Monroe Leovy=Martha Austin, of Baltimore
Progeny: Two Children

I   Thomas Monroe Leovy, Jr., b in San Diego, May 28 1916.

II   William Austin Leovy, b in San Diego, June 13, 1921.

Eliza Adair Leovy, another daughter of George J. and Lucy Leovy, married Thomas Crittenden Ackerman, Sept. 14, 1921. Mr. Ackerman was a winner of the Distinguished Service Cross for gallantry in action during the World War. They had one child, Elizabeth L. Ackerman, born 1922.

James Gillmore Leovy, the second son of George Julien and Lucy Leovy, was born in San Diego, Cal., Aug. 29, 1887. He graduated from a Los Angeles high school in 1906, and from the University of Southern California in 1912. And in the same year of 1912 he was admitted to the bar and has practiced law in the city of Los Angeles ever since, except the year he was in thew World War.

During the war Mr. Leovy enlisted as a private in the First California Field Artillery, became a sergeant, and in November, 1917, he was commissioned as First Lieutenant and ordered overseas immediately. He served in France with the 101st Field Artillery of the Twenty-sixth Division, the famous Yankee division, until wounded July 22, 1918, north of Chateau Thierry. He was gassed but recovered from it.

After being discharged from the army, Mr. Leovy was appointed in July, 1919, Deputy City attorney for the City of Los Angeles, a position which he still holds, acting as attorney for the Department of Water, Power and Light.

Before leaving France, Mr. Leovy was married.

1917

James Gillmore Leovy=Dulcebella Barbour, a native of San Diego

Louise and Katherine Leovy are the two remaining daughters of George Julien and Lucy Leovy.

Louise still lives in San Diego, her native city.

George Julien Leovy, Jr., was born in San Diego, May 8 1983, and was graduated from the University of Virginia in the spring of 1917, just in time to accept a commission as an Ensign in the Navy. His entire service was with the sub-chasers.

George Julien Leovy, Jr., commanded a division for more than a year in Albania, and commanded the first boat to enter the Austrian port of Durazzo during the Allied attack on that port.

He received the American Navy Cross, the Italian Medan of Valor, and the Greek War Cross.

After the Armistice, he volunteered to take a division to archangel, in Russia. Later he engaged in minesweeping, clearing out the mine barrage in the North Sea.

Mr. Leovy is now at Callao, Peru, as port superintendent for the Grace Steamship Company.

353. Victor Monroe, Jr., b March 8, 1959, died June 1875, just 15 years. Went to Hernando Miss., after the death of his parents, where he worked and studied with his cousin, Andrew Monroe. Was drowned in Lake Horn, Miss., while trying to save a boy's life. Buried at Hernando, Miss. Victor Jr., was the son of John Adair Monroe and M. E. Bacon Monroe.

354. Willie Monroe, daughter and eighth child of John Adair, and M. E. Bacon Monroe, born Dec. 29, 1963, at Frankfort, Ky. After the death of parents, she went to the Masonic Home with her sister Adair, who was a teacher there. Her father was a Mason, and hence that fraternity took an interest in her. She died two years later. Buried in Frankfort.

Thomas Bell Monroe, now senior, (as his grandfather and uncle are both dead,) Eldest son of John Adair, and Maria E. Bacon Monroe, born Oct. 28, 1848, in Frankfort, Ky. Married in 1872 Blandina Broadhead Hord, daughter of Judge Lysander Hord, of Frankfort, Ky. Was clerk in Insurance Bureau of Ky. Went to Logan Co., in 1877. Migrated to Lamar Co., Texas in 1880. A farmer.

380. Eliza Adair Monroe, daughter of John Adair Monroe and M.E.

Bacon Monroe, b July 24, 1852, at Frankfort, Ky. (South Side.) She taught a while in the Masonic Home. On October 1st, 1878 she married Gen. 381 Thomas H. Taylor, in Louisville, Ky. Died in Paris, Texas in 1902.

1878
380. Eliza Adair Monroe=Gen. Thomas H. Taylor
Progeny: Five Children

832.	I	Marie Louise Taylor, b May 10, 1880.
383.	II	J.A. Monroe Taylor, b Oct. 1881, d 1886, of Scarlet Fever, buried in Frankfort.
384.	III	C.J. Taylor, b May, 1883 (Changed to Thomas H. in 1990.)
385.	IV	Adair M. Taylor, b 1885.
836.	V	T.H. Taylor, b in 1887, only lived a few hours.

1907
382. Marie Louise Taylor=W.R.J. Zimmerman
Daughter of Gen. T.H. Taylor and   Residence, Charleston,
Eliza Adair Monroe Taylor Married   W. Va.
at the residence of Her sister, Mrs. 388
Wyatt Aikin, Abbeyville, South Carolina.
Progeny: None

384. Thomas H. Taylor (C.J.) was employed in the L. & R. R. R. office at Louisville, Ky.; Then went to the Standard Oil Co.'s office in N.O., La. Now Sales Manager of the Standard Oil Co., N.O., La. In the meantime, had been transferred to Cincinnati, O., then Chicago and back to New Orleans, La.

1905
384. Thomas H. Taylor=389 Fern Norris
Progeny: Tow Daughters

390.	I	Ruth Adair Taylor, b 1906.
391.	II	Maria Louise Taylor, b 1915. N.O., La.

1906
385. Adair Monroe Taylor=Hon. 392 Wyatt Aiken
Daughter of Gen. T.H. Taylor and   of Abbeville, S.C.
Eliza Adair Monroe Taylor.   Member of Congress

Progeny: Four Children
393. I Thomas Taylor Aiken, b Feb. 24, 1908.
394. II Adair Aiken, b Oct 24, 1910.
395. III Martha Aiken, b   16, 1912.
396. IV David Aiken, b Sept. 1, 1917.
347. John Adair Monroe, Jr., son of J. A. Monroe, Sr., and
M. E. Bacon Monroe, b in Frankfort, Ky., Sept. 26th, 1853. He worked with Prof. Shaler, Geologist in Ky. Then went for a while to Texas, about 1880; was Cowboy in Lady Adair's Ranch in the Panhandle of Texas. He next drifted into Mexico, and was interpreter in Court when Diaz was President, (he spoke Spanish fluently.) He got interested in mines in Mexico and other Spanish-American countries; was in one or more Revolutions in Central America. Was injured in a Copper Mine in Mexico, and was brought to Paris, Texas, where his brother l8ived, and died two weeks later. Thus, passed away one of the most lovable and brightest men of the family, in 1909, and was buried in the Paris cemetery.

1878

349. Mary Temple Monroe=Rev. 380 W.C. Clark
Daughter of John Adair Monroe   at Pass
Christian, Miss.
And M.E. Bacon Monroe
Progeny: One Son, Four Daughters

381 I William Monroe Clark, b 1891, graduate of Princeton, J.J. m 1907, Ada Hamilton, Progeny: 4 children, to wit; I 381 Carter Clark, b 1908. II William Hamilton Clark, b 1911. III 381 Francis Adair Clark, b 1915. IV 383 Janie Christine Clark, 1917

383. Janie Christine Clark, 1917.
Wm. Hamilton died in infancy.

384. Monroe and Ada Clark went to Korea as Missionaries from the Presbyterian Church in 1909. On a visit home in 1922, Ada died; buried in Newport, Ky. Monroe and family returned to Seoul, Korea, and at present is translator of important Books.

388. Kate Adair Clark, b 1880, in Ala. M 192, Prof E. A. Young of Livingston, Ala. 6 children, to wit: I 390 Wm. Crawford Young. II 391 Katherine Adair Young. III 392 Mary Monroe Young. IV 393 Martha McConnell Young. V 394 Agnes Ash Young. VI 395 Gessner Harrison Young.

366. Bessie Brawner Clark, b 1886, Shelbyville, Tenn. Went over with her brother as a Missionary to Korea.

397. Agnes Young Clark, b 1890. M R.G. Fulerod in N.Y. City A soldier in World War; one son, 399 Wm. Crawford Fulerod. Agnes did efficient war work in N.Y. City and is still engaged in it.

401. Marry Bessy Clark, a graduate of College and of Domestic Science is teaching that now in Wilmington, N.C. Single.

400. Victor Monroe, b March 8, 1859, at Frankfort, Ky. Went to Hernando, Miss., after the death of his parents, he worked and studied with his cousin Andrew Monroe; in June 1875 he was drown in Lake Horn, Miss., while trying to save a boy's life. Victor was only 16 years of age.

402. Willie Bacon Monroe, a daughter. B Dec. 19, 1863, d Feb, 1875. After the death of her parents, went to the Masonic Home where her sister, 403 Adair, was teaching, and died two years later; her father was a Mason, hence the kindness of the Fraternity. She was buried at Frankfort where she was born.

1872

342. Thomas Bell Monroe=404 Blandina B. Hord
Son of John Adair Monroe and   Daughter of Judge Lysander
M.E. Bacon Monroe   der Hord of Frankfort, Ky.

Progeny: Nine Children

405. I   John Adair Monroe, b 1873. M Elizabeth Stallings, 4 sons. (see biography.)
406. II   Annie Brown Monroe, b 1874. M Charles A. Poteet. 6 Children.
407. III Lysander Hord Monroe, b 1876. D 1884.
408. IV   Marie Catherine Monroe, b 1878. M. Oscar Rucker. Four children.
409. V   Mary Adair Monroe, b 1880. M Justine M. Neathery. 2 children.
410. VI   Thom. B. Monroe, Jr., 3d. b 1883. M Elizabeth Geron, Paris, Tex. 3 children.
411. VII Victor Monroe (girl,) b 1885. Graduate Paris High School. D 1908.
412. VIII Blandina Hord Monroe, b 1887. M Sam Bezhack, 1 son, Sam B. Bezhack, Jr.
413. IX   Benjamin James Monroe, b 1889. Single. Educated in Paris, Tex., d 1914.

405. John Adair Monroe, Jr., born in the southern part of Texas, in Austin. He taught school, was Superintendent of Schools of Lamar County, Texas. Entered as clerk in the First National Bank of Paris, Texas. In due time was transferred to the Federal Reserve Bank in Dallas, Texas. He is now President of the Hunt County Bank in Greenville, Texas.

He married in 1899, Miss Elizbeth Stallings. His parents are 342 Thomas Bell Monroe and 404 Blandina B. Hord Monroe.

1899

405. John Adair Monroe=414 Elizabeth Stallings
Progeny: Four sons

- 415. I John Adair Monroe, Jr. b 1901, graduated in Paris High School, 1917. Methodist University at Dallas, 1922 Now in Banking business in Greenville, Tex. For the most part worked his way through School and College.
- 416. II Stanley Monroe, b in Paril, Tex., 1903, graduated at Paris High School, also the Methodist University at Dallas. He also did his part about work. M Louise Majors of Midlothan, Tex.
- 417. III James Monroe, b June 13, 1910.
- 418. IV Alford Fall Monroe, b Dec. 9, 1912.

1896

406. Annie Brown Monroe=Charles A. Poteet
Daughter of T.B. Monroe and wife,   in Lamar County.
Blandina Hord Monroe.

Progeny: Six Children

- 420. I Annie Adair Poteet, b Nov. 1897. Graduated Paris High School, 1915, also Normal School, Denton. Now teaching in San Angelo, Texas.
- 421. II Lucretia Poteet, b Nov. 1900. M Henry A. Heitzler 1909, in San Angelo. Civil Engineer. One son, Henry A. Jr.
- 422. III Thomas M. Poteet, b Aug. 1902.
- 423. IV Charles Hord Poteet, b March 1905, now in Center College, Daneville, Ky.
- 424. V Gibbons Poteet, b Sept. 1906.
- 425. VI Victor Poteet, b Dec. 1909.

1903

408. Maria Catherine Monroe=426 Oscar Rucker
Daughter of T.B. Monroe and Blandina B. Monroe.
She was born Sept. **1878**. Educated in Louisville, Ky.

Progeny: Four Children

- 427. I Augusta Rucker, b Dec. 1904. Will graduate in the University of Texas in 1924.
- 428. II Samuel Rucker, b 1906.
- 429. III M. Katherine Rucker, b 1908.
- 430. IV Oscar Rucker, Jr., b 1910.

1903

409. Mary Adair Monroe=431 Justin M. Neathery

Daughter of T.B., and
Blandina B. Monroe

Live out on the Old Monroe place near Paris, Texas.

Progeny: Two Children

432. I   Sam Monroe Neathery, b Oct. 1914.
433. II Blandina Hord Neathery, b Jan. 19, 1919.

(410) Thomas B. Monroe, Jr., born Feb. 1883 on the old Click Place in Lamar Co., Texas. The sixth child of T.B. and Blandina B. Monroe. He was educated in Pass Christian; Miss. Was trained in Engineering. Manager of Cotton Press. Now a farmer.

1913

410. Thomas B. Monroe, Jr=434 Elizabeth Geron, near Paris

Progeny: Three children

I   Benjamin Geron Monroe, b June, 1916.
II   Carry Annie Monroe, b April, 1917.
III Thom. B. Monroe, Jr., b Oct. 13, 1922.

435. Victor Monroe, a daughter, the seventh child of T.B. and Blandina B. Monroe. B Jan. 10, 1885. She was educated in business after graduating in the Paris High School. In 1906, she died of pneumonia and was buried in Paris cemetery.

1910

436. Blandina Monroe=436 Sam B. Bejack

Eighth child of T.B. and
Blandina Monroe b on the Monroe place in Lamar
Co., Jan **1887**. Graduated Paris High school.

From Memphis Tenn.

Progeny: One Child.

437. I   Sam B. Bejack, Jr., b Oct. 1915.

(413) Benjamin James Monroe, nineth child of T.B., and Blandina B. Monroe; born Aug. 1889 at the home of her parents in Lamar, Co., and was educated in Paris, Texas. He was Contractor by trade, died of blood poison in 1914, and was buried in the Paris Cemetery.

102. Children born in Monroe branch and 44 marriages.

305. MAJOR THOMAS BELL MONROE, LAWYER AND SOLDIER—Fourth son of Judge Thomas B. Monroe, was born July 3, 1883, at Frankfort, Kentucky.

He waws thoroughly educated, graduating at the University of Louisiana at New Orleans, when his father was a professor in that institution;

in 1849 settled in Lexington, Kentucky, and entered upon the practice of law; rose rapidly in is profession; in the 1859 was elected Mayor of that city; became the editor of the "Kentucky Statesman,: and continued as its editor until the commencement of the Civil war; was made Secretary of State under Governor Magoffin; in September, 1861, having sent his family Morth, he went into the Confederacy, and soon after commissioned Major of the Fourth Kentucky Confederate Infantry, and fell, mortally wounded, April 6, near Burnsville, 1862, and his body was buried by the Federal soldiers on the field. He was a brave and noble officer.

Major Monroe was married in 1859, to Miss Elizabeth C. Grier, daughter of Judge Robert C. Grier, of Philadelphia. She survives him with one son (Grier Monroe).

(306). CAPTAIN BENJAMIN JAMES MONROE, LAWYER AND SOLDIER—was born August 7, 1839, at his father's residence, Montrose, near Frankfort, Kentucky, and was the fifth son of Judge Thomas B. Monroe.

He was educated under the care of his father, and at Sayre Academy and at the Western Military Academy, at Drennon springs, then conducted by Bushrod Johnson, who afterwards became a Confederate general. ** He also studied law with his father and was admitted to the bar at Frankfort. In 1858, he located in Leavenworth, Kansas,*** he returned to west life not being congenial to him, *** he returned to Kentucky, and resumed practice in Frankfort.

He was, soon after, sent on professional business to New Mexico; reached home when the war had been fully inaugurated, and when Kentucky was halting as to her course in the great conflict; soon after began recruiting men for the Confederacy; was finally made Captain of Company E., of the Fourth Kentucky Infantry, under Col. Trabue; was first engaged at Shiloh; was hot in the leg on the second day of the battle*** and was totally incapacitated for active service, in part by disease which had been preying on him for months; after a short trip to New Orleans in the interest of the army, he returned to Corinth, but was soon forced to resort to his friends in Marshall Co., Miss., where he died as a Christian, October 4, 1862, as was buried in the family burial-ground of his father's sister, Mrs. Hardin. (Was afterwards brought to Frankfort, J.T.C.)

(The sketches of Judge Thomas B. Monroe and his two sons, have been copied from the "Biographical Encyclopedia of Kentucky," pages 547-548—J.T. Cannon.)

CHAPTER XV

ADAIR-HARDIN GENEALOGY.

Lineage from first American ancestor—Mary Palmer Adair 4, Governor John Adair 3, William Adair 2, Thomas Adair 1.

1805

76 Mary Palmer Adair=Mark Hardin 134, a Lawyer
Daughter of the Governor of Kentucky.
Progeny: 3 Children.

135.	I	John Hardin, b 1807, studied medicine, located in Louisville.
136.	II	Jane Hardin. b. was twice married.
137.	III	John Adair Hardin, died unmarried.

135. Doctor John Hardin=Marthy Ward, 138
Oldest Son of Mark and Mary Adair Hardin.
Progeny: 5 children.

142.	I	Edward E. Hardin, a West Point graduate.
143.	II	Augusta Hardin, married Edward Dunn.
144.	III	Martha Hardin, who married D.A. Fredericks, of the U.S. Army.
145.	IV	Arthur Hardin, d, Young un-married.
146.	V	John Hardin, d, --

140. John Adair Hardin=Julia Carlin 147, of Carlton, Ill.
2d son of Doctor John Hardin niece of Governor Carlin 148
and great Grandson of of that State, and Sister
Governor of Kentucky. of General Wm. Carlin 149,
a West Point graduate 1852,
U.S. Army.

Progeny: 2 daughters.

150.	I	Miss Adair Hardin, a very devoted member of Sacred Hearth Religious Order, stationed at St. Charles, Mo.
151.	II	Miss Emily Carlin Hardin, d at age of 21.
142.		Col. Edward E. Hardin is a son of Doctor John Hardin and Gertude Dunn Hardin, and great grandson of Governor Adair. He was a Colonel in the U.S. Army, a graduate of West Point, Government Military Institute. He resigned from the Army on account of the health of his wife.

142. Col. Edward W. Hardin=Miss Julia Hutchins 152
Progeny: none.
Address, West New Brighten, Staten Island, N.Y.

136. Jane Hardin=Doctor Thomas Saunders 153, of Shelbyville
Kentucky

Daughter of Mark Hardin, and
Mary Adair Hardin.
granddaughter of Governor Adair.

136. Jane Hardin and Doctor Thomas Saunders 153; 1st marriage.
Progeny: 2 children

154.   I   Doctor Thomas Saunders, Jr.
155.   II   Judith Saunders.

136. 2d marriage, Jane Hardin=Alexander Logan 156
Progeny: 2 children

157.   I   James Logan.
158.   II   Jane Logan.

154. Doctor Thomas Saunders, Jr.-Ellen Owesly 159
Great grandson of Governor Adair   Daughter of prominent
Ky. Family, Shelbyville,
Kentucky
Progeny: none.

155. Judith Saunders=Alfred Bernondy 160

Great Granddaughter
of Governor Adair.

Progeny: 6 children

161.   I   Mary Adair Bernondy, twice married.
162.   II   Baudry Bernondy of St. Louis.
163.   III Mark Bernondy, never married.
164.   IV Fred Bernondy, is single, and living in California.
165.   V   Ednar Bernondy, married and has 2 children; Jane and Edner.
166.   VI Alfred Bernondy, died and left 2 children.

1900

(1st marriage)

161. Mary Adair Bernondy=William Wallace 167, d 1904
Progeny: none.

1917

(2nd marriage)

168. William Hall==Mary Adair Bernondy 159
Progeny: none.

1915

162. Baudry Bernondy=Elizabeth Maddox 167
Son of Judith Saunders and Alfred Bernondy.
Progeny: 2 children.
- 168.   I   J. Farmer Bernondy.
- 169.   II   Wm. Adair Bernondy.

157. James Logan=Marie Maddox 170
Son of Alex Logan and Jane Hardin Logan.
Progeny; 5 children, 4 daughters, and one son
(their names not stated.)

158. Jane Logan=John Bell 171

Great granddaughter of Governor Adair.   Was a Widower, and father of 172 General J. Franklin Bell of the U.S. Army.

Progeny: 2 children.
- 173.   I   Mark Hardin Bell, a bright young lawyer of Chicago, but died young, unmarried.
- 174.   II   Mary Wilson Bell.
- 175.   Alex Bell. D.

174. Mary Wilson Bell=Edgar Vaughn 176
Lived on Old mark Hardin farm near Shelbyville.
Progeny: 3 sons, 2 daughters.
- 177.   I   Margaret Douglas Vaughn.
- 178.   II   Edgar Vaughn, Jr.
- 179.   III   Hardin Bell Vaughn.
- 180.   IV   Mary Bell Vaughn.
- 181.   V   B Franklin Bell Vaughn.

None of these children are married.

143. Augusta Hardin=Edward Dunn 182
Daughter of Doctor John Hardin's 2d marriage.
Progeny: 4 children
- 183.   I   One daughter married Doctor Gaston Edwards.
- 184.   II   Next daughter married Doctor McEwen, both live in Orlando, Florida.
- 185.   III   A Son, Erwin Dunn also lives in Orlando, Fla.
- 186.   IV   And their youngest daughter lives in Jacksonville, Fla.

CHAPTER XVI
COL. WM. PRESTON ANDERSON

188. William Preston Anderson was a native of Botetourt County, Virginia, and was born about the year 1775. During the second term of General Washington's administration, he received from the President, a commission of Lieutenant in the U.S. Army. Abou this time or soon after, he removed to Tennessee and at one time was United States District Attorney for the Judicial District of Tenn. And was subsequently Surveyor General of the district of Tennessee. In the War of 1812, he was Col. Of the 24th, United States Infantry, and engaged in the battle of Fort Harrison. Col. W.P. Anderson's home in Tenn. was Winchester, franklin County, but while his children were small, he moved to his farm, six miles distant where he resided until his death in April, 1831.

188. Coll. Wm. P. Anderson, 1st=Miss Nancy Bell, 192
Progeny: 3 children.

189. I Musadora Anderson.
190. II Rufus King Anderson.
191. III Caroline Anderson.

1814

188. Col. William P. Anderson, married 2d=Miss Margaret L.
Adair 75,
B 1794 Daughter of Gen. Adair,
Afterward Governor of Kentucky.
Progeny: 7 children.

194. I Nancy Belle Anderson, married Capt. James Murrey 205, a sheriff.
195. II Catherine Adair Anderson, m Col. Skipwith.
196. III John Adair Anderson, died in infancy.
197. IV James Patton Anderson, afterwards a General.
198. V John Adair Anderson, (again).
199. VI Thomas Scott Anderson.
200. VII Butler Preston Anderson, married Ione Head.

193. Mrs. Margaret Adair Anderson, m 2d=Doctor Joseph M. Bybee
194

One child, a daughter, Caroline Bybee 186, who married H.D. Buckly 195, several of their children survive.

CHAPTER XVII
MAJOR GENERAL JAMES PATTON ANDERSON
Of the Confederacy

197. Major General James Patton Anderson, son of Colonel William Preston Anderson, and grandson of Governor Adair of Kentucky, was born at Winchester. Tenn., on Feb. 16th, 1822.

He got his primary education in country and village schools, then graduated in the Jefferson College at Connersville, Penn., in 1840. Returned to Miss. and studied Law with Delafield and04 Delafield and was admitted to the pbar in 1843. General Anderson says, "that in the summers of 1844-45 he spent three months each summer in the Law School of Judge Thomas B. Monroe at Montrose over Frankfort, Kentucky, and have always regarded these months as more profitably spent than any others in his life."

Returned to Miss. To practice law but needed financial support, s took the office of Deputy under his brother-in-law, Col. James H. Murray 205, for a year, then began the law practice, but hardly started before the Governor of Miss. Called him out to go to the war in Mexico, was elected Lieut.-Colonel, and commanded at Tampico. He returned at the close, his health broken with malarial fever. He resumed the practice of law and was elected to the Legislature.

He got military training in the Mexican campaign which stood him in lieu of a West Point Course in the art of war.

Anderson's health still being precarious, he was advised to change climate. His friend, Jefferson Davis 206, was just appointed Sec'y of War in President Peirce's 207 Cabinet, and Washington Territory was just organized. Mr. Davis 206 secured for him the position of U.S. Marshall of Washington, and also Census taker, though this was not a census year, 1853.

General Anderson was married on the 30th of April and started immediately on their bridal trip to Washington Territory, by way of Nicaragua. He regained his health in that great climate, and was popular with the people, and was elected to Congress as Delegate from that Territory. Just before his two-year term expired in Congress, President Pierce 207, appointed him Governor of Washington, but he declined; then when Mr. Buchanan 208 was inaugurated, he appointed General Anderson Governor of Washington and Indian Agent. He, Gen. Anderson consulted his wife, and they decided to resign the appointment, because they anticipated that the succession question would come up before his term of office was out.

Instead of going back as Governor of Washington he went to Florida and engaged in raising cotton and sugar with a big Plantation and Negro slaves.

Major Gen. J. Patton Anderson

197. Major General James Patton Anderson, like many other enterprising American citizens, lived in so many different sections of the Union, that it is a difficult matter to decide to which State he should be assigned in his record of Confederate Generals. At the beginning of the Mexican war, he was living in Mississippi and became Lieutenant-Colonel of Mississippi volunteers, although he had not had the advantage of a military education at the U.S. Military Academy, the Mexican conflict proved a good schooling for him in the military art. The good use he made of his opportunities in that practical training school was afterwards evidenced by the skill with which he managed troops upon the great arena of war between the states, 1861-65, and General Anderson 197 kept abreast with the most illustrious military men of his time.

Just before the Civil war came on General Anderson was living in Florida and in 1860 when Lincoln was elected, the Southern States were all frightened and panic stricken over what their fate would be, General Anderson was a member of the succession convention of Florida, and a delegate from there to the convention of delegates from all the seceding States at Montgomery, Ala., where the Confederacy was formed and launched. Gen. Anderson was not only a member, but a member of the committee to draft the ordinance of secession.

In April, 1861, he was Col. Of the first Florida Regiment of Infantry ready to go wherever the Confederate President might order. Stationed for some time at Pensacola, he was in Command of one of the Confederate columns in the fight on Santa Rosa Island on October, 1861. Early in 1872 he was promoted to Brigadier-General, his command having been transferred to Corinth, Miss. At the battle of Shiloh his Brigade was composed of the 17th, L., the La. Guards Response Battalion, the Florida Battalion (1st Regiment) under Maj. T.A. McDonnell, 9th Texas, 20th La., and a company of the Washington artillery.

Of his service General Bragg said: "Brig.-Gen. Patton Anderson 197 was among the foremost where the fighting was hardest and never failed to overcome whatever resistance was opposed to him. With a brigade composed almost entirely of raw troops his personal gallantry and soldierly bearing supplied the place of instruction and discipline.":

At Perryville he commanded a division of Hardee's 209 Corps and was in charge of the extreme right. At Murfreesboro he commanded Walthall's brigade of Wither's Division of Polk's 210 Corps.

His participation in the magnificent right wheel of the Army was inferior to that of none of the general officers who won fame on that day. It was his brigade which was ordered to take tree batteries "at any cost," and succeeded under the lead of its cool, steadfast, and skillful commander.

Subsequently he commanded Chalmer's 211 brigade, and during the

18th and 19th of September was in command of Hindman's 212 Division in the Chickamauga campaign. Anderson 197 was mentioned by Longstreet as distinguished for conduct and ability. He commanded the same division at Missionary Ridge. On Feb. 17th, 1864, he was promoted to Major-General and Assigned to the command of the district of Florida. After serving five months in that capacity he was ordered to report to General Hood 213 at Atlanta, Ga., in July, 1864, and on his arrival was assigned to his old division, which he commanded in the battle of Ezra Church; during the siege until wounded in the battle f Jonesboro, when he had to leave the Army until March 1865, on account of his wound.

Then, much against the advice and approval of his physician, he returned to the Army in North Carolina and was assigned to command of Taliaferos 214 division, Rhett's 215 and Elliot's 216 brigades from Charleston and was with it when surrendered at Greensboro, North Carolina.

General Anderson was in, and took part in, nearly all the larger battles between Virginia and the Mississippi River, and was in active service during the whole war, except the five months he was laid up with wounds.

The following letter was written to a member of Gen. Anderson's family, and is self-explanatory. It was written by General E.C. Walthall a, Confederate General of Mississippi.

Grenada, Miss., Sept 20th, 1872.

Dear Sir:

I was greatly shocked to receive your telegram announcing the death of Gen. Patton Anderson. I had not even heard of his illness. I am called away to Jackson by a telegram on a most imperative matter of business, otherwise I would certainly be with you on Sunday, and if by traveling all night tomorrow night I can reach Memphis in time after getting through in Jackson, I will go anyhow.

Few men have ever been known to me for whom I had the same respect and affection that I bore for him from the time I first knew him, and for non-had I more. He was true, unselfish and honorable in all things, and with all men, and the manliness with which he bore up under misfortune without murmur or complaint, and the submission of his proud spirit when adversity was on him, excited the admiration of all who knew him.

He was a genuine and pure-minded a man, as proud and brave a one as ever lived, and withal was so accomplished and amiable and gifted that he was to me and to most men who knew him, irresistibly attractive. I loved him and took him to my heart, and I cannot express to you how keenly I feel his loss.

Mrs. Etta Adair Anderson, Wife of Gen. Anderson.

I have written you a rambling letter—just saying imperfectly what I feel. I only wish I could say one word to break the force of this blow which has fallen so heavily on his family and on his friends, and the country. But his virtues and high qualities and rare gifts, when we contemplate them, have to make us feel the loss by the more.

But we can draw some solace from the full knowledge that he whom we loved—as a gentleman of honor has no superior—as a soldier he stood high among the highest—as a patriot he was true, devoted and uncompromising—as a friend he was faithful, staunch and purely unselfish—and as a brave, proud, quiet, cultivated man, he led a blameless life, filling well his place in his family, in country and in the world at large.

Are there many now among us like him? Is there anyone with all his high qualities and no low or bad ones? I confess I fail just now to call to mind one single one.

In am just getting over a sever attack of illness, and am all nerves, as my bad writing shows.

Your friend,
(signed) 242 Edward C. Walthall

(237) Henriette Buford Adair Anderson
(MrsJames Patton Anderson)

Was born at Tomkinsville, Ky., June 3d, 1834. When a small child moved with her parents to Morgansfield, Ky., (She was taught by her mother until she was 12 years old; Then she accompanied her father across the State to Herrodsburg to visit her grandmother; her father only remaining a few weeks, but Henriette remained and went to school a year. Then her grandmother carried her home in her carriage. There were no railroad in the country then.

One of her father's sisters, (Mrs. 82 Florida White,) lost her husband. She had no children—the whole family thought it a great affliction to be childless. She was very wealthy and lonely and wanted to adopt Henriette, or another one of Doctor Adair's children, (He had two daughters and one son.) Her father said he could never give up one of his children, but one or another might spend some time with her at different intervals, as it might suit her convenience. Mr. (82) White's first husband was Col. J. M. White, a good lawyer, who represented Florida in Congress many years. President Jackson sent Col. White on a special mission to Spain to adjust old Spanish claims in Florida. Of course, his wife went with him, and she spent much time abroad and had met all the people of note at that time. (See sketch of Mrs. (82)

Florida on another page in this vol.)

In April 1849, Mrs. (82) White took this niece, (Miss (137) Henriette,) for a year's educational travel in this country and Europe, besides sending her to school a year in Brooklyn. When she returned home, she found that her mother and grandfather 235 Cromwell were both dead, was very sad indeed as she had not heard of it before, the means of communication were so poor in those days.

Miss Henriette needed another year at school, so her father sent her to Memphis to school. Before going to Memphis to school, there was a green spot in their home in the back woods of Kentucky, to wit; a visit at the home of Doctor (84) Wm. H. M. Adair by Col. James (197) Patton Anderson, a nephew of Doctor Adair, and cousin of his children.

Shortley after this visit, which was the first time the Adair children had seen their cousin Patton since they were babies (Patton had just returned from the Mexican War), Colonel (197) Patton Anderson began his courtship of his cousin Henriette, which resulted in their marriage in April 1853. Miss (237) Henriette was still in school in Memphis; Col. Patton Anderson had just returned from Washington, D.C., where he got the appointment of U.S. Marshall of the new Territory of Washington. Immediately after the ceremony they took a steamer for his new field of official duties; by way of New Orleans, Nicaragua, and San Francisco, to Astoria, Oregon. Mrs. (237) Anderson had an uncle, General (85) John Adair, Collector of Customs at Astoria; So, she visited with them while her husband was taking the federal census in the southern side of the Territory.

Mrs. (237) Anderson's first night in Washington was spent at a ranch house of one room with an open shed on one side. There were about a dozen persons sleeping in the house on the floor, some of the party were Indians. Everyone spread their blanket on the floor, and the room was chuck full, but everybody slept good and all enjoyed their meals next morning.

Mrs. Anderson was, after this experience, a constant companion of her husband in taking the federal census, (which seems to have been one of the duties of a Territorial federal Marshal.)

Through with the census, they settled in Olympia, and became comfortably fixed; but it seems that at first they had rather a hard time roughing it. But they made friends of everybody and became popular and both of them were charmed with the people and the climate.

Col. (197) Patton Anderson got rid of the chronic malarial poisoning which had impaired his health since he was in Mexico.

By and by it came time to elect a delegate to represent the Territory of Washington in the National Congress. Col. Anderson was a candidate and was opposed by Judge 217 Strong, a former federal Judge.

The campaign was hotly contested but Col. (197) Patton Anderston won by a very handsome majority, so the Andersons were off for Washington, D.C. in due time; back by steamer, as they came out.

After Col. (97) Anderson's congressional term expired, President 207 Pierce offered him the position as Governor and Indian Agent, but Anderson declined the appointment; then a few days later when 208 Buchanan was inaugurated, that President appointed him Governor and Indian Agent of Washington Territory, and Anderson was inclined to accept it, but after consulting Mrs. Anderson, they declined it because they foresaw the approach of a dissolution of the Union, and Col. Anderson wanted to be in the South when the break came.

Being out of office, the Andersons went to florid and took charge of a big cotton plantation for their aunt, Mrs. (82) Florida White. They were thus engaged when the Civil War came on.

Col. Anderson took a prominent part in Succession, being one of the delegates from Florida to organize the Confederacy at Montgomery. Col. Anderson ranked as Major General in the Confederate Army. Mrs. Anderson and their children were with General Anderson and lived in tents in the army and were often near the great battles.

After her husband's death, she moved back to her old home, Morganfield, and remained there until her sons were grown, when she removed to Palatka, Florida, where her sons went into business, and died there on Feb 18, 1917. She was always interested in the general affairs of life, her principal interest, next to her church (presbyterian), being the United Daughters of the Confederacy. She organized the local Chapter (Patton Anderson Chapter) which was named for her husband, and of which she was the president, from the time of its organization until her death, aged 83 years.

GENERAL ANDERSON GENEALOGY
1853
197. Gen. James Patton=Henrietta Buford Adair
Son of Col. Wm. P. Anderson and   Daughter of Doctor Wm. H.M.
Adair
Margaret Adair Anderson   b 1834, d 1917
B 1822, d 1872

Progeny: Three Sons and Two Daughters
- 251.   I   William Preston Anderson, b July 14, 1856.
- 252.   II   Theophilus Beatly Anderson, b July 27, 1858.
- 253.   III   James Patten Anderson, b Oct. 2, 1860.
- 254.   IV   Elizabeth Cromwell Anderson, b Jan. 20, 1864.
- 355.   V   Margaret Bybee Anderson, b June 12, 1866.

Single, living in Palatka, Fla. Stenographer and Bookkeeper.

1891
251. William Preston Anderson=256 Calpurnia Mahala Garrett
Son of Gen. J. Patton Anderson and   d in Palatka, Fla. 1897
Henrietta Adair Anderson

Progeny: Two Children
- 257.   I   James Patton Anderson, III, b Palatka, May 23, 1892, served during the World War in U.ˑ Navy.
- 258.   II   Martha Adair Anderson, b Palatka, Jan. 21, 1896. Musician, Served in Secret Service Department, Washington, D.C., during the World War.

1888
252. Theophilus B. Anderson=Margaret Bailey Johnson
Son of Jen. J. Patton and Henrietta Adair Anderson   d in
Palatka, Jan. 1, 1906.

Progeny: Four Children
- 260.   I   Julia Etta Anderson, b Palatka, July 7, 1890. Died Sept. 3, 1890.
- 262.   II   Charles Everett Anderson, b.
- 263.   III   Theophilus Beaty Anderson, Jr., b Palatka, April 4, 1895. Died at 8 years
- 264.   IV   Cromwell Adair Anderson, b Palatka, Dec. 21, 1897.

Charles Everett Anderson, the 2d child of Theophilus B. Anderson, volunteered immediately upon declaration of War in April, but was refused on account of under-weight. Finally enlisted July 18, 1917, at Jacksonville. Left for overseas, Sept. 10, 1917. Returned from overseas Feb. 1, 1919. Rans: Corporal in Company B, 10th Engineers. Honorable discharged.

Miss Margaret B. Anderson

1919
Charles Everett Anderson=Marie Estella Browning
Born at Francis, Fla., Mar. 1896.
1921
Cromwell Adair Anderson=Marie Antoinette Richardson
Born, Micanopy, Fla, Feb 18, 1901
Second marriage 1909
252. Theophilus Beaty Anderson=265 Myrtle Land
at Morganfield, Kentucky.
Progeny: One Daughter
266.　I　Clara Land Anderson, b Jan 1910.

CHAPTER XVIII
GENEALOGY OF BYBEE AND BULKLEY

267. Cara Anderson Bybee=**268** Henry Walbridge Bulkley
Daughter of Margaret Adair   Born Jan. 12, 1831, in
And Doctor Bybee. Born in Herrodsburk, Ky. Charleston S.C. Died
Aug 16, **1840.** Died in New York City, in Baltimore, 1909. Served
April 30, 1883   as Major in Confederate Army, Civil War.

Was accused by a Mrs. 269 Wolf of being a southern spy, during the Civil war, and was imprisoned in Fortress Monroe (then I charge of General 270 Butler,) from about March 1, 1964, for about six weeks, when she was exonerated.

(This record taken from the U.S. War Department and from letters written by her while in prison.)

Progeny: 7 Children; 3 Sons, 4 Daughters
- 271. I   Margaret Adair Bulkley, b July 16, 1858.
- 272. II   Henry Walbridge Bulkley, Jr., b Dec. 13, 1860.
- 273. III Cara Bybee Bulkley, b Jan. 18, 1866, died Aug. 4, 1867.
- 274. IV   Joseph Norman Bulkley, b Sept. 17, 1868.
- 275. V   Helen Witherspoon Bulkley, b June 25, 1870.
- 276. VI   Patton Anderson Bulkley, b Nov. 6, 1872, died July, 1873
- 277. VII Cara Lockwood Buckley, b Nov. 6, 1872, died May, 1873.

1884

271. Margaret Adair Bulkley=**278** James Madison Gardinier
Daughter of Cara A. Bybee and Henry W., Bulkley.

Progeny: Two Children
- 279. I Cara Leslie Gardinier, b March 31, 1886. Went to France two months before the Armistice, as business manager of the Barnard College until (of which College she is a graduate) under the A.R.C., at Bordeaux, until Dec. 1918, when under the French Government that did reconstruction work for a year at the village of Marcoing, near Cambrai.
- 280. II Lion Madison Gardinier, b March 8, 1889.

1884

272. Henry Walbridge Bulkley, Jr.=**281** Maud Muller Haddock \ Son of H.W. Bulkley, Sr., and Cara Anderson Bybee.

Progeny: One Child, a Son
- 252. I Clinton Walbridge Bulkley, b June 19, 1889.

282. Clinton W. Bulkley=**283** Ethel Roberts

Son of H.W. Bulkley, Jr.
Progeny: Two Children
284. I Clinton W. Bulkley, Jr., b 1916.
285. II Jane Bulkley, b 191.

274. Joseph Norman Bulkley=286 Marion Walton McLean
After being divorced.

274. Joseph Norman Bulkley=287 Charlotte Hapgood
In South Africa, where they now live.
Progeny: None

1892

275. Helen Witherspoon Bulkley=Fred Hinkley Smith
Daughter of Cara A. Baybee and   In Morristown, N.J.
Henry W. Bulkley, Sr.
Progeny: Two Children
291. I Adair Smith, b Sept. 1, 1893. Died the same day.
292. II Margaret Deming Smith, b July 22, 1894.

1917

293. Margaret Deming Smith=280 Clarenden Waite Smith
Daughter of Helen Witherspoon
Buckley and Fred Hinkley Smith
Progeny: One Child
286. I Deming Waite Smith, b in Worchester, Mass., July 1, 1923.

(275) Helen Witherspoon Smith served in France from February 18, 1918, to August, 1918, with A.R.C. Was stationed at a line Canteen at Dijon Cote d'Or most of the time. Was three weeks in Paris during the bombardments by the Big Bertha. Returned to America on account of ill health.

CHAPTER XIX
BUTLER P. ANDERSON

200. Butler P. Anderson, that brave, noble and chivalrous gentleman, was born at Cragy Hope, the old family homestead near Winchester, in Franklin County, Tenn., on the 17th day of Sept. 1828. His father, Colonel 188 William Preston Anderson, a Virginian by birth, of the lineage of the Floyds, Breckinridges and the Prestons—a man of great culture, of strong and war attachments. He was a lawyer by profession, but a colonel of the 24th Regiment in the regular Army during the War of 1812, continuing in Command for several years after the cessation of hostilities.

He married Miss 75 Margaret Adair, a daughter of Governor John Adair of Kentucky. (For biography, see page   .) Governor Adair commanded the Kentucky troops at the battle of New Orleans, represented Kentucky in Congress, in the Senate and was one of the most useful and popular Governors the state ever had.

Six children were born to Colonel 200 W.P. Anderson and his Adair wife: two daughters and four sons; the eldest daughter married Col. 415 James H. Murray, a prominent citizen of De Soto County, Mississippi. The other daughter married 416 Peyton H. Skipwith, a successful merchant of New Orleans, before the war between the states. The sons were: Major General 417 J. Patton Anderson of Confederate Fame; Col. Scott Anderson, who moved to Austin, Texas, when a young man and became one of the most prominent lawyers in Texas; the 3d son, 418 John Adair Anderson was also a lawyer of prominence, but died at the age of 30. The youngest son, 200 Butler P. Anderson, the honored subject of this sketch, was only 2 years old when his father died, and his widowed mother returned to her old home in Kentucky.

His mother married a second time, Doctor Joseph N. Bybee, of De Soto County, Mississippi; and it was there, at his Stepfather's house that he received his preparatory education. During his school days he was noted for his strong attachments, scrupulous integrity, and rigid adherence to the truth under all circumstances. The foundations of his education was laid under the care of Mr. Frank Johnson, the dear old gentleman who survived his pupil some years. He entered and graduated from the Jefferson College at Connersburg, Penn., which was the alma mater of his brothers, Patten and John.

Butler P. Anderson, inheriting a love for the legal profession, entered the famous law school of his uncle, 296 Thomas B. Monroe, at Frankfort, Ky., and was graduated in 1849.

Butler P. Anderson, Yellow Fever Martyr.
Courtesy of Mrs. Kate Adair Hines of Athens, Alabama

In 1850, he and his brother set out for the Pacific coast. The stopped temporarily in San Francisco but finally settled in Astoria at the mouth of the Columbia River, in the Territory if Oregon.

He soon became influential and very successful in his profession, and his name was prominent throughout the Territory. He filled nearly every position that was strictly in keeping with his profession, the most important being clerk of the Legislative Council, district clerk, clerk of the Supreme Court, Register of the Land Office, Prosecuting Attorney for the Second Judicial district, and the U.S. District Attorney for the Territory, the latter appointment being made by President Pierce. His popular manners, natural kindness of heart, and stern integrity made him hosts of friends.

In 1855, in his 27th year, he married Miss Ione Head, a native of Kentucky, a young lady of great force of character, and during their 23 years of married life she proved herself a wise and affectionate wife and mother.

At the close of the war, he settled in Memphis; he resumed the practice of law and was actively engaged in it when the dread summer of 1878 with his plague, came over our land. For some years he held the position of revenue commissioner and back tax collector.

In the epidemic of Yellow Fever, of 1873, he became a "HOWARD."

At this point we will digress to explain the Yellow Fever plague. Prior to 1900 Yellow Fever, which was a mostly deadly epidemic disease, prevailed in the summer season in the tropical and semi-tropical cities; mostly in the cities around the Gulf of Mexico. The disease was hardly ever absent from all Gulf Cities at once but prevailed in some of them every summer. The disease was carried by ships and propagated in filth and bad sanitation. And about 1900 Doctor 420 Gorgas, an American Physician, of Tuscaloosa, Ala., working and studying the disease in Havana discovered and proved that the germs of contagion were carried by a certain kind of mosquito which were inoculated into a well person in the bite of those insects. These discoveries paved the way to stamping out the disease. Since 1900 there has been no epidemic of yellow fever in any American city, and not much in the Spanish-American cities.

Memphis had a sever epidemic in 1967, another in 1873, and again a most terrible one in 1878 followed by a lighter one in 1879.

The Howard Association. In 1867, in Memphis, a few gentlemen led by the medical profession, understanding and appreciating the work of the immortal philanthropist, John Howard, resolved to follow his example, and devote themselves, under his name, to the succor of the sick, the relief of the suffering and the burial of the dead. The epidemic of 1867 came, and their services were most opportune and welcome. They did good work in 1873, and again in 1878. We have not the space to enumerate the members of the

Howard Association, but it was composed of the best element of the population of Memphis and some of the surrounding town. Trained professional Nurses were few in numbers in those days and it was necessary for the best citizens to take this work in hand.

About the middle of the epidemic of 1873, the Howards ran out of money and supplies; they announced this fact to the nation through the Associated Press; then Mr. 421 Jay Gould, the noted financier and railroad builder, came forward. Jay Gould told the Howard Association to draw on him for all the money they needed to defray the expense of their campaign to the end of the epidemic. The only condition Mr. Gould made was to keep the donation a secret until his death, which they did.

During the epidemic of 1873, Major 200 Butler P. Anderson, the subject of our sketch, became a Howard, and was one of the most faithful and devoted of that association of noble men; feeding the hungry, ministering to the sick and caring for the dead; with cheering words tendering sympathy to bereaved ones, imitating the Divine example, "he went about doing good." From 1873 to August, 1878 his life was well known to the people of Memphis. Deeply interested in the material and moral advancement of the people of this section, his voice and pen were ever ready to be used in their interests. He was a man of strongest sympathy, and the purest philanthropy, and when the wail of distress from stricken Grenada, in 1878, caught his year, he could not restrain himself, nor refuse to go to her succor.

Home, Wife, Mother—the dearest and sweetest words God ever voiced in spoken language—these magic words had an enduring lodgment in his great and manly soul, and his heart ever turned to his home—the mecca where he found the endearments of life. There was the abode of his wife and children whom he loved so well. He bade them farewell to go on what he well knew was a perilous mission of mercy. Brave man and true Howard that he was, he did not pause to consider the risk, nor what the result would be. The people of Grenada asked for Succor, and he was among the few who responded, and when he reached that ill-fated town, he found the people in a carnival of death far worse than bloody war.

He was a higher order of courage than was required to march in forefront of the battle, for he fought an unseen foe whose deadly arm cuts own all alike, and against whom there is no protection.

It was fated that this hero should fall, that he should become a martyr to his human impulses, and his sense of duty. He sacrificed his life in trying to save others, but in dying he immortalized himself and made for the association a name far beyond the limits of his own state. As long as August, 1878, and Grenada, Miss., is remembered, so long will the name and memory of 200 Butler P. Anderson be cherished.

Soon after Major Anderson was stricken with the fever, his devoted wife was notified and she immediately went to him, staying with and nursing him until the last, and then following his remains to the grave. Their separation was of short duration, and in a few days, she too was stricken with the malady and was laid to rest beside the husband of her youth, in dear Elmwood.

"But when the sun in all his state
Illum'ed the eastern skies,
She passed through glory's morning gate,
And walked in Paradise."

The following children now survive: (422) Kate Adair, now Mrs. Ernest Hine, of Athens, Ala. (423) Ione, who was adopted by W.L. Huse, of St. Louis, and is now Mrs. (423) Hedges; and (424) John Adair Anderson, whose home is now in Memphis, and who holds a responsible position with B. Loweinstein & Bro.

188. Col. Wm. P. Anderson=79 Margaret Adair
Daughter of the Governor
Progeny
(200) Butler P. Anderson, and Others

200. Butler P. Anderson=423 Ione Head
Grandson of Governor Adair
Progeny: Five Children

422.	I	Kate Adair Anderson, b 1862. M 424 Ernest Hine.
197.	II	Patten Anderson, b 1865. Died unm, at 26 yrs.
425.	III	John Anderson, b 1868. M Annie Dillard.
426.	IV	Scott Anderson, b 1870. Died at 2 years.
427.	V	Ione Anderson, b 1873, m Issac Hedges.

1881

422. Kate Adair Anderson=Ernest Hine
Daughter of Butler P. and Ione Anderson
Progeny: Five Children

428.	I	William Hine, b 1883, Single.
429.	II	Everlyne Hine, b 1885, m Robert S. Beattie.
430.	III	Clara P.A. Hine, b 1881.
423.	V	Henrietta E. Hine, b 1894.

429. Everlyne Hine=433 Robert S. Beattie
Daughter of Kate A. and Ernest Hine.
Progeny: Three Children

435.	I	Robert Adair Beattie, b 1910.
435.	II	George Wm. Beattie, died.

436. III Ernest Sloss Beattie, b 1914.

427. Ione Anderson=437 Issac Hedges
Daughter of Ione and Butler P. Anderson
Progeny: Three Children

438. I William H. Hedges, b.
439. II Dorathea Hedges.
440. III Isaac Adair Hedges.

BAILEY GENEALOGY
1784

Katherine=Governor (4) John Adair
Progeny:
Margaret Adair and others.

1814

75 Margaret Adair=Col. 188 William P. Anderson
Progeny:
240. Belle Anderson and others

240. Belle Anderson=Capt. 205 James Murray
Progeny:
241. Ellen Murray, and others

1887

241. Ellen Murray=Hon. 241 Joseph Weldon Bailey
Daughter of Belle Anderson And Capt. James Murray. Grand-Daughter of Margaret Adair, and Col. Wm. P. Anderson. Great grand-Daughter of Katherine and Governor John Adair, of Kentucky.

Mr. Bailey was Representative in Congress from the Sherman district in Texas for a number of terms. Then he was Senator, and was the ablest expounder of the Constitution on the Democratic Side.

Progeny: Two Children

243. I Weldon M. Bailey, born ----- Married?----
241. II Joseph W. Bailey, Jr., born ---. Is a lawyer associated with his father.

(243) Mr. Weldon M. Bailey was a lawyer, but came out of the army deaf in one ear; and thus, unable to hear all that transpired in the trial of a case, he abandoned the practice.

245. Mr. Welden M. Bailey=Electra Waggoner
Daughter of Mr. 246 and Mrs. 247 W. T. Waggoner of Fort Worth, Texas.

CHAPTER XX

GENEALOGY OF ISABELLA MCCALLA DAIR PLEASANTS
Daughter of
Governor John Adair of Kentucky

Was born at Whitehall, Ky., in 1800. Married 414 Benjamin Franklin Pleasants, March 4th, 1817. Celebrated her Golden Wedding in Washington in 1867. Died 1869 at the home of her daughter, in Brooklyn, N.Y.

(414) Benjamin Franklin Pleasants was born in Goochland Co., Virginia. Family moved to Kentucky in his early childhood; Spent most of his life as a Clerk in the office of the Solicitor of the Treasury, in Washington, D. C., where he died June 2d, 1879.

1817
81 Isabella McCalla Adair=414 Benjamin F. Pleasants
Daughter of Governor Adair of Ky.
Progeny: Five Children

415.	I	Paulina Pleasants, b Dec. 13, 1817; d, June 23, 1829.
416.	II	Ann Catherine Pleasants, b, May 28, 1820. M, Mason Noble, Aug. 31, 1836.
417.	III	George Washington Pleasants, b, Nov. 24, 1823, m, Sarah T. Bulkley, in 1850.
418.	IV	John Adair Pleasants, b, May 17, 1826, m, Virginia C. Mosby, May 1852.
419.	V	Matthew Franklin Pleasants, b Sept. 17, 1829, m, Lydia Octavia Mosby, 1852.

(420) Rev. Mason Noble was born in Williamstown, Mass., March 18th, 1809. Was a Presbyterian Minister; during his active life he was pastor, successively of the following Churches: Fourth Presbyterian of Washington, D.C.; Eleventh Presbyterian Church of New York; was Naval Chaplin after 1853, lived in Washington when waiting orders, and after retirement at age of 62 years, acted as pastor of the Sixth Presbyterian Church of Washington, D.C., until his death in October, 1881.

1836
416. Ann Catherine Pleasants=Rev. 420 Mason Noble
Granddaughter of Governor Adair of Ky.
Progeny: Four Sons

422.	1	I Josep Franklin Noble, b, Aug. 1837, m, Emma M. Prime, June 4, 1862.

422. II   Mason Noble, Jr., b, Sept. 12, 1842, m, Mary Eliabeth Adam, Sept. 12, 1867.
423. III George Pleasants Noble, b, Jan. 4, 1845, m, Elisabeth T. Ketcham of Brooklyn, N.Y., Sept. 15, 1858. D, March 15, 1918.
424. IV   Charles Noble, b, in N.Y., Dec. 3, 1847, m. Alice Thomas, Jan. 21, 1874.

(421) Rev. Joseph Franklin Noble, served as Pastor of the following Churches, in succession: Presbyterian of Sandusky, Ohio; the Congregational Church, Torrinford, Conn.; Church of the Covenant (Congregational) Brooklyn, N.Y.; Presbyterian Church, Hemstead, Long Island, N.Y.; Congregational Churches, Falls Church and Vanderwerken, Virginia. On Editorial Staff of Appleton's Eyclopaedia, and Editor of the "Treasure Magazine," New York. Published "Thoughts for the Occasion,:" in several volumes, and "Sermons in Illustration." He died April 25, 1922.

1862

421. Rev. Jospeh Franklin Noble=Emma Matilda Prime
Son of Rev. Mason Noble, Sr.
Progeny: Four Daughters, Two Sons

426. I   Harry Noble, b, Sept. 22, 1863, m Fred Dudley, June 8, 1892. R.F.D., Rosslyn, Va.
427. II   Isabella Pleasants Noble, b, Dec. 22, 1864. M, Henry McKeag, Aug. 16, 1893, 172 Union St., Montclair, N.J.
428. III Kate Paulina Noble, b, July 5, 1872. Died Jan. 22, 1878.
429. IV   Henry Prime Noble, b, May 27, 1874, m, Letitia Merriweather Demarest, 1905, at Falls Church, Ca.
430. V   Alice Noble, b, May 24, 1878, m Francis Mallory Ball, Nov. 28, 1906, in Hollywood, Calif.
431. VI   Mason Franklin Noble, b, Aug. 15, 1882, m, Louise F. Kelley, April 18, 1908.

(432) Rev. Mason Noble, Jr., was Pastor of Congregational Churches at the following places: Cannan, Conn., Sheffield, Mass., Oriole and Lake Helen, Florida. He was born in 1842 and died in 1916.

1867

422. Rev. Mason Noble, Jr.=422 Mary Elizabeth Adam
Son of Rev. Mason Noble, Sr.
Progeny: Five Sons, Two Daughters.

426. I   George Adam Noble, b, June 23, 1868, at Inverness, Fla.
427. II   Katherine Pleasants Noble, b, Feb. 2, 1870, at Canaan, Conn.
428. III Rose Noble, b, Sept. 6, 1872, at Inverness, Fla.
429. IV   Mason Noble, 3d, b, Oct. 17, 1874, m, Millie Catherine Cake, Aug. 22, 1906.

430. V   John Adair Noble, b, Dec. 20 at Inverness, Fla.
431. VI   Samual Charles Noble, b, Dec. 26, 1881, m. Aileen Butler,
           Nov. 16, 1912. She died June 14, 117, at Jacksonville, Fla.
431. VII   Joseph Franklin Noble, b, March 20, 1886, d, Aug. 16, 1888.
(423) George Pleasants Noble, born Jan. 4, 1845, married
Elizabeth T. Ketcham, of Brooklyn, N.Y., Sept 15, 1868. Was Pastor of
           the following Presbyterian Churches successively:
           Weehawken, N.J., Malden, N.Y., Mendham, N.J., Carmel,
           N.Y. Died March 15, 1918

1845

423. Rev. George Pleasants Noble=433 Elizabeth T. Ketcham
Son of Rev. Mason Noble, Sr.
           Progeny: Four Sons, One daughter
434. I   Henry Herbet Taylor Noble, b, Jan. 27, 1870. M, Dec. 30,
           1896, Carolin Leslie Place.
435. II   Franklin Pleasants Noble, b, March 25, 1872, m June 19,
           1998, Jennie F. Bokoven.
436. III   Fanny Ketcham Noble, b, Oct. 19, 1873.
437. IV   Charle Noble, Jr., b, Jan. 8, 1877, m, Oct. 22, 1902, Grace
           Charlick.
438. V   George Pleasants Noble, Jr., b, May 29, 1881. Died Sept. 3,
           1882.

429. Henry Prime Noble=429 Letita Merriweather Demarest
Son of J.F. and E.M. Noble   at Falls Church Va.
           Progeny: Two Sons, One Daughter
440. I   Herny Prime Noble, Jr., b, Jan. 30, 1907.
441. I   Beartha Demarest Noble, b, Jan. 19, 1909.
442. III   Merriweather Adair Noble, b, Dec. 19, 1919.

Nov 28, 1906

430. Alice Noble=Francis Mallory Ball
Daughter of J.F. and E.M. Noble   at Hollywood, Calif.
           Progeny: One Son, Two Daughters
444. I   Francis Mallory Ball, Jr., b, Aug. 9m, 1907.
445. II   Alice Delany Ball, b, July 3, 1913.
446. III   Emma Matilda Ball, b, Feb. 21, 1919.

April 19, 1908

431. Mason Franklin Noble=447 Louise F. Kelley
Sixth Child of J.F. Noble
           Progeny: Three Daughters
448. I   Mary Noble, b, July 23, 1910.
449. II   Stephanie Louis Noble, b, May 29, 1912.
450. III   Virginia Adair Noble, b, May 29, 1914.

August 22, 1906
429. Mason Noble, 3d=451 Minnie Catherine Cake
Son of Mason Noble Jr., and Mary Adam Noble.
Progeny: One Daughter, Two Sons
452.   I   Mary Elizabeth Noble, b, Aug. 31, 1907.
453.   II   Mason Noble 4th, b, May 9, 1909.
454.   III   Hugh Noble, b, Oct. 7, 1911.
All born in Canaan, Conn.

1912
431. Samuel Charles Noble=455 Eileen Butler
Son of Mason Noble, Jr.   She died June 14, 1917, at Jacksonville, Fla.
Progeny: Two Daughters
456.   I   Carldeen Noble, b, Dec. 20, 1913.
457.   II   Aileen Noble, b, May 27, 1917.

(448) George Washington Pleasants, a grandson of Governor Adair, married 45x Sarah T. Buckley, and lived all his active life in Rock Island, Ill. He was a Practitioner of Law, then Judge of the District Court, and finally Justice of the State Court of Appeals. He died at an advanced age in Rock Island, Ill.

1850
488. George Washington Pleasants=451 Sarah T. Buckley
Progeny: One Son, Two Daughters
452.   I   Adair Pleasants, b, in Rock Island, April 8, 1854, m, 453 Sarah Mary Crawford, May 2, 1888. Was a lawyer in Rock Island.
454.   II   Nannie Pleasants, b, Rock Island, Jan. 8, 1858. Married 455 Samuel Adam Lynde, Aug. 27, 1879. Present Address, 155 West 58th St., New York.
456.   III   Belle Pleasants, b, Rock Island, April 16, 1860. Married Benjamin F. Orton, April 10, 1888. Present address: The New Port, 16th and Spruce St., Philadelphia.

John Adair Pleasants was a grandson of Governor John Adair o Ky. He was born 1826; Married in 1852; Was a lawyer in Akron, Ohio, for a few years; for the most of his life he was in the Insurance business in Richmond, Virginia, where he died in 1893.

1852
449. John Adair Pleasants=458 Virginia Cary Mosby
Progeny: Five Daughters
559.   I   Mary Webster Pleasants, b. Feb. 21, 1853. D, March 13, 1884
460.   II   Louise McLain Pleasants, b, Oct. 24, 1855. Lives at 508 E. Franklin St., Richmond, Virginia.

463. III   Kate Noble Pleasants, b, April 8, 1857, m, Edmund Christian Minor, 1877.
464. IV   Lydia Mosby Pleasants, b, May 18, 1960, m, Benjamin f. Purcell, 1893.
465. V   Rosalie Harrison Pleasants, b, Sept. 6, 1864, m, William W. Archer, 1893.

(450) Matthew Franklin Pleasants, was a son of B.F. and I.M. Pleasants, and a grandson of Governor Adair of Ky., born Sept. 29, 1829. Married Oct. 6, 1852. In mercantile business in New York till 1860; Pardon Clerk in the office of the Attorney General, Washington, D.C., till 1870; then Clerk of the U.S. Circuit Court, Richmond, Virginia, till his death in 1906.

1852

450. Matthew Franklin Pleasants= 466 Lydia Octavia Mosby

Progeny: Two daughters, Three Sons

467. I   Isabella Adair Pleasants, b, Oct. 21, 1853. M, Reginald Gilham in 1888. Address 11 E. Franklin St., Richmond, Va.
488. II   Virginia Mosby Pleasants, b, Jan. 10, 1856, d. 1921.
489. III McLain Pleasants, b, June 21, 1868, m, Hester Kyle, 1893, d, 1903.
490. IV   Matthew Pleasants, b July 22, 1865; d 1867.
492. V   John Adair Pleasants, b, 1870, d, 1904.

1888

452. Adair Pleasants=493 Sarah Mary Crawford

Son of Geo. W. and Sarah M.G. Pleasants.   Address Adair Pleasants Esq, Rock Island Ill.

Progeny: One Son, One Daughter

494. I   Dorothy Pleasants, b, March 18, 1889.
495. II   Matthew Pleasants, b, Feb. 21, 1892.

1879

454. Nannie Pleasants=496 Samuel Adams Lynde.

Daughter of Geo W. Pleasants   155 West 58th St. N.Y.

497. I   Cornelius Lynde, b, Feb. 20, 1881, m, Bertha Pollock.
498. II   Isabella Adair Lynde, b, Oct. 9, 1883. M. John Francis Danman, Jr.
499. III George Pleasants Lynde, b, March 13, 1887. M, Sarah Gibson.

1888

456. Belle Pleasants=500 Benjamin F. Orton

Daughter of Geo W. Pleasants.

Progeny: One Daughter

502. I   Ellen Adair Orton, b, Dec. 12, 1890.

463. Kate N. Pleasants-503 Edmund Christian Minor
Daughter of John Adair Pleasants   508 E. Franklin St.,
Richmond Va.

    Progeny: Five Daughters, One Son

560.   I   Louise McLain Minor, b, 1878. Died 1880.
561.   II   Kate Pleasants Minor, b,1879, died 1887.
562.   III Virginia Adair Minor, b, 1882, m Edw. Gilchrist.
563.   IV Edmund Christian Minor, b, 1885. Died 1890.
564.   V   Caroline Minor, b, 1887. M, Richard S. Ely, 1914. Address R.F.D, Alexandria, Va.
565.   VI Annie Hyde Minor, b, 1889. Died 1922.

1893

464. Lydia M. Pleasants=Benjamin F. Purcell.
Daughter of J.A. Pleasants   He died in 1923

    Progeny: Four Sons

571.   I   Adair Pleasants Archer, b, 1894. Died 1918 at Camp Grant, Ill., U.S. Service, World War; Influenza the direct cause.
572.   II   Sheppard Archer, b, 1898, died 1899.
573.   III William W. Archer, Jr., b, 1902.
574.   IV Edmond Minor Archer, b, 1904.

1893

489. McLain Pleasants=575 Hester Kayle.
Son of Matthew F. Pleasants

    Progeny: Two Sons, One Daughter

576.   I   Matthew Franklin Pleasants, Jr., b, 1894.
577.   II   Robert Kyle Pleasants b, 1895. M, C.M. Chichester, 1917. He died 1918.
578.   III Catherine Sellers Pleasants, b, 1898, C.M. Butterworth, 1922.

1893

497. Cornelious Lynde=580 Bertha Pollock.
Son of Nannia Pleasants and S.A. Lynde

    Progeny: One Daughter, One Son

581.   I   Margaret Lynde.
582.   II   Samuel Adams Lynde, Jr.

1903

498. Isabell A. Lynde=584 J.F. Danman
Daughter of Nannie P. and S.A. Lynde.

    Progeny: Three Sons, One Daughter

585.   II   Samuel Lynde Danman, b.
586.   II   John Francis Danman.
587.   III Nancy Danman.

AMERICAN ADAIRS—Line A

588. IV   Peter Adair Danman.

499. George Pleasants Lynde=589 Sarah Gibson.
Son of Nannie Pleasants and S.A. Lynde.
Progeny: One Son
590.   I   Charle McGill Lynde.

562. Virginia Minor=592 E. Gilchrist.
Daughter of Kate N., and E.C. Minor
Progeny: One Daughter
593.   I   Katherine Caroline Gilchrist, b, 1909.

1915

504. Caroline Minor=594 Richard Ely
Daughter of J.A., and E.C. Minor
Progeny: Two Sons, One Daughter
595.   I   Richard Edmund Ely, b, 1915.
596.   II   Adair Anderson Ely, b, 1921.
597.   III   Anna Morris Ely, b, 1923.

566. Martha Purchell=598 Philip S. Barba.
Daughter of Lydia P., and B.F. Purcell
Progeny: One Son
599.   I   William Philip Barba, b 1922.

1917

577. Robert Kyle Pleasants=600 C.M. Chichester
Son of McLain and Hester Kyle Pleasants.
Progeny: One Son
602.   I   Robert Kyle Pleasants, Jr., 1915.

1922

579. Catherine S. Pleasants=603 C.M. Butterworth
Daughter of McLain and Hester Kyle Pleasants
Progeny: One Daughter
604.   I   Roberta Kyle Butterworth, b, 1923.

1922

605. Kathleen McKeag=606 Burdette O'Conner
Daughter of Isabella P. and H.C. McKeag.
Progeny: One Daughter
607.   I   Isabella Noble O'Conner, b, July 1, 1923.

103. Children Born in the Pleasants Branch. 31 Marriages

CHAPTER XXI
SKETCH OF MRS. ANNETTA SCOTT FOX

Mrs. Annetta Scott Fox, second daughter of Doctor Robert Scott and his wife, Mary Adair, was born in Monticello, Florida, July 12th, 1861. She married in 1886 to James Albert Brandon of Thomasville, Georgia, where they resided until his death in 1895. A year later Mrs. Brandon took her niece, Harriet Newcomb, an art student, to New York City, and made her home there until her marriage in 1902 to Hon. A.F. Fox, Member of Congress from the Fourth Mississippi District. As the wife of a Congressman, Mrs. Fox, by her many charms and brilliant attainments, was easily a leader in the social and official life of the capitol city, and after Mr. Fox's retirement from Congress, and their return to Mississippi, though a stranger, with the same ability and charm, she soon made for herself a wide circle of friends and an influence which was felt, not only locally, but in all parts of the state. She presided with a gracious dignity at their home, "Elm View," widely known as one of the most beautiful estates in Mississippi, and with the generous hospitality dispensed b her it became famous as a center of the social, political and intellectual life of the State, entertaining as its frequent guests the leading men and women of the commonwealth.

Mrs. Fox has been prominently connected with the patriotic organizations, both state and national, notably the Daughters of the American Revolution of which she served for many years as State Regent and National Vic President General, and Colonial Dames of America, of which she is at this time State Vice President. These organizations have enjoyed splendid growth and progress under her leadership. During the world war, Mrs. Fox was a leader in various branches of relief and patriotic work actively responding to all calls made upon her.

HON. ANDREW FULLER FOX

Andrew Fuller Fox, son of Hally Fox and his wife, Sarah Hughes, was born on the 26th of April, 1849, in Pickens County, Alabama. Both the Fox and Hughes families were for several generations' residents of South Carolina, and members of both are mentioned in records of the Revolutionary War. The Foix family came to South Carolina from Virginia and was originally English.

When Andrew Fuller was four years old his father moved to Calhoun County, Mississippi, settling near the old town of State Springs, where other members of his family had homes. Before Fuller was twelve years old the Civil War came on and all the male members of the family, of fighting age, enlisted; he was most anxious to take part in it and at the age of fourteen, with a young cousin, slipped away from home and walked thirty-five miles to Grenada, Miss., where a regiment was encamped; he was taken by the commanding officer into his tent for the night, and the next day, to his infinite chagrin and disappointment, was sent back to his home.

During the war there was little opportunity in the South for boys to obtain an education, but Fuller, always devoted to books, used every spare moment for study, his older sisters his instructors; so, at the age of seventeen he, having acquired an unusually good literary and classical education for that time, accepted a position as a teacher. Later he went to a college in Mansfield, Texas, from which two years afterwards he was graduated. He then returned to Mississippi and founded a small college at State Springs, which for many years enjoyed a good standing and patronage. It had been his intention to devote himself to a life of teaching, a profession for which he had great respect, but finding that it was a strain upon his nerves and threatened to undermine his health, he decided when twenty-seven years of age, to give it up. He moved to Grenada and studied law in the office of Gen. E.C. Walthall, for whom he had a great attachment. The devotion and intimacy between these two continued until the death of Gen. Walthall in 1898.

With his well-trained mind, Mr. Fox soon finished his law course, and was admitted to the bar, beginning his practice in Calhoun and Webster counties. In 1883 he accepted an invitation from Hon. Frank White, who afterwards moved to Alabama and later became U.S. Senator from that state, to form a partnership for the practice of law in West Point, Miss. When Mr. White removed to Birmingham, Mr. Fox not wishing to leave Mississippi, formed a partnership with S.M. Roane, and for many years the firm "Fox and Roane" was one of the best known and most successful in the state.

In 1891 Mr. Fox was a member of the State senate, an office which he accepted solely for the purpose of securing the re-election to the U.S. Senate of Gen. E.C. Walthall and Gen. J.Z. George. This accomplished, Mr. Fox resigned the office of State Senator to accept from President Cleveland the appointment as U.S. District Attorney. Before the expiration of one term in this office, Mr. Fox was urged to become the nominee of his party for Congress from the 4th Mississippi District. Though always much interested in the politics of his state, Mr. Fox did not care for office holding and only accepted this nomination when tendered from a sense of duty and devotion to his state, and at great sacrifice personally and financially. At that time the

4th District had a strong populist element, there being decided indication of the election of a populist for Congress. With his strong personal following Mr. Fox was elected by a splendid majority, and re-elected twice, almost without opposition, though never a candidate, and never having made a canvass of his district. After six years he announced that he could not serve longer. A demand was then made upon him to become a candidate for Governor of Mississippi, by the conservative element of that state to oppose Jas. K. Vardaman, a man of the most radical views and tendencies. This, however, Mr. Fox was forced to decline to do because of the death of his partner, Mr. Roane, which made it imperative that he again take up their large practice.

In 1911 Mr. Fox was elected by acclamation president of the Mississippi State Bar Association. He continued in his profession until 1924 when he retired and has since spent much time in travel.

Mr. Fox as married in 1873 to Miss Augusta Branson of Mansfield, Texas, who died in 1900. In 1902 he was married to Mrs. Annetta Scott Brandon, daughter of Doctor Robert Scott and his wife, Mary Catherine Adair.

CHAPTER XXII
DOCTOR WILLIAM HENRY MOORE ADAIR

The subject of this sketch was the eldest son of Gov. John Adair of Kentucky, and his wife, Katherine Palmer, and was born on the family estate, "White Hall," near Harrodsburg, on July 9th, 1805. He received a college and professional education and began the practice of his profession in his home county. He was married on September 28th, 1830, to Elizabeth Ann Cromwell, a descendant of the Craddocks, Cromwells, Risteaus, Worthingtons, and many other well-known families who made the early history of Baltimore County, Maryland.

The had six children, three of whom died in infancy. The eldest, Stephen Cromwell, is still living.

In 1838, Doctor Adair moved with his family to Morganfield, Union County, to be near his wife's father who was quite old and wished to have his daughter with him. There Doctor Adair practiced his profession and also found much other work to engage his attention. At that time this part of Kentucky was quite primitive, being settled largely by Roman Catholics. Doctor and Mrs. Adair did a great deal of educational and missionary work, organizing Presbyterian churches and Sunday schools. He assisted in the organization of the church at Morganfield of which he was an elder up to the time of his death. He had the misfortune on October 8th, 1851, of losing his wife, who was a splendid and capable woman, a real helpmate to him in his buy and useful life. He seemed never to have recovered from the effects of the loss, though he continued to practice his profession until in February, 1859, when he had a severe illness. As his two daughters were married and living in Florida, his son, Cromwell, took him South as soon as he was able to travel, hoping the mild climate would be beneficial. But he did not regain strengths and died on March 15th, 1859.

ROBERT SCOTT, M.D.

Robert Scott, the son of James Scott, and Margaret Bailey, his wife, was born in Jefferson County, Florida, on March 25th, 1833. His father had moved some years before from the family home near St. Mary's Ga., to join relative and friends and make a new home in the then territory of Florida. One of the most thrilling recollections of Robert's childhood in this wild country was an unexpected attack one evening open the home by a band of Seminole Indians when, but for the prompt and ready action of his father and his slaves, the family would no doubt have been massacred. Some years later his father bought and moved his family to another plantation only a short distance from the town of Monticello.

Robert and his brother, William, were educated by private teachers and later sent to the University of Virginia; but before he had taken his medical course the father died, leaving Robert the care of Mother and three younger sisters, as well as the responsibility of the plantation and slaves. He established a home in the town for the family, arranged the business affairs for his absence and went to Philadelphia where he finished his medical course two years later at Jefferson College. He at once began to practice his profession in his home town, where in February, 1859, he was married to Mary Katherine Adair, daughter of William Adair and Elizabeth Cromwell, his wife; the mother having died, Mary spent much of her girlhood with her aunt Ellen Adair Beatty at "Casa Bianca," a few miles from Monticello, and it was in this interesting old home that the wedding took place.

Two years lat3er the Civil War came on, and Doctor Scott enlisted in a local company, organized by Colo. Bird, and was elected 1st Lieutenant. Very soon after they joined the army, however, a petition was sent to the authorities by the citizens of town and country to have Doctor Scott returned, as some of the older physicians, who had been expected to care for the people, had accepted hospital appointments. Later a small hospital was established in Monticello for the care of sick and wounded soldiers, to which work Doctor Scott devoted himself during and after the war.

His wife died in August, 1872, leaving six daughters, all of whom are living at the present time except the youngest who died in infancy.

Doctor Scott died January 3, 1886. He was a man of great strength of character and gentleness of disposition, a devoted husband, father, brother and friend. He led a most unselfish life, doing much good in the community, ready with sympathy and help for all in trouble and need, often at great sacrifice to himself.

WILLIAM HENRY PALMER MOORE ADAIR, M.D.

Lineage—Doctor 4 Wm. H.M. Adair (3 John Adair, 2 William Adair, 1 Thomas Adair,) son of Governor Adair of Kentucky; was born July 9, 1805.

1830

85 Doctor William Henry Moore Adair=608 Elizabeth Cromwell

Progeny:
- 609. I   Cromwell Adair, the oldest, born 1831.
- 610. II   Henrietta Adair, born 1834.
- 611. III   Mary Katherine Adair, born Feb. 1839.

612. Cromwell Adair married 613 Katherine Cromwell, a distant cousin. Progeny: none. Both are living at this time at Morganfield, Ky. (239) Henrietta Adair, born about 1834, married her cousin, Gen. 197 James Patten Anderson.

Mary Katherine Adair was born 1839.

611. Mary Katherine Adair=614 Robert Scott, M.D.
She died in Aug. 1872.   Of Monticello, Fla.
He died in 1886
Progeny: Five Children

615.	I	Margaret Elizabeth Scott, born Dec. 1859.
617.	II	Annetta Scott, born July 12, 1861.
618.	III	Adair Scott, born Feb 3, 1864.
619.	IV	Minnie Scott, born Oct. 12, 1866.
620.	V	Julia Scott, born July 27, 1869.

1879

615. Margaret Elizabeth Scott=621 Orlando Newcomb
Progeny:

622.	I	Henrietta Adair Newcomb, March 8th.
623.	II	Molly Newcomb.
624.	III	Robert Newcomb.

623. Henrietta Adair Newcomb, 625 Eugene Smith
Born 1880   of Thomasville, Ga., where they now live.

623. Molly Newcomb=626 Frederick Warrington Bull
Born 1882   Died 1920
627.   One son, Frederick Bull, Jr., born 1913.
            Mrs. Bull resides with son, mother and brother in N.J.
            The third child, Robert Newcomb, was born 1885, and is not married.

(617) Annetta was born 1861.

1886

617. Annetta Scott=628 James Albert Branden
of Thomasville, Ga., died 1895
Progeny: None
2d Marriage

617. Annetta Scott=629 Andrew Fuller Fox
A lawyer and Congressman from West Point, Mississippi.
Progeny: None

1881

618. Adair Scott=630 John Denham

Born 1864 of Monticello, Fla. Died 1908

Progeny: One Son

631. Robert Scott Denham.

1916

631. Robert Scott Denham=632 Margaret Hubbard of Montgomery, Ala.

Progeny: One son

Robert Scott Denham, Jr., b. 1917.

Minnie Scott, 4th daughter of Doctor Scott, born 1866.

1884

619. Minnie Scott=633 Emmet Smith of Florida

Progeny: Two Children

634. I Robert Smith, b 1885.
635. II Minnie Smith, b 1891.

634. Robert Smith=637 Fletcher Farrell of Ala.

Lived in Columbus, Ga.

Was recently killed in an auto Accident.

She now lives with her parents in Moultre, Ga.

Julia Scott, 5th daughter of Doctor Scott, b 1869

1891

620. Julia Scott=638 James Mason Dyer

Progeny: Three Children

639. I Adair Dyer, b, 1892, not married, lives in Dallas.
640. II James Mason Dyer, Jr., b, 1894, not married. Living in Corsicana, Texas.
641. III Annetta Baldwin Dyer, b, 1897. Married Carrell Miller, lives in Corsicana, where his parents also reside.

Hon. Stephen Cromwell Adair

Stephen Cromwell Adair, the son of Doctor Wm. H.P.M. Adair and Elizabeth Cromwell, his wife, was born at Harrodburg, Ky., July 18th, 1831. The family removed to Morganfield, Union County, in 1838.

Cromwell's education began at home, was continued at the high school at Henderson, Ky. For four years he was at college in Hanover, Indiana, where he was graduated in 1854. He then accepted a position to teach in a school in Memphis, Tenn., studying at the same time. Having finished the law course, he returned to Kentucky and began his practice in Union and adjoining counties, where he soon became widely known as an able and conscientious lawyer and financier, and where he enjoyed a splendid practice for many years.

Mr. Adair served for a number of terms in the state Senate and was a leader in that body when much constructive legislation was accomplished, the most notable of which was the adoption of the present constitution of Kentucky. He was a candidate for Congress in 1876 but was defeated by Mr. Laffoon. Mr. Adair, with his splendid training, personal integrity and unusual ability, would have brilliantly represented his state in our nation's capital had he been elected.

Mr. Adair was married Nov. 13th, 1860, to Katherine Cromwell, a daughter of a cousin of his mother. Both are living at this time, enjoying a beautiful old age among the friends of a lifetime in the home they made for themselves when on the threshold of life's journey together.

CHAPTER XXIII

AMERICAN ADAIRS—LINE A

CHAPTER XXIII

CROMWELL GENEALOGY

Morgan Williams, ap Morgan, ap Yevan (Welch princes) = Elizabeth Cromwell, Sister of Thos. Cromwell, Earl of Essex.

Richard Cromwell Williams Knighted by King Henry VIII, "Sir Richard Cromwell" (dropping the Williams) in compliment to his mother's brother, the Earl of Essex. = Frances, daughter and co-heir of Thos. Murfyn, Knt.

Henry Cromwell was knighted by Queen Elizabeth 1563. Served in the House of Commons. Was known as "The Golden Knight" because of his munificence. = Joan Warren, daughter of Sir Ralph Warren, of Lord Mayor of London in 1536.

Oliver (Sir) of Hinchenbrook, Uncle of Oliver—the "Protector." = Elizabeth Bromley, dau. of Sir Thos. Bromley, Lord High Chancellor of England. He presided over the Commission that tried Mary, Queen of Scots. Is buried in Westminster Abbey.

Henry Cromwell Came to Virginia about 1620. = Wife unknown

William Cromwell Member of the Legislative Council of the Lord Proprietor. = Elizabeth Trahearne

William Cromwell II = Mary Howard

Joseph Cromwell = Comfort

Capt. Stephen Cromwell Born 1747, Died 1783 = Elizabeth Murray

Stephen Cromwell II = Mary Cradock, dau. of Maj. John Cradock, who served in Revolutionary War

Elizabeth Cromwell = Dr. Wm. H. M. Adair, Son of Governor John Adair of Kentucky.

Henrietta Buford Adair = James Patton Anderson, Lieut. Col. in U. S. A. during Mexican War, and Maj.-Gen. in Confederate Army.

Adair Lineage from first American ancestor—Henrietta B. Adair, Dr. Wm. H. M. Adair, Gov'r John Adair, William Adair, Thomas Adair.

CHAPTER XXIV
GENERAL JOHN ADAIR OF ASTORIA

John Adair, (3 Governor John, 2 William, 1 Thomas Adair), was born at White Hall, Ky., Aug. 8th, 1808. He was the youngest child in a family of eleven children of Governor John Adair and Anna Palmer Adair, his wife. John Adair was a small boy when his father was Governor of Kentucky.

After he finished his education, he married, in 1834, Miss Mary Ann Cockburn Dickerson, b Feb. 15th, 1816.

He was naturally a pioneer and wanted to go west. After he was a grown man, he tired of slavery and emancipated his negro slaves, moved to Indiana, and settled on the Wabash near Terry Haute, with his family and some of his emancipated slaves. This was in 1884. This proved to be an unhealth climate and he lost three of his children there, and he and his wife determined to move. At this time, 1848, President Polk appointed him Collector of Customs at the port of Astoria, Oregon. This occurred before the discovery of gold in California was known on the Atlantic side of the country. So on the 18th of Dec. of that year John Adair took his wife and six children aboard the steamer Falcon at New Orleans, bound for Oregon, via the Isthmus of Panama. Before the boat sailed, the news of the discovery of gold in California had spread over the country, so the boat became crowded to the limit with passengers. Among the passengers was Gen. Percifer F.F. Smith and his staff, including Gen. E.R.S. Canby. The Falcon landed her passengers at Chagres, from which point they had to make their way by canoes and muleback across the isthmus to Panama. This journey was particularly difficult and dangerous; the trails were almost impassable, and the cholera broke out among these six hundred passengers while they were making this perilous journey. When they reached Panama, they had to wait for the steamship California to take them to San Francisco.

The Adairs had six children, and while waiting, the old town of Panama was filled to overflowing with Americans, who were wild to get on to the gold mines, but many of this eager crowd yielded up their lives to cholera before getting beyond Panama. At last, after nearly two months of weariness and expense, the steamship California reached Panama, and Adair was, with great difficulty, able to get his family aboard for San Francisco. Tickets were re-sold for as much as fifteen hundred dollars. This Pioneer steamship reached San Francisco on Feb. 28th, 1849, having been 29 days out of Panama, out of fuel twice, on fire twice, and poorly fitted at any time for

Gen. John Adair of Astoria

Mrs. John Adair of Astoria

the immense load of passengers. Arriving in San Francisco, the Golden City, Adair found everyone going, or wanting to go, to the mines. Many prominent men urged him to remain in San Francisco and report back to Washington that a Collector of Customs was vastly more needed than such an officer could be needed at Astoria; but Adair thought it clearly his duty to push on to his destination.

He therefore set about getting transportation to the mouth of the Columbia River. After trying various vessels, he fortunately met Capt. Nathaniel Crossby, an early Portlander, who was going to Oregon with the little brig Valdora and took passage on that. The little vessel had been 28 days in making the trip, and her passengers were indeed glad to get ashore, having served 24 days their turns at the pumps, in order to keep the Valdora afloat.

General John Adair was made welcome to his new home by the few white people living there, and during the summer of '49 moved his family into their permanent home.

Adair was so successful as Collector of Customs, and his services were so well appreciated by the authorities at Washington City that he was continued in office for twelve years, during the administrations of Polk, Taylor, Pierce and Buchanan.

Adair was a leading Democrat, yet no efforts of his opponents were sufficient to have him removed as Collector of Customs at Astoria. He retired voluntarily at the end of President Buchanan's terms. After his retirement from the collectorship, he engaged in stock farming and other lines. He was never a military man but was dubbed "General" in honor of his distinguished father, the Governor of Kentucky. General John Adair led a pure and upright life and was universally revered and respected accordingly.

He died on the 9th of April, 1888, at his home in Astoria, age 80 years.

1834
John Adair=Mary Ann C. Dickinson

At Whitehall, KY. The Dickinsons were a distinguished family.

Progeny: 13 Children, 8 Girls, 5 Boys

626. I Elizabeth Adair, b July, 1835. M Charles J. Brenham 1855, d 1875.
627. II Ellen Adair, b Dec. 1836. M Geo H. Mendell October, 1838.
628. III Katy Adair, b March, 1838. M Wm. T. Welker, July, 1857, d Dec., 1910
629. IV John Adair, Jr., b July, 1839. M Bethenia A. Owens, July, 1884, d Nov. 1914.
630. V Joseph Palmer Adair, b Nov., 1840, d Jan., 1846.

631. VI   Anna Pindell, b Dec., 1841, d Jan., 1846.
632. VII   Mary Ann Adair, b Feb., 1844, m Wm. H. Jordan Nov., 1865.
633. VIII Sarah Adair, b Feb., 1845, d Jan., 1846
634. IX   Samuel Dickenson Adair, b Jan. 1847, m Mary Rodney Morris, Jan. 1880. D. 1916.
635. X   Wm. Butler Adair, b. June, 1849, m Mary Louise Jorand, Sept, 1887.
636. XI   Henry Buford Adair, b Sept. 1851, d Aug. 1871
637. XII   Laura Pindell Adair, b. Aug., 1854, m. Bishop Wm. Morris Barker, July, 1892.
638. XIII Isabelle Pleasants Adair, b. Oct., 1856, d. Dec. 1867.

626. Elizabeth Adair=639 Charles J. Brenham in 1855 B 1817, d. 1875

Progeny: 4 Sons, 2 Daughters

640. I   Louisa Brenham, b. Aug., 1858, d. June, 1881.
641. II   Robert Bernard Brenham, b. Dec., 1860, m. Jan. 1890, Annie K. Dowsett.
642. III Mary Dickinson Brenham, b. Sept, 1862, d. 1879.
643. IV   Betty M. Brenham, b. Nov. 1864, d. April, 1899.
644. V   Charles J. Brenham, b. Jan., 1867, d. Apr., 1868.
645. VI   Laura J. Brenham, b. July, 1870.

641. Robert Bernard Brenham=646 Annie K. Dowsett, m. Jan. 27, 1890.

Progeny: One child

647. Charles James Brenham, b. April, 1895.

627. Ellen Adair=**648** George Henry Mendell, b. 1831, d. 1902, m. 1858; 1st Lieut., U.S. Eng. Corps.

Progeny: 5 Children

649. I   Mary Adair Mendell, b. Dec. 1862, d. Nov., 1863
650. II   George Henry Mendell, Jr. b. Aug. 1868.
651. III Ellen Mendell, b. July, 1871, died in infancy.
652. IV   John Adair Mendell, b. Sept., 1873.
653. V   Clarence Mendell, b. Oct., 1875, d. Dec., 1900.

649. George Henry Mendell, Jr.=**654** Mary Kelknap Janin m. Aug. 1st, 1901.

628. Katy Adair=**655** William T. Welker, m. July 23rd, 1857, b. 1830; d. 1900. 1st Lieut. U.S. Ordinance.

Progeny: 9 Children

656. I   Adair Welker, b. May 1858.
657. II   William Welker, b. Oct., 1859, d. Jan., 1865.
658. III Mendell Welker, b. Apr., 1862, d. June, 1904. Married Eliza Gay, 1901.

659. IV   Mary Welker, b 1864, d. 1865.
660. V   Katy Welker, b. Dec., 1865.
661. VI, VII Louise and Lily, twins, b. Aug., 1869; both died in infancy.
662. VIII Nelly Welker, b. Sept., 1872, died in infancy.
663. IX   Henrietta Welker, b. Sept., 1874, d. Dec., 1903
664. X   Louise Welker, Oct., 1877, d. Jan., 1878.

1899

660. Katy Welker=Herman G. Wilson

Progeny: 2 Daughters

665. I   Rosalie Adair Wilson, b. _____
666. II   Eleanor Nimmo Wilson, b. _____

Mr. Wilson is a successful orange grower and business man, and his family are most elegant people. Home at Riverside, California.

1884

629. John Adair, Jr.,=**667** Bethenie A. Owens

Progeny: One Child

668. Anna Adair, b. 1887. Died in infancy.

1865

632. Mary Ann Adair=667 William H. Jordan, Capt. U.S. Infantry. b. 1837, d. 1909.

Progeny: 5 Daughters, 4 Sons

670. I   Mary Adair Jordan, b. Sept., 1866.
672. II   Julia Cady Jordan, b. Nov. 1867, d. May, 1920
673. III   John Adair Jordan, b. 1869, d. 1870.
674. IV   Elizabeth Adair Jordan, b. Aug., 1871, d. April. 1891.
675. V   Ella Jordan, b. Dec., 1873, d. March, 1896.
676. VI   William Henry Jordan, b. Jan. 1, 1876.
677. VII   Samuel Dickinson Jordan, b. Dec., 1873.
678. VIII Laura Jordan, b. Sept., 1880.
679. IX   David Jefferson Jordan, b. Feb., 1884.

1887

670. Mary Adair Jordan=680 Henry Fletcher Kendall, 1st Lieut, 8th U.S. Calvery

Progeny: 2 Daughters, 1 Son

682. I   Elzabeth Adair Kendall, b. March, 1895, died in infancy.
683. II   Adeline de Valcourt Kendall, b. Aug., 1898.
684. III   William Henry Kendall, b. Dec., 1901.

1902

676. William Henry Jordan, Jr.=685 May Evelyn Ball (1st Lieut. 18th U.S. Inf.)

1905
678. Laura Jordan=686 Carl Daniel Lewis
Progeny: 2 Children

687. I   Carl Daniel Lewis, Jr., b. Nov., 1905.
688. II Elizabeth Adair Lewis, b. April, 1911.

1907
679. David Jefferson Jordan=689 Clara Ella Root. (Died May 6th, 1910).

Progeny: One Child

699. David Hadon Jordan, b. Jan., 1909.

Second Marriage:
679 David Jefferson Jordan=700 Edna Kindred, Feb. 6th, 1918.

1880
634. Samuel Dickerson Adair=701 Mary Rodney Morris. Of a distinguished family.

Progeny: 6 Children

703. I   Hannah Adair, b. Dec., 1880.
704. II   Henry Rodney Adair, b. April, 1882, Lieut. In U.S. Army, killed in battle in Mexico, June 1st, 1916.
705. III John Adair, b. Oct., 1883, d. Dec., 1885.
706. IV   Wistar Morris Adair, b. Jan., 1886.
707. V   Mary Ann Adair, b. Aug., 1889.
708. VI   Alexander Adair, b. May, 1892. Lieut. In U.S. Army in World War.

1909
190. Hannah Adair=709 Lausset Richter Rogers
Progeny: One Daughter, Two Sons

710. I   Daniel Rogers, b. Aug., 1910.
711. II   Adair Rogers, b. March, 1912.
712. III Diana Rogers, b. May, 1918.

1917
709. Alexander Rogers=713 Irene Patiani
Progeny: One Child

714. Alexander Morris Adair Rogers, b May, 1919.

1887
635. William Butler=715 Mary Louise Jorand
Progeny: One Daughter, Two Sons

716. I   Robert William Adair, b. Jan., 1892.
717. II   Joseph Alexander Adair, b. Sept., 1894.
718. III Margaret Ellen Adair, b. Feb., 1898.

1892

637. Laura Pindell Adair=719 Rev. Wm. Morris Barker Bishop of Olympia. B. 1854, d. 1901.

Progeny: Two Daughters

720. I Anna Ellis Barker, b. Oct. 1894.
721. II Mary Adair Barker, b. Nov., 1896, d. June, 1897.

Lieut. Henry Rodney Adair was born in Astoria, Oregon and got his High School education at that place. His father was 634 Samuel Dickinson Adair, grandfather, General 85 John Adair, and his great-grandfather was Governor of Kentucky. His mother was Mary Rodney Morris, daughter of the Bishop of Oregon. He entered the U.S. Military Institute at West Point in 1900. In 1912 he graduated from the Mounted Service School, where he won honors in the international competition in horsemanship.

Lieutenant Adair was with the Regular Army in its invasion of Mexico in 1916, when President Wilson ordered the army to use blank cartridges in harmony with his goody-goody policy towards Mexico. Lieut. Adair and his comrades had to hold still and let Gen. Villa and his army shoot them down in carrying out Wilson's whimsical policy of "watchful waiting."

634. Samuel Dickinson Adair, who lived in Portland, Oregon with his family, was ill at the time and died after his son was killed but never knew that his son was dead.

CHAPTER XXV
LINE B

THOMAS ADAIR, WITH HIS FAMILY
The first Adair Family to arrive in America
1 Thomas Adair, with his family.

Adairs began to migrate to America during the first half of the 18th Century; they came from the Ulster counties in Ireland, and from Galloway, Scotland. In America some of them stopped in Maryland, some in New Jersey, but the larger number went to Pennsylvania, and they scattered from that State to South Carolina and other States.

The Adairs were Scotch-Irish emigrants, with not much love for the mother country, but an intense patriotism for their adopted country. Hence, they made good soldiers for the American Independence Cause.

Most of the Adair emigrants were single men who left their sweethearts behind and married in America.

It was about 1730 that Thomas Adair with his family from Ireland, County Antrim, landed in Pennsylvania, Chester County. The history of Thomas Adair is rather meager; but enough is known to establish the fact that Thomas was a son of Alexander Adair, and grandson of Rev. Patrick Adair of County Antrim in Ireland. Rev. Patrick married his cousin, Miss Jean Adair, daughter of the first Sir Robert Adair. Rev. Patrick Adair had four sons and one daughter. His third son was Alexander Adair, the Father of our Pioneer, Thomas Adair. We do not know the name of Alexander's wife, nor the name of the wife of Thomas Adair, but we know his children, all of whom were born in Ireland, County Antrim. Thomas Adair was born in 1680.

Following is the Progeny of Thomas Adair and wife:

2   I   James Adair, the oldest, was born about 1709, built up and carried on an enormous trade with the Indians. He also wrote the best book ever published on the Indians. His descendants are in Arkansas and Oklahoma.

3   II   Joseph Adair Sr., born 1711. Most of the Adairs of South Carolina, George, Alabama and Tennessee are his descendants.

4   III   William Adair, the youngest, was born 1719, settled in the Waxaw Colony of South Carolina, and after the Revolutionary War his whole family moved to Kentucky, where one of them became Governor, and all of them became prominent.

Between 1750 and 1755, Thomas Adair and his three sons moved from Pennsylvania to South Carolina and settled on Duncan's Creek in the 96th district, now Laurens County.

James Adair, through his commercial influence and patronage, being a wholesale buyer for his Indian trade, got access to the King, and that Monarch, King George II, made a large grant of land to him, i.e. James Adair, who located the patent on this beautiful Duncan's Creek, in Laurens County, located away out beyond the frontier in the Indian Country. James Adair had his father and brothers to move from Pennsylvania to South Carolina to settle on this land. In going from the settlements to see this land, they found no road, no surveys and no white settlements, just a virgin forest, but a beautiful country. So, they cut out a road as they went up and in order that they might find their way out again.

After examining the land, and selecting their locations, some of the party went to work to build houses and clear land for cultivation, while others were sent back to Pennsylvania after their livestock which they drove overland on foot from the Susquehanna Rover to Duncans Creek. Their corn mill was also brought along and set up for operation by nailing it to a tree. It was something like an old-fashioned coffee mill. It was a curiosity to the Indians, who had been accustomed to grind their corn by rubbing it between two stones. This Colony obtained their supply of corn the first year by trading with the Indians.

Shortly after the Adair Colony was established, another noted Colony was located to the east of it called SAXAW Colony, composed of Scotch-Irish settlers from Pennsylvania. According to McGrady's history of South Carolina, the Adairs were considered as prominent members of this WAXAW Colony. We suppose the two colonies were considered as one and the same because of their proximity, the same type of settlers, and being settled at the same time. McGrady mentions a few samples of the products of this colony in the way of prominent men and women, to wit:

Names of some of the prominent men born and reared in the WAXAW colony, to-wit: Doctor J. Marion Sims; Hon. John C. Calhoun; Gen. Wade Hampton; Governor John Adair of Kentucky; Gen. Andrew Jackson; Governor Crawford of Georgia; Right Rev. Alexander Gregg, D.D., Bishop of Texas, and m ay others.

When the American Colonies began their struggle for independence the Adairs sided with the Americans, and there were no less than ten Adairs in the American Army from South Carolina, and about the same number of

Adairs in Washington's Army from Pennsylvania. When James Adair went to London in 1775 to have his book on the Southern Indians published, he appealed to members of the British Cabinet to conciliate the American Colonies and settle matters peaceable. He also appealed to the British Government in this behalf, in the introductory chapter of his book. During the War of the Revolution, and afterwards, South Carolina kept its own records, muster rolls, and so forth, and paid its own soldiers for military services, and its own citizens for supplies for the military and distressed civil population. These records were never in the hands of the general government at Washington but were retained at Columbia. Therefore, any inquiry for the war record of any soldier, or supposed soldier, of the Revolution in South Carolina should be addressed to the State Historical Commission of South Carolina, at Columbia, but not to Washington, where the records of other States are kept.

Joseph Adair Sr. was a soldier in the Revolution, was Commissary of Co. D. Col. Casy's Regiment, at the age of seventy years.

During the hottest part of the Revolutionary War, about 1780, the Tories burned the Courthouse at Laurens, also the private residences of many of the prominent Adairs and thus destroyed the priceless records up to that date. Therefore, we have depended for data on the later County Records, Histories of South Carolina, Civil, Military and Religious; Family Bible Records, and Traditions.

JOSEPH ADAIR, SR.
Sterling L 96-5-8
Received satisfaction.

The State of South Carolina, in account with William Adair. Sept 19th, 1781

Receipt of William Adair, 1070 cwt. Of Flour; 5 ½ bu of Wheat; 5 bu of Corn for the use of widows and distressed families in Col. Casey's Regiment.

Per Joseph Adair   D Company

Sworn to by Colonel Casey

Another Commissary's pay bill of Joseph Adair, Commissary, commencing the 20th day of August, 1781, and ending in March, 1782, both days included. A Full itemized expense list is on record and has been photographed by Lyles Studio in Colombia.

This itemized list is certified by Levi Casey, Col. Jan. 6th, 1786.

Joseph Adair was married twice.

1732

3 Joseph Adair=Sarah Laferty of Pennsylvania
Progeny: Six Children

Three sons: Joseph, Jr., 5; James, 6, and Benjamin, 7. Three daughters: Leah Ramage, 8; Sarah Adair, 9, and Mary Owens, 10.

Second Marriage:

Joseph Adair=Susana Long of South Carolina
Progeny: One Son
Died Young, Unmarried

The present stone building of Duncans Creek Church was built in 1767. Joseph Adair Sr. served this Church as Elder for forty years.

In 1788 he made and filed his "Will" in the Court House at Laurens, S.C., and died in 1801, aged 90 years. Was buried in Duncans Creek Graveyard. Following is a copy of his "Will."

"I give and bequeath to my wife, Susanna, all Cattle, Hogs, and Pewter; $160 Continental dollars, all grain, farming tools, beds and bedsteads.

I give to my sons, James and Joseph Jr., the remainder of the Continental money, Imported bedsteads, and the Arm Chairs.

I give to my son Benjamin, half of my Cooper tools; also, twenty pounds old currency.

I give to my daughters, Leah Ramage, Sarah Adair, and Mary Owens, each twenty pounds old currency.

Signed Joseph Adair Sr."

JOSEPH ADAIR, JR.

5   Joseph Adair, Jr., was the oldest son of Joseph Adair, Sr., and Sarah Laferty; was born about 1733, in Pennsylvania, and was about 17 years of age when the whole family moved to South Carolian. Therefore, he got part of his education in Pennsylvania, and more education and training in South Carolina. He seemed to have been a successful farmer and businessman, judging from the way he bought Negro slaves and improved his lands.

Joseph Adair, Jr., was a soldier in the American Army during the Revolutionary War, and was with Col. Lacy at Hauk's defeat.

1758

5 Joseph Adair, Jr.=Sarah Dillard
Progeny: Four Sons and Four Daughters

11	I	John Adair, a Revolutionary Soldier, migrated to Morgan County, Ga., 1800.
12	II	James Adair, moved to Tennessee, settled S.E. of Nashville, in 1800.

13	III	Robert Adair, a bachelor, schoolteacher, in 1800 settled in Bedford Co., Tenn., and taught school. The late Confederate General and U.S. Senator Isham G. Harris was one of his pupils.
14	IV	Elisha Adair, his progeny moved to Alabama, Perry County, then to Texas, where they now live, and are prospering.
15	V	Elizabeth Adair, m Houston.
16	VI	Jane Adair, m Holland.
17	VII	Casy Adair, m McCrary.
18	VIII	Charity, m Daivd Little.

We have the genealogy of all of Joseph Adair's family except Casy McCrary.

Joseph Adair, Jr., died Oct. 17, 1812, age 79 years, and was buried in Duncans Creek graveyard. His WILL was recorded in Laurens Court House, Auditor's office, box 44, 1812, as follows:

"I will to my son, John Adair, wife Jane Jones, One Parcel of land.

To my son, James Adair, wife Elenor, one tract of land.

To Robert Adair, my son, money and silver breeches buttons.

To Elisha Adair, my son, one tract of land.

To Joseph Alexander Adair, by Grandson, silver coat buttons.

To Elixabeth Adair Houston, my daughter, one Negro girl.

To Jane Adair holland, my daughter, one Negro woman.

To Charity Adair Little, my daughter, One Negro woman.

Signed, Joseph Adair, Jr."

JOHN ADAIR
The Revolutionary Soldier

John Adair was the oldest son of Joseph Adair, Jr., and Sarah Dillard Adair. He was born at his father's farm home on Duncans Creek, Laurens County, South Carolina, about 1759. He got a common school education, learned agriculture and the saddle maker's trade. John Adair entered the American Army sometime in 1779 and served till the end of the war. He was in numerous battles, and was captured once near Charlotte, N.C., but by the efforts of General Smallwood, Adair and seven of his fellow prisoners were exchanged.

"General W. Smallwood to Lord Cornwallis;

Camp, October 24th, 1780.

Sir: The prisoners taken in the neighborhood of Charlotte, whose names you will observe below, I understand are very solicitous to obtain an exchange. Perhaps your Lordship would have no objection to admit of a partial exchange of those persons for a like number now in our possession, whose situation and circumstances may not be altogether dissimilar. If this proposition should meet with your approbation, you will be so obliging as to signify it, that the exchange may take place.

Respects &c, &c,

W. Smallwood

The right Honorable Lord Cornwallis,
Commander of the British Forces, Southern Department.

The following were their names:

John Adair, Richard Thomas, Wm. Rankin, Andrew Baxter, John McKay, Wm. Wyley, Wm. Wallace, Alexander Brown.

As stated elsewhere in this volume, South Carolina paid its own soldiers, and the stub receipts of the State Authorities were prime evidence of service in the Revolutionary Army.

The State of South Carolina.

In account with John Adair:

His account of military duty as private, since the reduction of Charleston.

Sterling L 60-00-0

Sterling L 8-11-5

Received satisfaction June 14th, 1783.

The State of South Carolina, In account with John Adair, Esq.

"His account for sundries for military use amounts to Sterling L 268-14-1/4 in the Revolutionary War."

John Adair had his full share of hardships in the war, and especially in prison.

Soon after the Revolutionary War ended, John Adair married Miss Jane Jones, his cousin, as her mother was Adair stock.

1783

John Adair=Miss Jane Jones
Progeny: Twelve Children

19 I Joseph Alexander Adair, b 1784 in Laurens County, S.C. He was the boy who received the silver coat buttons by will, from his grandfather, Joseph Jr.

20 II John Fisher Adair, b 1786, Laurens Co., S.C. A wheelwright and first-class mechanic. He was the father of Col. George W. Adair, of Atlanta.

21 III Capt. Hiram Adair, b 1788, Laurens Co. Lived many years in Upson Co., Ga. He was a soldier with General Jackson in Indian wars, also in the battle of New Orleans in 1815.

He left a large family, and died in Upson Co., Ga., age 84 years.

22 IV Jones Adair, b 1790, in Laurens Co., S.C. Was a farmer and trader in Morgan Co., Ga. His grandchildren and great grandchildren number near 100 at this time.

23 V Elizabeth Adair, married Miles Garrett, a farmer in Chambers Co., Alabama.

24 VI William Adair, b about 1792, in Laurens Co., S.C. was a fine mechanic; lived in Morgan Co., Ga. Had a son named John, who lived in Clayton Co., G., and a daughter Elizabeth, married Mr. Burk in the same county.

25 VII Mary Adair married John Apperson, a farmer at Selma, Ala. Left a large family.

26 VIII Farmer Adair, lived at Autoga, Ala. He was a tanner by trade, and the father of Capt. James Adair, ticket agent at the Union Depot, Atlanta

27 IX Susan Adair married Mr. Ethridge, a farmer, who lived and died near Demopolis, Ala.

28 X Sallie Adair, d young, unmarried.

28 XI James Adair, b in Morgan Co., Ga., father of the late Hon. A.D. Adair and Green B. Adair, both of Atlanta, was a merchant and farmer, and Captain of the Militia.

30 XII Joel Hayden Adair. While at school, in his teens, the teacher thought to punish him by knocking his head against the wall, but the blow was too heavy; it killed him.

This family were all upright and good citizens; most of them attained great age and raised numerous families.

John Adair died at the age of 59, in 1812, as was buried in Jenkins Cemetery at Apalachee, Morgan Co., G., where his tomb now stands. His South Carolina estate was administered by his younger brother, Elizha Adair, in 1813, at Laurens, L.C. Jane Adair, the widow, moved to Perry Co., Ala., where she married Green Jackson, and died 40 years later, at the age of 96 years.

In the year 1800 John Adair and his family moved from Laurens Co., S.C., to Morgan Co., Ga.

The children of John Adair and Jane, his wife, were a wonderful family of worthy citizens. At least nine of them reached great age, about 80 years or more. They were prolific, too, for there were about a hundred grandchildren, and as many great grandchildren, at this date, 1922.

John Adair was born about 1759; went into the Army at the Age of 20. He was a farmer and saddle-maker by trade. He was married in 1783; migrated to Morgan Co., Ga., in 1800, and died in 1812, in that county.

19 JOSEPH ALEXANDER ADAIR

Joseph Alexander Adair was the oldest son of John and Jane Adair, was born in Laruens Co., S.C., in February, 1784. He was 16 years old in 1800, when the family moved to Morgan Co., Ga. He got good training as a mechanic and could make anything out of wood or iron. When he was a mature man he opened a shop in Walton Co., Ga., at a place then called Jug Tavern, now called Winder. In 1811 he married Miss Elizabeth H. McCord.

Adair was reasonably successful at his business in Walton Co., but he became restless, sold out and moved to what was then the frontier, DeKalb County, and settled and opened a farm three miles west of the present center of the city of Atlanta, on Proctors Creek. Of course, there was no city there at that time, just a wild country over which the wild Indians roamed. Adair hardly got his farm opened up when the Indians stole all of his horses, and he was so disgusted that he sold out and moved back to his hold location in Walton Co. The two moves and the loss of his horses almost broke him up. This was in 1827 to 30 and subsequent years.

Gen. Andrew Jackson was president of the United States for two terms, and what was called Jackson's panic was on the country. The banking system of the nation was bad. There was one chief bank called the United States Bank, located in Philadelphia. It was chartered by Congress for a term of two years and was due to expire in 1826. But Congress renewed this charter by special act, several years before it expired, and President Jackson vetoed this renewal bill without devising a suitable scheme to take its place, and it produced a widespread panic that ruined business and lasted many years. This environment, coupled with the fact that the schools for higher education were few and far between and expensive, was Adair's excuse for giving his children only a common school education.

1811
Joseph Alexander Adair=Elizabeth McCord
Progeny: Five Sons and Two daughters

31	I	James McCord Adair, b 1812, left a large family, and died in Confederate Army in 1864.
32	II	John Adair, b 1814, m Mary Ann Scott, had several children, and d in middle life. His youngest son was John Benjamin Adair.
33	III	William Adair, b about 1815, m Polly Palmer; had two daughters, the second one being posthumous, her father having died.
34	IV	Joseph Adair, d young, unmarried.
35	V	Robert, m and d; widow m Robert B. McCord.

36	VI	Jane Adair, m her cousin, Robert B. McCord.
37	VII	Nancy Adair, m Wm. Mitchell, who, with two of his sons, Robert and William, died in the Confederate Army. Tehri three daughters, Lizzy m Johnson; Jane m Dilmus Nix, and the youngest m Davis. James Mitchell and Andrew Mitchell were the two youngest sons.

After Adair and his wife got too old to keep house, and their children all married who were living, they broke up and went to live with their children and visit their kin. His mother was still living, so he lived with her until she died; then he visited his niece, Mrs. Griffin, near Selma, Ala., where he died and was buried age 80 years. Elizabeth H. Adair, the widow, spent her last years with Nancy Mitchell.

CHAPTER XXVI

GENEALOGY OF JAMES ADAIR, SR.
FROM 1 THOMAS ADAIR, THE PIONEER
BORN IN ANTRIM COUNTY, IRELAND, 1680
SONS

2   James Adair, the Indian author and trader, b 1709,
3   Joseph Adair, Sr., father of South Carolina-Georgia-Alabama Adair, b 1711.
4   William Adair, father of the Kentucky Adairs, b 1719.

173. 2

3 Joseph Adair, Sr.=Sarah Laferty, of Pennsylvania

Progeny

5   I   Joseph Adair, Jr., Revolutionary soldier.
II James Adair, Sr.
III Benjamin Adair.
VI Leah Ramage.
V Sarah Adair.
VI Mary Owens.

17—

6 James Adair, Sr.=Hannah_____

Progeny

38   I   James Adair, Jr., b 1781.
39   II   Hannah, m Ruben Meadows.

1781

38 James Adair, Jr.=Delilah Holland

Progeny

40   I   Robert J. Adair, m Sarah Jacks.
41   II   Edmond Adair, m Susan Dillard.
42   III   Isaac Adair, m Sarah Dillard.
43   IV   Nancy Adair, m – Ramage, and moved west.
44   V   Henry Adair, m Elizabeth Pitts.

41 Edmond Adair=Susan Dillard

Progeny

45   I   James W. Adair, m Elizabeth Little.
46   II   Sarah E. Adair, m Robert Briggs.
47   III   Isaac W. Adair, m Francis Nelson.
48   IV   Francis Adair, m Rennick Anderson, 2d wife.
50   VI   Susan Adair, m Harrison Copeland.
51   VII   John Adair, m Margaret Stone. (John is the only one living at present, 1922).

46 James W. Adair=Elizabeth Little
Progeny
52   I   Margaret Adair, m A.M. Hays.
53   II   Emma Adair, died.

52 Margaret Adair=A.N. Hays.
Progeny
54   I   Leslie St. Clair Hays, m Hellen Hopp.
55   II   Elizabeth Hays, m W.W.B. Owens.
56   III   Pearle Hays, m James Sprunt.

54 Leslie St. Hays=Hellen Hopp
No Children

55 Elizabeth Hays=William W.B. Owens
56   I   William Bailey Owens, Jr.

56 Pearl Hays=James Sprunt
Progeny
57   I   Edward Sprunt.
58   II   Margaret Sprunt.

50 Susan Adair=Harrison Copeland
Progeny
39   I   John Copeland, m – (wife's name not given).
60   II   Clarence Copeland, m, widower (no children).

47 Isaac Weyman Adair=Frances Nelson
Son of Edmond and Susan Adair
Progeny
61   I   Edmond J. Adair.
62   II   William J. Adair.
63   III   Claud B. Adair.
64   IV   Eugene Adair (Migrated west).

61 Edmond J. Adair=Lois Meadows
Progeny (None Reported)
65   William J. Adair, not married.

66 Claud B. Adair=Bertie Brant

51 John E. Adair=Margaret Stone
Son of Edmond Adair.
Progeny
67   I   Lloyd Adair.
68   II   George Adair.
69   III   Iva Adair.
70   IV   Lois Adair.
71   V   Lorice Adair.
72   VI   William Adair.

AMERICAN ADAIRS—Line B

48 Frances Adair=Majes Rennick Anderson
Daughter of Edmond Adair
Progeny

73   I   Mattie Susan Anderson.
74   II   John Edmond Anderson.
75   III   William Rennick Anderson.

73 Mattie Susan Anderson=William M. Myers
Progeny

76   I   Fannie Inez Myers.
77   II   William Hugh Myers.
78   III   Edmond Anderson Myers.
79   IV   Pierce Maurice Myers.
80   V   John Vernon Myers.
81   VI   Ruth Elizabeth Myers.
82   VII   W.M. Myers.
83   VIII   James Saxon Myers.

76 Fannie Inex Myers=James Early Tinsley
Progeny

84   I   James Earl Tinsley, Jr. Dead.
85   II   Frances Myers Tinsley.

81 Ruth Elizabeth Myers=Jack Launis

75 William Rennick Anderson=Mollie Owens
Progeny

86   I   Blanche Davis Anderson.
87   II   Frances Rebecca Anderson.
88   III   Mattie Lee Anderson.
89   IV   Fay Owens Anderson.

49 Nancy Adella Adair=James Rennick Anderson (2d wife)
Progeny

90   I   Fannie Adair Anderson.
91   II   Mary Lake Anderson, d age 4.
92   III   Nina Dillard Anderson.
93   IV   Roy Holland Anderson.

90 Fannie Adair Anderson=Perry Taylor Hawkins.
Progeny: Miriam Adella Hawkins

92 Nina Dillard Anderson=Edgar Marshall Atwell
Progeny

94   Edgar Marshall Atwell, Jr.

Robert Pressie Adair=Usilla Jacks
Son of Robert J. Adair Sr.
Progeny

94   I   Robert Adair. Jr.

AMERICAN ADAIRS—Line B

95	II	Mollie Adair.
96	III	Sallie Adair.
97	IV	Nannie Adair.

Robert J. Adair, Jr.=Minnie Copeland
Progeny

98		Nine children:
99	I	Rhett P. Adair.
100.	II	Irene Adair.
101.	III	Mayme Adair.
102.	IV	Lena Adair.
103.	V	Posey Adair.
104.	VI	Ralph P. Adair.
105.	VII	Sara Adair.
106.	VIII	Louise Adair.
109.	IX	Robbie Adair.

99 Rhett P. Adair=Madge York
Progeny

108.	I	Madeline Adair.
109.	II	Forrest Adair.
110.	III	Dorothy Adair.
111.	IV	Bobby Adair.
112.	V	Hubert Adair.

100. Irene Adair=John G. Pitts
Progeny

113.	I	Joyce Pitts.
114.	II	Martha Pitts.
115.	III	John G. Pitts, Jr.

101. Mayme Adair=Doctor R.W. Johnson
Progeny

116.	I	Gerrard Johnson
117.	II	R.W. Johnson, Jr.
118.	III	Otha Johnson.

102. Lena Adair=Doctor James Ray
Progeny

119.	I	Lena Bell Ray
120.	II	James Ray, Jr.

103. Posey Adair=William King.
Progeny

121.	William King, Jr.
122.	Ralph Adair, a bachelor.

105. Sarah Adair=Olin Thomas Lowing
Louis Adair and Robbin Adair not married
95 Mollie Adair=William McMillian

AMERICAN ADAIRS—Line B

Progeny
- 122. I Louilla McMillian.
- 123. II Sallie Belle McMillian.
- 124. III Pressie McMillian.

122. Louilla McMillian=Albert Galloway
Progeny
- 126. I William Albert Galloway.
- 126. II Kathleen Galloway.

123. Sallie Belle McMillian=John W. Finney
Progeny
- 127. One Child, John W. Finney, Jr.

124. Pressie McMillian=Louis Glasgow
Progeny
- 128. William McMillian.

96 Sallie Adair=James M. Pitts
Progeny
- 129. I Hubert J. Pitts.
- 130. II Raymond Pitts.
- 131. III Louis Pitts.
- 132. IV James M. Pitts, Jr.
- 133. V Emmie Pitts.

129. Hubert J. Pitts=Huddie Mae York
Progeny: None

97 Nannie Adair=E. Lee Pitts
Progeny
- 134. I Stanley Pitts.
- 135. II Sterling Pitts.
- 136. III Davis Pitts.
- 137. IV Carroll Pitts.
- 138. V William Denny Pitts.
- 139. VI Jannett Pitts.

134. Stanley Pitts=Ethel Russell
No Children

135. Sterling A. Pitts=Kate Hargrove
Progeny
- 140. Sterling A. Pitts, Jr.

Robert Pressie Adair=Jessie Bell Westmoreland
(Second Marriage)
Progeny
- 142. Vivian Parks Adair

Paschal Meadows=Sarah Miller

(Won of Ruben and Hannah Adairs Meadows. James and Oney are brothers of Paschal)

Progeny
143. I Martha Meadows.
144. II John Meadows.
145. III George Meadows.
146. IV Margaret Meadows.
147. V Turmia Meadows.

143. Martha Meadows=Griffin Pitts
Progeny
148. I John Mack Pitts.
149. II Lee James Pitts.
150. III George Pitts.
152. V Guy Pitts.

132. James Pitts=Sallie Adair
Daughter of Pressie Adair

153. Mary Elizabeth Adair=George Henry Davidson
Progeny
154. I Lawrence Holland Davidson.
155. II Sarah Alice Davidson.
156. III Augustus B. Davidson.
157. IV Mattie Lou Davidson.
158. V Annie Robinson Davidson.
159. VI George Robert Davidson.

154. Lawrence Holland Davidson=Mary Isabella Henry
Progeny
160. I Wm. Henry Davidson, d
161. II Earl A. Davidson, d
162. III Essie E Davidson.
163. IV Ruth B. Davidson.
164. V Joe McDavidson.
165. VI Louise Davidson.
166. VII Martha Davidson.
167. VIII Bee Davidson.

160. William Henry Davidson=Lula Finney
Progeny
168. I L.H. Davidson.
169. II Willie Earl Davidson.

155. Sara Alice Davidson=Joe C. McMillan
Progeny
170. I Marie McMillan
171. II Annie Lou McMillan.
172. III Lizzie C. McMillan.

AMERICAN ADAIRS—Line B

173. IV   John C. McMillan.
174. V   William M. McMillan
175. VI   Sara Lois McMillan

171. Annie Lou McMillan=Doctor Henderson Henry
Progeny
176. I   Rogert Henry.
177. II   Lois Everlyn Henry.

172. Lizzie C. McMillan=W.P. Baldwin
Progeny
178. I   Sara Frances Baldwin
179. II   W.P. Baldwin, Jr.
180. III   Mary Elizabeth Baldwin.

173. Jodie C. McMillan=Louise Tayler
Progeny
183. I   Joe F. McMillan

156. Augustus B. Davidson=Maggie Mason
Progeny
184. I   Mollie Irene Davidson.
185. II   Ethel Mason Davidson.
186. III   Lizzie Ruth Davidson.

184. Mollie Irene Davidson=Hugh Donnor
Progeny
187. I   Joseph D. Donnor.
188. II   Miriam Donnor.

186. Lizzie Ruth Davidson=Edgar L. Little
Progeny
189. I   Margaret Little.

157. Mattie Lou Davidson=Thompson Richard Owens
Progeny
190. I   George Robert Owens.
191. II   Susie D. Owens.
191. II   Susie D. Owens
192. III   Thomas P. Owens.
193. IV   Mary E. Owens.
194. V   Hubert Owens.
195. VI   Roy Owens

190. George Robert Owens=Inez Ruth Hutchinson
Progeny
196. I   George Robert Owens, Jr.
197. II   Albert Davey Owens.

191. Susie D. Owens=Claude Lawrence Vaughan
Progeny

198.   I   Claude L. Vaughan, Jr.
199.   II   Dorothy Vaughan.

158. Annie Robbinson Davidson=Benjamin Franklin Copeland
Progeny
200.   I   Leslie Lawrence Copeland.
201.   II   Bessie Thompson Copeland.
202.   III   George Elbert Copeland.
203.   IV   Lena C. Copeland.
204.   V   Alice H. Copeland.
205.   VI   Benjamin F. Copeland, Jr.
206.   VII   Mildred Copeland.
207.   VIII   Posey W. Copeland.

200. Leslie Lawrence Copeland=Lou Belle Pitts
Progeny
208.   I   Leslie L. Copeland, Jr.
209.   II   Allene Copeland.

201. Bessie Thompson Copeland=Caldwell Weir
Progeny
210.   I   Caldwell W. Weir, Jr.

190. George Robert Davidson=Sara Eumira Bell
42 James Isaac Adair=Sara Dillard
Progeny
211.   I   Martha Holland McElroy Adair.
212.   II   James Robert Adair.

211. Martha Adair=David Copeland
Progeny
213.   I   James Isaac Copeland.
214.   II   Fannie Copeland.
215.   III   John McElroy Copeland.
216.   IV   Sallie H. Copeland.
217.   V   William David Copeland.

212. James Robert Adair=Lizzie Mason
Progeny
218.   I   Maggie Adair
219.   II   Mattie Adair.
220.   III   Augustus Adair.
211.   IV   Ida Adair.
222.   V   Camilla Adair.
223.   VI   Jessie Adair.
224.   VII   James Isaac Adair.
225.   VIII   Lizzie B. Adair.
226.   IX   Banna Adair.

213. James Isaac Copeland=Lula Casey
Progeny
227. I   Nan McElroy Copeland.
228. II Marion Copeland.

214. Fannie Copeland=John Pitts
Progeny
229. I   John H. Pitts.
230. II   David T. Pitts.
231. III Sarah H. Pitts.
232. IV   Martha Pitts.

215. John M. Copeland=Lena Bell
Progeny
233. I   Isaac Blufford Copeland.
234. II   John David Copeland.
235. III Mattie L. Copeland.
236. IV   James Copeland.
237. V   Donigan Copeland.

216. Sallie H. Copeland=W.B. Farr
Progeny
238. I   William Beatty Farr.
239. II David T. Farr.

217. William David Copeland=Laura Vance
(Nena Martin, second wife)
Progeny
240. I   James Isaac Copeland.

218. Maggie Adair=Y.A. Copeland
Progeny
241. I   J.D. Copeland.
242. II   Larue Copeland, d age 2.
243. III Little Page Copeland.
244. IV   Rubie Copeland.
245. V   Elizabeth Copeland.

219. Mattie Adair=John Flow
Progeny
250. I   Annie Martin Flow.
251. II   Leslie Harold Flow, d.
252. III Bonnie Lavello Flow (Killed accidentally).
253. IV   Walter Flow.
254. V   Oran Adair Flow.

220. Augustus Adair=Ephee Wood
Progeny
255. I   Audrey Parks Adair.

256. II   Ethel Adair.
257. III Sterling Adair.
258. IV   Hellen Adair.
259. V   Flow Adair.

221. Ida Adair=Edd. Acklin
Progeny

260. I   Nora Mae Acklin.
21   II   Banna Acklin.
262. III Irene Acklin.
263. IV   Zane Elizabeth Acklin.
264. V   Horace Edmond Acklin.

222. Camilla Adair=Ernest Wood
Progeny

265. I   Maurice Wood.
266. II   Elizabeth Wood.
267. III Ernest Mason Wood.
268. IV   Jeff Sypert Wood.
269. V   Marian Price Wood.
270. VI   Camilla Ophelia Wood.
271. VII Margaret Wood.

224. James Isaac Adair=Melky Mabley
Progeny

272. I   Melk Marie Adair.

223. Jesse Lola Adair=D.A. Nastom
Progeny: None

226. Fannie Banna Adair=Fred C. Gillespie
Progeny

273. I   Fred Hamilton Gillespie.

225. Lizzie B. Adair=Robert R. Weiner
Progeny

274. I   Robert Adair Weiner. (Grandchildren of)

218. Maggie Adair=Y.A. Copeland
Son of J.D. Copeland=Sena Kemp
Progeny

275. I   Wilma Oneita Copeland.
276. II   La Ru Wicklin Copeland.
277. III Hellen Floyd Copeland.

Little Page Copeland=Desta May Johnson

The Children, Grandchildren and great-great-grandchildren of James Robert Adair and Elizabeth Mason Adair, His Wife.

Family Record of Isaac J Adair.

Isaac J. Adair=Annie Dillard (1st wife)

AMERICAN ADAIRS—Line B

Progeny

278. I   Thomas W. Adair.
279. II Nancy L. Adair.

278. Thomas W. Adair=Ella Joess (1st wife)
Progeny

280. I   Joe Adair.
281. II   Thomas Adair.
282. III Sam Adair.
283. IV   Ella Adair.

280. Joe Adair=Annie May Copeland.
Progeny

284. I   Cecil Adair.
285. II   J.K. Adair.
286. III Watts Adair.
287. IV   Copeland Adair.

282. Sam Adair=Marie McMillian
Progeny

288. I   Elizabeth Adair.
289. II   Sam Y. Adair.
290. III Archie Sam Adair.

289. Sam Y. Adair=Lorena O'Dell (2d wife)
Progeny

291. IV   William Earnest Adair.
292. V   Colie Adair.
293. VI   Johnnie Mae Adair.
294. VII   Floyd G. Adair.
295. VIII Marie M. Adair.
296. IX   Dillard Adair.
297. X   Clifton Adair.

279. Nancy L. Adair=Tom Ray
Progeny

298. I   Sallye Ray.
299. II   Minnie Ray and (III) Nannie Belle Ray.

298. Sallye Ray=P.M. Pitts
Progeny

300. I   Floyd Pitts.
301. II   Ray Pitts.
302. III Josephene Pitts.
303. IV   Clair Pitts.

299. Nannie Belle Ray=J.H. Bell

Isaac J. Adair=Annie Hollingsworth (2d wife)
1852

Progeny

- 304. I William P. Adair.
- 305. II Mary Addie Adair.
- 306. III Robert Franklin Adair.
- 307. IV Isaac Edmond Adair.

304. William P. Adair=Etta Adair

Progeny

- 308. I Luther Adair.
- 309. II Leila Adair.
- 310. III Mattie Adair.
- 311. IV Carson Adair.
- 312. V Desdy Adair.

William P. Adair=Ella Duckett (2d wife)

Progeny

- 321. VI Grover Adair.
- 322. VII Clara Adair.
- 323. VIII William Adair.
- 324. IX Adgar Adair.
- 325. X Lily Adair.

309. Leila Adair-Will Gillam (died)

Progeny

- 313. I William Clye Gillam

309. Leila Adair Gillam=G.F. Cooley (2d husband)

Progeny: One Child, Grover Cooley

1908

310. Mattie Adair=Grover Cleveland Neighbors, b July, 1885 B Oct., 1891

Progeny

- 314. I Thelma Neighbors, May, 1909.
- 315. II Etta Neighbors, Jan. 4, 1912.
- 316. III Ruit Neighbors, Sept., 1914.
- 317. IV Luther C. Neighbors, Jan. 22, 1917.
- 318. V John Henry Neighbors, Oct., 1918.
- 319. VI William Neighbors, Sept., 1922.

1919

312. Desdy Adair=Irby Holland

320. One Child, Luther Holms Holland.

305. Mary Addie Adair=J.D. Dillard

Progeny

- 326. I J. Will Dillard.
- 327. II S. Gay Dillard.
- 328. III Nettie Dillard.

226. J. Will Dillard=Lydee Henry
Progeny

I J. Will Dillard, Jr.

1919
327. S. Gary Dillard=Lilian Salters
Progeny

329. I Virginia Dillard, b June 28, 1922.

1912
328. Nettie Dillard=George H. Ellis

330. I Dillard Ellis, b Aug. 30, 1916

1892
306. Robert Franklin Adair=Donna Young
Progeny: Eight Children

331. I Blanche Adair.
332. II Robert Christopher Adair.
333. III Rutledge P. Adair.
334. IV Oscar Ducket Adair.
335. V Annie B. Adair.
336. VI James F. Adair.
337. VII Mae Adair.
338. VIII Ernie Young Adair.

1914
331. Blanche Adair=Lewis Henderson
Progeny: Three Children

339. I Robie Adair Henderson.
340. II Lydea D. Henderson.
341. III Edith Henderson.

1897
307. Isaac Edmond Adair=Bessie Neighbors
Progeny: Three Children

342. I Myrtle Adair, b Jan. 2, 1900.
343. II Gladys Adair, b Dec. 18, 1908.
344. III Keith Adair, b March 12, 1912.

1920
342. Myrtle Adair=Guy Tumblin
Progeny: One Child

345. I Guy Tumblin, Jr.

1924
332. Robert Christopher Adair=Luella Leaman

1922
333. Rutledge Adair=Agnes Henry

CHAPTER XXVII
SARAH E. ADAIR

(46) Sarah E. Adair was the second child of Edmond Adair and Susan Dillard Adair. Lineage—Her lineage runs thus: 7 Sarah E. Adair, 5 Edmond Adair, 4 James Adair, Jr., 3 James Adair, Sr., 2 Joseph Adair, Sr., 1 Thomas Adair. She was born Oct. 24, 1840, and married Oct. 7, 1858, at Clinton, S.C.

46 Sarah E. Adair=Robert P. Briggs

Progeny: Nine Children; Six Daughters, three sons

345. I Orella S. Briggs, married Charlton C. Cromer of Newbery, S.C.
346. II Nancy L. Briggs, married Bachman J. Cromer of Newbery, S.C.
347. III Robert E. Briggs, died in Texas, unmarried.
348. IV James R. Briggs, m, 1 son, 1 daughter; son died in infancy, daughter m Bryan Holt.
350. V James W., m and lives at Hammon, Okla.
351. VI Julia, the youngest, was only 15 at her mother's death; returned to S.C. and married to William Lynn and had issue of 2 sons and 4 daughters.

There were three other children in the Briggs family, whose names are not mentioned, from which we presume they died unmarried, making nine in all.

Orella Briggs Cromer, who married Charlton Cromer, had one son and three daughters, all married; the son married, and died, survived by a daughter, Robie Cromer. The eldest daughter, Drucy Cromer, married Mr. McSwain of Columbia, and has one son, 253 Charlton McSwain.

Sarah, her second daughter, married Wright Spoon, and lives at Monroe, N.C. She has three daughters and one son.

Frances Cromer, the third daughter, married Richard Furgusson, and has one son, 353 Richard Butler Furgusson.

Nancy L. Briggs, who married Bachman Cromer, had nine sons and two daughters. Two sons died in infancy and one, 354 Haskell Briggs Cromer, was killed in France in 1918 in the World War.

Six of the Cromer boys are still living at this date (1922), to wit: 355 Arthur, 356 John Wallace, 357 Carl, and 358 Walter, at Newbery, S.C.; 359 Elmer C., at Columbia, S.C., and 360 Bachman D. is in Ohio.

The two daughters are married and live in Newbery, S.C., to wit; Mrs. T.C. Chalmers and Mrs. Clyde McCarley. The latter has one son and one daughter.

Arthur Cromer, the eldest son, is married and has two sons and two daughters.

Mr. Robert P. Briggs died in the fall of 1877 at Clinton, and in the following winter Mrs. Sarah E. Adair Briggs moved back to their old home, which is now the little town of Whitmire, S.C. While there, her two eldest daughters married two Cromer brothers of Newbery, S.C.

In the fall of 1886, Mrs. Sarah Briggs, with three sons and one daughter, moved to Arkansas, and she died there six years later, Aug. 24, 1892, aged 52 years, after a very eventful career.

CHAPTER XXVIII
ROBERT PRESSE ADAIR
OF CLINTON, SOUTH CAROLINA
An Autobiography

Lineage—Robert J. Adair, James Adair, J., James Adair, Sr., Joseph Adair, Sr., Thomas Adair.

I was born December 19, 1841, and raised within four miles of Clinton. My father was named Robert J. Adair. My mother was named Sallie Jacks before marriage. My father died in 1864. My mother died in 1897. I started to school when I was about six or seven years of age. I did not get a college education. I got all of my education in an old field schoolhouse. The last school I went to was in 1858. I had a very good grammatical and mathematical education. In 1858, 1859 and 1860 I stayed at home and helped my father on the farm. He gave me one bale of cotton a year. He kept that cotton for me until I came home from the war.

I left home at went to the War Between the States on August 6, 1861, at the age of nineteen, and served in the army four years. I belonged to Company "A," 13th Regiment, South Carolina Volunteer, McGowan's Brigade.

Our company was sent to Lightwood Know Springs, seven miles north of Columbia, S.C., on the old Charlotte Railroad. This was a camp of instructions for drill, etc. We remained here until the latter part of October, 1861. Our regiment was then ordered to Charleston. Here my company and one or two others of the regiment were sent to Edisto Island to keep back the Yankee gunboats. There we had a great time killing fox-squirrels, the first I had ever seen. We stayed here four or five days, then took the Stearn boat and were sent back toward Charlston. We were sent to Coosahatchee, Adams Run and other points on the coast, guarding trestles, rice mills, boat landings, ferries, etc., during that winter.

In April, 1862, we were ordered to Virginia via Richmond. We were sent to within a few miles of Fredericksburg, Va. Here a good many of my company, including myself, were taken sick. We were sent back to a place called Ashley, Va., where several of our company died. I was sent from here to Richmond, Va., where I had an attack of typhoid fever. I was very will for several weeks and unconscious most of the time. After being in a hospital for three or four months, I was sent back to my company just before the battle of Harper's ferry. Here we captured 11,000 prisoners, besides provisions, ammunition, etc. I was in the battles of Sharpsburg, Fredericksburg, Falling Waters, Wilderness, Spottsylvania Court House, Jericho Ford, Riddle Shop, Fussell's Mill, Deepbottom, Jones Farm and some skirmishing southeast of Petersburg. Reams Station charged our picket line near Petersburg. I was on picket at the time.

I was in the fight on the right of Petersburg the day before the command left our breastworks. I was wounded in this fight, having been shot in the abdomen. Was sent back to the hospital and from there to Appomattox Court House and then to Danville, Va. Here I got a furlough and reached home April 18, 1865. The company began coming in from the surrender on the 22nd and 23rd of April, 1865.

I had not been home long before gangrene set in and I was dangerously ill for several months. My life was almost despaired of during this time. I also had a buckshot buried in my temple in the battle of Chancellorsville. These were the only times I was ever hurt by the Yankees.

Our army was successful in all the above battles except Gettysburg and Petersburg. Lee surrendered April 9, 1865, at Spottsylvania Court House.

When I returned home my father had died. I went to work with my mother on the farm. Had no way of making money, only wagoning. Railroads were all stopped at that time and the only way we could get anything was to do hauling from Newberry, Colombia and other places. After two years we went to making some cotton. When we came home from the war people had plenty to eat. All we wanted was some money. On August 10, 1865, I married Miss Ila F. Jacka. We lived happily together for eleven years. She died September 18, 1876, leaving four small children, as follows: Robert J. Adair, Molly S. Adair, Sallie Lee Adair and Nannie A. Adair. My mother helped me to raise these four children. I lived a widower eleven years. I then married Jessie Blle Westmoreland on December 8, 1887. We lived happily together for thirty-five years. She died June 14, 1923. Had one child, V. Parks Adair, with whom I am now living at Clinton, S.C. I have been living in Clinton since 1900.

In 1892 my friends insisted that I run for County Commissioner of Laurens County, S.C., which I did. I was elected. I served as County Commissioner for two years. I was then elected Supervisor of Laurens County, S.C. I served as Supervisor for five years. I was then put on the State Equalization Board and served in this capacity for twelve or fifteen years. I then went out of politics. I had a good deal of farmland. I had always been a farmer. When I was elected Supervisor I turned my farm over to my son, Robert J. Adair. He looked after my business until he died, September 11, 1911.

After that I gave up the most of my farming and commenced selling off my land. Sold all of my land except the lots I owned in Clinton. Since that time I only looked after my little patches, helped about my garden and helped my wife. Did very little manual labor. For the last year I haven't been able to do much, a my health failed me. I am thankful that I'm am still living.

Four of my children, twenty-five grandchildren and twenty-two great-grandchildren nearly all live here in Clinton. I am now 82 years of age.

1896

361. Nannie A. Adair=E. Lee Pitts, a merchant in Clinton
Daughter of Robert Presse and Usilla Jacks Adair
Progeny: Eight Children, including two sets of twins

- 362. I   Stanly L. Pitts, b 1897, m Ethel Russell Oct. 5, 1919; car motorman.
- 363. II   Sterling A. Pitta, b 1899, m Kate Hargrove, Nov. 5, 1920. His occupation, manager W.U. Telegraph Office at Clinton.
- 364. III Davis V. Pitts (Twins)
- 365.   Carroll L. Pitta, b 1904. These two both work in drug stores.
- 366. V   Mary Pitts, b 1908.
- 367. VI   W. Denney Pitts, b 1912.
- 368. VII Jeannette Pitta, b 1914.
- 369. VIII Jean Pitts, b 1914 (twins). Jean died at age of 6 months.

The three youngest are in school.

CHAPTER XXIX

LINE B—THE WEYMAN ADAIR LINE

FIRST AMERICAN ANCESTOR, THOMAS ADAIR

A Native of Antrim County, Ireland. In America about 1730.

1 Thomas Adair=---
Progeny: Three Sons

2	I	James Adair, b 1709 in County Antrim, Ireland. Indian author and trader.
3	II	Joseph Adair, Sr., b 1711—father of the Carolina=Georgia Adairs.
4	III	William Adair, b 1719—father of the Kentucky Adairs.

1731
Joseph Adair=Sarah Laferty of Pennsylvania
Progeny: Three sons, Three Daughters

5	I	Joseph Adair, Jr., b 1732 in Penn; a soldier in Revolution.
6	II	James Adair, Sr., b 1734.
7	III	Benjamin Adair, b 1736.
8	IV	Leah Ramage.
9	V	Sarah Adair.
10	VI	Mary Owens.

Joseph Adair, Sr., married, second, Susana Long, in South Carolina. One son, died young, unmarried.

1765
Benjamin Adair=Nancy George
Son of Joseph Adair, Sr.
Progeny: Six Sons, One Daughter

370.	I	Zadock Adair, father of Rev. Weyman Adair.
371.	II	William Adair, father of Doctor William W. Adair, late of Dallas.
372.	III	John Adair. Was executor of his father's estate.
373.	IV	Isaac Adair.
374.	V	James Jamison Adair.
375.	VI	Benjamin Adair, Jr.
376.	VII	Margaret Adair.

Benjamin Adair's will was dated 1823, and probated at Laurens, South Carolina.

1796
370. Zadock Adair=Sarah Kelley

Born about 177, son of   Daughter of Peter Kelly and

Benjamin Adair. Zadock died 1856   Jane Ewing, both of South Carolina.

Progeny: Two Sons, One daughter

377.   I   William Adair, b Nov. 1, 1803, m Sarah Ewing of Kentucky; settled nr Rodney, Miss., and raised a large family.
378.   Weyman Adair, b Feb. 22, 1805.
379.   III Mary Adair, b Sept. 29, 1807.

All born in Laurens Co., S.C.

Rev. Weyman Adair, born about 1805, has the following lineage: Zadock Adair, Benjamin Adair, Jospeh Adair, Sr., Thomas Adair.

Rev. Weyman Adair was a Cumberland Presbyterian Minister, a follower of his uncle, Finis Ewing. He was a graduate of Lebanon College, Tennessee, a man of great and profound learning, a consistent Christian, broad in his views and toleration, and a magnetic orator. He was an old line "Whig," and later a Democrat. His wife was a brilliant and beautiful woman, wrote exquisite verse, was a splendid housekeeper in spite of the fact that she was a great reader, and exerted a benign influence around her. She was musical as well as literary.

Rev. Weyman Adair was like most ministers in that he lived in one place after another, no more than two of his children being born in the same county. From Sumpter County, Ala., where he was married, he took his bride to Winston County, Miss., where their two oldest children were born. The next two children were born in Sumpter County, Ala., near Warsaw. And the youngest child was born in Sharon, Madison County, Miss., in 1850. Between this date and 1853 he moved to Huntsville, Texas.

From Huntsville he went out to preach, even in distant communities. He was the first minister of any denomination to preach in several sections.

Rev. Weyman Adair and Gen. Sam Houston, President of the Republic of Texas, were close friends and neighbors. Upon one occasion, when they were traveling together, Doctor Adair fell ill, and Gen. Houston Nursed him tenderly and faithfully. A got foot bath being deemed helpful in the case, Houseton waved aside the slave who brought the water, and performed the deed himself, replying to his friend's remonstrances that his Master had set an example which he could do no less than follow.

After Weyman Adair's death, on Nov. 28, 1853, from yellow fever, his family moved to Cincinnati, Texas, where they remained until that town was devastated by the yellow fever, when they returned to Huntsville.

1836

378. Rev. Weyman Adair=Delthia Staunton De Berry
Progeny: Three Sons, Three Daughters

380.	I	Mary De Berry Adair, b 1837, m John Magruder Wynne.
381.	II	Sarah Pricilla Adair, b 1840, m Cowper Sheldon Taliaferro.
382.	III	Weyman Limiel Adair, b 1842, Single. D in 1872.
383.	IV	Hartwell Horn Adair, b 1844, d 1855.
334.	V	William De Berry Adair, b 1847, m, 1st, Kate Norton, who died 1887; m 2d, Lula Norsworthy.
385.	VI	Delthia Fancis Adair, B 1850; killed while riding a spirited horse just the day before she was to go away to boarding school.

380. Mary De Berry Adair was born in Winston County, Miss., Nov. 19, 1837. Graduated from Andrew Female College, at Huntsville, Texas, in 1855. Married at the home of her mother in Cincinnati, Texas, Jan. 14, 1858, to John Magruder Wynne, son of Erasmus Wynne and Jane Sophronia Anderson, of Wynnewood Plantation, near Huntsville.

1858

380. Mary De Berry Adair=John Magruder Wynne
Progeny: Four Daughters, One Son

386.	I	Gustavus Adair Wynne, m Samuella Gibbs.
387.	II	Jane Sophronia Calmes Wynne, m Doctor Joseph Revis Lay.
388.	III	Mamie Staunton Wynne, m Wm. D. Cox; have one son, Wm. Adair Cox.
389.	IV	Florence Magruder Wynne, m Charles Granderson Barrett. Child, d infancy.
390.	V	Ara Adair Wynne, m Tyler Haswell; one daughter, Ara Wynne Haswell.

Eleven years after the death of her first husband, Mr. Magruder Wynne, the widow married Capt. George Washington Farris, a Mexican War veteran, and a Confederate army Captain, an old friend and neighbor, much respected and loved by the stepchildren.

Progeny: None

1872

381. Sarah Priscilla Adair=Cowper Shelton Taliaferro of Navasota
Second Child of Rev. Weyman   Of a distinguished
Virginia family.
Adair and Delthia Staunton De Berry Adair;
b 1840 Graduated at Andrew Female
College in Huntsville, Texas

Progeny: One Child
391.   I   Weyman Tell Taliaferro.

1897

391. Weyman Tell Taliferro=Annie White
Progeny: None

1903

391. (2d marriage) Weyman Tell Taliaferro=Katie White
Progeny: Two Children

392.   I   Katie Priscilla Taliaferro. Student in Methodist University at Dallas.
393.   II   Louise De Berry Taliaferro, in grammar school.

384. William De Berry Adair, fifth child of Rev. Weyman Adair and Delthia Staunton De Berry Adair, was born March 12, 1847, at Sharon, Madison County, Miss. Too young to enlist in the war between the States as a soldier, he determined to serve the Confederacy in some way and was accepted as Courier. He was fearless and daring, and performed distinguished service, for which he was mentioned in dispatches.

After the war he has been a member of the Legislature, and prominent in State affairs.

1884

384. (1st marriage William De Berry Adair=Kate Norton
Daughter of Colonel Hiram Norton of Austin. died in 1887.
Progeny: None living

384. (2d marriage) William De Berry Adair=Lulu Norhworthy
Daughter of a prominent family living on Buffalo Bayou, just below Houston
Progeny: Two Daughters

394.   I   Katie Adair.
395.   II   Caroline Louise Adair.

382. Weyman Lemiel Adair, third child of Rev. Weyman Adair and Delthia Staunton De Berry Adair, was born in 1842 in Sumpter County, Ala., near Warsaw. Was trained in Austin College. He served in the Confederate Army in Hoods' Texas Brigade. He died near Marlin, Texas, May 13, 1872. His last words were, "Tell mother that I am not afraid to die." He was buried in Marlin, but later his body was brought to Huntsville to rest beside his mother.

383. Hartwell Horn Adair, the fourth child or Rev. Weyman Adair and wife, died at the age of eleven years in Crockett, Texas, at the home of Doctor Lewis Meriwether, to whom they had taken him for medical treatment.

385. Delthia Francia Adair, the youngest child of Rev. Weyman Adair and wife, was born in Sharon, Missi., and was killed when thrown from a horse near Huntsville, Texas, Feb. 12, 1865. She was a magnificent horsewoman, but the saddle girth broke when her spirited horse shied at a pile of lumber.

She was a beautiful and intelligent girl and was to leave for boarding school the next day.

396. Gustavus Adair Wynne, only son of John Magruder Wynne and Mary De Berry Adair Wynne, was born at Wynnewood Plantation on San Jacinto River, near Huntsville, Texas. He is a banker in Huntsville and has large interests in East Texas. He is a man of wide charities and a great influence for good; a graduate of Austin College; a very brilliant amateur geologist; a Shriner and Knight Templar, and a Steward in the Methodist Church.

G. Adair Wynne married a daughter of Capt. Hiram Gibbs and Mary Bayliss of Gibbsland, Ja. She was a graduate of Andrew Female College, a fine Latin Scholar, much beloved by all. She came of the Gibbs family of South Carolina. She was also descended from --- Turner, the only woman to whom a monument was been erected over an American battlefield. This is a Guilford Court House, N.C.

She died Sept. 21, 1921, at Houston, while on a visit to her married daughters living there. She was buried two days later at Huntsville.

396. Gustavus Adair Wynne=Samuella Gibbs
Progeny: One Son, Three Daughters

397.	I	Mae Samuella Magruder Wynne, b---, m Ike Barton McFarland.
398.	II	Florence Sanford Wynne, b---, d in childhood.
399.	III	Gibbs Adair Wynne, b--, m Lela Mae Brown; have two daughters.
400.	IV	Samuella Porter Wynne.
401.	V	Mary Ruth Wynne.
402.	VI	Sabra Lois Wynne, b--, m Wm. Armaunt Reynaud; one child, Sabra Adair Renaud.

387. Jane Sofronia Calmes Wynne=Doctor Jospeh Revis Lay
A Practitioner of medicine of Houston
Formerly Surgeon to A&M College, later
At Huntsville, a prominent M.D.
Progeny: One Son

403. Magruder Wynne Lay. Graduate of University Texas; District Manager of American Book Company.

Florence Magruder Wynne, a granddaughter of Rev. Weyman Adair, was State Historian of the Texas Division of the United Daughters of the Confederacy, very prominent in club, musical and social circles, and one of the most influential women in the whole State, a brilliant historian and distinguished in literary pursuits.

Her husband, Charles Granderson Barrett, was a prominent lumberman, Mayor of Huntsville, and stockholder of director in numerous and various enterprises in this section of the State. Was educated in Texas Military Institute. A 32d degree Mason. He died Feb. 7, 1921.

398. Florence Magruder Wynne=Charles Granderson Barrett
Progeny: None

388. Mamie Staunton Wynne, daughter of John Magruder Wynne and Mary Adair Wynne, is very prominent in literary, patriotic and social circles in Texas. She is First Vice-President of the Penwoman of Texas, an officer in the Texas Women's Press Association, member of the United Daughters of the Confederacy, formerly an officer in it; one of the Daughters of the American Revolution, American Clan Gregor Society, Sam Houston School Alumni Association, etc. Having been a widow for many years, she has been free to devote her remarkable talents to literary pursuits and patriotic endeavor and has been very successful as a writer of feature stories and historical articles.

Her husband is W.D. Cox, editor and publisher, and at one time President of the Texas State Press Association.

368. Mamie Staunton Wynne=W.D. Cox
Progeny: One Son

404. Willam Adair Cox is a young businessman of Dallas; is a Shriner and a Scottish Rite Mason.

390. Ara Adair Wynne, daughter of John Magruder and Mary Adair Wynne, in distinguished as a church woman and a social leader of Bryan, Texas. During the World War she was Red Cross Chairman and worked tirelessly. She was educated at Price's Seminary and Baylor College, is a member of the U.D.C. and D.A.R. societies and local clubs.

Her husband, Mr. Tyler Haswell, is Mayor of the City of Bryan, Senor Warden of the Episcopal Church, and a public-spirited citizen as well as a prominent businessman.

390. Ara Adair Wynne=Tyler Haswell
Progeny: One Child

405. I Ara Wynne Haswell.

405. Ara Wynne Haswell, daughter of Ara Adair Wynne and Tyler

Hasell, was born in Bryan, educated in the University of Texas, Whitis School and Sargeant's School in New York. She is a Pi Beta Phi. She was married April 29, 1922, to Stiles Giraud, a wholesale jeweler of Houston and New York.

1922
405. Ara Wynne Haswell=Stiles Giraud

397. Mae Samuella Magruder Wynne, daughter of G.A. Wynne and Samuella Gibbs Wynne, was born and reared in Huntsville, Texas, and educated in the University of Texas. She is State Regent Texas Daughters of the American Revolution and has held other offices in this society; is one of the Board of Directors of the Y.W.C.A. of Houston, member of Pi Beta Phi, Colonial Dames, Daughters 1812, U.D.C., Order of LaFayette, National Officers Club, College Women's Club, and two local literary clubs.

Her husband is general manager of yards of Temple Lumber Co.; President of the Houston Building and Loan Association; ex-President of Young Men's Business League, Presbyterian Elder and Sunday School Superintendent, Chairman of the Board of Directors of the Houston Social Service Bureau, graduate of University of Texas, class of 1904; Phi Delta Theta; member of local clubs.

397. Mae Samuella Magruder Wynne=Ike Barton McFarland

398. Florence Sanford Wynne, daughter of G.A. and Samuella Wynne, a beautiful and bright girl, died in childhood.

399. Gibbs Adair Wynne, son of G.A. and Samuella Wynne, was born and reared in Texas where he and his father are both officers and directors in the Gibbs National Bank, thus being the third generation of bankers in this town, the first bank there having been established by his grandfather, Magruder Wynne. He served a while in the First National Bank of Houston. He is a Shriner, Knight Templar, and Scottish Rite Mason.

He married Lela Mae Brown, a graduate in music, daughter of Charles David Brown and Ida Porter Brown of Sedalia, Mo., a descendant of the distinguished Quaker family named Jenney, which came to America with William Penn.

399. Gibbs Adair Wynne=Lela Mae Brown
Progeny: Two Children

406.   I   Samuella Porter Wynne, b---
407.   II Mary Ruth Wynne, b---.

401. Sabra Lois Wynne, daughter of Gustavus Adair Wynne and Samuella Gibbs Wynne, was educated at Sam Houston Institute, University of Texas and Columbia University. She is a member of Kappa Alpha Theta,

U.D.C., D.A.R., American Clan Gregor Society, and local clubs. On August 10, 1919, she married William Armount Reynaud (a descendant of an illustrious French family and a son of Pierre Reynaud and Lelia Riddick). He is a Shriner, a Knight Templar, and a Scottish Rite Mason, a Rotarian, and an Episcopalian. He is secretary and treasurer of O.P. Jackson Seed Company of Houston, and a member of local clubs.

1919
401. Sabra Lois Wynne=William Armaunt Reynaud
Progeny: One Daughter

408.   I   Sabra Adair Reynaud, b ---.

395. Katie Adair, daughter of William De Berry Adair and Lulu Norsworthy, attended Sam Houston Institute and Whitis School in Austin, Texas. She is said to resemble the beautiful Frances Adair, her aunt.

395. Katie Adair, daughter of William de Berry Adair and Lulu Norsworthy Adair. She attended Sam Houston Institute and the University of Texas. Pi beta Phi.

Weyman Tell Taliaferro, son of Pricilla Adair and Cowper Shelton Taliaferro, was born in Navasota, Texas where he still resides. He, like his father, is a banker, and is cashier of the Citizens National Bank. He is a Steward in the Methodist Church, and a man of wide influence and large interest. He has been married twice. After the death of his first wife, he volunteered for service in the Spanish-American War, and was made Quartermaster-Sergeant.

Katie Priscilla Taliaferro graduated at the Navasota High School with the highest honors and is now a student at the Methodist University at Dallas. Kappa Delta.

Louise de Berry Taliaferro is a student in the grammar grades of the Navasota public schools and gives promise of being a fine scholar when she enters high school and college.

Doctor Wm. Washington Adair.

CHAPTER XXX

DOCTOR WILLIAM W. ADAIR'S BRANCH

DESCENDED FROM BENJAMIN ADAIR

1 Thomas Adair, born about 1680, in County Antrim in Ireland. Settled in Pennsylvania about 1730 and moved to South Carolina about 1750.

Progeny: Three Sons, all Born in Ireland

2	I	James Adair, b 1709. Indian trader and Indian author.
2	II	Jospeh Adair, Sr., b 1711. Father of the South Carolina-Georgia-Alabama Adairs.
4	III	William Adair, b 1719. Father of the Kentucky branch of the Adairs.

Joseph Adair, Sr., was a soldier and Commissary in the American Army, War of the Revolution, at the age of 70.

1731

Joseph Adair, Sr.=Sarah Laferty, in Pennsylvania

Progeny: Three Sons, Three Daughters

5	I	Joseph Adair, Jr., b 1732. Soldier in the Revolution; was with Lacey at Hauk's defeat.
6	II	James Adair, Sr., b 1734. The will of Joseph Adair, Sr., was probated at Laurens, S.C. in 1801.
7	III	Benjamin Adair, b 1736.
8	IV	Leah Adair, b 1738.
9	V	Sarah Adair, b 1740.
10	VI	Mary Adair, b 1742.

1777

Benjamin Adair=Nancy George

Progeny: Six Sons, Daughter

370.	I	Zadock Adair, b 1778. Father of the Rey. Weyman Adair.
371.	II	William Adair, b 1780. Father of Doctor W.W. Adair, late of Dallas.
372.	III	John Adair.
373.	IV	Isaac Adair
374.	V	James Jamierson Adair.
375.	VI	Benjamin Adair, Jr.
376.	VII	Margaret Adair.

Benjamin Adair's will was probated at Laurens, S.C., in 1823, and his son, John Adair, was the executor under the will.

371. William Adair's lineage runs back to his first American ancestor, Benjamin Adair, Joseph Adair, Sr., Thomas Adair.

After locating in Alabama, William Adair went back to Laurens County, in South Carolina, and married his old sweetheart, Elizabeth May Robertson, on May 2, 1806. William Adair died in 1851, and was buried in Union Town, Perry County, Ala.

1806

371. William Adair=Elizabeth May Robertson
Son of Benjamin Adair.   Of Laurens County, S.C.
            Progeny: Seven Daughters, Two sons
  409.   I   Elvira Adair, b April 18, 1807, d at 18 years, unmarried.
  410.   II   Polly Adair, b Oct. 12, 1808, m Scott.
  411.   III Nancy Adair, b Sept. 28, 1810, m McLemore
  412.   IV   Pernesy Adair, b Aug. 2, 1812, m Motes, the photography.
  413.   V   Benjamin Franklin Adair, b Sept. 29, 1914. Settled at Hot Springs, Ark.
  414.   VI   Rebecca Long Adair, b Aug. 10, 1816, m Goodwin
  415.   VII Doctor William Washington Adair, b May 17, 1818. Settled in Texas.
  416. VIII   Martha Elizabeth Adair, b Sept. 14, 1821, m Terry.
  417.   IX   Emeline T. Adair, b March 29, 1824, m Stead.

414. William Washington Adair, M.D., the seventh child of William and Elizabeth May Robertson Adair, b May 17, 1818, at Union Town, Perry County, Ala.

He got his first year of medical training at the Transylvania University in Lexington, Ky., then finished his medical education at one of the well-known medical colleges in Philadelphia, where he got his medical degree.

About 1855 Doctor W.W. Adair and most of his sisters moved off to Texas. Their brother, Benjamin Franklin Adair, settled in Hot Springs, Ark., Their father died in 1851, but their mother went with them to Texas, and died in 1869, age 83 years. They settled in Crockett, Houston County, Texas.

Doctor Adair practiced medicine, conducted a large cotton plantation, and prospered at it. Just before the war between the States terminated, he owned nearly a hundred negro slaves, which were, of course, emancipated, but it left him with large holdings of land.

About 1869 he sold out his holdings and moved to Lone Oak, in Hung County, where he conducted a general store and practiced medicine as well. He remained at Lone Oak about fifteen years, and prospered. During the early eighties he moved to Kallas and gave all his time to real estate to the end of his life, and died on the 4th of January, 1890, age 72 years. He was buried in Greenwood Cemetery in Dallas.

Being a successful physician, Doctor Adair performed a vast amount of work for the relief of suffering humanity and did his full share of charity work.

Doctor Adair was an Elder in the Presbyterian Church for nearly fifty years and was sincere and zealous in his church work. He was truly an upright man, one whom everybody loved and respected.

Doctor W.W. Adair married twice.

414. Doctor W.W. Adair=Candia A.H. Lockett (1st wife)
B May 16, 1827, d Nov 23, 1851
Progeny: Two Sons, One Daughter
All born at Union Town, Perry County, Ala.

- 410. I Caroline Elizabeth Adair, b July 10, 1845, m J.B. Rounsaville.
- 417. II George Washington Adair, b April 21, 1848, in Alabama, d April 4, 1881.
- 418. III William Franklin Adair, b June 23, 1851, d November 21, 1920.

414. Doctor W.W. Adair=Jane Elizabeth Rentz (2d wife)
B March 4, 1835, d Sept. 9 1894, at
Fayetteville, Tenn., and was buried there.
Progeny: None

George Washington Adair=Willie Cole, of Lone Oak, Texas
Son of Doctor W.W. Adair and Candia
A.H. Lockett Adair.
Progeny: Two Sons

- 419. I Benjamin Lockett Adair, b May, 1876. Presbyterian Evangelist. (See Biographic Sketch.)
- 420. II William Edward Adair, b September, 1877. (See Sketch.)
- 421. III Eddie Lee Adair, a daughter, now lives at Ardmore, Okla., with her aunt, Center.

416. Caroline Elizabeth Adair=J.B. Rounsaville, of Lone Oak
Daughter of Doctor W.W. Adair and first wife
Progeny: Six Sons and Three Daughters

- 422. I Ella Rounsaville, m Doctor John T. McMillan; 4 children; Texarkana.
- 423. II George T. Rounsaville; 1 child; alto, Texas.
- 424. III William W. Rounsaville; 1 child; R.R. Agent, Tyler, Texas.
- 425. IV John Rounsaville; 2 children; R.R. Agent, Ft. Worth.
- 426. V Florence Rounsaville, m Jackson Cade; 2 children living; La Port, Texas.
- 427. VI Gus Rounsaville; 5 children; Banker, Alto, Texas

428. VII   Ora Rounsaville, m Eddins; 3 children; Auto business, Detroit, Mich.
429. VIII   Lonnie Rounsaville, Bachelor; salesman, Houston, Texas.
430. IX   Cone Johnson Rounsaville; R.R. Agent, Hamilton, Texas.
(See Sketches of this Family.)

1897

419. Benjamin Lockett Adair=Sallie Cason, both of Lone Oak
Son of George W. Adair.

Progeny: Five Children living

435. I   Willie Olivia Adair, b 1898, m Doctor M.H. Starns in 1921; one child, Sarah Elizabeth Starns, b 1922; live in Lubbock, Texas.
436. II   Emmet C. Adair, b 1899.
437. III Ben Elmore Adair, b 1903.
432. IV   Frank Jackson Adair, b 1906.
439. V   Virginia Lockett Adair, b 1913.

William Franklin Adair was born at Uniontown, Perry County, Alabama, June 23, 1850. He moved to Texas in 1856, accompanied by a colony of immigrants, most of whom were aunts, uncles and neighbors. They first settled at Crockett, Houston County, Texas, and established some plantations on a place called Cochenio Bayou, which they settled up for about six miles. In 1870 his father, Doctor William Washington Adair, and family moved to Lone Oak, Hunt County, Texas, and purchased a ranch. Doctor Adair also entered into the mercantile business. In the fall of 1870, William Franklin Adair entered the Trinity University for a term of five years, where he was educated. Trinity University in those days was located at Tehuacana, in Limestone County, Texas, but has since been moved to Waxahachie, Ellis County, Texas. In 1875 he moved to Dallas and entered the employ of Richard V. Tompkins & Company, which at that time was one of the largest cotton factors, commission merchants and agricultural dealers in the Southwest. While connected with Tompkins & Company he married Miss Mary Lillie Robberson of Terrell, Texas, to which union two sons were born, being William Walter Adair and Robin Adair, both of whom reside in Dallas. In 1880 he formed connection with the sales forces of B.F. Avery & Son of Louisville, Ky., as southern representative, with headquarters at Houston, Harris County, Texas. After serving five years with Avery & Son, he entered into the wholesale grocery business in Dallas, which he continued for thirty years, most of the time being connected with the Schneider-Davis Company. During the time that Mr. Adair was engaged in the wholesale grocery

W.W. Adair of Dallas

Reekes Adair

business out of Dallas he was considered one of the highest-powered grocery salesmen in the territory, as he possessed natural sales ability, which enabled him to get a larger volume of business than other salesmen. He was very loyal to his employer, and the weather never got so bad that he did not make his territory regularly. At the expiration of the thirty years in the wholesale grocery business out of Dallas he had made such real estate investments as to permit him to retire from the business for the last fifteen years of his life. He died at 3:25 a.m., November 22, 1921, at 3603 Swiss Avenue, in Dallas, Texas, where he had made his home since 1884. Rev. W.D. Bradfield, of the Grace Methodist Church, who was a former schoolmate at Trinity University, performed the burial service, and he was buried at Grove Hill Cemetery in Dallas, Texas

1878

418. William Franklin Adair=Mary Lillie Robberson

Son of Doctor W.W. Adair, born June 3, 1850, at Uniontown, Ala. b Dec. 8, 1858, at Springfield Mo. Married at Terrell, Texas.

(See Sketch of W.F. Adair.)

Progeny: Two Sons

431.   I   William Walter Adair, b Jan 23, 1880, in Dallas. (See Sketch.)

432.   II   Robin Adair, b Feb. 11, 1884. (See Sketch.)

March 29, 1911

431. William Walter Adair=Lucile B. Reekes

Son of William Franklin and Lillie Robberson Adair

Progeny: One Son

433.   I   William Reekes Adair, b Feb. 27, 1919.

1919

423. Robin Adair=Mrs. Edna Cecelia Jones Berry Nold

Son of William Franklin and Lillie Robberson Adair.

Progeny: One Son

434.   I   Robin Adair, Jr., b June 4, 1921.

Mrs. Ella Rounsaville McMillan and her Progeny

Mrs. Ella Rounsaville McMillian was born in Crockett, Houston County, Texas, June 2, 1866. She is the daughter of J.B. and Caroline Adair Rounsaville, and granddaughter of the late Doctor W.W. Adair of Dallas.

1882

422. Ella Rounsaville=Doctor John T. McMillan, of Loan Oak, Texas
Progeny: Four Children

440.   I   Charles Homer McMillan, b June 11, 1884, at Potsboro, Texas; m Opal Bryant at Pittsburg, Texas, March 17, 1907; two children.
441. Norma McMillan, b June 23, 1908 and
442. George McMillan, b Dec 30, 1910, at Tyler, Texas.
443.   II   Ollie Robin McMillan (a daughter), b Feb. 24, 1886, at Chandler, Texas; m J.W. Sutherland at Chandler, Sept 3, 1905. Res. Texarkana. Two children.
444.   Lucine Sutherland, b June 16, 1906.
445.   Robin Sutherland, b January, 1910.
446.   III   Wayne Rounsaville McMillan, b at Chandler, Texas, Feb. 14, 1888, m at Tyler to Annie Laura Templeton, Nov. 8, 1898; two children, both girls:
447. Jewel McMillan, b Sept. 27, 1909.
448. Mary Ella McMillan, b Aug. 30, 1916. Both born at Tyler.
449.   IV   Florence Gerturde McMillan, b Feb. 24, 1890, at Chandler, Henderson County, Texas. Married L.E. Morgan, dental surgeon, July 26, 1908, at Hamlin, Jones County, Texas; Two children:
450.   Mildren Morgan, b July 10, 1909.
451.   Eugene Morgan, b Feb. 12, 1917. Res. Hamlin, Texas.

All these children and grandchildren are living, in five health, and prospering. The two sons are and have been employed by the St. Louis & Southwestern Railroad ever since they were boys, and since they attained the ages of 18 and 20, respectively, they have been conductors.

Doctor John T. McMillan, the father of this family, died Nov. 11, 1893, leaving these four children, ranging in age from 3 to 9 years, to be reared by their widowed mother, who was only 27 years old, with limited means and no business training. But with good sense and good judgement with teaching music, she succeeded admirably and won universal praise for her success. Her children are noted for their good moral character, energy and ambition. She was not able to give them more than a high school education, but their aptitude and ambition enabled the children to profit to the fullest extent from their training. They are exemplary citizens. Mrs. Rounsaville McMillan deserves all honor and praise for the noble work she accomplished in raising and educating such a family of children, and this is the greatest honor we can bestow on her. She is a consistent member of the Baptist Church, and hence a good Christian.

William W. Rounsaville, son of Caroline Adair and J.B. Rounsaville, and grandson of Doctor W.W. Adair, was born Feb. 2, 1871, at Lone Oak, Hunt County, Texas, where he was raised to 13 years; then the family moved to

Wm. Franklin and Wife of Dallas

452. I   Flora Rounsaville, b 1900, died at age of 6 months.
453. II Olo Rounsaville, b 1902.

William Walter Adair, born Jan. 23, 1880. Son of William Franklin and Marrie Lillie (Roberson) Adair. Lived in Dallas all of his life. Attended private and public schools, also business college locally; also attended military school short time at Boonville, Mo. Being ambitious, he took up the work of traveling salesman like his father, at the age of 19. Has traveled re represented some Eastern concern in Texas, Oklahoma, Louisiana and New Mexico for the past twenty-five years. At one time he was Texas representative for the National City Company, a subsidiary of the National City Bank of 55 Wall Street, New York, which is the largest banking institution in the United States. He had charge of their bond sales in Texas. During the war he resigned his position with the National City Company and accepted service with the Magnolia Petroleum Company, which is the Standard Oil Company in disguise in Texas. While with the Magnolia Petroleum Company he rendered and paid all of the taxes for this large company in Texas, Oklahoma, Kansas and New Mexico. He was later transferred to the purchasing agent's department, where he made the adjustments of discrepancies between the company and firms from whom they purchased on all purchases in Oklahoma and Kansas.

Since leaving the oil company he has spent his time in looking after his real estate investments and in promoting the widening and illuminating of Dallas city streets with ornamental lighting systems of "white ways."

Early in life his brother, Robin Adair, age 5, fell head first into a tub of chow-chow, and it happened to be William's good fortune to pull him out. He saved one man form drowning and one from discouragement.

He is a member of Keystone Lodge. 1142, A.F. & A.M.; Dallas Consistory No. 2; Hella Temple, A.A.O.N.M. Shrine; Post F., Travelers' Protective Association; Illinois Commercial Men's Association; Lakewood (Golf) Country Club of Dallas.

He was above the draft age, but volunteered in the Quartermaster's Department, U.S. Army, on Sept. 25, 1918; was examined at Camp Bowie (Fort Worth, Texas) on Oct. 7, 1918, but was never called for service.

He married Miss Lucile Reekes of Dallas on March 29, 1911. William Reekes Adair, their only son, was born Feb. 27, 1919.

ROBIN ADAIR, second son of William Franklin and Mary Lillie (Robberson) Adair. Born Feb. 11, 1884. In early life he was connected with the auditor of receipts of the Texas & Pacific Railway at Dallas. For many years he has been engaged in adjusting work and also in looking after his real estate investments. Married Edna Cecelia Berry Nold, a widow with one child. He has one son, Robin Adair, Jr. Attended the public schools in Dallas and then a stenographic course at a local business college. Lived in Dallas all his life. Member of the Illinois Commercial Men's Association and the Lakewood (Golf) County Club of Dallas. Great lover of fine stock.

Information on the children of James Rounsaville and Caroline (Adair) Rounsaville:

George T. Rounsaville, oldest son, lived in Chicago He is an invalid with brain disease, and his brother, Gus, cares for him.

(425) Ohn Rounsaville, third oldest son, lives on Pennsylvania Avenue in Fort Worth, Texas. He spent the major portion of his life working for the St. Louis & Southwestern (Cotton Belt) Railway in various capacities. He started in as helper, then telegraph operator, station agent, brakeman, train auditor, and then city passenger agent at Fort Worth, Texas for several years; then joint city passenger agent for the St. L. & S.W. and International & Great Northern Railways at Waco, Texas. He is a very steady fellow, and a member of the Masonic order. Has a wife and several children.

(427) Gus Rounsaville, fourth oldest son. This fellow is the steadiest, most dependable son of the Rounsaville family. In early life he taught school. Later started in as a helper around a St. L. & S.W. railway station, later telegraph operator and then station agent. While station agent at Alto, Texas, he accepted service as cashier of the Alto state Bank at Alto, Texas, since that time he has become president of this bank. He still lives at Alto, Texas. Has a wife and four or five children. He is superintendent of the Sunday school in his town. Very dependable in every way.

Lonnie Rounsaville, fifth oldest son, is a bachelor.

Cone Rounsaville, sixth son, started in as a helper around the St. Louis & Southwestern Railway offices. Later became telegraph operator and then station agent. Now agent for this road at Hamilton, Texas. Consider him a very dependable boy. Married.

Mrs. Ora (Rounsaville-Smith) Eddins has been married twice. Frist husband Tom Smith. Three Children by Smith. She has since their changed their names to Eddins. Second husband's name is Dan Eddins. This girl is a fine character and a good woman in every way. She lives in Detroit, Michigan. Dan Eddins is with the Maxwell Automobile Co. Dan Eddins was born and raised in Waco, Texas.

Benjamin Lockett Adair was born at Lone Oak, Hunt County, Texas, eldest son of George Washington and Willie (Cole) Adair. Left an orphan when quite young. Raised by his grandfather, William Washington Adair, who moved from Lone Oak to Dallas. Attended Dallas schools. A great many have expressed themselves as saying that Lockett Adair was a cross between Moody and Sam P. Jones of Cartersville, Ga., in his preaching. He is one of the best "go-getters" to get them into the church that I have every seen.

William Edward Adair, born at Lone Oak, Texas, was the son of George Washington and Willie (Cole) Adair. He was born sixteen months after Lockett's birth. He has spent most of his life either as a real estate man or a traveling salesman with headquarters at Dallas. He now represents the Hanson Glove Company of Milwaukee in Louisiana, Arkansas and Mississippi. He has one child living, a girl, Eddie Lee Adair. His wife died about fifteen months ago at Greenville, Texas, and is buried at Cumby, Texas, her old home.

Florence Rounsaville Cade, daughter of J.B. and Caroline (Adair) Rounsaville, and granddaughter of Doctor W.W. Adair, was born at Lone Oak, Hunt County, Texas. Married Jackson Cade. He died Aug. 14, 1914.

426. Florence Rounsaville=Jackson Cade
Progeny: Three Sons

I Weldon Cade, b Jan 6, 1909.
II Maxwell Cade, b July 14, 1910; died Dec. 20, 1914.
III Edward Jackson Cade, b Sept, 14, 1912.

REV. ROBERT F. ADAIR

463. Rev. Robert F. Adair is a retired Presbyterian minister, living at Goodletsville, Tenn., North of Nashville. Has the following lineage:

463. Rev. Robert F. Adair, 457 John Evans Adair, Wm. Adair, James Adair, Jospeh Adair, J., Joseph Adair, Sr., Thomas.

James Adair, mentioned above was a son of Joseph Adair, Jr., raised in Laurens County, South Carolina. James Adair Moved to Tennessee about 1800 about thirty miles southeast of Nashville. They drifted to Arkansas about forty years later.

CHAPTER XXXI

ELISHA ADAIR

AND HIS GENEALOGICAL LINE

Thomas, the first American ancestor of Elisha, was born in Ulster, Ireland, about 1680. He migrated to America about 1730 and settled in Pennsylvania but moved to South Carolina in 1750. He brought with him three sons, all born in Ireland, to wit:

2	I	James Adair, born 1709. Indian Author and trader.
3	II	Joseph Adair, Sr., b 1711, father of the Adairs of S.C., Ga., Tenn., Ala.
4	III	William Adair, b 1719, father of the Kentucky branch of Adairs.

1732

3 Joseph Adair., Sr.=Sarah Laferty of Pennsylvania
Progeny: Three Sons, Three Daughters

5	I	Joseph Adair, Jr., b 1733.
10	II	James Adair, Sr., b 1735.
7	III	Benjamin Adair, b 1737.
8	IV	Leah Adair.
9	V	Sarah Adair.
10	VI	Mary Adair.
3		Joseph Adair, Sr., married, second, Susanna Lond; 1 son died unmarried.

1757

5 Joseph Adair, Jr.=Sarah Dillard
Son of Joseph Adair, Sr.
Progeny: Four Sons, Four Daughters

11	I	John Adair, b 1758, m 1783, d 1812.
12	II	James Adair, b 1760.
13	III	Robert Adair.
14	IV	Elisah Adair, b 1775.
15	V	Elizabeth Adair, married Houston.
16	VI	Jane Adair, married Holland.
17	VII	Casey Adair, married McCrary
18	VIII	Charity Adair, married David Little.

1799

14 Elisha Adair=-_____
Son of Joseph Adair, Jr., and Sarah Dillard Adair.
Progeny: One Son and perhaps others

471.	I	Isaac Adair, b 1800 in Laurens County, S.C.

Isaac Adair was a physician and a farmer. His wife, Jane Henry, was also born in Laurens County, S.C., where they were married. During the early years of their married life, they migrated to Perry County, Ala., where their son Elisha was born; subsequently they moved to Scott and Nashoba Counties, Miss. In 1852 the family moved to Houston County, Texas. In 1858 his first wife, Jane Henry Adair, died at their farm home west from Crockett, Texas.

1827

471. Doctor Isaac Adair=Jane Henry

Progeny: Four Daughters, Six Sons

472.	I	Margaret Adair, m George Hopper.
473.	II	Milinda Adair, m Henry Varner.
474.	III	John Pinkey Adair, m Martha Weldon.
475.	IV	Elisha Young Adair, m 1st Martha Gaston; 2d Lucy Freeman.
476.	V	Henry Adair, m Talitha Conner.
477.	VI	Hosea Adair, m Cynthia Conner.
478.	VII	William Adair, m Puss Wallace.
479.	VIII	Albert Adair, died in infancy.
480.	IX	Sarah Jane Adair.
481.	X	Almina Adair.

1859

471. (2d marriage) Doctor Isaac Adair=Miss---Thompson

Near Crockett, Texas.

Progeny: One son

I David Thompson Adair, m Eliza Hill, who died shortly. Names of his 2d and 3d wives not known.

Doctor Isaac Adair died in 1863, and his second wife died six weeks later at Crockett, Texas./

415. Elisha Young Adair, son of Doctor Isaac and Jane (Henry) Adair, was born in Perry Co., Ala., April 22, 1832. The next move the family made was to Nashoba and Scott counties, Miss. In 1852 the family landed at Crockett, Houston County, Texas.

Elisha served in the War Between the States under Capt. D.A. Nunn of Crockett. After serving one year in the ranks, he was detailed to superintend the government tan yard.

He was a skillful saddle-maker. He made the writer a saddle in 1874 that was more valuable than an ordinary saddle-horse.

Je was a merchant in this hometown of Alvarado, Texas. He was a consistent member of the Cumberland Presbyterian church and a prominent

Mason; his funeral being conducted by that fraternity. He died in 1905, aged 73 years.

1859

415. (1st Marriage_ Elisha Young Adair=Martha Gaston
Progeny: Two Children. One of them died in infancy the other in childhood.

1865

415. (2d marriage_ Elisha Young Adair=Lucy Frances Freeman
Progeny: Seven Children

582.	I	Mary Milinda Adair, b 1866, d 1869.
483.	II	Pollie Jane Adair, b 1869, m William Campbell Glasgow, retired banker of Alvarado.
484.	III	Ida May Adair, b 1872, m Monroe Turner Crawford, grocery merchant, 3008 Pickett St., Greenville, Texas.
485.	IV	Weyman Collier Adair, b 1875, m Stella Childress, Rio Vista, Texas.
486.	V	Virgil freeman Adair, b 1880, m Louise Evans, Corsicana, Texas. Mfg. auto supplies, Lindsey, Cal.
487.	VI	Herman Elisha Adair, b 1883, m Viola Venable of Alvarado, Texas. Is a bookkeeper, 3008 Picket St., Greenville, Texas.
488.	VII	Lilian Francis Adair, b 1891, m Marvin Gaines Monoghan, chief clerk to gen. Supt. Of Fort Worth & Denver R.R., 1315 Giddings St. Wichita Falls, Texas.

1888

483. Pollie Jane Adair=William Campbell Glasglow
Daughter of Elisha and   Banker, retired,
Lucy Adair   Alvarado, Texas

Progeny: Five Children

489.	I	Very Inex Glasgow, b 1889, d 1889.
490.	II	Robert Adair Glasgow, b 1890; merchant in Alvarado, Texas. Was Lt. of Inf., World War, service in France.
492.	III	Sula Mae Glasgow, b 1892, m Roy Douglass, banker, 407 Douglas Ava., Cleburne, Texas. Two children: William Brown Douglas, Eugene Roy Douglas.
492.	IV	Herschel Glasgow, b 1895, banker, Stock Yards Nat. Bank, Fort Worth. Married Grace Miller, Fort Worth, Texas. Herschel was sergeant Aviation Corps, World War.
493.	V	Hazel Francis Glasgow, b 1900, d 1907.

1892

484. Ida May Adair=Monroe Turner Crawford
Daughter of Elisha and Lucy Adair   Grocery Merchant,
                                        Greenville, Texas.

Progeny: Eight Children

494. I   Pollie Crawford, b 1893, d 1894.
495. II   Ralph Adair Crawford, b 1894. Grocery merchant, Greenville, Texas. Married Edith Lyons of Great Falls, Mont.
496. III   Pauline Elizabeth Crawford, b 1900. A teacher of Spanish and Latin; residence 3008 Pickett St., Greenville, Texas.
497. IV   Ruth Crawford
498. V   Mary Crawford (twin sisters), b 1903. Students in Asberry College, Wilmere, Ky. Home, Greenville, Texas.
499. VI   Lawrence William Crawford
500. VII   James Laird Crawford (twin brothers), b 1908. Students.

485. Weyman Collier Adair=Stella Childress

Son of Elisha and Lucy Adair.   Home, Rio Vista, Texas.

Progeny: Four children

502. I   Gladys Adair, b 1903, m Dewy Reeves, a farmer, Rio Vista, Texas. One child, Lawrence Reeves.
503. II   Seaburne Young Adair, b 1905. Student.
504. III   Mary T. Adair, b 1911. Student.
505. IV   Charlie Francis Adair, b 1915.

All Live at Rio Vista, Texas.

1907

486. Virgil Freeman Adair=Louise Evans of Corsicana, Texas

Son of Elisha and Lucy Adair.

Progeny

506. I   Noel Phillips Adair, b 1908. Student.
507. II   Elvis Yount Adair, b 1910. Student.

1903

487. Herman Elisha Adair=Viola Venable of Alvarado, Texas.

Son of Elisha and Lucy Adair.

Is a bookkeeper in Greenville, Texas.

Progeny: Nine Children

508. I   Robin Adair, b 1904. A farmer; home, Greenville, Texas.
509. II   Maurine Adair, b 1906, d 1920.
510. III   Richard Adair, b 1908. Student.
511. IV   Lucile Adair, b 1920. Student.
512. V   Frank Adair, b 1912. Student.
513. VI   Hazel Adair, b 1913; d 1915
514. VII   Iena Faye Adair, b 1915. Student.
516. VIII   Ida May Adair, b 1917, d 1917.
517. IX   Viola Hermione Adair, b 1919.

The Family home is 3008 Pickett St., Greenville, Texas.

19---?

488. Lilian Francis Adair=Marvin Gaines Monahan
Daughter of Elisha and Lucy Adair.
Progeny: None.
Mr. Monahan is chief clerk to the Gen. Supt. Of the Fort Worth & Denver R.R.
Home, 1315 Giddings St., Wichita Falls, Texas.

CHAPTER XXXII
HUGHSTON-WALKER GENEALOGY AND WALKER BIOGRAPHY

5 Joseph Adair, Jr., in his will, dated Jan. 12, 1812, which is on file in the probate judge's office at Laurens, S.C., says; "Likewise I give and bequeath unto my daughter, Elizabeth, and her husband, John Huston, one negro girl names Clavius."

15 Elizabeth Adair=John Huston (Later spelled Hughston)
Progeny: Seven More Children

516. I Joseph Hugston.
517. II Jean Hughston.
518. III John F. Hughston.
519. IV Archibald Hughston.
520. V Elisha Hughston.
521. VI Casey Hughston.
522. VII Leroy Hughston.

520. Elisha Hughston=Margaret Norman

Born Oct. 4, 1788.   Born Oct. 8, 1795.
Died July 20, 1868.   Died May, 1867.

Progeny: Nine Children

523. I Jesse Hughston.
524. II David Farmer Hughston.
525. III Martha Louisa Hughston.
526. IV Elizabeth Jane Hughston.
527. V William Leroy Hughston.
528. VI Julia Frances Hughston.
529. VII John Marion Hughston.
530. VIII Elisha Melton Hughston.
531. IX George Newton Hughston.

525. Martha Louisa Hughston=Newton Pinckney Walker

Born Aug. 2, 1820.   Born Nov. 27, 1816.
Died June 19, 1900   Died Nov. 13, 1861.

Progeny: Seven Children

531. I Louisa Caroline Walker.
532. II Sabra Jane Walker.
533. III Margaret Ann Walker.
534. IV Newton Farmer Walker.
535. V Albert Pickney Hughston Walker.
536. VI Idalia Martha Seabrook Walker.
537. VII Horace Walker.

1867
534. Newton Farmer Walker=Virginia Eppes
Born Jan. 12, 1845.   Born Nov. 25, 1842.
Progeny: Five Children
538. I   Horace Eppes Walker.
539. II   Albert Hayne Walker.
540. III Newton Pinckney Walker.
541. IV   William Laurens Walker.
542. V   Virginia Eppes Walker.

Horace never married. Born Nov. 22, 1867.
1896
539. Albert Hayne Walker=M. Elizabeth Rawlings
Born March 27, 1870.   Sept. 14, 1896.
Progeny: Two Children
543. I   Virginia Walker.
544. II   Lilah Walker.
340.   Newton Pinckney Walder died unmarried, June 24, 1895.

541. William Laurens Walker=Nelia D. Dailey
Born July 6, 1873   Nov. 1   Born Feb. 24, 1877
Progeny: Six Children
545. I   William Laurens Walker, Jr.
546. II   Louisa Booker Walker.
547. III Nelia Dailey Walker.
548. IV   Newton Pinekney Walker.
549. V   Robert Wood Walker.
550. VI   Newton Farmer Walker, Jr.
1900
542. Virginia Eppes Walker=Robert M. Hitch
Born April 11, 1875   Nov. 21
Progeny: Two Children
551. I   Virginia Hitch.
552. II   Robert M. Hitch, Jr.

BIOGRAPHICAL SKETCHES

Newton Pinekney Walker was born in the southern part of Spartanburg County on Nov. 27, 1816. At that time there was not public school system in South Carolina, and the "free schools" of the Piedmont region were widely scattered and offered very limited opportunities along the lines of education. However, the subject of this sketch determined to secure an education, and early in life he began the hard undertaking of self-education. He succeeded so well at this that we find him as a young man a teacher in his community and an ordained minister of the Baptist Church.

On April 20, 1837, Newton Pinckney Walker married Martha Louisa Hughston, who had two deaf brothers and one deaf sister. Being a teacher and a minister, he naturally became deeply interested in these deaf children and took steps to make his interest practical. There being no school for the deaf in South Carolina at that time, he visited Cave Spring, Georgia, where there was a small school housed in a few log cabins, which had just been opened for the instruction of deaf children. He remained in this school for several months or until he had mastered all that was there known concerning the education of the deaf.

Upon his return home he purchased the present site of the South Carolin School for the Deaf and the Blind, and in 1849 opened a private school with five deaf children. In 1855 a department for the blind was added, and in 8157 the property was sold to the State and made a State institution. On Nov. 13, 1861, he died of measles, being then only 45 years of age. He was survived by his wife and seven children, all of whom, with two exceptions, were educators of the deaf or the blind.

It is interesting to note in connection with the life of the founder of the South Carolina School for the Deaf and the Blind that, at the time of his death, he was making arrangements to place this labor of special education upon the shoulders of others in order that he might again devote himself to his chosen profession of the ministry. He was a man of advanced religious thought and desired to organize a church to promulgate his religious belief. He spent his very last days writing an outline of his proposed church organization.

While he was not permitted to study for any great number of years the problem of his epical work of educating the deaf and the blind, still he mastered these problems with wonderful accuracy. The South Carolina School for the Deaf and Blind stands as a monument to perpetuate his memory. In the central part of the Administration Building there is a bronze tablet erected to his memory by the General Assembly of South Carolina. At the bottom of this tablet the following quotation from his writings is reproduced: "All increase in in virtue tends to complete success."

Newton Farmer Walker, the eldest son and fourth child of Martha Louisa (Hughston) and Newton Pickney Walker, was born in Spartanburg County on Jan. 12, 1845. His education was received in his father's home, the neighborhood school and St. John's Classical and Military School of Spartanburg, S.C. He was a student at this school when, having reached the age of 16, he joined the Confederate Army in Virginia. In the spring of 1862, he was given a furlough in order that he might return home to improve the condition of his health and to assist in the management of the School for the

Deaf and the Blind—his father, the superintendent of the school, having died the year previous.

From that time forward his life has been spent controlling, organizing and developing South Carolina's school for her deaf and blind children. He carried this school through the trying days of the Civil War and through the more trying days of the Reconstruction period.

Early in life Newton Farmer Walker married Virginia Eppes of Laurens County, and from this union there were born four sons and one daughter. All these sons, except one who died in early manhood, have followed their father in the work of educating the deaf and the blind. He is still the superintendent of this school (1924) and is active in the control of its affairs.

Superintendent Walker has received many honors at the hands of his friends throughout Spartanburg County and South Carolina. For many years he has been a ruling elder in the First Presbyterian Church of Spartanburg, a life trustee at Converse College, a member of the Crust Breakers' Club, a member of the Spartanburg County Pension Board and commander of the local chapter of Confederate Veterans.

Many years ago, the South Carolina University conferred upon him the honorary title of Doctor of Laws in recognition of his services as an educator in this State. The General Assembly of South Carolina, by concurrent resolution, conferred upon him the title of Doctor of Philanthropy and Charity—the only degree that has ever been conferred by any General Assembly in the United States.

Doctor Walker has been an active Mason for a long term of years and is a Past Grand Commander of Knights Templar of South Carolina.

But his is best known throughout his State and the United States as an educator of deaf and blind children, and in 1923 was elected President of the American Association of Instructors of the Deaf.

Horace Eppes Walker is the oldest son of Doctor and Mrs. N.F. Walker and was born in Spartanburg on Nov. 22, 1867. He graduated from the University of South Carolina in 1887 and began his life work of educating the deaf that fall in the State School at Fulton, Missouri. After teaching the advanced class in that school for twenty years, he came to the Tennessee school at Knoxville as principal. Later, in 1918, he was made superintendent of the Tennessee school but after serving three years he was forced to resign, owing to his physical condition. Up to the present he has not been able to resume his labor. He has never married. At the time of his retirement, he was recognized as one of the best teachers of the deaf in the United States.

Albert Hayne Walker, the second son of Doctor and Mrs. N.F. Walker, was born in Missouri on March 27, 1870. He, like his older brothers, was educated at the University of South Carolina, where he was graduated in 1889. His first work as an educator of the deaf was in Austin, Texas. In this school he labored for seven years, and in 1896 went to the Tennessee school. He remained here but one year and next entered the Florida school at St. Augustine—first as a teacher, later as the principal, and in 1906 was made president of this school. He has been very successful as the head of the Florida school for the deaf and blind and has built for the State of Florida one of the best schools in the United States.

In 1896 he married Elizabeth Rawlings of Columbia, S.C., and from this union there are two daughters.

About ten years ago the University of Florida conferred upon President Walker the Honorary title of Doctor of Literature as a token of its appreciation of his work as an educator.

Doctor Walker is an active worker in the Episcopal Church, having served his local church as vestryman for several years. As a Rotarian he enters actively into the business life of St. Augustine. He is vice-president of the American Conference of Superintendents and Principals of Schools for the Deaf.

William Laurens Walker, the fourth son of Newton Farmer Walker and Virginia (Eppes) Walker, was born in Spartanburg County on July 5, 1873. To be exact, he was born in the school for the deaf and the blind at Cedar Springs, S.C. He was educated in a private school in Spartanburg, the Wofford Fitting School and Wofford College—graduating from the latter in 1894. Immediately upon his graduation he accepted work in the West Virginia School for the Deaf and the Blind located at Romney. The following year he accepted work in the Missouri School for the Deaf but remained there only a few months. The South Carolina school secured his services on Jan. 1, 1897. Since that date, except for one year when he practiced law in Spartanburg, he has been with the South Carolina School for the Deaf and the Blind. At present (1924) he is principal and assistant superintendent.

On Nov. 1, 1900, he married Nelia DuPuy Dailey of Romney, W. Va., and five children survive from this union.

Mr. Walker has been active in Masonic Circles of his county and state, having been at the head of every branch of Masonry in the city of Spartanburg, and at present (1924) in Grand Commander of the Grand Commandery of Knights Templar of South Carolina and is Potentate of Hejaz Temple at Greenville, S.C.

He is chairman of the board of deacons of the First Presbyterian Church of Spartanburg and is an enthusiastic member of the Spartanburg Kiwanis Club.

CHAPTER XXXIII

GENEALOGY OF CHARITY ADAIR LITTLE
And Her Descendants in South Carolina

Lineage
4 Charity Adair, 3 Joseph Adair, Jr., 2 Joseph Adair, Sr., 1 Thomas Adair.

1797

18 Charity Adair=David Little
Daughter of Joseph Adair.   B 1767, d 1812.
B about 1773, e 1826.

Progeny: Nine Children

517. I   David Little, Jr., b 1798.
518. II   Elizabeth Little, b Aug. 27, 1800.
519. III   Joseph Little, b July 24, 1801. Moved to Deckert, Tenn.
520. IV   James Little
521. V   Jane Little (Twins), b July 12, 1803. Moved to Madison, Texas.
522. VI   John Little, b Feb. 23, 1806.
523. VII   Nancy Little, b Sept. 28, 1807, Married Alex Fairbarn, moved West.
524. VIII   Thomas Little, b Aug. 1, 1809; m 1840; d 1872
525. IX   Holland Little, b 1811; d 1873.

1820

518. Elizabeth Little=James Copeland
Second child of David Little   of Laurens Dist., S.C.
And Charity Adair Little

Progeny: Six Children

526. I   George Copeland, b about 1821.
527. II   Margaret Copeland, b 1823.
528. III   Elbert Copeland, b 1825.
529. IV   William Copeland, b 1827.
530. V   John Copeland, b 1829.
531. VI   David Copeland, b about 1831.

526. George Copeland=Frances Young
First Child of James and
Elizabeth Little of Copeland.

Progeny: Eight Children

532. I   Mary Copeland.
533. II   Duckett Copeland.

534. III James Copeland.
535. IV Fannie Copeland.
536. V Rebecca Copeland.
537. VI Mason Copeland.
538. VII Rhett Copeland.
539. VIII Luda Copeland
540. IX Guy Copeland.

About 1867

532. Mary Copeland=Mr. Bell

Daughter of George and   of Brevard, N.C.
Frances Copeland

533. Duckett Copeland=Bee Johnson

Second child of George and Frances Copeland

Progeny: Four Children

541. I George Copeland, Jr.
542. II James Copeland.
543. III Annie Copeland.
544. IV Duckett Copeland, Jr.

541. George Copeland, Jr.-Lou Jones

First son of Duckett and
Bee Johnson Copeland

Progeny: Four Children

545. I Amy Copeland, m Ferdinand Jacobs; 2 children.
546. II Bee Copeland is in Chicora College, Columbia, S.C.
547. III and IV are twins (don't know names).

542. James Copeland=Mayme Little

Second son of Duckett and
Bee Johnson Copeland

Progeny: None

543. Annie Copeland=Walter Furgerson

Third Child of Duckett and   Clinton, S.C.
B.J. Copeland.

Progeny: Two Children

547. Duckett Copeland, Jr.=Lena ---, Clinton, S.C.

Progeny: Two Children: (names not given)

534. James Copeland=Lydia Vance

Third Child of George and
Frances Copeland

Progeny: None Mentioned

536. Rebecca Copeland=Doctor Bill Shands

Fourth child of George and Frances Copeland

Progeny: Two children (Names not given)

537. Mason Copeland=Sarah Ball
Sixth child of George and Frances Copeland
Progeny: One Child

538. Rhett Copeland=Mamie Hunter
Seventh child of George and Frances Copeland

539. Luda Copeland=Dick Copeland
Eights child of George and Frances Copeland.

440. Guy Copeland=Mary Bowen
Ninth child of George and Frances Copeland.
Progeny: Several Children (names not given)

527. Margaret Copeland=Guss Mason
Second child of James and
Elizabeth Little Copeland
Progeny: Four Children

548. I   Miss Pell Mason, m Say Gary; have children
549. II Will Mason, m Emma Finney.
550. III Sallie Mason, m Belton Holland.
551. IV Ida Mason, unmarried.

528. Elbert Copeland=Charlotte Ferguson
Third child of James and Elizabeth Little Copeland
Progeny: Several Children

529. William Copeland=Miss McCarley
Fourth child of James and
Elizabeth Little Copeland.
Progeny: Several Children

530. John Copeland=Miss Thomp Finney
Fifth child of James and
Elizabeth Little Copeland.
Progeny: Four Children

552. I   David Copeland.
553. II James Copeland.
554. III Sallie Copeland.
555. IV George Watt Copeland.

531. David Copeland=Martha Adair
Sixth child of James and   Daughter of Isaac Adair
Elizabeth Little Copeland
(Duplicated on another page)
Progeny: Four Children

556. I   Isaac Copeland.

557. II William Copeland.
558. III Janie Copeland.
559. IV Hamp Copeland.

Children of John and Thomp Copeland

Sallie Copeland, m a Mr. Johnson; one child; husband dead.
Jime Copeland, a bachelor.
George Watt Copeland, a bachelor.

520. James Little=Matilda Williams

Fourth child of David and Charity Adair Little

Progeny: One Child

560. I John W. Little (nicknamed Chaney Little), b 1833; d 1914. He married Eliza Little, his cousin.

Progeny: Three children

561. I Preston Little, m Eula Blakely; they have children and live in Phoenix, Arizona.
562. II Thomas Little (is unknown), out West.
563. III Orrah Bess Little, m; 1 child.
564. IV Joe Hickson Little, m; 2 children.

565. Thomas Little=Miss Henry

Second child of John W. and
Eliza Little

Progeny: Four Children

566. I Janie Little, m Lloyd McCrary; 2 children.
567. II Mary Hunter Little, m MacHipp; 4 children.
568. III George Little, m Miss Davidson; 1 child.
569. IV John Little, m.

563. Orrah Little=Mike Peake

Third child of John W. and Eliza Little.

Progeny: Two Children

570. I John Peake, dead.
571. II Theodore Peake, a physician in Clinton, S.C. Married Mary Simpson; has 2 children.

527. Susan Little=William Leak

Daughter of James and
Matilda Little.

Progeny: Six Children

573. I Will Leake, m Bessie ---; 2 children.
574. II Tom Leak, m; no children
575. III Lidie Leak, m Clayte Baily; no children.
576. IV Al Leak, m Elbert Stone; 2 children.
577. V Ed Leak, and engineer; killed on train.
578. VI Mayme Leak, unmarried.

569. John Little=Sarah Wolf

Sixth child of David and

Charity Little, b Feb., 1806

Progeny: Three Children

579.   I   Ludy Hamilton Little, m Mary Reid; have 3 children
580.   II   Nancy Allen Little, m John Jacks; have 4 children.
581.   III Ophelia Little, m Haste Dial; no children.

582. Thomas J. Little, Jr.=Eliza Craig

Progeny of Thomas J. Little, Jr., a Soldier in Civil War, and

Eliza Criag Little

Two Children

583.   I   Will Little.
584.   II   Annie Lou Little, both single.

1840

524. Thomas Little=Jane Eleanor Craig

Eighth child of David and

Charity Adair Little

Thomas Little was born Aug. 1, 1809, and was too old for field service in the Civil War, but rendered great service at home, providing supplies for the Confederate Army, furnishing negro labor to throw up breastworks in Charleston. He suffered great losses by depredation of soldiers, and just after the was by carpetbaggers and scalawags who came down from the North to pilfer. He died in 1872.

Progeny: Eight Children

585.   I   Sarah Little, b July 9, 1841; m 1861; d 1878.
586.   II   Elizabeth Little, b March 22, 1843; m April 20, 1865; d July 1, 1906.
587.   III Margaret Little, b May 16, 1845; m June, 1865; d Feb., 1905.
588.   IV John Pinckney Little, b March 4, 1848; m June, 1868; d 1874 in Ala.
589.   V   Emma Little, b April 29, 1857; m April 18, 1872.
590.   VI Thomas Perrin Little, b June 28m, 1853; d 1875 in Ala.
591.   VII James Hamilton Little, b Aug. 12, 1855; m; d Sept. 13, 1892.
592.   VIII David Downs Little, b 1857; m Sept. 21, 1881.

585. Sarah Little=Isaac Finney

First Child of Thomas Jane E. Craig Little

He served 4 years in the Confederate Army, Co. I, 3rd S.C. Reg., 1861-64.

Progeny: Seven Children

592.   I   Janie Finney.
593.   II   Isaac Finney, Jr.
594.   III Thomas Finney.

595. IV   John Finney.
596. V   Minnie Finney.
597. VI   Emma Finney.
598. VII Joe Finney.

1877

592. Janie Finney=Roland Ray
First Child of Isaac and
Sarah Little Finney.

Progeny: Three Children

599. I   Lille Ray.
600. II   Lydia Ray.
601. III Inez Ray.

599. Lillie Ray=Ross Young
First Child of Roland and   Laurens County in **1910.** Has held said
Janie Finney Ray.   Office continuously for 12 years and was
Elected in 1922 for another 4-year term.

Progeny: Four Children

602. I   Doris Young, b March 4, 1901; graduated at Chicora
           College, Columbia, B.A. Degree, 1922.
603. II   Grace Young, b Nov. 7, 1903.
604. III Duckett Young, b Oct. 13, 1906. Residence, Laurens, S.C.
605. IV   George H. Young, b Oct. 16, 1910

599. Lydia Ray=Pink Horton, Albemarl, N.C., have 2 children.
601. Inez Ray, single.

593. Isaac Finney Jr., second son of Isaac and Sarah Finney, was
bitten by a rabid dog while at school, in Jun, 1875, and 60
days later took hydrophobia and died a most horrible
death.

594. Thomas Finney, third child of Isaac and Sarah Finney, died with
typhoid fever at the age of 16 years.

595. -596 John and Minie Finney, the fourth and fifth in the Finney
family, both died the same day. They had malaria and took
morphine by mistake for quinine.

597. Emma Finney=Will Mason
Sixth child of the Finneys.

Progeny: Seven Children

602. I   George Mason.
603. II   Gus Mason.
604. III Loree Mason.
607. IV   Dorcus Mason.
608. V   Willie Mason.
609. VI   Joe Mason.
610. VII Flemming Mason.

AMERICAN ADAIRS—Line B 223

All are single except Loree.

Loree, third child, married Jodie Chandler; they have 2 children, Sadie and Jodie, Jr.

Jo Finney, the seventh in the Finney family, is a bachelor. All lived in Clinton.

953. Isaac Finney, the father of this family, died suddenly with a congestive chill. The mother, Sarah Little Finney, died soon after, from grief.

587. Margaret=Milton Little

Third Child of Thomas and   1st cousins, son of Holland Little
Jane E. Craig.

Progeny:

611.	I	Minnie Little, b April 6, 1868; m at Emelle, Ala.
612.	II	Alice Little, Nov. 20, 1872; m Gregory and have 2 children.
613.	I	James Gregory, b 1907.
614.	II	Margaret Gregory, b Oct., 1909.

588. John Pinkney Little=Alice Little, 1st wife

588. John Pinkney Little=Virginia Little, 2d wife, sisters

Fourth child of Thomas and Jane   Daughters of Holland
Little E. Little.

One child born by 2d wife, Virginia Little, named Julia Little. She married Collet Griffin. The Griffins had one child named for his father, 615 Collet Griffin, Jr. The father died about the time this child was born.

616. Miss Collett Griffin (a feminine name in this case), is a student in Rock Hill College, and will graduate this year (1923).

Virginia Little=E.C. Briggs

She was twice a widow, and
this is her third venture

Progeny: Three Children

617.   Robert, Ell and William Briggs. It seems Ell Briggs is a bachelor living in Oklahoma, and the other two are dead.

1872

589. Emma Little=David A Glenn

Fifth Child of Thomas and Jane E. Craig Little

Progeny: Three Children

618.	I	William Simpson Glenn, b Feb. 15, 1873; m 1898.
619.	II	Thomas Little Glenn, b May 25, 1873; m April 20, 1900.
620.	III	John Perrin Glenn, b Nov. 5, 1878; m Nov. 5, 1908.

William Simpson Glenn was educated in Clinton Presbyterian College; took his A.B. Degree in 1893, and his M.A. Degree in 1894. He taught two years in Prof. Callett's High School in Wilmington, N.C. In 1897 he opened an office in Spartanburg, S.C., for real estate, stock and bond business. In 1904 he was elected President of Security Trust Co. and Vice-President of the Bank of Commerce. In 1922 he was elected President of the National Carolina Bank, in Spartanburg, S.C.

1898

518. William Simpson Glenn=Willetta Calloway
Of Wilmington, N.C.

Progeny: Four Children

621. I Martha Glean, b March 7, 1899; m James Sartor. One child, Willetta Sartor. They live in Atlanta, Ga.
622. II Gemma Glenn, b July 20, 1901. She graduates his summer in Hollin's College, Bourtetort Springs, Va.
623. III William S. Glenn, Jr., b Feb 29, 1903. Is now in Davidson Presbyterian College, S.C.
624. IV Frances Glenn, b Sept. 20, 1907, Is in Spartanburg High School, 1923.

619. Thomas Little Glenn=Ellie Lou Robinson
Second child of David and Emma Little of Savannah, Ga.
Glenn, a traveling salesman, residing in
Athens, Ga., for educational advantages
for his children.

Progeny: Three Children

625. I Thomas Little Glenn, Jr., b April 20, 1902. Graduates this summer (1923) in Law at Athens, Ga.
626. II Henry Robinson Glenn, b 1904. Student in Georgia Tech., Athens, Ga.
627. III Ella b. Glenn, b 1907. Student in Lucy Cobb Institute, Athens, Ga.

John Perrin Glenn, third son of David and Emme Glenn, graduated at Clemsen College, S.C., 1903; graduated in dentistry in Vanderbilt University, Nashville in 1907, and located and established himself in the practice of dentistry in Spartanburg, S.C. In 1923 he is establishing the Glenn-Ayers Floral Co., Spartanburg, S.C.

620. John Perrin Glenn=Bessie Joy
Of Nashville, Tenn.

Progeny of John Perrin Glenn and Bessie Joy Glenn: Two Children.
628. I John Perrin Glenn, Jr., b Nov. 14, 1914.
629. II Thomas Joy Glenn, b March 24, 1919.

David A. Glenn, husband of Emma Little Glenn, died May 10, 1894.

AMERICAN ADAIRS—Line B

Lineage

The Glenn lineage, from the earliest American ancestor on the Adair side runs thus: Emma Little Glenn, Thomas Little, Charity Adair Little, Jospeh Adair, J., Joseph Adair, Sr., Thomas.

1881

591. James Hamilton Little=Emma Finney

Seventh child of Thomas and Jane Craig Little, b Aug. 28, 1855

Progeny: Four Children

630. I John Thomas Little, b Sept. 6, 1878; m Nov. 26, 1908, Lyde Milam. Two children, Emma Milam Little, b 1909; Janie, b 1912.
631. II Minie Little, b Sept. 17, 1880. First marriage 1888, to Harvey Brannen; second marriage Jan. 4, 1919, at Statesboro, Ga. No progeny.
632. III Mayme Little, b --- 20, 1882; m Doctor J.R. Copeland of Clinton, S.C., on June 28, 1908. Progeny, none.
633. IV James Hamilton Little, Jr., b July 21, 1889; m Antonette Thompson of Abbeville, S.C., April 30, 1919. Have one child.

1881

592. David Downs Little=Eva Meyers

Eights Child of Thomas and Jane Craig Little, b Nov. 4, 1885. Born April 9, 1863.

Progeny: Two Children

634. I Hugh F. Little.
635. II Craig S. Little.

634. Hugh F. Little=Mildred Lindsey

First child of D.D. and Eve Meyers Little of Jonesville, S.C.; b Oct. 18, 1905.

Progeny: Five Children

635. I Hugh Francis Little, Jr., b Sept. 7, 1906, at Spartanburg, S.C.
636. II David Downs Little, Jr., b May 7, 1908, at Spartanburg, S.C.
637. III James Edward Little, b Oct. 17, 1911, at Marion, N.C.
638. IV Carroll Baldwin Little, b Feb. 1, 1915, at Marion, N.C.
639. V Herbert Lindsey Little, b Dec. 1, 1918, at Marion, N.C.

Craig S. Little is single and an invalid.

592. David Downs little and his brother, 637 James Hamilton Little, son of Thomas and Jane Craig Little, formerly did a dry goods business in

Clinton, S.C. After the death of James H. Little, David D. Little moved to Pacolet Mills, S.C. Here he bought cotton for the mills. After these mills were destroyed by fire in 1903, David D. Little moved to Spartanburg and opened a cotton office, taking as a partner his son, Hugh F. Little, who was a graduate of Clemson College. Besides the local business of the firm, they built and operated cotton mills in Marion, N.C.

There is at present a decided movement among cotton manufacturers in New England to move their business south to the cotton fields, where raw material is at hand, the climate is mild, and waterpower is abundant. The Littles, father and son, have proved their capacity to operate, construct and manage such enterprises, which gives confidence to capital; hence, millions of dollars are being invested for New England cotton manufacturers by David D. Little and son, Hugh F. Little, in the foothill counties of South Carolina and North Carolina. Such a movement has been expected for the last forty years, because the raw material is at hand and the climate is mild.

Summary of the Little Family

One hundred and seventy-two marriages; 150 children born in 130 years' time, in Laruens and Spartanburg Counties, N.C.

MRS. EMMA LITTLE GLANN, daughter of Thomas and Jane Craig Little, was born at Clinton, S.C., April 29, 1851; married David A. Glenn, April 18, 1872, and became the mother of three children, William S., Thomas Little, and John Perrin Glenn.

Left a widow when these children were small, Mrs. Glenn devoted her efforts to rearing and educating her sons. With a degree of courage and perseverance she faced a task, difficult at any time, but doubly so during Reconstruction.

Mrs. Gleann's mother was Jane Eleanor Craig, fifth of the nine children born to Thomas and Elizabeth Craig. Thomas Craig married his cousin, Elizabeth Craig, and was, for this marriage, disinherited by his father, William Craig. With his young wife he went to the home of his bachelor brother, John Criag, to live. He made wooden spoons and forks for their use, and after ploughing throughout the day it was his custom to split rails or make shoes at night. By dint of energy and economy, he accumulated 200 slaves, who were a total loss at the close of the Civil War. In spite of his great loss, however, his estate was worth more than $100,000.00 at his death, February 8, 1873.

Thomas Craig was the son of William and Jane Logan Craig, William being the oldest son of the John and Eleanor Craig who came to South

Carolina from Ireland in November, 1773, landing at Charleston, and locating near Enoree River, in what was then Ninety-Six District, now Laurens County. John Criag was born some time prior to 1740, and after coming to South Carolina served in the Revolution as a private in the South Carolina Militia. He died in 1785, and was buried in the old Duncan's Creek Presbyterian churchyard, near Clinton. The will of Eleanor Craig, his widow, is recorded in (Old) Book B, at page 79, of the court records at Laurens, S.C.

An interesting paper, still in the family's possession, is the receipt given b the shipmaster for the passage of John Craig and his family to Charlston. It reads as follows:

"Rec'd. from John Crage One Pound Two Shillings and nine pens in earnest for seaven passengers for their passage on board the Betty from this porte to Charleston South Carolina, their allowance to be seaven pounds of Beef, seaven pounds of Bread or meal, and one pound of Butter or Molasses each week and two Quarts of Water each Day for each passenger.
Larne 19th Oct. 1773.
Abm. Woodside."

Another interesting document is the certificate of good character given to John Craig by the head of his local church in Ireland. It reads as follows:

"I certify that the Bearer, John craig and Ellen his wife are Protestants of the Presbyterian Persuasion and are free of all public scandal or Church censure, and having a mind to remove to the Province of South Carolina with their six children are hereby recommended to all he may apply to as sober, honest people and worthy of Encouragement. Dated at Ahoghill in the Kingdon of Ireland this 6th day of November 1773.

Sam Cuming, Dip. MoDoctor"

The staunch Presbyterianism of the family was an honest inheritance. It had its roots in the convictions of that John Criag who was condemned to death because of his Protestantism in the sixteenth century, and of whom the Encyclopedia Britannia has the following account:

"Craig, John, one of the Scottish Reformers, was born about 1512. He was educated at the University of St. Andrews, and entered the Dominican Order. But, being suspected of Heresy, he was cast into prison. Retiring to the continent, he obtained the patronage of Cardinal Pole, and for some years taught in Dominican schools, and performed other services for the order.

"He was converted to Protestantism by the Institutes of Calvin, and having made a brave confession of his heresy before the Inquisition, he was condemned to be burnt. But, on the eye of his execution, Pope Paul IV died,

Mrs. Emma Little Glenn.

and the mob broke open the prisons. Craig fled to Vienna, where the Emperor, Maximilian II, refused to surrender him to the Inquisition. He now returned to his native country, and after preaching for some time in Edinburg became Coadjutor to Knox. It was he who proclaimed the banns of marriage between Queen Mary and Bothwell, but he openly denounced their union. On the death of Knox in 1672, he naturally succeeded to the leadership of Scottish Church. He took the most prominent part in drawing up the second Book of Discipline, and he was the author of the First Covenant, otherwise called the King's Confession (1581), and of Craig's Catechism (1592), which was for half a century in general use in Scotland. But, though he was bold enough to rebuke the King in his sermons, he yielded to his commands, and signed a declaration, promising obedience to the bishops and submission to an Act that had been passed forbidding the assembling of the church courts without royal license. Craig's coadjutor and successor was Andrew Melville."

Mrs. Emma Little Glenn, mother of William S. Glenn, well-known financier, and Doctor J.P. Glenn, dentist, has succeeded in raising in Clinton, her old home, an endowment fund of $2,000 for the permanent upkeep and attention of the graves and walks of the cemetery of Duncan Creek Presbyterian church—the oldest Presbyterian church in Laruens County, and the mother of ten churches of that denomination, scattered throughout Laruens and adjacent counties. Mrs. Glenn has selected a board of six trustees to handle his sum, which will be invested in government bonds, the interest being used annually to pay for the labor of cleaning up the cemetery and keeping it attractive in every way. Duncan Creek Presbyterian church was founded in 1752, and among its organizers were: Anderson Me-Logan, were ancestors of Mrs. Gleann. Her father, the late Thomas Creary, Joseph Adair and Homas Logan. The latter two, Adair and Little, were members of this church and served for years as one of its deacons. His body sleeps in the church cemetery. Duncan Creek church is six miles northeast of Clinton, and for years was the place of worship of the Presbyterians of that town. Subsequently the Clinton Presbyterian church, of which Doctor W.P. Jacobs was for nearly fifty years pastor, was established.

Mrs. Glenn is state genealogist of the South Carolina Daughters of the American Revolution, having held that position since 1913. In line with her work of tracing the birth, ancestry and family line of county officials throughout the state. The probate judge's office and that of the clerk of court, where wills and land papers are guides to the family connections and continuity, she inspects the old records and papers. In speaking of her work to The Herald's correspondent yesterday she stressed the condition in which these papers are found in many of the county offices. There is no provision for their permanent preservation. This is due to the lack of any appropriation from any source, according to the officials. At the state meeting of the D.A.R. source, according to the officials. At the state meeting of the D.A.R. in Greenville on the 14th and 15th of November she will bring before that body the importance of making an appropriation for this specific purpose. According to her experience of a decade in this work she is impressed with the indifference of people towards preserving family history and tradition. The general attitude towards the subject of tracing family history, as she finds it, is: "Everybody's business is nobody's business."

CHAPTER XXXIV

JANE ADAIR HOLLAND
AND HER DESCENDANTS

Joseph Adair, Jr., in his will, dated Jan. 12, 1812, which is on file in the Probate Judge's Office at Laurens, S.C., says: "Likewise I give and bequeath unto my daughter Jane, and her husband, Thomas Holland, one negro girl." Jane Adair was born in 1765, in Laurens District, S.C.

16 Jane Adair=Thomas Holland
Progeny: One Daughter
639.   I   Asenath Holland, b 1795.

639. Asenath Holland=Samuel Copeland
Daughter of Thomas and Jane Adair Holland
Progeny: One Daughter
640.   I   Louisa Copeland, b 1821; d 1871.

640. Louisa Copeland=George Holland
Daughter of Samuel and   (were cousins)
Asenath Copeland
641.   Asenath Holland, b 1840; d 1872

Asenath Holland=Henry Midleton Hunter
Daughter of George and
Louisa Copeland Holland.
Progeny: Three Children
643.   I   Guy Hunter Copeland, b 1886.
644.   II   Frances Copeland, b 1889.
645.   III Asenath Copeland, b 1896.

643. Guy Hunter Copeland=Margaret Stewart
Son of John Rhett Copeland
And Mary Hunter Copeland
Progeny: Two Children
646.   I   Guy Copeland, Jr.
647.   II   Stewart Copeland.

644. Frances Copeland=James B. Frazier
Daughter of John Rett Copeland
And Mary Hunter Copeland.
Progeny: Two Children
648.   I   James B. Frazier, Jr.
649.   II   John Rhett Frazier.

645. Asenath Copeland=Eugene Bethea

Daughter of John Rhett and
Mary Hunter Copeland
>Progeny: None

646. Clara Holland, daughter of George Holland Louisa Copeland Holland, granddaughter of Samuel Copeland and Asenath Holland Copeland, and great granddaughter of Thomas Holland and Jane Adair Holland, daughter of Joseph Adair, Jr., was born Dec. 2, 1852, at Clinton, S.C.

Dec 2, 1869

646. Clara Holland=William Albright
Sept 6, 1846, at Morristown, Tenn.
>Progeny: Two Children

- 647. I Doctor George Copeland Albright, b Sept. 6, 1876, at Clinton, S.C.
- 648. II Texas Cate Albright, b Aug. 9, 1873 at Paris, Texas.

Dec 27, 1899

647. Doctor George Copeland Albright=Nannie Vance
>Progeny: Three Children

- 649. I George Copeland Albright, Jr., b Nov. 21, 1902, at Laurens, S.C.
- 650. II William Vance Albright, b June 6, 1905, at Laurens, S.C.
- 651. III Clarence Holland Albright, b Aug. 7, 1907, at Laurens, S.C.

Dec 27, 1893

648. Texas Cate Albright=William Hale Shands at Clinton S.C.
>Progeny: Two Children

- 652. I Evie Louise Shands, b Oct. 24, 1894, at Clinton, S.C.
- 653. II Kate Shands, b Sept. 24, 1896, at Clinton, S.C.

Dec 20, 1920

652. Evie Louise Shands=Roger Le Hew Coe
Daughter of Texas Cate and at Blackburg, S.C.
William Hale Shands.

>Progeny

- 654. I Louise Albright Coe, b Nov. 5, 1921, at Rome, Ga.

June 19, 1918

653. Kate Shands=Thomas P.P. Carson
Daughter of Texas Cate and
William Hale Shands.

>Progeny:

- 655. I Katherine Shands Carson, b Dec. 23, 1919, at Clinton, S.C.; d Jan. 8, 1922, at Clinton, S.C.

Col. Geo. W. Adair, Father of Atlanta

CHAPTER XXXV
COL. GEORGE W. ADAIR OF ATLANTA

Lineage: George Washington Adair, John Fisher Adair, John Adair, Joseph Adair, Jr., Joseph Adair, Sr., Thomas Adair.

Thomas Adair was born in Antrim County, Ireland, in 1711, and came to America in 1730.

Joseph Adair, Sr., was born in Antrim County, Ireland, in 1711 and came to America in 1730.

Joesph Adair, Jr., was born in Pennsylvania in 1735, and went to South Carolina in 1750.

John Adair was born in South Carolina in 1758 and went to Georgia in 1800.

20 John Fisher Adair was born in South Carolina in 1786 and went to Georgia in 1800.

656. Joseph Adair, Sr., Joseph Adair, Jr., and John Adair were all soldiers in the American Army, War of the Revolution, in South Carolina. George W. Adair was born in Morgan County, March 1, 1823. His father was John Fisher Adair, and his mother was Mary Slaven Adair, of a Virginia family of French descent.

When George was two years of age his parents moved with him to DeKalb County, Ga., and bought a farm five miles south of Decatur. His mother died in 1834. Owing to the lack of school facilities the boy's education was limited. At the age of twelve his father placed him with Mr. G.B. Butler in his general store at Decatur, Ga. The boy proved to be faithful and trustworthy, and Mr. Butler had confidence in him.

The banking system was crude in those days. The merchant had to take the cash with him to the wholesale market, or to pay a debt where credit had been extended. Mr. Butler had to meet a debt on one occasion, in Augusta. He could not leave home at the time, so he sent the boy, George W. Adair, with the money to Augusta. Mrs. Butler sewed the money up in Gorge's clothes and put him on the stagecoach and started him on the long, tedious trip (there were no railroads in those days). He attended to it promptly and correctly and returned on time.

"*To be reliable is a fortune*" was George W. Adair's motto. It was a fortune to him, for everybody had confidence in him. He remained with Mr. Butler in the store until 1840, during which time he had the advantage of only a few months at school.

After Mr. Butler retired form business, Col. James N. Calhoun, Charles Murphey, Wm. H. Dabney and Doctor Ephriam M. Poole, having noticed that he was unusually sprightly boy, made up a syndicate among themselves, each taking stock equally in the expenses, and sent George to school for two years, where he obtained the best education that could be had in the village academy of that day. At the end of that time he went to Covington and read law with Floyed & Williamson, and was admitted to the bar in 1844, but, being in debt for his education, and having no capital, and as the people were just passing out of a panic or financial depression, he abandoned the idea of practicing law, and accepted a position as passenger conductor on the Georgia Railroad, which was just being completed into Atlanta. The late Richard Peters was Superintendent, and J. Edgar Thompson was Chief Engineer of this railroad. Adair ran on this road until he paid benefactors all the money, with interest, and that they had advanced for his education.

He then accepted a situation in Covington, Ga., as a clerk with Cary Wood, who was his relative and with whom he boarded during the time he was studying law in the place.

After a short while he accepted a situation in a wholesale house in Charleston, S.C., where he remained two years.

In 1860 he took an active part in politics and was delegate from the state at large to the convention in Baltimore which nominated Bell and Everett for President and Vice-President, respectively, whose motto was, "Union, the Constitution, and Enforcement of the Laws." Political excitement ran very high at this period in history.

The fire-eaters had determined on succession as a remedy for the evil complained of, especially the constant war that was made on the institution of slavery by the Republican party, or as it was then called the Abolition party. He took the same view that was entertained by Alexander H. Stephens, Benjamin H. Hill, and many other leading members of the Whig party, and made the stump speeches vigorously on the line of co-operation or contending for our rights within the Union, and with his friends, Col. Calhoun and Thomas Moore, no of this county, was a candidate for the State Convention on the cooperation side, but just a few days before the election FORT SUMTER was fired upon, which so inflamed the public mind that no conservation could resist the tidal wave of succession, and these candidates were defeated. Doctor James F. alexander, Col. Luther Glenn and Doctor J.T. Logan were the successful candidates on the succession side.

At the commencement of the war, he associated with J. Henry Smith in launching a new daily paper called The Southern Confederacy, which was published in Atlanta. This paper was published with marked ability. It had bright and reliable correspondents in every army corps in the country, and built up the largest circulation that any army paper had ever had in the South previous to that time. Its policy was to sustain the Confederate Congress, and to vigorously prosecute the war of defense.

At the battle of Chickamauga, Capt. N.B. Forrest was wounded, and came down to Atlanta, where he remained with Col. Adair until he recovered. Forrest, being restive, disliking to serve under the ranking generals, was given, by President Davis and the war department, the privilege of forming an independent calvary command. Col. Adair sold out his newspaper interests, and Gen. Forrest made the following appointment:

Headquarters, Atlanta, Ga., Nov. 16, 1863, --G.A. Adair has this day been appointed Aid de camp on my staff and will be respected and obeyed as such.

N. B. FORREST,
Major General.

Colonel Adair accepted the appointment and proceeded, accompanied by Governor Isham G. Harris, to West Tennessee, where Forrest soon rallied his famous cavalry command that so distinguished themselves until the close of the war.

After the surrender Col. Adair returned to Atlanta and went actively into business as a dealer in real estate in which he continued to the end of his business career. He developed a great talent as a salesman and auctioneer. He was the first to introduce subdivisions of blocks and tracts of land and public sales of real estate at auction, in which he continued to be very successful. Col. Adair conducted large sales in Alabama and Tennessee also.

He took an active part in every movement that tended towards the promotion, building up and improvement of the city. He was not an office hunter, but served the city as councilman and water commissioner, and the county as county commissioner, and was elected to the constitutional convention in 1865 upon his return to Atlanta.

Colonel Adair was one of Atlanta's best known and most popular pioneer citizens. He saw the city grow from a small village to its present size and was one of those who worked for the best interests and welfare of Atlanta. He was a public-spirited man, with more than the ordinary foresight into the future, and from the first predicted great things for the growing community. Having been conductor of one of the first trains that ever ran out of Atlanta, he evinced considerable interest in the development of the city as a railroad center.

Colonel Adair was best known, however, as a real estate dealer, and as such sold more Atlanta property than anyone else in the city. He established himself in this line just after the Civil War and continued it through his business career.

As an auctioneer, his reputation was more than local, and he was accounted one of the brightest wits, as well as one of the most genial personalities, in the business. As a story=teller he was without a peer, and no barbecue was complete without his presence. He was always the life of the party, and some of his best stories have traversed the continent.

His native gift of oratory, ready wit, clear analysis, genial nature and public spirit qualified him for public office. Energetic, administrative, discerning, and with broad views, he was a progressive and influential citizen and a powerful factor of public growth.

1854

656. Col. George Washington Adair=Miss Mary Jane Perry

Progeny: Seven Children

657.	I	Mary Adair.
658.	II	Robin Adair.
659.	III	Jack Adair.
660.	IV	Forrest Adair.
661.	V	Sallie Adair.
662.	VI	Annie Adair.
663.	VII	George Adair.

1876

657. Miss Mary Adair=Mr. G. A. Howell

Daughter of Col. G.W. Adair

And Mrs. Jane Perry Adair

Progeny: Four Children

663.	I	Mary Howell, m McCarley.
664.	II	Carry Howell, m Milner.
665.	III	G.A. Howell, Jr.
666.	IV	Ruth Howell, d young, unmarried.

1907

663. Miss Mary Howell=P.D. McCarley

Daughter of G.A. and Mary

Adair Howell

Progeny: Three Daughters

Forrest Adair, Financier of Atlanta

667. I   Mary Adair McCarley, b 1908.
668. II   Annie Elizabeth McCarley, b 1910.
669. III Alice Caroline McCarley, b 1915.

1907

664. Carrie Howell=Mr. N. Milner
Daughter of G.A. and
Mary Adair Howell

Progeny: None

665. Mr. G.A. Howell, Jr.=Catherine Mitchell
Son of G.A. and Mary
Adair Howell.

Progeny: Two daughters

670. I   Katherine Howell, b 1911.
671. II   Mary Adair Howell, b 1913.
672. III G. Arthur Howell, b 1916.

660. Forrest Adair=----------
Son of Col. G.W. Adair

Progeny: Four Children

673. I   Elizabeth Adair, m Robert Gregg; one child, Bettie
674. II   Frank Adair, m Margaret Ladson; no children.
675. III Forrest Adair, Jr.
676. IV   Robin Adair, m Mary Butler; one child, b 1918.

661. Miss Sallie Adair=Marshall Eckford
Daughter of Col. G.W. and
Jane Perry Adair

Progeny: Two Sons

677. I   George Adair Eckford, b 1898.
678. II   Errol Eckford, b 1902.

662. Miss Annie Adair=W.E. Foster
Daughter of Col. G.W. and
Mrs. Jane Perry Adair.

Progeny: None

George Adair=---
Son of Col. G.W. Adair and
Mrs. Jane Perry Adair.

Progeny: Seven Children

679. I   Perry Adair, b 1899.
680. II   George Adair, b 1901.
681. III Sarah Adair, b 1912.
682. IV   Jack Adair, b 1913.
683. V   Mary Jane Adair, b 1915.

684. VI   Forrest Adair, b 1917.
685. VII   Glenn Adair, b 1921.

FORREST ADAIR THE NOTED FINANCIER

Forrest Adair is a son of the late Colonel George W. Adair of Atlanta, and the following is his lineage: George W., John Fisher, John Joseph, Jr., Joseph, Sr., Thomas Adair.

John Adair, Joseph Adair, Jr., and Joseph Adair, Sr., were all soldiers in the American Army, War of the Revolution, in South Carolina.

The Adair Realty and Trust Company, of which Mr. Adair is president, is often referred to in national conventions of real estate and insurance men as one of the best organized real estate businesses in America. It has departmentalized the real estate business, and is, in fact, a sort of real estate department store, which will sell you a lot, lend you the money to build anything from a cottage to a skyscraper, modern hotel or department store; build the cottage, skyscraper, modern hotel, or department store for you; insure the property for you; sell your bonds for you, and act as your trustee.

This company operates in every city of 20,000 inhabitants between Washington and El Paso, and it knows the South and every Southern city as it knows Atlanta. It was probably the first to induce the big insurance companies in the East to lend their millions in the South.

This works for the upbuilding of the South, as illustrated in the case of Lakeland, Florida.

It is said that there are not many pieces of active real estate in Atlanta that haven't at some time passed through the hands of the Adairs. Its annual business today runs to $12,000,000 or $15,000,000, which doesn't begin to represent the values of the properties handled in the course of a year.

Forrest Adair has done as much as any other one man to reduce the real estate business in the South to something like a science. He suggested that the Gorgia School of Technology put in a chair of real estate and outlined a course of study in real estate for that college that has since become a pattern for many other colleges and universities.

There is no bronze grille, no partitions of oak and glass, separating the desk of Forest Adair from the rest of the works, or from the public. He is the most accessible man in the place.

We were chatting about some of the things he is interested in, especially his activities outside of his business.

"You know," he said, with great earnestness, "I believe profoundly in the law of compensation, and I believe that a Supreme Being keeps books on us—a Supreme Being who has the only perfect system of bookkeeping ever invented.

"You get out of his life exactly what you put into it; no more., no less. You can't fool the bookkeeper. Many of your rewards and punishments will be meted out to you right here.

"If you desire happiness for yourself, you must create happiness for others; if you desire health, you must pay for it; if you would sow wild oats, you must resolve to go back over our ground and grub the very last one of them. If you sow your wild oats too young in life, and wait too long to dig them up, you will find they have grown thick and rough and taken deep roots, making the grubbing all the harder for you.

"You can't expect to plant weeds and thistles and have shade trees grow up and shelter and bless you in your old age. And you can't expect life to be a bed of roses for you unless you plant a few rosebushes.

"The farmer who takes everything out of the soil and puts nothing back finds himself in his old age starved on barren acres. It's the way of all life. You reap exactly what you sow; that's not only the gospel truth, it's scientific truth."

"The real estate business is a science," Mr. Adair insists. "Real estate values used to be based entirely upon somebody's opinion, and that somebody's opinion may have been not worth a hang.

"This was first brought home to me in a forcible way in a court trial here in Atlanta twenty-five years ago. I wasn't interested in either party in the litigation, but I dropped into the courtroom because the case involved a real estate transaction. Each side had a formidable array of witnesses, and each witness had been summoned to give his opinion as to the value of the property in litigation. The side that had the most witnesses won.

"The stupidity and injustice of the thing aroused me. I advised the attorney for the losing side to take on appeal and told him to cut out most of his witnesses next time, and put two or three real estate experts on the stand. He took an appeal, got a new trial, and with expert testimony won his case in the new trial. He won because the jury got facts and not opinions.

"Real Estate values are not guessed at anymore. They are accurately determined. For instance: We put a young man with a clicker on any business corner in any city South. He clicks off every man who passes that corner in a day. We know that 30 percent of the men who pass would enter a cigar store placed there, and we know that the average purchase of these men would be twenty cents apiece.

"Given the exact number of men who pass that corner, we can

determine with fair accuracy the amount of sales a tobacco stand on that corner will make in a year, and we know that a cigar store or drug store can afford to pay ten percent of its gross sales for rent. The value of that stand as a cigar or drug store location is thereby scientifically determined.

"Of course, the two I have mentioned are exceptional businesses. Many other lines probably couldn't pay more than five percent. Department stores, as a rule, cannot afford to pay more than one and a half percent of their gross sales for rent."

There are upward of a hundred men and women in the Adair organization in Atlanta. They are mostly young people. Some who have been with the firm nearly a quarter of a century are still young. There is a glow of good health and friendliness in every face, and everybody is full of orderly pep.

"We catch 'em young, and then we keep 'em young." Says Mr. Adair. "Young folks are easy to teach. They don't have too many fool theories and mistakes to unlearn. Take a man of forty-five years and put him in here, and you would have to spend months and months unteaching him before you could begin to teach him.

"Before we employ young men or young women we get their personal and family history. Then we require them to undergo a physical examination to determine the state of their health. At the end of six months, we give each of them a thousand-dollar life insurance policy. That calls for another physical examination. At the end of two years, we give another thousand dollars' insurance, and that gives us another examination, making three examinations in two years. By that time each individual is a conscious part of the organization and has caught the good-health idea. Then he ought to be capable of looking out for himself.

"I choose new employees as carefully as I would choose companions for my wife and daughter. In fact, there isn't a boy or a girl in the business who is not a welcome associate of my wife and daughter.

"We believe in training our own employees for every responsible position in the firm. I have found that we draw our best assistants from the ranks of college-bred men. The college man usually has a keener mind and an ability to grasp things more quickly than a man who has had no college training. We take young men during the summer vacation period, principally young fellows who are working their way through college, and who need summer employment to help them out. Many of these develop rapidly and are equipped for full-time employment with us when they finish at college.

"That's better than picking men up anywhere and everywhere and trying them out, only to have to fire a lot of them. It's easy to discourage and handicap a young fellow starting out in life by putting him in the wrong job and then telling him he's no good for it. It's you who may have made the mistake; but you may send that young fellow away with the idea that the mistake is his, and that he is a failure. That's an injustice to him."

Getting him back to the story of his own life, Mr. Adair said:

"I was graduated at the Boys' High School in Atlanta when I was fifteen years old. That was in 1879. I came home from the graduating exercises, and the family was sitting around waiting for bedtime. Mother was doing some knitting, and Father was reading a book.

"Presently Father turned down the corner of a page, laid his book said and said, 'Son, you have finished high school, and now we've got to plan to send you to college this fall.'

"'Father,' I replied, 'I've been thinking it over, and I've decided I don't want to go to college. I want to go in the office with you and learn the real estate business after I have had my vacation.'

"Next morning Father came up to my room and woke me up, asking me to have breakfast with him. We ate in silence. After breakfast he hitched the old horse to the buggy and asked me to climb up in the buggy with him. We had no automobiles and no street cars in those days. He drove down to the office, and all the way down we didn't say a word to each other.

"We got to the office. Father took me in and introduced me to one of his men, a Mr. Evans. He told Evans I wanted to learn the business, and to take me in hand and use me just as he would use any other boy, forgetting I was the son of the boss.

"I did an office boy's work around the place until night. On my way back home with Father I said, 'I think you misunderstood me last night. I said I wanted to learn the real estate business after I had my vacation.'

"'I didn't misunderstand you at all,' he answered. 'But businessmen don't have vacations. Vacations are for schoolboys, and you told me you didn't want to be a schoolboy anymore.'

"I relate this incident because it is characteristic of the training I got under my father. He was something of a philosopher.

"Now let me say right here that the sooner a man acquires a philosophy of life, the longer he will live, the happier he will be, and the more use he will be to himself, his family, his friends and humanity. A very fortunate thing happened to me when I was thirty-five years old and going good and recklessly, giving no thought to my health. I was suddenly fetched up with an attack of biliousness that laid me up for a week. Then I began to think.

"There are lots of factories that work twenty-four hours a day, seven days in the week. The result is every now and then something goes wrong, and they have to shut down, which means laying everybody off. They haven't given their firemen and stokers a chance to clean out the boilers. The boilers wear out and they have to get new ones.

"Here I had been going like one of those factories. But I had only one boiler and, if that played out, I wouldn't know where to shop for another. I began to use a little common sense about my stomach. I found out what it was for and what I could reasonably expect of it.

"Ever since that time I have given that organ so much work to do, and no more. I eat three meals a day, and when my stomach has taken care of them it lays off and stores up the necessary gastric juices to take care of the next meal. In twenty years now I haven't eaten a sandwich, a piece of candy, a plate of ice cream, a bag of peanuts or a piece of fruit between meals.

"The man who runs out to a soda fountain and gets a sandwich and a heavy drink between meals, or who eats and apple every time he passes a fruit stand, or who goes to the ball game in the afternoon and eats hot-dogs and peanuts to help pass away the time, is simply punishing his stomach, wearing out his digestive apparatus unnecessarily, and crippling his efficiency.

"A man must keep his health if he is going to love is work, or love anything else.

"I love my work so that I had rather take a vacation at my desk than anywhere else in the world. That desk is the most desirable place on earth to me, outside my own hearth.

"A man must keep his health to love his work, and he must love his work if he is going to enable it and make a genuine 'go' of it. My father taught me that, and I have taught that to my boys. I have three sons, and every one of them is here in this business, the head of some department of it, and every one of them the master of his job.

"In the very beginning of our married life Mrs. Adair and I threw a certain old-fashioned motto out of our home—if it was ever in our home. It was that one about 'A child should be seen and not heard.' They used to hand-embroider that fool notion, frame it, and hang it up in the sitting-room to stare at the kids from morning until night.

"Now, augmentative ability, the art of expression, should be the most important part of a child's education, and where under the sun can a child learn that so readily as in his own home, with his own parents? My children were always taught to talk back; not to be saucy, impudent, or insolent, you understand; but just to come right out with anything that was on their minds. If they disagreed with me, they were supposed to say so, and I would fight it out with them in an argument—not with a razor strap or a hickory switch.

"In that way, not only were their own wits developed, but we developed a bond of sympathy and understanding that has made us good pals through life. The bests way to awaken and invigorate a child's mind is by keep discussion, and the best place in the world to stage this is around you own fireside or dining table."

If you should go to Atlanta and look up Forrest Adair and not find him at his desk, you would likely find him in some hospital ward in that Southern metropolis, for ministering to the sick is his hobby.

"I never saw another man like him," a famous orthopedic surgeon of Atlanta said to me. "Other rich men send us a case and tell us to send them the bill, and that is their final interest in it. But not so with Forrest Adair. He had brought me many cases, and every time he follows them up from day to day.

"Somehow, he finds time every day to run out to the hospital and see how his protégés are getting along, and when they are discharged from the hospital he follows them out into life and sees that they do not lose heart or have a relapse."

Five thousand crippled children in Georgia call him "Papa Adair." Hundreds of poor people look upon him as a benefactor. Almost every man, woman and child in Atlanta knows him. He has given the equivalent of several fortunes to the sick, the halt, the lame, the blind, and the purely indigent, making no fuss about it.

It is known, moreover, that he carries a fund of several thousand dollars in his private vault, to have the cash always handy when someone needs his help.

He is a familiar figure in many hospital wards in Atlanta, and his most intimate friends are physicians, surgeons, and nurses. He is one of the richest men in Atlanta, is called the busiest man in Atlanta, has as many friends as any other man in that Southern city; and if there is anyone in these United States who gets more out of life at sixty years of age than Forrest Adair, his name just isn't in the books, that's all.—Abstract of an article written by W.O. Saunders for the American Magazine.

CHAPTER XXXVI
JONES ADAIR

22 Jones Adair (John, Joseph, Jr., Joseph, Sr., Thomas Adair), was born in Laurens County, S.C., about 1798, and in 1800 was brought to Georgia with the family by his father, who settled in or adjoining Morgan County.

Jones Adair was a farmer and trader, and very genial and kind, consequently, very popular. He was very strongly opposed to succession at the outset of the war between the States. His oldest son of the younger set of children, Leander Adair, was killed in the Confederate Army in the battle of Chickamauga. His father went in as soon as the battle was over and got the body of his son, brought it home and buried it. Lee was one of nature's nobleman, a very worthy son, and his death was a source of great and continued grief to his father and mother. Adair never ceased to blame the Confederate leaders for the horrors of the war between the States.

Jones Adair was married twice, and was the father of twelve children, seven by his first wife and five by his second wife, but he lost two or three of them in infancy and childhood. It seems that he lived for quite a while in an unsanitary location, and hence his children died from malarial disease, and not from any hereditary ailments.

(First Marriage) Jones Adair=Miss Woods
(Second Marriage) Jones Adair=Polly Ann Shields

The following were his children who lived to be grown:

686. I William Franklin Adair was a civil and locomotive engineer. He helped to survey and construct the Georgia Railroad from Madison to Atlanta, then took a locomotive and ran the first train into Atlanta and ran as a locomotive engineer for many years. He married, first, Mary Melton. She died and he married Miss Thrasher. Two girls born to this marriage. He died in Morgan County in 1919.
687. II Mary Adair, m Tom Estes; buried at Lemiel's Church.
688. III and IV were girls and both died in infancy.
689. V Mandy Adair, m a Skelton; buried at Prospect.
690. VI Fannie Adair, m Tom Welburn; buried at Prospect.
691. VII Virgil Jones Adair, m Miss Moore; d in 1905, age 74, and was buried at Prospect.

JOSEPH BENJAMIN ADAIR

691. Joseph Benjamin Adair was the son of Jones Adair and Polly Ann Shields Adair.

Lineage from His First American Ancestor

6 Joseph Benjamin Adair, 5 Jones Adair, 4 John Adair, 3 Joseph Adair, Jr., 2 Joseph Adair, Sr., 1 Thomas Adair.

He was born in Morgan County, Ga., and spent his whole life there, except the time he was in the Confederate Army. He was a cotton planter and his whole time was taken up with that work and the rearing of his children.

He was opposed to the War Between the States, but when it became necessary for him to fight for his State or against it, he of course went into the Confederate Army with the Georgia troops and remained there until the end of the war.

He was a worthy citizen, honorable in all the relations of life. He was born about 1841, and died Feb. 21, 1916, age about 75 years. Was married twice.

1866

691. Joseph Benjamin Adair=Lizzie Stovall, b —; d 1867.

Progeny: One child

Lizzie Adair, who married Ben Chappell of Carroll County. They have one child.

692. Mamie Chappell, who married John Summerville on April 17, 1917, a civil engineer; home in Washington, D.C.

Second Marriage, April 22, 1869

691. Joseph Benjamin Adair=Amanda Cordelia Stovall
Sister of his first wife.

Progeny: Fourteen Children

693.	I	Mary Ann Adair, b Nov. 25, 1870; m J.H. Harper; 4 children, 2 of them d.
694.	II	Sally P. Adair, b Dec. 11, 1871; d 1872.
695.	III	Cornelia Amanda Adair, b March 4, 1873; m George L. King.
696.	IV	Jones Adair, b Aug. 4, 1874; m Mamie Harris June 2, 1922. Have 1 son, Jones Harris Adair, born May 18, 1924.
697.	V	John Patrick Adair, b Dec. 3-, 1876; m Bessie Lee Young of Madison, 1917; 2 children: First, Susan Frances Adair, b Nov. 8, 1917; second, Martha Ellen Adair, b Jan. 23, 1921. The family lives near Rutledge.
698.	VI	Fannie E. Adair, b Jan. 6, 1879; m W.G. Williams of

Atlanta, April, 1911. Home, Atlanta; 7 children: First Bessie Evelin Williams, b April 7, 1902; m James B. Bryson of Atlanta, June 11, 1921; no children; home, Atlanta. Second, Donie Williams, b Sept. 15, 1903. Third, Cordelia Williams, b Feb. 16, 1906. Fourth Howard Williams, b Oct. 23, 1908; d 1912. Fifth, Herbert Williams, born Nov. 12, 1910. Sixth, Wesley Williams, b Dec. 25, 1912. Seventh, Perry Williams, b Dec. 14, 1914.

699. VII Alvin R. Adair, b March 13, 1880; m Corine Shaw of Rutledge, April 24, 1921; lives near Farmington, Ga.

700. VIII Donnie Adair, b Feb. 17, 1882; d in infancy.

701. IX Inez Melvina Adair, b April 17, 1884; me L.P. Banks, July, 1908; home, Columbus, Ga. No children.

702. X James Franklin Adair, b July, 1887. He was a soldier of the World War, and after being honorably discharged, came home and he and his brother, Alvin R. Adair, married sisters at the same time, with the same ceremony, at Rutledge; Alvin R. m Miss Corine Shaw, and James Franklin m Miss Thelma Shaw, April 24, 1921; all live in the same house. James Franklin and wife have 1 daughter, Clemathene, b July 22, 1923.

703. XI Joseph Benjamin Adair, Jr., b March 20, 1889; m Maggie Hinton of Covington, Ga., Jan 2, 1916; have 2 children; First, Mindelle Hinton Adair b Oct. 31, 1916. Second, James Nimon Adair, b Sept 15, 1918. Third, Sarah Barnes Adair, b Aug. 4, 1920. Joseph Benjamin Adair's family now live at Farmington, Ga.

704. XII Zida Una Adair, b Feb. 4, 1891; graduated a Westlian Female College, Macon, Ga., May, 1918. Taught school until 1921; m G.A. Lakey of Fort Gains, Ga., where they now reside.

705. XIII Alonzo Burnett Adair, b Aug. 19, 1892; d March 11, 1998 (diphtheria).

706. XIV Radford Riden Adair, b Oct. 11, 1895; he served about a year in the World War, of which six months were in France. After returning home he married Miss Sue Simpkins of Asheville, N.C., May, 1920. Residence, Asheville, N.C.

Recapitulation

Fifteen children, two of whom died in childhood.

Seventeen grandchildren, of whom two died in infancy.

One great-grandchild

JAMES WILLIAM ADAIR

707. James William was the third son, the second family of Uncle Jones Adair. He was born about 1848 and is married to Nannie Malcom of Morgan County. The live near Fairlay, same county.

707. James William Adair=Nannie Malcom
Progeny: Thirteen Children

708.	I	Eddie, m Nannie Mitchell; 6 children living and 1 dead.
709.	II	Mattie Lue, m Lit Howard; 7 children; live near Bostwick, Ga.
710.	III	Augustus Gainway, m Maud Peters; 1 son; live near Fairplay.
711.	IV	Hardy, m Mood Peters; 2 daughters
712.	V	Anna, m C.F. Riden, M.D.; 7 children and live in Bostwick.
713.	VI	Eva, m Frank McHugh; have 5 children and live near Bostwick.
714.	VII	Virdie, m John Peters; have no children; live near Goodhope Ga.
715.	VIII	Jeffie Shields; m Jewel Curtis; have 3 boys; live near Rutledge.
716.	IX	Lonnie Lou, died unmarried; buried at Prospect.
717.	X	Claud, m Mabel Herron; no children; live near Rutledge.
718.	XI	Maud, m Hugh Herron; have 2 children and live at Hazelhurse, in South Georgia.
718.	XII	Grady, m Model Malcom; have 1 boy and live near Fairplay
719.	XIII	Zilla, m S.V. Garret, April 27, 1916; live near Logansville.

720. Augustus R. Adair was the fourth son of Jones and Polly Ann Shields Adair. Was born about 1852; died 1916. Was a farmer and postmaster at Waco, Ga., for many years. Twice married.

(First Marriage) **720** Augustus R. Adair=Eliza Adams
Daughter of Hyram Adams of Clayton Co.
Progeny: Three Children

720. Augustus R. Adair=Annie Styles
Progeny: Four Children
Children, First Family:

721.	I	Beffee, m H.G. Entrekin and lately died at Bremen, her home; 2 boys, Harry and Lenard Entrekin.
722.	II	Willie, m Johnnie Riggs; 1 girl, Willie Jewel Riggs; d about 1911.
723.	III	Lealia, m Emery Upchurch; they live at Bremen and have 2

girls, Eunice and Virginia, live in Carrolton, Ga.

Second Family:

724. IV   Gussie Adair.
725. V   Bennie Jewel Adair.
726. VI   Josie Adair.
727. VII   Allain Adair.

PATRICK L. ADAIR

Patrick L. Adair is probably the youngest grandson of John Adair, the Revolutionary soldier, who was a grandson of Joseph Adair Sr., who was a quarter master in the Revolutionary Army at the age of 70 years. His lineage would run back as follows:

6 Patrick, 5 Jones, 4 John, 3 Jospeh, Jr., 2 Joseph, Sr., 1 Thomas Adair.

Patrick Adair was born March 17, 1854. He is a farmer and lives near Farmington, Ga. He married Florence W. Harper, born May 2, 1867, a daughter of Jeeb Harper. They have 11 children (at this date, May 23, 1916), all living and only 1 married.

1890

728. Patrick L. Adair=Florence Harper

Progeny: Eleven Children-four sons, seven daughters

729. I   James Baldwin Adair, b March, 1891.
730. II   Marther Graves Adair, b Sept. 10, 1892.
731. III   Apheals Everline Adair, b Sept. 26, 1893.
732. IV   Neelie Amanda Adair, b Jan. 7, 1895.
733. V   George Lee Adair, b May 3-, 1897.
734. VI   Augustus Reed Adair, b 1899.
735. VII   Ruby Sumaria Adair, b March 5, 1901.
736. VIII   Sallie Claud Jones Adair, b March 4, 1902.
737. IX   Frances Jane Adair, b April 28, 1905.
738. X   Mary Anton Adair, b April 28, 1905.
739. XI   Silby Harris Adair, b June 4, 1908.

Uncle Jones died in 1883, age 85 years. At the present date, 12 children, 61 grandchildren, 50 great-grandchildren. Total, 123 descendants.

CHAPTER XXXVII

AUGUSTUS DIXON ADAIR
Merchant Prince of Atlanta

Lineage

A.D. Adair, 5 James Adair, 4 John Adair, 3 Joseph Adair, Jr., 2 Joseph Adair Sr., 1 Thomas Adair.

Thomas Adair, born in Antrim Co., Ireland, 1680, came to America, 1730, to Pennsylvania.

Joseph Adair, Sr., born in Antrim Co., Ireland, 1711, came to America, 1730, to Pennsylvania.

Joseph Adair, Jr., born in Pennsylvania, 1733; came to South Carolina 1750.

John Adair, born in South Carolina, 1758; came to Georgia 1800.

James Adair, born in Georgia, 1806; came to Alabama 1820.

Joseph Adair, Sr., Joseph Adair, Jr., and John Adair were all soldiers in the American Army, War of the Revolution, in South Carolina.

James Adair, eleventh child of John Adair, the Revolutionary soldier, was born in Morgan County, Ga., in 1806; he migrated a few years after the death of his father, to Alabama, and lived with his brother, Farmer Adair. Soon after this he commenced his mercantile career at Independence, Ala.

He bought a stock of goods on credit and did a large business a few years at Independence and Hambleton, Autoga County. He soon paid all his debts and made money by the thousands. He also ran a tannery in connection with his mercantile business. In 1835 he moved to Talladega, Ala., and bought a farm, becoming a planter. He intended building a store and carrying on his business there but suffered a sunstroke soon after his removal to Talladega, which resulted in his going blind. He continued to live for ten years after this stroke, but never recovered his sight, and finally died in 1845 with inflammation of the brain.

1826

740. James Adair=Sarah Dean of Ga., at Independence, Ala.
Son of John Adair and Jennie Jones Adair.
Progeny: Ten Children

Augustus Dixon Adair, Late Merchant Prince of Atlanta

741.	I	Infant, d unnamed.
742.	II	Jefferson Hayden Adair, Captain in Civil War, d in 74th year in Arkansas.
743.	III	Emily Tinsley Adair, m Mr. Derick.
744.	IV	Hamilton Weyman Adair; d age 34 in Federal prison at Elmira, N.Y.; was a Confederate soldier, captured at the battle of Petersburg, VA. He left a wife and 3 children.
745.	V	Augustus Dixon Adair (we called him Cousin Dick); served in the war on the staff of Gen. N.B. Forrest.
746.	VI	Green Buron Adair, served through the war, army of Virginia.
	VII	Amanda Jane Adair; first m W.A. McCarty and was mother of McCarty Brothers (firm of A.D. Adair and McCarty Bros.), and daughter, Willie Dunson. M 2nd F.A. Moore.
747.	VIII	Walter Dean Adair, a war veteran and former partner in the mercantile firm of Adair & Bros.
748.	IX	Martha Susan Adair, m J.L.R. Barrett; mother of Walter Green Barrett and Edward Dixon Barrett.
749.	X	Sarah Alabama Adair, m Warren H. Campbell at Gainesville, Ga. Mother of Mrs. L.D. Watson of Atlanta and Mrs. Charles West of Savanah.

About 1869 or 1870 the Adair Brothers built a new residence in Gainesville, Ga., and moved their mother and sisters there from Talladega, Ala.

745. Augustus Dixon Adair, the fifth child of James and Sarah Dean Adair, was born at Talladega, Ala., July 17, 1835, just before the removal of the Indians from there to the Territory. He was born and raised on a farm and had to work, although his father had a plantation and several slaves. His father died when he was 10 years of age, and his mother had the work and responsibility of raising and educating the family of little children, and she made a wonderful success of it. Too much praise cannot be bestowed in such a case.

Five sons in the family were Confederate soldiers. One of them died in a federal prison, but none of them was killed in battle. A.D. Adair (his mother called him Dixon) received a grammar and high school education in the neighborhood school and town academy. After he attained his majority, he left the farm in charge in younger brothers and he began clerking for George Butler at Childressburg, Ala. This was in 1856. He left his employment in 1857 and began teaching school in the bend of the river, known as the Ferguson settlement in Talledaga County, Ala. He continued to teach this school until the following year. At that time, at the invitation of his cousin,

George W. Adair, he came to Atlanta, Ga., to commence his business career. Cousin George secured him a position with Halfin & Meyers (dry goods), where he remained one month. Then he secured a position with a new house, Salmons and Simmons, on Whitehall Street, and remained with these people three years until 1861. After Dixon came with them, they moved down to what is known as the Brown & Allen corner, southeast corner Alabama and Whitehall streets. After leaving this firm He was taken into partnership with the firm of Anderson, Adair & Co., composed of A.T. Anderson, G.W. Adair and A.D. Adair as the junior member. This firm did a general commission business for two years and then sold out to Anderson & Johnson in the winter of 1863.

Then Dixon Adair went out West with his cousin, G.W. Adair, to join Gen. N.B. Forrest. George W. Adair was appointed to the General's staff, and A.D. Adair joined his escort, and was detailed as a non-commissioned officer to run the blockade business and buy cotton and sell the same in Memphis, and to get out army supplies. This he did successfully until the spring of 1864, when the Federal General Warren was placed at Memphis and ordered by General Grant to stop all blockading. A.D. Adair was in the enemy's lines at the time and was captured by the Federal troops and taken to Memphis to Warren's headquarters for trial as a spy. Testimony could not be found sufficient to convict him, however, and he was released. A guard was sent to escort the prisoner through the lines, which they did, after first relieving him of all the money on his person. Adair had exchanged his uniform with the telegraph operator and left his side arms at Senatobia, Miss., so that when captured he was in citizen's clothes and unarmed.

On being released, he gathered all the goods and money out on the line and took them to Verona, Miss., where General Forrest was encamped at the time, and making his report, fell back in line, where he remained during the remainder of the war, and surrendered at Gainesville, Ala., on the Tombigbee River, in May, 1865.

A.D. Adair says he was at twenty or thirty skirmishes and several of the large battles, including Murphreesboro, Tenn,; Columbia, Tenn.; Franklin, Tenn.; Athens, Ala.; Sulphur Trestle, Ala., and Selma, Ala.

At the close of the war Mr. A.D. Adair returned to Atlanta, after spending two months in Alabama. On his return to Atlanta, July 3, 1865, he found the city in ruins but was fortunate enough to find a house on this lot on Calhoun Street (now known as Piedmont Avenue, near where the medical college now stands—southeast corner of Piedmont Avenue and Gilmer Street).

This house he rented to his cousin, Col. George W. Adair, and he lived there with Col. G.W. Adair for the space of one year, the G.W. Adair residence in West End having been burned during the war.

In 1866 A.D. Adair entered into partnership with L.C. and T.L. Wells, under the firm name of Wells, Adair & Co., but in the fall of 1867, Adair sold out to Wells and formed a partnership with Judge W.W. Clayton under the name of Clayton & Adair. At the expiration of a year and a half, Judge Clayton's interest was bought out, and the business was continued on Whitehall Street under the name of Adair and Brother, A.D. Adair having taken his brother, Green B. Adair, into the firm. Shortly afterward they took in their younger brother, Walter Dean Adair, and the name then read Adair and Brothers. Walter D. Adair die in 1876, and Green B. Adair retired in 1891. Then A.D. Adair took two of his nephews, George W. and James D. McCarthy, into partnership under the name of A.D. Adair and McCarthy Brothers, as it now stands.

(The foregoing is an abstract of the autobiography of Augustus Dixon Adair, the merchant prince of Atlanta. This abstract written since his death in 1922 at the age of 87 years.)

Cousin Dick Adair was only 10 years old when his father died; therefore, his mother raised him and looked out for his education to the best of her ability, and Dick always looked out for his mother and assisted her in the care and education of the younger set of children. He started all his younger brothers and some of his nephews in business.

A.D. Adair was a model husband and father. He was broadminded, liberal and honorable in his dealings with the public, and the business world had confidence in him; his credit was unlimited. During the panic in the early nineties, when he needed operating capital in his business, it was no trouble for him to borrow $50,000 through brokers in New York. Of course, that would be considered a small sum now in this flush and prosperous period, but it was extraordinary under the conditions prevailing at that time.

A.D. Adair was elected treasurer of the Southern Baptist Convention and re-elected many years. It was a pleasure to correspond with him, because he was always punctual and attentive.

Augustus Dixon Adair knew more Adairs and more Adair traditions than anyone else.

He amassed quite a fortune, the amount of which the writer does now know. A.D. Adair, Jr., takes his father's place in the firm of A.D. Adair and McCarthy Brothers in Atlanta. They are miners and manufacturers of phosphates and wholesale dealers in fertilizers.

745. Augustus Dixon Adair=Octavia Hammond
Son of James and   Daughter of Judge Dannis
Sarah Dean Adair.   F. Hammond of Atlanta

Progeny: Six Children

750.	I	Adelene Adair, m Julian of Atlanta, June, 1893.
751.	II	Sarah Catherine Adair, d in infancy.
752.	III	Laura Isabell Adair, m S.G. Bonn of California, March 31, 1903.
753.	IV	Octavia Adair, d in infancy.
754.	V	Barbara Adair, m C.M. McClung of Knoxville, Tenn., March, 1905.
544.	VI	Augustus Dixon Adair, Jr., M Miss Boline Clark, April 22, 1911.

CHAPTER XXXVIII
JANE J. ADAIR-MCCORD
AND HER DESCENDANTS IN GEORGIA AND FLORIDA

Lineage from Her First American Ancestor
5 Joseph Alexander Adair, 4 John Adair, 3 Joseph Adair, Jr., 2 Joseph Adair, Sr., 1 Thomas Adair

1844

746. Jane J. Adair=Robert B. McCord
Daughter of Joseph Alexander and Elizabeth McCord Adair.

Progeny: Four Daughters, Two Sons

- 757. I Louisa Jane McCord, b March 29, 1846; m W.J. McMillian.
- 748. II James Washington McCord, b July 1, 1848; m Cornelia Walker.
- 749. III Fannie Elizabeth McCord, b Oct. 15, 1851; m R.T. Hinson.
- 750. IV Nancy Everlyn McCord, b Nov. 15, 1853; m John T. Dixon.
- 751. V Sallie Catherine McCord, b March 5, 1856; m W.T. Asbell.
- 752. VI Columbus Howard McCord, b May 18, 1862; m Mattie Cox.

1873

748. James Washington McCord=Cornelia Walker.
Son of Jane and Robert McCord
Occupation: Hotel business.

Progeny: Three Sons, One Daughter

- 753. I Mather M. McCord, b 1874. A physician in Rome, Ga.
- 754. II Robert B. McCord, Jr., b about 1876. Is Superintendent of Children's Home Society in Atlanta, Ga. Address, Hapeville, Ga.
- 755. III Guyte P. McCord, b about 1878. Is a lawyer and former Mayor of Tallahassee.
- 756. IV Pearl McCord, b 1880; m Paul Nicholson, a jeweler

1866

750. Nancy Everlyn McCord=John W. Dixon
Daughter of Robert and Jane McCord. A Contractor at Thomasville, Ga.

Progeny: Two Sons, Four Daughters

- 757. I Alma Dixon, b 1887, a nurse in Tallahassee, Fla.
- 758. II Clifton Dixon, d in infancy.

759. III   Mattie Howard Dixon, b 1880; m Frank L. Callender, a Methodist minister, at Freeburn, Minn., in Minnesota Conference. Have 2 children: Everlyn Jane Callender, b 1917; Frank P. Callender, Jr., b 1920.
760. IV   Mary Elizabeth Dixon, b 1892; a teacher and Satsuma orange grower.
761. V   Blanford Dixon, b 1894; m Robert L. McKenzie, fruit grower and naval stores operator of Panama City, Fla. They have 1 child, Annie Elizabeth MeKenzie, b Nov. 19, 1921.
762. VI   Orin K. Dixon, b Feb. 19, 1898. He served three years in the Navy during the World War; was in the mine-sweeping division that cleared the North Sea of mines after the Armistice was signed. Married Blanche Murphy of Boston, Mass. They have 2 children, Orin K., Jr., b Jan. 19, 1919; Paul Norman Dixon, b May 24, 1922. They live in Boston Mass.

GENEALOGY OF LOUISA MCCORD MCMILLAN
1865

757. Louisa Jane McCord=W.J. McMillan
Daughter of Robert and   A Planter
Jane McCord

    Progeny: Four Sons, Five Daughters

763. I   Olivia Matilda McMillan, b Oct. 12, 1866; m J.A. Sarrett.
764. II   David S. McMillan, b 1869; m Lucy Brown.
765. III   Beaulah H. McMillan, b 1871; m W.D. Golding.
766. IV   Charles W. McMillan, b 1871; m Ola Hicks.
767. V   Jessie D. McMillan, b 1876; m R.H. Mash.
768. VI   Thomas Hiram McMillan, b 1871; m Viola Norton.
769. VII   Hannah Jane McMillan, b 1881; m S.C. Sholas.
770. VIII   Minnie Lee McMillan, b 1884; m H.C. Barrett.
771. IX   William G. McMillan, b 1887; m Rosa Levern.

1887

763. Olivia Matilda McMillan=J.A. Sarrett
Daughter of W. J. and   A Mechanic
Louisa Jane McMillan.

    Progeny: Four Sons, Five Daughters

772. I   Allie May Sarrett, b June 15, 1888; m J.M. Richards
773. II   Lillie Belle Sarrett, b July 22, 1890; m J.T. Billingsly.
774. III   Mary Elizabeth Sarrett, b Feb. 28, 1893, m W.S. Gay.
775. IV   Samuel Hiram Sarrett, b Jan. 10, 1895; d March 17, 1913.
776. V   William Edward Sarrett, b March 18, 1897; d June 18, 1913.
777. VI   Martha Louise Sarrett, b Sept. 4, 1899; m T.H. Lewis

778. VII James Albert Sarrett, b April 30, 1902; machinist.
779. VIII Mabel Claire Sarrett, b Oct. 1, 1904; nurse.
780. IX Paul Clendenson Sarrett, b Jan. 1, 1909; student.

1894

764. David S. McMillan=Lucy Robinson

Son of W. J. and Louisa McMillan.

Occupation: Farmer in Mitchell Co., Ga.

Progeny: Three Sons, Two Daughters

781. I Georgie Lou McMillan, b 185; m ----.
782. II James Mack McMillan, b 1897; in U.S. Army.
783. III Edith McMillan, b 1899.
784. IV Harriet McMillan.
785. V Velia McMillan.

765. Beula H. McMillan=W.D. Golding

Daughter of W.J. and Louisa McMillan   A Farmer in Grady Co., Ga.

Progeny: Five Sons, Six Daughters

786. I Annie Mae Golding, b Dec. 2, 1891; m T.L. Hoetyin, a farmer, 1910.
787. II Carrie Belle Golding, b Jan. 18, 193; m A.J. Gilliard, farmer, 1913; 6 children.
788.
789. III Vilanta Golding, b Dec. 29, 1895; m Jessie Gillard, a farmer, in 1913; 6 children.
790. IV Laura Lou Golding, b Feb. 25, 1897; m Floyd Cameron, a farmer, in 1923; 1 child d in infancy.
791. V Malcolm Golding, b July 20, 1900; is a farmer and m Mattie Lee Dupree, 1921; 2 children.
792. VI William H. Golding, b Dec. 10, 1902; m Girtha Bodiford in 1920; a farmer
793. VII Lester B. Golding, b Jan. 24, 1903; a farmer.
794. VIII Eugene C. Golding, m Aug. 6, 1906.
795. IX Inez Golding, b Aug. 9, 1909.
796. X Paulene Golding, b Oct, 30, 1913.
797. XI Robert Golding, b Sept. 16, 1916.

1898

766. Charles W. McMillan=Ola Hicks

A farmer, Son of W.J. and Louisa McMillan.   Live in Grady Co.

Progeny

798. I Olva Bush McMillan; b Jan. 1, 1903; m J.B. Pelham, a farmer, in 1922.
799. II Fondren M. McMillan; b 1905.

800. III   Byron O. McMillan, b 1907.
801. IV   Hannah McMillan.
802. V   ---McMillan
803. VI   ---McMillan

1896
767. Jessie D. McMillan=R.H. Marsh
Daughter of W.J. and   A sawmill operator
Louisa McMillan.

Progeny: Four Sons, Two daughters

804. I   William Monroe Marsh, b 1897; d in infancy.
805. II   Rosa Lee Marsh, b 1899; d in infancy
806. III   Johnnie E. Marsh, b 1902; m Joe Hannell, telephone lineman, in Albany, Ga.
807. IV   Arthur Marsh, b 1905.
808. V   Shelley Marsh, b 1908.
809. VI   T.L. Marsh, b 1912.

1904
768. Thomas Hiram McMillan=Viola Norton
Truck farmer in Wauchula, Fla.
Son of W.J. and Louisa McMillan.

Progeny: Three Sons, Three Daughters

809. I   Clara McMillan, b Oct. 17, 1905.
810. II   Sadie McMillan, b Sept. 24, 1907.
811. III   Myrtice McMillan, b Sept. 22, 1908.
812. IV   Emory McMillan, b Sept. 8, 1910.
813. V   George McMillan, b Aug. 25, 1913.
814. VI   Edward McMillan, b April 21, 1918.

1903
769. Hannah Jane McMillan=S.C. Sholar
Daughter of W.J.   A Farmer of Grady Co., Ga.
And Louisa Jane McMillan.

Progeny: Three Sons and Two Daughters

815. I   Bascom Sholar, b Sept. 6, 1906.
816. II   Margaret Louise Sholar, b 1910; d in infancy.
817. III   Marvin Sholar, b 1912.
818. IV   Robert Lee Sholar, b 1914.
819. V   Lucine Sholar, b Nov., 1916.

1919
770. Minnie Lee McMillan=H.C. Barrett
Daughter of W.J. and   A Printer of Birmingham.
Louisa McMillan.

Progeny: Two Daughters
820. I Louisa Barrett, b Sept. 15, 1920.
821. II Norma Barrett.

1915
771. William G. McMillan=Rosa Laverns
Youngest son of W.J. and
Louisa McMillan.
Was in U.S. Navy four years. At present, employee of fire department of Birmingham, Ala.

1910
772. Allie Mae Sarrett=M. Richards
Daughter of J.A. and   A machinist of Mt. Pleasant, Fla.
Olivia Sarrett.
Progeny: One Son, Three Daughters
822. I Alline Richards, b --- 18, 1910; d Jan. 18, 1912.
823. II James Everett Richards, b Feb 7, 1913.
824. III Elsie Mae Richards, b Oct. 20, 1915.
825. IV Virginia Belle Richards, b Dec. 3-, 1917.

1916
773. Lillie Belle Sarrett=J.T. Billingsley
Daughter of J.A. and   A Farmer in Thomas Co. Ga.
Olivia Sarrett.
Progeny: One Son, One Daughter
826. I Joseph Earl Billingsley, b July 12, 1917.
827. II Lillie Edna Billingsley, b Jan. 19, 1920.

1914
774. Mary Elizabeth Sarrett=W.S. Gay
Daughter of J.A. and   A Carpenter of Thomasville, Ga.
Olivia Sarrett.
Progeny: Two Sons
828. I Harry Loyd Gay, B June 12, 1915.
829. II William Hugh Gay, b Dec. 16, 1922.

1923
777. Martha Louise Sarrett=T.H. Lewis
Daughter of J.A. and   A Druggist of Knoxville, Tenn.
Olivia Sarrett.

Louisa Jane McMillan died April 12, 1918, of paralysis. W.J. McMillan died April 15, 1921, of high blood pressure.

The living descendants of Louisa Jane McMillan are: Children, 9; grandchildren, 48, and great grandchildren, 27. The dead ones are:

Grandchildren, 5; great grandchildren, 5.

749. Fannie Elizabeth McCord=R.T. Hinson
Daughter of Robert B. and
Jane J. McCord
A Planter.

Progeny: Two Sons, Two Daughters

830. I   Nettie L. Hinson, b 1875; m J.H. Vinson, a farmer in Grady Co. Ga., 1893.
831. II Mattie J. Hinson, b 1877; d 1881
832. III James A. Hinson, b 1879; m India Waldron, 1904. He is a truck farmer at Ft. Meyers, Fla. One daughter, seven sons.
834. IV John Robert Hinson, b 1882; m Ollie Hughes, 1906 Railroad employee at Climax, Ga. Has three sons.

1888

751. Sallie Catherine McCord=W.T. Asbell
Daughter of Robert and
Jane McCord
A machinist in Thomasville, Ga.

Progeny: Two Sons

835. I George H. Asbell, b Sept. 30, 1889; m Mrs. Charlotte April, of Gutterberg, Iowa. He is a construction engineer, and lives in Atlanta.
836. II James R. Asbell, b Aug. 6, 1892. He is a contractor in Panama City, Fla.

JAMES WASHINGTON MCCORD

748. James Washington McCord, second son of Robert Bowles McCord and Jane Adair McCord, was born in Walton County, Ga., July 1, 1848, and died in Tallahassee, Fla., June 15, 1923. After his elder brother, David, was killed in battle during the Civil War in 1863, their father and mother, with James and the younger children sacrificed the old home place in their native North Georgia county, and with about a dozen slaves moved in a train of wagons carrying everything to new scenes in the extreme southern part of the state. They settled on a considerable body of woodland purchased at small cost in Thomas County, bordering the Florida boundary. James barely missed active service in the war, but his father, having lost his oldest son, was not anxious for this other boy to be called out.

They, with their slaves, began clearing land in a wilderness of yellow pine. There was no railroad in all that section, and public schools were unknown. Private schools could not be maintained for lack of teachers and a sufficient number of pupils. So, James' schooling stopped about the time the war started, when he was twelve years old. The boy worked right along with the slaves and was, when grown, really a giant in physical strength as he was in his six four inches height and hiss two-twenty-five in weight. At the age of twenty-four the young man went a=courting down there on the banks of the Ochlocknee where, beside the river, with its snow-white sand banks, lived Mary Walker, a handsome girl of fifteen. They married next year, and she went to live with him in the farmhouse, yes, of logs, in which he had "bached" alone for more than a year.

After they had borne two boys in the log-pen house, the sawmill had come in, a public road had been established on a line through their land a mile away. There, on the crude highway of the times, they built a neat frame house, and in it lived until they had borne two other children. The question of schooling for the children was then becoming a problem. The young parents did not have much education, but from the beginning were ambitious that their children should become strong wherein they themselves were weak. Out there in that sparsely settled community Mather, the first born, started, at the age of six, on hikes of three and four miles to the nearest log cabin school, that would run for a term of three months. He did not go alone, for his little brother next in size, and three years younger, always went with him, starting to these little old schools at the age of three. The two little boys, Mather and Robert, sat from eight till four every day on those backless slab seats, which did not let their feet touch the floor, until they worried together through several of the first readers.

The father had found a demand for brick out there in the country and had supplied it by making a kiln of soft mud brick, such as his father had long since taught him to make. His success with that little kiln urged him to move to the nearby town of Cairo and engage in the business of making brick for the public, while having better opportunities for the education of his children, who then numbered three boys and one girl. During the five year's residence in Cairo another child was born but lived only a few years. This was Ralph, who died at the age of three and was buried in the cemetery at Cairo. The other children, in the order of their age, were:

(837) Mather Marvin,
(838) Robert B.,
(839) Guyte Pearce and
(840) Pearl,

All of whom are now living and have families of their own.

A series of rains and storms, in connection with panicky conditions in the country, practically whipped out the brick business of James McCord in Cairo in 1892, and with little of material goods left the family moved first to the undeveloped section of West Florida, where they pioneered for five more years, but always carrying on the education of their children. When no school was available, Mather and Robert studied together systematically in the rooms every day until they had gone ahead of the instruction in the local schools and had themselves passed the examinations for teachers and had, as boys, taught several of the public terms, which lasted in each instance only four or five months.

Since education was uppermost the whole family was then ready to pull up stakes and move to the vicinity of the best school of which they know. They trusted the Lord and their willingness to labor for a living, and they reached Tallahassee, the capital city, with scarcely enough funds to get their freight out of the depot. The cook stove was smashed in moving, and for several weeks the family meals were prepared, as in olden times, in the open fireplace. But the neighbors knew nothing of this, for the family had brought along their pride, and did not let those capital city folks know their financial condition.

Through all these other years the parental home of these three boys and one girl has remained in Tallahassee, under the moss-hanging live oaks, among the red hills peculiar to this particular section of Northern Florida, and close by those numerous lakes common to all parts of Florida. There, and from there, under the constant stimulation of their parents, the boys and their young sister have secured the educational opportunities for which they were all ambitious. Their father lived to the age of seventy-five and died in 1923. He always insisted that he did not make much financial success and attributed it to the lack of training in early years. But he insisted that his children had the "Blood" in them and could succeed, because of their greater opportunities. He had particular ambitions for his three boys: hoped one would be a doctor, one a preacher, and the other a lawyer. His ambitions in that respect were almost literally realized.

Mather Marvin, the oldest, studied at the University of Georgia and graduated in the Atlanta College of Physicians and Surgeons, now a part of Emory University. He later did post-graduate work in New York and at Harvard University at Cambridge. He is now, and has been for a number of years, a highly esteemed physician, specialist in children's diseases, in Rome, Ga. He was born Oct. 31, 1877, in Thomas County, Ga.; married Bessie Maybelle Butler, daughter of Doctor and Mrs. John Augustus Butler in the same county. Three children have been born to them:

    Mildred Cornelia, b June 5, 1905,
    841. Ralph Butler, b March 21, 1907, and
    842. Malcolm Marvin, b March 25, 1920.

Doctor Mather M. McCord was the founder of the Children's Free Clinic of Rome, Ga., in 1918. He is now president of the Floyd County Medical Society. He has been secretary of the Seventh Congressional District Medical Society since 1917, and a Counsellor for the Seventh Congressional District of Georgia in the Medical Association of Georgia since 1921. Socially, he is a member of the local Kiwanis Club, the Coosa Country Club, and the Presidents Club.

838. Robert B., the second son of James W. McCord, was named for his grandfather, Robert. But his mother would not consent for him to have the middle names, "Bowles." It was left "Robert B." until such time as he should fit the middle name on. During the first running for president of Wm. Jennings Bryan, the older brother. Mather addressed him by letter one day as "Robert Bryan McCord" and he has carried that name on his college degrees and legal papers to this day, but says he has never been satisfied with it, since Bryan wasn't elected president. He was born Oct. 11, 1880, in Thomas County, Ga. He pioneered here and there, getting the early years of his schooling, but later attended the high grade schools of Tallahassee, and then graduated with the A.B. Degree from the University of Florida in 1905.

Robert was the one marked for a preacher, but, like Moses, kicked against it. But, not like Moses, he readily did dodge it entirely. He says he once had what he then considered a remarkable call to preach, and, therefore, he does not know what the consequences someday will be. But he is confidently expecting to be excused from that, just as he believes he must be divinely excused for many other instances of disobedience.

He still had in mind to be a preacher when he graduated at the University of Florida in 1905. He determined, if he must enter the ministry, that he would not go to the denominational school to be taught what to believe, but would choose a great school in which they were only seeking the truth in the light of all that could be known without regard to any particular doctrine of a sect. So, from the University of Florida Robert went to Yale in 1905, and studied there three years, graduating in the class of 1908 with the degree of Bachelor of Divinity. He had decided before he graduated at Yale that he was not going to choose the church for his career but determined to finish what he had started. As soon as school was out at New Haven he said good-bye to any thought of the ministry as a profession, and bought his ticket for the Rosebud Indian Reservation of South Dakota, where he spent four months of summer riding bronchos, associating with the Indians, and organizing Sunday Schools among the squatters and settlers that were coming over the border, for the Boston Sunday School Society. While there he was offered a fellowship in the graduate school of the University of Chicago, and to that school he returned in the fall, and pursued courses in sociology and political economy for two years, closing his school career in 1910, when he took the Master of Arts Degree in the Department of Sociology. He had spent four summer vacations in the North, not exactly "vacating," but engaged in remunerative employment. One summer was spent in rural Connecticut, one in Northern Vermont and Canada, that one on the Indian Reservation, and the last traveling Ohio and Indiana in the selling game. He says he did this last work largely to gain ability and self-confidence in the selling game before he should offer to sell some social service down home in Georgia.

When Robert B. McCord gave up the idea of the church as a profession he had not lost his religion in its essential features, or thrown down his call to a life of ministry and service to his fellow creatures, and when he finished his schooling at the University of Chicago in 1910, in the Department of Sociology, he might have had what he would consider a very remunerative employment if he had chosen to stay in the North. But just as he felt loyal to God, Who had called him to what he now interpreted in a larger way as a life of service rather than one of material accumulation and self-gain, so now also felt a loyalty to the home people down south, who ought to have the benefit of anything worthwhile he had gained in these years of schooling, since the South had long been somewhat handicapped in certain respects.

He had a strong conviction from his studies that home conditions or environments and opportunities largely determine the kind of man or woman the child will be. If then we could shape the influences over the child through its growing period, we could largely determine the kind of citizen he would be. With that thought in mind, Robert went back to Georgia and incorporated, with leading citizens behind it. The Georgia Children's Home Society, not an orphanage, but a child-placing agency on a state-wide scope. He has built up a strong child-welfare organization, with headquarters in Atlanta, and he has been its executive head while it has each year been growing stronger for twelve years. Hundreds of the most handicapped children in the State have been given by this agency a new and wholesome environment, devoted foster parents, and a big chance to find life worthwhile.

While answering the call of a stranded group of youngsters at Dalton, just one hundred miles north of Atlanta, in 1915. Robert ran upon the town's volunteer social worker, Clara Brown, and he gave her no more peace or freedom from annoyance until she promised to marry him and kept her promise on June 21, 1916. Clara Brown was doing a great work in the free kindergarten of Dalton and persisted that she must not lay down the services she had begun. But Robert promised that if she would come on with him down to Atlanta, he would soon get her up a little school down there. He has kept his promise, and in eight years four little ones have come to be in her school.

841. Robert B., Jr., was born April 28, 1917.
842. Clara Brown, b Dec. 14.
843. Adair, b Dec. 28, 1921.
844. Edward James, b March 23, 1923.

They live in Hapeville, a residential suburban town just outside of Atlanta, and Robert drives in to Ormewood Court, the headquarters of the State's child-placing system in Atlanta, every morning.

As a college man, Robert is a member of the Kappa Alpha Fraternity (Southern). He says he has no time now for strictly social organizations. He loves home, his gardens, and his radio programs too well to be away from them unnecessarily. He is a member of the Atlanta Lions Club, Atlanta Masonic Club, and the Atlanta Social Workers Club, all weekly luncheon clubs for community improvement. He is also a member of the American Association of Social Workers and the Southern Methodist Church.

839. Guyte Pierce McCord, youngest of these three brothers, obtained his education under fewer difficulties than in the case of Mather and Robert. He had the advantage of the best city schools earlier in life, getting his preparation for college mostly in Tallahassee. He finished his pre-law schoolwork in the State College of Florida and pursued his legal training in the law school of Washington and Lee University in Virginia, from which school he graduated in June, 1907.

Guyte has always been built more like his father, tall and solid. He is six feet two inches, that last two inches taller than Doctor Mather, who is two inches taller than Robert. But even Guyte has always been two inches shorter than his father. Guyte was an intense and successful football player throughout his career at the Florida School and at Washington and Lee University. While on the eleven as the heaviest man in the Florida school, his institution won over all Florida competitors, as well as some outside. While on the Washington and Lee eleven his school beat the University of Virginia for the first time in several years. He does not claim all the credit for the victories but considers himself fortunate in having been on the winning team. He was also a member of the baseball teams at both schools. Guyte

Guyte P. McCord, Mayor of Tallahassee.

obtained his board at Washington and Lee by guaranteeing to his landlady peace and quiet among a bunch of some thirty or forty student boarders. The boys were generally loyal to him and made his board thus come easy. But when it became necessary, he did not hesitate to "use the big stick."

On graduation he returned to his home city and put out his "Lawyer" single in Tallahassee, where it has since remained. He was immediately, in that same year of his graduation, made U.S. Commissioner for the Northern District of Florida and Deputy Clerk of the U.S. District Court, and these relieved him from having to pass through that starvation period which is the experience of most young lawyers. He held these positions while building up a substantial law practice and gave them up when they were in the way of his career.

Guyte was the beau of many visiting girls to Tallahassee through a period of several years as a young lawyer, as well as having his "steady" always on the ground. He finally believed he had fallen hopelessly in love with one of these visiting girls at the Methodist parsonage. He kissed her while telling her the state of his feelings on the night before she was expected to leave for her own home the next day. While he felt there was no doubt in his mind, and none whatever in his heart, about the next step, he told her that he would not like to act hastily in the matter and declare his positive intentions to marry her until she had prolonged her visit another week. At least, that is what Jean Patterson McCord, the parson's niece and Gutye's little wife, tells on him now. She admits that she prolonged her visit another week, and that it was the happiest one of her unmarried life, for Guyte did not practice much law, only made life sweet those seven days, and she went back then to Pensacola to get ready for the wedding. They were married in January, 1912, and since then two children have come, another Guyte and Jean. The former was born Sept. 23, 1914, and his little sister came May 1, 1918.

Guyte, and most of his known antecedents, were members of the Methodist Church, but after he married he concluded that Jean's membership in the Presbyterian Church meant more to her than his connection with the Methodist Church did to him, so he put his membership in her church, and much of the time since then has been superintendent of the Sunday School of the First Presbyterian Church of Tallahassee.

Guyte McCord's most conspicuous work outside the practice of law is the overhauling he has given the city government of Tallahassee. He got some practice in going up against opposition in the football arena; he got some other practice while prosecuting attorney of his city running out the tigers and their kind. Then, when he was elected Mayor of Tallahassee six years ago on a ticket for better city government, he found that he could not give what the city needed without overturning the existing charter and starting the whole thing from the beginning, At that time Tallahassee was generally known as a "fogy old town," made up of people who cared nothing for progress or modern methods in the management of their city affairs. The municipality was deeply in debt and getting deeper while the streets remained unpaved and unworked. The old buildings, the cluttered-up sidewalks and the muddy streets gave the impression of a boy with a dirty face, and untrimmed and unbrushed hair. Guyte as mayor studied commission a manager form of governments about the country, and concluded Tallahassee needed just that thing. Scarcely anybody else thought so, they feared any change, and he had to begin an educational campaign. He took it to the public, to the Chamber of Commerce, and finally to the legislature for a new charter. After a fight with the people ratified the charter, and the new government was put in with Guyte again as mayor, or head of the three men who were to run the city through their chosen manager. As the campaign waged the opposition had set forth that Guyte McCord was seeking to feather his dirty face, and untrimmed and unbrushed hair. Guyte, as mayor, the charter that the mayor, who heretofore had been on salary, would, under the new government, receive no salary at all, and likewise the other two commissioners. They put up a good salary, after they had won the fight, for a competent city manager, and the opposition said, "He is fixing to take that job and its salary." But he was always far from leaving his lucrative law practice for any such position. He devoted as much of his days and nights for five years in making a new city charter for the capital of the State of Florida, which anybody will now recognize by a visit, that his law practice was suffering. Last year, when he resigned, 1923, he received the plaudits of press and people for the remarkable change he had brought about in the general conditions of the city. They gave him the credit, petitioned him to remain as mayor, apologized for ever thinking he expected to make a dollar for himself by the things he had advocated and accomplished for the city, and spread his picture over one-half the front page of the local daily paper. But he resigned, and for the last year has given more intensive interest to the practice of his profession, has become a better player of golf out at the country club links, and has caught more fish and bagged more ducks than in any year since he came back from law school in Virginia. He is a member of the local Elks, Kiwanis Club, Golf and Country Clubs, but is not a member of any secret order except his college fraternity, Sigma Alpha Epsilon, joining at Washington and Lee. Guyte was born Sept. 2, 1884.

840. There is just one left, the youngest child and only daughter, Pearl Eugenia, born Sept. 1, 1887. The boys have sometimes expressed regret for their sister's sake that she could not as they, on account of being a girl, plunge into a career and have the satisfaction of fighting it out. On the other hand, they would not for anything miss the pleasure of having this one sister. She admits that she demanded of these older brothers that they do all her mathematical calculations during her school years, but she has always felt that it was nothing more than right that they save her from bothering her brain with unnecessary figuring. She had two years in the State College, now for women only, in Tallahassee, and then quit to marry a childhood playmate, who had come back from Philadelphia a fully trained jeweler and had set up for himself in Tallahassee. She married Paul T. Nicholson in Tallahassee, June 24, 1908, about the time her brother Robert reached the Rosebud Indian Reservation in South Dakota for that summer with the bronchos and coyotes and prairie dogs. Two daughters were born to them: Eunice Cecile, Oct. 20, 1910, and Mary Elinor, March 31, 1912. Their father died, following an operation for appendicitis, in May, 1916, leaving his young wife and two little daughters. But he had sufficient foresight and business ability not to leave them stranded. Pearl had no experience with business up to the time of her husband's death, but she soon acquired it and has considerably increased the accumulations left her. She never did leave her parental home but made it a condition of her marriage that her husband come in with her family. Paul Nicholson was an exact fit into the family, and to Pearl's father and mother always seemed as one of their own boys. Her father died in 1923, but Pearl McCord Nicholson and her mother are living there in Tallahassee now at the corner of Capitol Square. In addition to the income from her property, Pearl and her mother have no inconsiderable income from the sale of fine cakes which they bake for filling local and out-of-town orders. They have been ordered by people in all parts of the United States, because they have made a reputation as bakers of fine cake such as one does not often find for sale.

COLUMBUS HOWARD MCCORD

752. Columbus Howard McCord, son of Robert B. and Jane Adair McCord, was born in Walton County, Ga., May 8, 1862. He was licensed to preach and admitted into the South Georgia Conference of the Methodist Episcopal Church, South, Dec. 1, 1888. He continued in the active itinerary for eight years, when he retired from the Conference and engaged in farming. He was widely known as a very earnest, deeply pious minister. He was much in demand for marrying and burying people. He died Nov. 28, 1914, in Nashville,

Ga., and was buried in the cemetery of that city.

1883
Columbus Howard McCord=Mattie Evans Cox
Progeny: Ten Children

- 847. I John Dwight McCord, b Aug. 12, 1884; became a minister in 1909.
- 848. II Eliza Jane McCord, b June 15, 1886; m J.F. Bradford Oct. 20, 1915.
- 849. III Mary Elizabeth McCord, b Nov. 25, 1887; m J.L. Rogers.
- 850. IV Rachel McCord, b Jan. 21, 1890; m M.R. Riggs Dec. 23, 1906.
- 851. V William Didge McCord, b July 4, 1891; became an optician.
- 852. VI Osie Bell McCord, b July 24, 1893; m W.N. Whidden Feb. 2, 1915.
- 853. VII Fannie Lou McCord, b Sept. 21, 1895; m W.R. Smith Oct. 25, 1915.
- 854. VIII James Thomas McCord, b 1897; d in infancy.
- 855. IX James Lovett McCord, b April 15, 1900; became an optician.
- 856. X George Matthews :McCord, b May 22, 1904. Still a student at this date, June, 1924.

1911
847. John Dwight McCord=Elizabeth Taylor

Son of Columbus H. and Mattie McCord   In Americus, Ga.

Progeny: Five Children

- 857. I Minie McCord, b May 21, 1913.
- 858. II Ruth McCord, b Nov. 18, 1915; d April 12, 1916.
- 859. III John Dwight, Jr., b April 13, 1917.
- 860. IV Mary, and
- 861. V Martha. The twins were born March 10, 1919.

847. John Dwight McCord graduated at Emory University with an A.B. Degree in 1909 He joined the South Georgia Methodist Conference the same year, and is serving as pastor the Bartow, Ga., charge.

848. Eliza Jane McCord=Jacob Frank Bradford

Second child of Columbus H. and Mattie McCord.

She was educated at the Georgia Woman's College.

A Farmer; lives near Nashville, Ga.

Progeny of the Bradfords: Two Children

- 862. I Thomas Howard Bradford, b July 29, 1916.
- 863. II Lou Hazel Bradford, b Sept. 20, 1918.

1918
849. Mary Elizabeth McCord=John Leroy Rogers
Third child of Columbus H. and Mattie McCord.
She was graduated At Worthem College, and attended a Special training school in Kansas City.
A farmer at Glenville, Ga.

Progeny: Four Children, but two died in infancy
- 864. I Sue Nell Rogers, b Dec. 23, 1921.
- 865. II Charles Edwin Rogers, b March 24, 1923.

1906
850. Rachel McCord=Marvin R. Riggs
Fourth child of Columbus H. Mattie McCord.
A Farmer of Manassas, Ga.

Progeny: Ten Children; two of the sons died in infancy
- 866. I Wilmer Lee Riggs, b May 18, 1908.
- 867. II Elma Fay Riggs, b Oct. 27, 1909.
- 868. III Timothy Clyde Riggs, b Feb. 24, 1911.
- 869. IV Mather Marvin Riggs, b April 5, 1913.
- 870. V Mary Francis Riggs, b Jan. 26, 1915.
- 871. VI John Paul Riggs, b Sept. 15, 1918.
- 872. VII Joseph Harald Riggs, b Oct. 8, 1919.
- 873. VIII Clare Ruth Riggs, b Nov. 16, 1922.

William Dodge McCord, the fifth child of Columbus H. and Mattie McCord, was a graduate of Needles Optical Institute in Kansas City, Mo. He served about two and one-half years in the U.S. Navy as a volunteer during the World War. He is now an optician in Thomasville, Ga.

1918
851. William Dodge McCord=Mollie Purdom
Progeny: One Child
- 874. I William Dodge McCord, b Jan, 29, 1920.

1915
852. Osie Bell McCord=W. Nichols Whiddon
Sixth child of Columbus H. and Mattie McCord. a merchant in Tifton, Ga.

Progeny: Two Sons
- 875. I Hubert Paige Whiddon, b Nov. 1, 1915.
- 876. II Harald Dwight Whiddon, b Dec. 28, 1919.

1915
853. Fannie Lou McCord=W. Reppard Smith
Seventh child of Columbus H.   A clerk in Metter, Ga.
and Mattie McCord.

Progeny: Three Children; one died in infancy

877.   I   Ruby Lee Smith, b Dec. 27, 1916.
878.   II   Marie Smith, b Oct. 13, 1922.

James Thomas McCord, 1897; d a few months later.

855. James Lovett McCord, ninth child of Columbus H. and Mattie McCord, was in Senior Class at Sparks College when he volunteered for service in the World War, but never saw foreign service. He is a graduate of the Optical College in Chicago and is now an optician in Atlanta.

856. George Matthews McCord, tenth child of Columbus H. and Mattie McCord, is a graduate of Sparks College and a student in Emory University, in Atlanta.

CHAPTER XXXIX

JAMES MCCORD ADAIR AND HIS DESCENDANTS

James McCord Adair (5, Joseph Alex Adair; 4, John Adair; 3, Jospeh Adair, Jr.; 2 Joseph Adair, Sr.; 1, Thomas Adair), was born in 1812 near Winder in Walton County, Ga., and spent his youth in working on his father's farm and shop. When he did get started to school, he made good use of his time and learned rapidly. Next, he took a course in mechanical engineering and machinery, with Claborne Harris, a noted machinist with shops near Jefferson, in Jackson County. This was before the days of cotton factories, and Harris was manufacturing spinning machines, which would turn out spool thread when fed on seed cotton and run by hand power. Harris had a standing premium of $100 to any of his students who could make a spinning machine the first year of their pupillage, and Adair won it, which was considered extraordinary. One hundred dollars was a big bonus in those panicky years during and after Jackson's administration.

When James M. Adair was a young man, the Government required every able-bodied young man to belong to a military company and drill at regular intervals. Adair was popular enough to be elected Captain of his company. His associates regarded him as a man of exemplary habits and high moral principles.

In 1838 or 39 James M. Adair visited his uncle, Jones Adair, in Morgan County, whose wife's maiden name was Polly Ann Shields. There he met a sister of his aunt, whose name was Martha Barnett Shields. The next year, 1839, they married, moved to Jackson County, and bought the Ben Thornton homestead on Little Turkey Creek, four miles south of the present town of Commerce. In this home they spent the remainder of their lives and raised their family.

Adair soon abandoned his machine shop, except for some occasion when he wanted to use it, and put all his time on this farm, and he prospered at it. He improved his land, bought more land, built a new residence, doing all the work of building the house himself. He also bought several negro slaves, mostly young negroes, which he could sometimes get cheap. He even bought one little negro in the time of the war, after Mr. Lincoln's emancipation edict, but the Confederate leaders taught the people that the land would be confiscated, as well as the slaves, in case the Confederacy lost its cause. There was nothing else in which to invest money, which was depreciating.

James McCord Adair

The subject which gave Adair and his wife most concern was the education of their children. They had eleven children to raise and educate, and it was a difficult problem with their environment. Every year their neighborhood had a primary school, lasting several weeks, taught by a teacher usually without special training. Beginners were here taught to spell, read and cipher. But there was only one high school in the county, located at Jefferson, seven miles away, and yet this County of Jackson was among the more intelligent and wealthy in the State. This school was endowed by James Martin, a wealthy citizen of the county, and named for him, "MARTIN INSTITUTE." Its income paid part of the tuition fees of the students. The State University was at Athens, where classics and mathematics were taught but not practical studies were taught. There was no free tuition, and it was a State institution only in name. Of course, it is better now, and my description of it applies to the whole of the nineteenth century. There were no public libraries, no free tuition, and the pupil's board bill was a heavy item. Notwithstanding these adverse conditions, the Adairs planned to give all of their children all the education they would take. The oldest son, Alexander, had spent one year at Martin Institute, and one year at Athens, and Hasseltine spent one year at Martin Institute, when the war between the States put a stop to the educational program. The two oldest sons went out into the army with the first company from that county. They were sent to training camp at Big Shanty, north from Atlanta. The sanitary conditions of the camp were bad, typhoid was raging, and Alexander was seized with typhoid and died, and his father took him home and buried him in the family graveyard. Alexander was a most noble fellow, and his death was a grievous blow to his parents and family. Oscar, the next oldest son, served through the war, and captured twice, and spent one winter as a prisoner in Camp Douglass at Chicago, and he says that Camp Douglass was just as bad as Andersonville, Georgia.

It was in 1861 that Alexander died at Big Shanty Camp. The next year, 1862, Henry, the third son, went into the army with Capt. Mintz's company, and died with a relapse of measles in a hospital in Chattanooga, Tenn., and was buried there.

In 1864 James M. Adair went himself into the army, at the call of the Confederate Government and the State of Georgia for men up to 55 years of age. He was sent to training camp at Milledgeville, the State Capital, and Capt. Prudence was his captain. An epidemic of camp diarrhea was in the camp, and Adair soon became a victim. The sanitation was bad and the diet was anything but good. Adair was sent home for treatment, but died three days after reaching there, September, 1864. His funeral was largely attended.

Physically, James M. Adair was a fine specimen of a man, six feet one inch in height, weighing 180 pounds. Mentally, he was broad-minded, with strong will and self-reliance, initiative, and energy, and his moral faculties were well developed. He inherited mechanical talent and transmitted it to most of his children.

When Adair died all his children, except one or two, were minors, the youngest being a baby in arms. The work and responsibility of raising and educating them devolved on the widowed mother alone. In addition, she had to look after the little negroes. Of course, when the war was over the negroes were emancipated. That relieved her of their care and responsibility. Emancipation was a greater blessing to the slave-owner than to the slave.

The mother was not able to send her children to college at Athens as she desired to do, but no less than five of the children were educated at Martin Institute, in Jefferson. High school studies were finally established at Commerce, and some of the younger ones pursued high school studies there. Four of the sons won the Doctor's Degree—three dentists and one physician. Robert also deserves credit for advising and encouraging his three younger brothers to take professions; however, the mother is entitled to all honor for encouraging and assisting all her children to acquire higher education when they wanted it. The whole family of children turned out to be honorable and worthy citizens.

(31) James M. Adair and wife, and the wife afterwards, were benevolent to the windows and orphans of other soldiers and to distressed persons during the war and for a year after the war was over. The supplied foodstuffs raised on their farm; the needy were numerous, and glad were the hearts of the many who were tided over by the Adairs at the end of the war between the States.

1839

31 James McCord Adair=Martha Barnett Shields **380**

| Of good lineage, and the Grandson of John Adair, the revolutionary soldier. | Of Morgan County. Scotch-Irish ancestry. |

Progeny: Twelve Children

881. I William Alexander Adair, b Sept. 15, 1840; educated at Martin Institute and at Athens; d of typhoid in Confederate Army in August, 1861; buried at home.

882. II Julius Oscar Adair, b April 9, 1842; m Julia A. Hix.

883. III Allen Henry Adair, b Oct. 15, 1843; d a Confederate soldier at Chattanooga, June 20, 1862; buried in soldiers' graveyard.

884. IV   Hulda Ann Hasseltine Adair, b April 30, 1845; m A.J. Harris; one son.
855. V   Minerva Cornelia Adair, b Sept. 29, 1847; m D.M. Nox January, 1867; d 1877.
866. VI   Robert Benjamin Adair, b May 27, 1849; m, first, Aline V. Moss, one son, Robin; m, second, Mattie Simms of Raleigh, N.C.
867. VII   Henrietta Josephene Adair, b Aug. 16, 1851; m Aug. 19, 1869, J.A. Hudson; five children; live in Atlanta.
888. VIII   James Barnett Adair, b July 5, 1853; graduated in medicine 1874; m 1883; two daughters, one son. Home, Los Angeles.
889. IX   Anderson Brantley Adair, b Dec. 5, 1855; d March 26, 1857.
890. X   Hamilton Stephens Adair, twin brothers; m Nov. 27, 1878, Susan M. Malcom; four or five children in 1898.
891. XI   Samuel Brownfield Adair, b March 5, 1858; m F. Augusta Thornton Dec. 19, 1888; five children; graduated in dentistry, 1881.
892. XII   Eugene Franklin Adair, b Sept. 5, 1861; graduated in dentistry in 1885; m Lula Westbrook Oct. 24, 1892; four daughters.

Their mother died Dec. 22, 1884, age 64 years and seven months.

JULIUS OSCAR ADAIR

882. Julius Oscar Adair, the second son of James M. and Martha R. Adair, was born April 9, 1842. His lineage runs thus: Julius O. (James M., Jospeh A., John, Joseph, Jr., Joseph, Sr., Thomas Adair).

He enlisted in the Confederate Army at the age of 18 years and served to the end of the war. He spent the usual period in the training camp at Big Shanty, just north of Atlanta. He and his older brother, Alexander, were companions until the latter died. Then Oscar was sent off to the Virginia Army, but he did not like his associates, nor the conditions that he had to contend with, so he got transferred to Gen. Joseph F. Johnson's Army, operating in the west, and remained with it until the end, when they surrendered in North Carolina. J.O. Adair was in most of the major battles of the Western Army; was wounded once and captured twice; was confined one winter in Camp Douglass, in Chicago, as a prisoner of war, where he was brutally treated, starved and frozen until he was a mere skeleton, and scarcely able to walk, when he was finally exchanged and sent home to recuperate. He says there was no excuse for starving the Confederate prisoners, because

James McCord Adair

Mrs. Martha B. Adair.

the Federals had plenty of foodstuffs. He thinks it was in retaliation for the reported starvation of Federal prisoners at Andersonville, Ga.,, where the Confederate authorities claimed they were short of foodstuffs. Anyhow, the prisons on both sides were a disgrace to civilization, and one side was no better than the other.

882. J.O. Adair was a mechanical and machinery engineer. He also tried his hand at farming, but did not like it.

Married November, 1865

882. Julius Oscar Adair=Julia Ann Nix, 892

Daughter of T.T. Nix, 893,

A Confederate soldier.

Progeny: Eight Children, Sixteen Grandchildren and Seven Great-Grandchildren (1923)

894.	I	Harriet L. Adair, b Oct. 26, 1866, a teacher; m David M. Dickson **(895)**, a merchant and farmer, Dec. 5, 1889. He was also a member of Board of Education of Morgan Co. They had 7 children, 3 of whom died young; 4 are living, 2 boys and 2 girls; Ora Dell Dickson, b Oct. 24, 1892, has high school education and 1 year at normal in Athens; taught 1 term at Greshamville, Ga., then married.
895.		Thomas T. Jones of Madison, Ga., Jan. 9, 1918, mechanic. Residence 67 Ponders Ave., Atlanta; children:
897.		Thomas David Jones, b Oct., 1918;
898.		John Reinhardt Jones, b Aug., 1921; d Oct., 1922.
899.	V	Henry Grady Dickson, b Sept. 7, 1895; has high school education, 2 years at agricultural college and graduated at college of technology, electrical engineering. Now engaged in real estate and building construction in Atlanta. Address, 98 Inman St. Married Dec. 25, 1919, 900 Emma Thurston, school teacher; 2 children born to them: 901 H.G. Dickson, b June 4, 1923; 902 Lillian Doris Dickson, b Aug. 3, 1920.
902.		Hoyt David Dickson, b April 6, 1900; has high school education; is merchant and farmer. Address, Rutledge, Ga. Single at present (1923).
904.		Claire Aline Dickson, b Oct. 1, 1905; has high school education and 1 year at State Normal School at Athens; may enter college again in September.
905.	II	James Thomas Adair, second son of J.O. and Julia Adair, b Sept. 2, 1869; was locomotive engineer for 28 years, but now is an automobile dealer. Married 907 Fannie Rickie, Feb. 26, 1891; 4 children born to them, all boys: First, Herman Garland Adair, b April 8, 1892; has high school

education and 1 year at technological college, Atlanta; vulcanizer. Married 908 Myrtle Bruce April 15, 1919. Have 3 children: 909 Martha Adair, b Dec. 21, 1917; 910 Chester Adair, b Dec. 21, 1920, and 910 Mary Adair, b Dec. 21, 1920. (Last 2 are evidently twins.) Second 912 Chester Priez Adair, b Nov. 14, 1894; high school graduate and 1 year at University of Georgia at Athens; also graduate Southern Business College, Atlanta. He volunteered into the service, World War, Sept. 12, 1917; died in France Sept. 14, 1918; brought back to Georgia and buried in Athens April, 1920, with great military honors. Third son, 913 James Thomas Adair, Jr., b June 26, 1902; has high school education and graduated at the university in Athens, June, 1923. Expects to study medicine. Fourth 914 Luther Carlton Adair, b Nov. 8, 1904, education not complete.

915. III Third son, William Henry Adair, b Jan. 9, 1871; d June 11, 1872.

916. IV Fourth, Ferdinand M. Adair, b Jan. 22, 1873; a farmer. Address, Garza, Texas, R. 2. Married 917 Callie Reynolds of Denton, Texas, Jan. 21, 1897. They have 6 children: First, Mabel Adair, b about Dec., 1897, married, no children. Second, 919 Louise Adair, b about 1899; m and has one child, a girl 2 years. Third, 920 Lillie Mae Adair, b about 1901; is single; has normal training. Fourth, 921 Herbert Adair, b about 1903. Fifth, 922 Oscar Adair, b about 1908. Sixth, Julia Adair, b about 1911.

924. V Fifth, Ethel Mae Adair, b Oct. 9, 1876; m Robert J. Poss, a mechanic, March 13, 1904. Address 108 Gramling St., Marietta, Ga.; no children.

926. VI Sixth, Rubel Montine Adair, b Oct. 20, 1878; high school education; a splendid musician, having taught music 6 years. Single, d Jan. 7, 1912.

927. VII Seventh, Aline B. Adair, b Oct. 22, 1881; high school education and 2 years at State Normal College at Athens; taught school 10 years; has a splendid musical education and taught music several years. Aline is a stenographer and is now working for the government. She married 928 R.E. Swilling of Cardele, Ga., July 5, 1914, who died a year later. She lives with her father in Marietta, Ga.

929. VIII Eighth, Morgan Carlton Adair, b Oct. 27, 1886; high school education and graduate of Georgia School of Technology at Atlanta and is an electrical engineer. P.O. 67 W. Ontario Ave., Atlanta. Mar-930 Maud O. Smith from Indiana. May 21, 1914; 2 children born: 931 Morgan Charles Adair, b June, 1915, and 932 Robin Adair, b 1921.

AMERICAN ADAIRS—Line B

884. HULDA ANN HASSELTINE ADAIR, daughter of James M. and Marta Shields Adair (called Tinie for short) was born in Jackson County, Ga., on April 30, 1845. She was educated at Martin Institute, in Jefferson, Ga. She married in 1870.

933. Tinie Adair=934 Andrew Jackson Harris
A farmer at Commerce, Ga. He was
A Confederate soldier and the grandson
Of a Revolutionary soldier.

Progeny: One Son

935.   James Walton Harris.

935. James Walton Harris=936 Miss Salers

Progeny: Three Daughters, One Son

937. I   Allie Lee Harris.
938. II Pauline Harris.
939. III Ralph Harris, b Oct. 16, 1900.
940. IV Laruene Harris.

885. MINERVA CORNELIA ADAIR

Was a daughter of James M. and Martha Shields Adair. She was born Sept. 29, 1847; died Feb. 10, 1878.

1867

941. Dilmus Monroe Nix=885 Minerva Cornelia Adair
A farmer and merchant; a son of   Daughter of James M and
T.T. Nix, a Confederate soldier   Martha Shields Adair.
And farmer.

Progeny: Four Children

942. I   Julius Benjamin Morgan Nix, b June 13, 1871; d Aug. 20, 1880.
943. II Evie McCord Nix, b Oct. 25, 1872; d July 19, 1919; m Charles Bennett.
944. III Robert Clarence Nix, b Aug. 8, 1874.
945. IV Dillard Monroe Nix, b May 16, 1876.

Cornelia Adair Nix died in 1878.

1897

943. Evie McCord Nix=Charles L. Bennett 946, a farmer
Daughter of Dilmus M. and
Cornelia Adair Nix.

Progeny: Three Sons, One Daughter

947. I   Frederick William Bennett, b April 13, 1900; a teacher in the Agricultural College of Georgia State University; m Lillian Mae Cates, Dec. 22, 1921; 1 son, Lester Robert

Bennett, b Jan. 6, 1923.
984. II   Altus Robert Bennett, b March 25, 1903.
948. III Onloe Cornelia Bennett, b Sept. 5, 1905.
950. IV   Charles Curtis Bennett, b Aug. 14, 1915.

1901

944. Robert Clarence Nix=Bonnie Mae Shirley
Son of Dilmus M. and
Cornelia Nix. A merchant

Progeny: Two Daughters, Two Sons

952. I   Imogene Nix, b July 19, 1902.
953. II   Tennell Nix, b Dec. 24, 1905; d May 8, 1907.
954. III Catheryne Nix, b May 12, 1908.
955. IV   Robert C. Nix, Jr., b May 5, 1923.

1899

945. Dillard Monroe Nix=Miss Clara Harris 956
Son of Dilmus M. and
Cornelia Nix. Is a merchant.

Progeny: Four Sons, Two Daughters

957. I   Lloyd Monroe Nix, b Dec. 13, 1901.
958. II   James R. Nix, b March 6, 1904.
959. III Martha Everlyn Nix, b Oct. 21, 1905.
960. IV   Edith Cornelia Nix, b May 21, 1908.
961. V   Joseph Nelson Nix, b Oct. 25, 1911.
962. VI   Dillard Lafayette Nix, b April 5, 1919.

1878

(Second marriage) **941** Dilmus Nix=Permelia Jane Mitchell 963
A Farmer and merchant   A cousin of his first wife.

Progeny: Five Children

964. I   Sidney Johnson Nix, b Oct. 2, 1879; m Lottie Appleby.
965. II   Dilmus Herbert Nix, b Oct. 11, 1882; m Lillian Gertrude Maley.
966. III Dora Maud Nix, b Feb. 29, 1884; m George Williamson.
967. IV   William Thomas Nix, b Oct. 25, 1888; m Alva Montgomery.
968. V   Nancy Elizabeth Nix, b June 4, 1890.

1907

964. Sidney Johnson Nix=Lottie Appleby 963
Son of Dilmus M. and Jane Nix.
Is a lawyer and solicitor of the
City Court of Jefferson, Ga.

Progeny: Four Children

970. I   Mildred Nix, b June 4, 1907.

971. II Charlotte Nix, b Oct. 12, 1913.
972. III S.J. Nix, Jr., b March 5, 1921.

1882

965. Dilmus Herbert Nix=Lilian Gertrude Maley 973
Son of Dilmus. A farmer.

Progeny: Four Children

974. I Joseph D. Nix, b Aug. 13, 1910
975. II Hal M. Nix, b Feb. 16, 1913.
976. III Ruth Nix, b March 21, 1916.
977. IV Moton Estes Nix, b Sept. 13, 1921.

1908

966. Dora Maud Nix=George Griffin Williamson 978
Daughter of Dilmus.

Progeny: Five Children

979. I George G. Williamson, Jr., b Dec. 17, 1908.
980. II Frances Jane Williamson, b March 18, 1910.
981. III Dilmus Nix Williamson, b Oct. 16, 1911.
982. IV Malcolm Lafayette Williamson, b Sept. 30, 1913.
983. V George Anne Williamson, b Dec. 6, 1922.

1914

967. William Thomas Nix=Alma Montgomery 984
Son of Dilmus M. and Jane Nix.

Progeny: Three Children

985. I Wilmer Nix, b Dec. 23, 1914.
986. II Dupree Nix, b Aug. 9, 1917.
987. III Woodrow Wilson Nix, b March 13, 1920.

1916

968. Nancy Elizabeth Nix=A. Kent Rosetter 988
Daughter of Dilmus M. and Jane Nix.

Progeny: Two Children

989. I Nancy Janette Rossetter, b May 23, 1920.
990. II Appelton Kent Rossetter, b Oct. 6, 1922.

DOCTOR ROBERT BENJAMIN ADAIR OF ATLANTA

(886) Doctor Robert Benjamin Adair was the son of James M. and Martha Shields Adair, and ranks in the middle, in age, in the family of his parents. He was in his teens during the War Between the States.

His three older brothers all went into the Confederate Army during the first year of the war, and two of them died, and finally his father went into the army, and soon died, leaving a house full of little children and the plantation and negro slaves. So Robert B. Adair became lieutenant to his mother in the management of the plantation and slaves. When the war came to an end, the negroes were confiscated and set free, some of the younger sons in the family were getting large enough to work in the field, so that the boys altogether were enough to run the farm, with some hired help in the busy seasons. Robert B. managed the farm well under the circumstances, but his education was being neglected. So, when he was 18 years old his mother sent him to school one year at Commerce. The next year she sent him to Martin Institute at Jefferson, and boarded him with the minister, the pastor of the church.

About this time Robert B. selected dentistry for his profession. He bought some books for preliminary reading in dentistry, and whereas his mother paid for his education through the high school, that was as far as she felt she could go. But Robert B. had the necessary ambition, energy and will to undertake the expense of a professional education himself, so he taught school in the country, and boarded at home, and carried on his preliminary dental studies at the same time. Finally, when he thought he could enter college, and also thought he had enough money to put him through, he went to the Baltimore College of Dental Surgery and took his course. Before he got through, however, he ran short of money, and his younger brothers made up a purse and loaned him enough to get through on. He appreciated it and showed his appreciation in many ways. When his younger brothers came to select professions, Robert B. counseled and advised with them, and afterwards, when they needed assistance, he was a willing friend.

Dentistry was in its infancy when Doctor Robert B. Adair entered the profession, and he had to educate the public to appreciate it.

Doctor Robert Benjamin Adair is a successful professional man. No let us make a psychoanalysis, and see where his strong points are, and his handicaps.

1st. Mechanical talent is fine, inherited from a long line of ancestors, and we understand is transmitted to his progeny.
2d. Will power is good, which is important.
3d. Optimism, good.
4th Ambition, splendid.
5th Affectionate, enough.
6th Egotism, in a way, is a handicap, yet it gives him self-confidence.
7th Irritable temper: in boyhood "was ready to fight at the drop of the hat," but ready to forgive and make friends again.

1873

886. Doctor Robert Benjamin Adair=Allene Victoria Moss 991
Progeny: One Child

992. I Robin Adair, b 1878.
1914
886. (2d marriage) Doctor Robert B. Adair=Miss Mattie Simms 993 of Raleigh, N.C.

Progeny: None

Achievements of (886) Doctor Robert Benjamin Adair

Coming in boyhood days, and lasting through life, was the one distinct call to the profession of dentistry. This call was followed with a zeal amounting to a passion.

His early years in the profession were spent in general practice in Gainesville, Ga., where he made a signal success both in a professional and financial way, but he desired to give himself more largely to the treatment of pyorrhea, or Riggs disease, so in 1895 he moved to Atlanta, taking up the special treatment of pyorrhea.

In the Journal of Dental Research (Dec., 1921), Doctor Arthur H. Merritt of New York City, writing on the History of Periodontology, says: "One whose name is worthy of special mention is that of 886 Doctor R.B. Adair. For more than half a century Doctor Adair has consistently maintained the essential correctness of the principles laid down by John M. Riggs, thus making him one the beacon lights in the early history of Periodontology."

In clinic, before the International Medical Congress in Washington city in 1887, Doctor Adair gave to the profession a post-operative treatment for use in oral surgical cases, known as Pyorrhea Treatment Nos. 1 and 2. This treatment came into extensive use throughout the dental profession.

Doctor Adair served his profession in Georgia as President of the Dental Society, 1890-91, and later as a member of the State Examining Board.

On May 15, 1923, in celebration of his fifty-five years in the practice of dentistry the Fifth District Dental Society of Georgia gave in his honor a testimonial banquet. Fellow dentists, who had worked with him from ten to forty years, commended him for unusual force of character, views far in advance of his generation, marked enthusiasm over every forward step in the profession, and constant encouragement of younger men to higher and better achievement. As an evidence of their love and appreciation, at the close of the banquet a beautiful silver water service was given him. The pitcher bore his inscription:

"Presented to Doctor R.B. Adair from the 5th District Dental Society in appreciation of his services in the advancement of dentistry in Georgia."

995. Doctor Robin Adair=Leona Ragland 996
Son of Doctor R.B. Adair.

Progeny: Four Children
997. I Frances Allene Adair, b ____
998. II Robin Adair, Jr., b ____
999. III Millard Adair, b ____
1000 IV Benjamin Adair.

995. Doctor Robin Adair is well educated, being an A.B. and D.D.S. He is a skillful dentist and enjoys a good practice in Atlanta.

887. Henrietta Josephene Adair Hudson, the youngest daughter, ranked about middle in the family of James M. and Martha Adair. She was just entering her teens at the close of the war between the States, when educational facilities were limited. She got training at the Martin Institute in Jefferson, and at Commerce, and her education ranked far above the average of the period for girls. She was bright, fine looking and popular. At the early age of 18 she married (1001) James Anderson Hudson, a son of (1002) Maj. James P. Hudson, who had been a member of the State Legislature, and was a leader in his community. He ranked as Major in the war between the States. (1001) James Anderson Hudson, Phenies husband, was raised on his father's farm and was an industrious farmer. He was fond of a joke and would go his whole length for a good joke on his neighbor or friends. By and by, they sold their farm and bought a home in Atlanta, and moved there, where their children could have better educational and social advantages. She is now a widow, and still occupies her Atlanta home, where she is surrounded by some of her children.

1869

887. Henrietta Josephene Adair=James Anderson Hudson 1001
Progeny: Seven Children, One Daughter, Six Sons
1002 I Lery O. Hudson, a minister.
1003 II James Lonie Hudson, a locomotive engineer.
1004 III Hamilton Cary Hudson, electrical engineer.
1005 IV Theodocio Eula Hudson, m Mr. Self; is now a widow, a teacher.
1006 V Eugene Calvert Hudson, in the Navy.
1007 VI Earley Halbert Hudson, railroad passenger conductor.
1008 VII Mercer Alberta Hudson, d, one month.

Lery Olney Hudson was born at Commerce, ga., July 20, 1870; was raised on a farm, and got his high school training at Commerce. He decided on the ministry as his calling from his youth up. He graduated at the Mercer University, the Baptist institution of Georgia, in 1894. In 1895 he graduated in the Southern Baptist Theological Seminary, Louisville, Ky. He then accepted a call to the First Baptist Church at Columbus, Kans., and has been there and in that vicinity ever since, and his church and community have the utmost confidence in his integrity and conscientious devotion to his work. The climate does not agree with him, and he has some ill health to contend with, which is a handicap.

On Jan. 1, 1897, he married Miss Maud Gresham of Columbus, Kans.

1897

1002 Rev. Lery O. Hudson=Miss Maud Gresham 1009

Progeny: Five Children; Two Sons, Three Daughters

1010	I	Paul Hudson, a ministerial student at college in Fort Worth; is married and has one child.
1011	II	Mildred Hudson.
1012	III	Eula Hudson.
1013	IV	Mona Hudson.
1014	V	Robert Lee Hudson.

All are being educated in high school and college.

James Lonnie Hudson was born in 1872. As a boy he worked on his father's farm. After his school training at Commerce, he served the required apprenticeship in locomotive engineering, a profession to which he aspired from his early youth. His ambition was to sit at the throttle of a great locomotive, pulling a long passenger train. He is employed by the Southern Railway, and pulls the first train out, Atlanta to Washington, and has always enjoyed the confidence of the railway company, and he is president of the American Brotherhood of Locomotive Engineers.

1895

1003 James Lonnie Hudson=Imogene Mayne 1015

Progeny: Eight Children

1016	I	Stella Hudson, m Walter Pullam; one child, Walter Pullam, Jr.
1017	II	Halbert Hudson, graduate Electrical Engineer at Georgia Technical Institute, and is an electrical engineer for Southern R.R.; m 1921; no children.
1018	III	Etta Virginia Hudson, a business girl.
1019	IV	Mildren Hudson, a business girl.
1020	V	Imogene Hudson, student in high school.
1021	VI	James Hudson, d, age two years.
1022	VII	Margarett Hudson, in Primary school.
1023	VIII	John Westley Hudson, schoolboy.

1007 Earl Halbert Hudson, son of J.A. and Josephene Adair Hudson, was born Sept. 5, 1886, at Commerce, Jackson County, G. His parents moved to Atlanta, Ga., in 1904. Since then, he has been with the Southern Railway, ranking as conductor. He is highly respected by all his higher officials, owing to his fine moral and business qualifications. He is a devoted churchman of the Baptist faith.

1907

1007 Earl Halbert Hudson=Miss Maud Thomas 1024

of Atlanta

Progeny: One Son

    1025   I   Charles Halbert Hudson, b Oct. 28, 1909. He is a bright high school boy and has developed musical talent.

1004 Cary Hamilton Hudson, the third son of J.A. and Henrietta Josephene Hudson, finished high school and sophomore year at Mercer University. He then went east and served the required apprenticeship in electrical telephone construction, and soon showed such skill and talent that he was placed in charge of a switchboard at Trenton, and at Atlantic City, N.J. He died of meningitis Sept. 20, 1894. He was not married.

1005 Theodocio Eula Hudson, the only living daughter, finished grammar school and high school at Commerce, Ga. She attended the senior class at Brenau College at Gainesville, Ga., and graduated in one year. As a teacher she shows some talent, and has been engaged in her profession almost continually, in grammar grades, high school, and as principal. She shows thrift enough to accumulate quite a lot of real estate and financial securities.

In 1909, August, (1005) Miss Eula married (1026) Mr. T.G. Self. He died in 1913.

She has traveled extensively in the United States and Canada, and is now teaching in Los Angeles, Calif.

1006 Eugene Calvert Hudson, the fifth child of J.A. and Henrietta Josephene Adair Hudson, after finishing grammar school, enlisted in the U.S. Navy and served two terms with credit, and touched at every port in the world. He married about 1918.

Mrs. Henrietta Josephene Adair Hudson deserves great commendation for her success in raising and educating her children.

888. James B. Adair, M.D., was born July 5, 1853, a son of James M. Adair and Martha Barnett Shields Adair, and was named for both of his parents. He got a high school course at Commerce, Ga. He selected the profession of medicine because he liked the study of scientific medicine, and from philanthropic motives. His professional Training was obtained in the Medical College, University of Georgia; Medical School, Columbia University; and the Bellevue Hospital Medical College, of New York, and the University of Pennsylvania, in Philadelphia. After practicing twenty years in Texas, he gave it up because he was no longer able, physically, to do a general practice.

Doctor James Barnett Adair, age of 60.

The Editor, James B. Adair at Age of 24,

Mrs. Opal Adair Gilmer.

Virginia Hare Adair and Capt. Herbert S. Adair.

Adair is an advocate of the advantages of membership in medical societies and was a member of half a dozen of them.

Doctor Adair feels that he has done his full share of philanthropic work for suffering humanity. He is a cripple and invalid, from being run over by an automobile in 1914. He served one year on the editorial staff of the Seattle Daily Times, and six years as editor of the Northwest Mining Journal.

The following is his lineage: James B. Adair, James M. Adair, Jospeh A. Adair, John Adair, Jospeh Adair, Jr., Joseph Adair, Sr., Thomas Adair. Three of these were soldiers in the American Army, War of the Revolution, in South Carolina.

Doctor Adair's wife was a daughter of Capt. Thomas J. Hare (1027), whose ancestry is traced back to heroes of the War for Independence in North Carolina. Mrs. Adair was noted for her beauty and intelligence, and her mother, Amanda Sherman Hare (1028) was a superior woman, mentally and physically.

1883

888. Doctor James Barnett Adair=Miss Virginia Hare 1029

| Son of James M. and Martha B. Adair, and compiler and author of this book. | Daughter of a Confederate Calvary Captain, and of good lineage. |

Progeny: Three Children

1020   I   Ninon Gertrude Adair, b Sept. 23, 1884.
1031   II   Opal Montine Adair, b Dec. 8, 1888.
1032 III Herbert Spencer Adair, b Nov. 6, 1892.

All born in Houston Texas.

1030 Ninon Adair was educated in Broadway High School and University of Washington, both in Seattle. Her major studies were English, music, bacteriology and stenography, in all of which she became very proficient. She is a fluent writer.

1913

1033 Mr. Edmond Rider Downs=Miss Ninon Gertrude Adair 1030

| An American banker living in Mexico | Daughter of James B. and Virginia Hare Adair. |

Progeny: One Child

1034   I Virginia Downs, b March, 1914.

1912

1035 Mr. Merritt Fisher Gilmer=Miss Opal Montine Adair 1031

| A lumberman, and son of Colonel James N. Gilmer. Of the Confederate Army. | Daughter of James B. and Virginia Hare Adair. |

AMERICAN ADAIRS—Line B

Progeny: Two Sons

1037   Ernest Adair Gilmer, b ---
1038   II James Merriwether Gilmer, b ---
         July 30, 1924

1032 Doctor Herbert Spencer Adair=Miss Mildred Gambrell 1039
Son of Doctor James B. and   Daughter of Judge James N.
Virginia Hare Adair.   And Mrs. Mary Gambrell
                                                        Of Lockhart, Texas.

HERBERT SPENCER ADAIR, D.D.S.

Doctor Herbert S. Adair, of Los Angeles, was born in the mansion of the last President of the Republic of Texas, in the city of Houston, the Capitol City.

His parents are Doctor James B. Adair and Virginia Hare Adair. When a boy his parents moved successively west and north, living in El Reno, Okla, in Salt Lake City, Utah, and in Washington. He spent fifteen years in Seattle, where he got his primary education and his high school training was obtained in the Broadway High School, where he graduated, gaining an enviable record in athletics, excelling in aquatic sports and football. He was lifeguard on the municipal beach at Alki Point for four years and is credited with saving many persons from drowning.

Young Adair arrived in Los Angeles in September, 1915 and matriculated at the Dental College of the University of Southern California, where he represented the dental branch in football, and on the debating team. He was recognized as one of the leaders in these sidelines of a college career. He was graduated at the Dental College with honors in June, 1918 and immediately entered for service in the World War in the Army of the United States as first lieutenant in the Dental Corps, and was stationed at Fort Oglethorpe, Ga., where he was thoroughly drilled. After the Armistice was signed, he was put on the Reserve Corps, but allowed to return to civil life, subject to a call to arms, and he has since been promoted to a captaincy.

He visited the principal cities of the United States and, incidentally, assisted his father in gathering data for the Adair Genealogy. He returned to Los Angeles, decided to make this city his permanent home, and opened an office on Broadway for the practice of dentistry. As a general practitioner, there is no better in the city. Adair inherits mechanical talent from a long line of ancestors. Other strong points are a good memory and attention to details.

Doctor Herbert S. Adair.

Doctor Adair served two terms as Secretary-Treasurer, and two terms as President, of the Texas State Society, and built up the membership from 50 to 500 members. He was Vice-President of the Federation of State Societies in 1922. He is a member of the National Exchange Club, Los Angeles Ad Club, Sons of the American Revolution, Sierra Club, The Association of the Army of the United States, L.A. Athletic Club. He is a Director in the Life Extension Service Bureau of Los Angeles, and numerous fraternal societies.

On the 30th of July, 1924, he was married to Miss Mildred Gambrell, daughter of a good family in Lockhart, Texas. She noted for intelligence as well as beauty.

Doctor Adair's office is Suite 713 Story Building, on Broadway at 6th Street, Los Angeles.

890. Hamilton Stephen Adair, son of James M. Martha Shields Adair, was one of the younger set in the family, and he was one of twin brothers. His mate, named Anderson Brantly Adair (1043) died, age 2 years.

890. Stephen, as he was called, was not only a delicate boy in his youth, but his tastes and affinities were more those of a girl. He had the same opportunities for education that his brothers had, and he selected agriculture as his avocation and the other members of the family assigned him part of the old homestead, where he spent the rest of his life. During his early manhood he became crippled up with articular rheumatism. He nearly recovered, but died in 1898, age 43 years.

1879
890. Hamilton Stephen Adair=Miss Susan R. Malcomb 1045
of Morgan County, Ga.
Progeny: Five Children

1046	I	Henry Adair.
1047	II	Cornelia Adair, m Mr. --- Harris, son of Laith Harris; have three children.
1048	III	Ethleen Adair, m Thomas Hutchins; have three children; live Birmingham.
1049	IV	Eugene Brownfield Adair, m and lives in Birmingham, Ala.
1050	V	Bennie Adair; was a soldier in the World War.

They are all worthy citizens.

891. Doctor Samuel Brownfield Adair, next to the youngest son of James M. and Martha B. Adair, was born March 5, 1858, got his primary education in short summer schools, and worked on the farm the rest of the year, until his eighteenth birthday, then he got his high school training by continuous study. He selected dentistry as his profession, studied with his brother, Doctor R.B. Adair, then attended the Baltimore College of Dental

Surgery, and graduated there in 1881. He finally settled in Elberton, Ga., as a permanent location. He did well there, but some years later, when his children needed school advantages, he moved to the neighboring town of Roman on account of better school facilities at the latter place.

About 1886 he took a post-graduate course in dentistry at his alma mater in Baltimore.

He was popular as a dentist, and successful as a financier, a natural born banker; in fact, he missed his natural calling by not going into the banking business.

1888
891. Doctor Samuel Brownfield Adair=Miss F. Augusta Thornton
1052   1052

Son of James M. and   A most excellent wife
Martha B. Adair.   And mother.

Progeny: Five Children

- 1053   I   Shields B. Adair, m; two children. Is a teacher in a junior college near Rome, Ga.
- 1054   II   Ruby T. Adair, m; one child, then died; babe in charge of its Grandmother Adair at Roman, Ga.
- 1055   III   Florence Augusta Adair, m; lives in Rome, Ga.
- 1056   IV   George Franklin Adair is taking an engineering and mechanical course in Pittsburg, Pa.
- 1057   V   Wilma Adair; is a pupil in school in Boman, Ga.

892. DOCTOR EUGENE FRANKLIN ADAIR

Eugene Franklin Adair was born Sept. 5, 1861, and was the youngest of twelve children of James M. and Martha Shields Adair. His father died when he was only three years old and left his mother to raise and educate him. He received his high school education at Martin Institute in Jefferson, spent one year in Vanderbilt University in Nashville, Tenn., and graduated at the Baltimore College of Dental Surgery in 1885, dentistry being his profession. He practiced for a time with his older brother, Doctor R.B. Adair, in Gainesville, Ga., then located at Commerce, Ga., where he did a good practice and prospered financially, being a director in a bank. Doctor Adair was an enthusiastic supporter of Chinese Missions and maintained a missionary himself for many years.

Doctor E. F. Adair and family now live in Gainesville, Ga.

Mrs. Ninon Adair Downs

Mildred Gambrell Adair

AMERICAN ADAIRS—Line B

892. Doctor Eugene Franklin Adair=Miss Lula Westbrook 1065
Of good lineage, and of of Franklin County, Ga.
Revolutionary stock.

Progeny: Four Daughters

    1058   I Lucile Adair, b May 5, 1894.
    1059   II Edith Adair, b Feb. 29, 1896.
    1060   III Rebe Adair, b ---
    1061   IV Faith Adair, b ---

Lucine Adair graduated at Lucy Cobb Institute in Athens, Ga.

1063 Rev. Mr. Read-Miss Lucile Adair 1062
Member of the North Georgia   Daughter of Doctor Eugene and
Conference, M.E. Church   Lula Westbrook Adair.

Progeny: Two Children

Edith Adair graduated in Lucy Cobb Institute in Athens, Ga., which is one of the best in Georgia. Then she and (1064) Mr. Wisenhunt, whom she afterwards married, both attended a missionary school in Louisville, Ky.

CHAPTER XL
S.C. HAYS, M.D.

Leslie Saint Claire Hays was the son of A.N. Hays and Margaret Adair Hays (his wife), and was born March 2, 1888, at Clinton, S.C., where he was raised, got his primary and collegiate education, and where he makes his permanent location. He graduated at Presbyterian College, 1906 (valedictorian).

He helped to pay the expenses of his education by work, first in a publishing and printing concern; then he taught school three years, to-wit: at Presbyterian College in Clinton, second, at Shady Grove, a third, at Dillon, S.C.

He got his medical education in New York at the following institutions: Four years in the College of Physicians and Surgeons, being the Medical Department of Columbia University, where he graduated in June, 1913, with honors. In 1912 and 1913 he was resident at New York Nursery and Child Hospital as resident pathologist, working the summer of 1912 and during spare time of school year. He won an appointment for two years' surgical service in Bellevue Hospital, March, 1913.

In June, 1913, he stood state examinations for licenses to practice medicine in New York and South Carolina.

He entered Bellevue Hospital in July, 1913, and served until July, 1915.

He located in Clinton, S.C., July, 1915, where he soon established a hospital.

He enlisted in the World War, Medical Department of the U.S. Army, in February, 1918, and served at General Hospital 14, Fort Oglethorpe, Ga., his entire service, and was discharged Dec. 16, 1918.

After the war Doctor Hays spent five months in post-graduate work at St. Bartholomue's Hospital, New York, in 1922, and also worked with Doctor G.S. King at Bay Shore, Long Island.

Finally, Doctor Hays reopened his hospital in Clinton, as Doctor Hays' Hospital.

Doctor Hays married Miss Virginia Owens, Dec. 20, 1916. His wife and baby died a year later. In May, 1919, he married the second time, Miss Helen Hopp of Illinois.

Doctor Hays is a member of all the regular medical societies, to-wit: Laurens County Association (President), S.C. Medical Association, The southern Medical Association, and the American Medical Association (Fellow).

He is a high-up Mason and a member of various other organizations, clubs and societies.

We predict a brilliant career for this scion of the Adair Stock. His widowed mother deserves the credit for his training.

CHAPTER XLI

MRS. DILLARD

AN INCIDENT SHOWING THE HEROISM OF A HEROINE OF THE REVOLUTION

Mrs. Dillard was a noble American woman, wife of Capt. Dillard, an American soldier, and the mother of Sarah Dillard, the wife of Joseph Adair, Jr., another American soldier.

One the day before this heroic act, Mrs. Dillard had entertained Col. Clarks' command of American soldiers by feasting them on milk and potatoes. On the evening of the same day Fergusson and Dunlop, British commanders, came along and stopped at her house. They inquired whether Clark and his party had not been there, what time they left, and their numbers. She answered that they had been there, that she could not guess their numbers, and that they had been gone a long time.

They ordered her to prepare supper for the officers with dispatch. They took possession of the house and took Mrs. Dillard's bacon for their men. She began preparing supper for them. In going backwards and forwards from the kitchen she overheard much of their conversation, and found that that they had determined to pursue Clark as soon as they had refreshed themselves a little, and she heard one of the Tory officers tell Fergusson that he had just been informed that the rebels with Clark were to encamp that night at the big springs, and it was at once resolved to surprise them before day. Upon this she hurried supper, and as soon as she had sit it on the table, slipped out of a back way, went to the stable, bridled a young horse that had been kept up, and without saddle,, mounted, and rode with all possible speed to apprise Clark of his danger, in the hope of being in time to make a safe retreat, believing that the enemy were too numerous to justify a battle with them.

She arrived just in time to put them in readiness for action, for Fergusson had dispatched Dunlop with 200 picked mounted men to engage Clark and keep him employed until his arrival. Dunlop's detachment attempted to rush in as ordered, but Ferguson was too late for the frolic—the Americans won the victory. It was the warning that Mrs. Dillard gave Clark that enabled him to be ready for the enemy, instead of being surprised by him.

This noble woman's heroic act ought to entitle her lineal descendants to membership in patriotic organizations, such as the D.A.R. and the Sons of the Revolution. (See Mills Statistics of S.C.)

Below we herewith copy some of the records of South Carolina, taken from the original copies just after the Revolutionary War.

Revolutionary Accounts Audited 1-100

State of S.C.
 To Alexander Adair.
    L 22-10-8
    L 12-12-10
   Charleston Army settlement.

State of S.C.
 To Benjamin Adair
    L 12-2-10
   For horse lost in 1770.

State of S.C.
 To Isaac Adair,
His account of Military duty as private in Charleston Army.
    L 192-10-8
    L 27-10-0
  Received from the Treasury, June 14th, 1785.

State of S.C. Received of James Adair Jr, Sept. 7th, 1783.

200 pounds of flour for the use of widows and distressed families in Col. Casy's Regiment,
  Joseph Adair D Company.

State of S.C.
  To James Adair Jr,
200 pounds of flour L 1-17-6
Paid for recovery of horses lost at Augusta in May,
 177. 9—L 8-6-7

  L-4-7 ¼
State of South Carolina, To
  `Joseph Adair Sr.
His account of number of days duty as Commissary, also for provisions, forage, hire of wagon, team et & for military account in 1781,
   The whole Charge L 673-10-9
         L 96-5-8
     Paid

A commissary pay bill of Joseph Adair, Sr., Commissary, commencing Aug. 20, 1781, ending March ?, 1782 (full itemized expense list is on record, and has been photographed by Lyles Studio at Columbia).

This itemized list is certified by Levi Casey, Colonel, Jan. 6, 1785.

LINE C

CHAPTER XLII

JAMES ADAIR
The Author and Merchant

2 James Adair, the son of 1 Thomas Adair, was born in County Antrim, in Ireland, about the year 1709. He was the oldest of three brothers, named as follows: James, the subject of this sketch; 3 Joseph, the father of the Carolina-Georgia Adairs; 4 William, the father of the Kentucky Adairs.

Thomas Adair migrated from Ireland, County Antrim, about 1730, with his three sons, and settled in Chester County, Penn., where they resided for twenty years, and then moved to South Carolina about 1750.

James was educated in Ireland before coming to America, but his younger brothers had to finish their education in Pennsylvania. James' training embraced mathematics and languages, and he had natural talent for business and diplomacy.

2 James Adair left Pennsylvania earlier than his father and brothers, and joined a partnership at Charleston, S.C., with 20 Golphin, the noted Indian trader, and was engaged in that business for about forty years, beginning about 1735. They imported from Great Britian, through the port of Charleston, such goods as the Indians wanted, and transported them by pack trains over trails to various stations located in various southern States as far west as the Mississippi River. They built up an enormous trade, which continued for a long period. They did not use wagons and roads, but packhorses and trails. Adair's travels and acquaintance with the Indians made him familiar with the resources of the country, and his trade and business relation with the wholesale business of Great Britian made him friends and got him the ear of the King. Adair saw a section of country in upper South Carolina, known as 96th district (afterwards named Laurens County), which pleased him. He therefore applied to 21 King George II for a grant, and it was given to him by the King. We do not know, at the present time, the number of acres contained in the Adair Grant, but it contained and embraced Duncans Creek and all the region around about.

Having secured this land, James Adair had his father and brothers move from Pennsylvania and take charge of it, improve, use, and occupy some of it, and sell the balance. The Adair family from Pennsylvania began to improve it in 1750.

James Adair was a traveling merchant. His business was everywhere. He had no local habitation. Therefore, he could not use nor occupy this land himself.

Adair had the confidence of the various Indian tribes occupying the Southern States from Virginia to the Mississippi. He acted as diplomat and peacemaker between tribes, and between Whites and Indians. One instance was where the French at New Orleans tried to negotiate with the Choctaws for land. Adair was appealed to, and he settled it in favor of the English. He was an authority on populations statistics of the Indians. He studied the Cherokee language and made vocabularies of the various dialects of the various Indian tribes, and he compared these languages with the Hebrew language, of which he was a scholar.

While living with the Indians he made a study of their manners and customs and, as far as possible, of their ethnology, and gathering together the material which he had prepared with much labor and work, his friends induced him to have it published, which he did in London, 1775. The volume was entitled "The History of the American Indians, particularly those nations living in the Southern States, from Virginia to the Mississippi River." This work is not only interesting, but valuable, on account of his careful description and elucidation of the customs and manners of the Indians, their rites and ceremonies. It has also especial value on account of its containing many facts showing a striking resemblance between the customs of Indians and those of the Jews.

On the existence of this resemblance Adair based a theory, which he sustained with arguments to prove, that the Indians of North American descended from the Jews.

These arguments included the fact of their division into tribes, their worship of Jehovah, their festivals, fasts and religious rites, their daily sacrifice, their prophets and high priests, their cities of refuge, their marriages and divorces, their burial of the dead and customs with regard to mourning, their language and choice of names adapted to circumstances, their manner of reckoning time and various other particulars which he investigated and escribed in detail.

In the course of the prosecution of his labors he made vocabularies of the Indian dialects, which, though unsatisfactory in many respects, have a distinct bearing on the theory he advanced.

The opinions and conclusions of Adair were afterward adopted by Doctor Elias Boudinot in his "Star of the West, Or an Attempt to Discover the Long Last Tribes of Isreal."

We intend to make copious extracts for this chapter from Adair's treatise on the Indians, but just before we were ready to write the extracts, someone stole the book from the Los Angeles Public Library. Being out of print for nearly 140 years, it cannot be replaced.

James Adair made a trip to London in 1775, and while in London he interviewed members of the British Cabinet in behalf of peace for the American Colonies, and in the introductory chapter of his book he urged the British government to conciliate the colonies and maintain peace.

About the time of his trip to London, or just before that time, Adair married a lady in North Carolina and finally settled in that state. (We do not know his exact location nor the maiden name of his wife.) His oldest son was James Adair, Jr., who married Miss Kilgor.

10 James Adair, Jr.=Miss Kilgore 10

12 John Kilgor Adair, b 1828 in N.C.

12 John Kilgor Adair moved to Alabama before the Civil War, was a Colonel in the Confederate army. Most of his children were born in Alabama, but he moved to Fayetteville, Ark., to educate his children in the State University.

12 John Kilgore Adair=Martha McTier Carter 13
Progeny: Eight Children

14	I	James Leonidus Adair; lives at Ada, Okla.; m Martha Bishop.
15	II	John Kilgore Adair, Jr.
16	III	William Clayton Adair.
17	IV	Preston Brooks Adair.
18	V	Ellafair Adair, m John Benn. Gunter.
19	VI	Ida Adair.
25	VII	Jennette Adair.
2	VIII	Franklin Pierce Adair, d.

27 Preston Brooks Adair was born in DeKalb County, Ala., in 1857. His father's family moved to Arkansas in 1858. Preston B. entered the University at Fayetteville, in 1878. Preston Brooks Adair has filled various county offices with credit and public satisfaction.

1884

(1st marriage) **27 Preston Brooks Adair=Alice Harmon of Miss. 28**
Four Children Living

29	I	Gertrude Adair.
30	II	Morvin Adair.
31	III	Oliver Adair.
32	IV	John Kilgore Adair.

1898

(2d marriage) **27** Preston Brooks Adair=Anna Wilks 33
Progeny: Six Children

34	I	Day Adair.
35	II	Dian Adair.
36	III	Randall Adair.
37	IV	Donald Adair.
38	V	Mary Adair.
39	VI	Ruth Adair.
40	VII	Vernon Adair, d at 6 months.

18 Ellafair Adair=John Benjamin Gunter 41
Progeny: One Daughter

42   Mildred McTier Rittenhouse of Baltimore.

LINE D

CHAPTER XLIII

HON. JOHN ADAIR OF KNOXVILLE
GENEALOGY OF PART OF THE DESCENDANTS OF
HON. JOHN ADAIR, SR., OF KNOXVILLE.

1 Hon. John Adair, Sr.=Ellen Crawford **2**
Born in Antrim County, Ireland, 1732.
Progeny: Mary Adair and others

3 Mary Adair=Robert Christian
Adair of Knoxville.   of Sullivan Co.
Daughter of Hon. John   Son of Col. Gilbert Christian
Progeny: 6 Maria Christian, b Feb. 2, 1802, d June 21, 1883, and others

1819

6 Maria A. Christian=John Smith **7**
Daughter of Robert and   Born 1795, d 1883; native
Mary Adair Christian   of Culpepper Co., Va.
Progeny: Two Sons, Seven Daughters

8	I	Israel Owen Smith, b Oct. 17, 1820.
9	II	Mary Ann Ellen Smith, b Nov. 25, 1822.
10	III	Martha Louisa Smith, b Sept. 1, 1828.
11	IV	Emily Alzira Smith, b March 4, 1832.
12	V	Sarah Maria Smith, b. Dec. 23, 1835.
13	VI	Margaret Prudence Smith, b Sept. 13, 1836.
14	VII	James Harvey Smith, b Jan. 17, 1840.
15	VIII	Harriet Virginia Smith, b March 9, 1842; d June 21, 1923.
16	IX	Matilda Adeline Smith, b Sept. 12, 1844; d Oct. 20, 1858.

September, 1884

15 Harriet Virginia Smith=**17** W. Templeton Mitchell
Daughter of John Smith and
Maria Christian Smith.
Progeny: None

9 Mary Ann Elender Smith=John Tillery
Second daughter of John and   Born Oct. 6, 1816.
Maria Smith

Progeny

17	I	Sarah Elmira Tillery, b Sept. 23, 1843.
18	II	Rebecca Maria Tillery, b Dec. 26, 1845.

Unveiling of Monument of Knoxville.

19 III Mary Teresy Tillery, b July 9, 1848.
20 IV   Samuel Loue Tillery, b April 22, 1851.
21 V   Isabella Parlie Tillery, b March 17, 1854; d Aug. 16, 1855.

1878

20 Samuel Loue Tillery=Eglentine N. Badgett
Fourth child of John Tillery and
Mary E. Smith.

Progeny

22 I   Rogers Tillery, b Jan. 1879.
23 II   Weller Tillery, b July 15, 1881.
24 III   Anna Tillery, b Sept. 26, 1883, d 1902.
25 IV   Lucy Tillery, m Crawford, b Sept. 24, 1886.
26 V   Stella Tillery, b Aug. 18, 1894; m Stepp.
27 VI   Nannie Tillery, b Jan. 4, 1896.
28 VII   Mary Tillery, b March 22, 1889.
29 VIII Samuel Tillery, b Sept. 17, 1901.

1908

25 Lucy Tillery=25 G.S. Crawford
Daughter of Samuel L. and
E. Badgett Tillery.

Progeny: Three Daughters

30 I   Nancy Evelyn Crawford, b April 24, 1908.
31 II and III   Jane and Hellen Crawford (twins), b June 9, 1911.

1920

26 Stella Tillery=J.F. Stepp
Fifth child of Samuel L. and
E. Badgett Tillery.

Progeny: One Daughter

32 I   Mary Clementine Stepp, b May 7, 1921.

1854

10 Martha Louis Smith=10 Stephen Henry Smith
Daughter of John and   b 1819, at Williamston, Mass.
Maria Christian Smith

Progeny: Five Children

33 I   Lucius Adair Smith, b June 8, 1822; d Sept. 1852.
34 II   Frances Jane Smith, b Jan. 15, 1856; d 1916.
35 III John Henry Smith, b March 20, 1864; d Sept. 3, 1884.
36 IV   Margaret Louisa Smith, b March 20, 1864; d June 1, 1923.
37 V   Ida Newland Smith, b Oct. 16, 1867; d June 18, 1899

1881

34 Frances Jane Smith=34 Elijah Elonzo Hackworth

Daughter of John and
Martha L. Smith.
Progeny: Four Children
38	I	Eleanor Adair Hackworth, b Dec. 4, 1881.
39	II	Blanche Louise Hackworth, b Jan. 27, 1883; d Dec. 27, 1910.
40	III	Rose Tanner Hackworth, b Nov. 1, 1886.
41	IV	Harry Smith Hackworth b Oct. 2, 1888.

1901

36 Margaret Louisa Smith=36 William S. McCulla
Daughter of Stephen H. and
Martha L. Smith

Progeny: None
1904

38 Eleanor Adair Hackworth=38 Louis L. Gouffon

Progeny: Two Children
42	I	Ruth Eleanor Gouffon, b Oct. 14, 1905; d April 13, 1919.
43	II	Charles Louis Gouffon, b Sept. 25, 1910.

39 Blanche Louise Hackworth=39 Doctor W.T. Flanagan
Daughter of Elijah Alonzo and
Frances J. Hackworth.

Progeny: Two Children
44	I	Mary Frances Flanagan, b Aug. 4, 1909.
455.	II	Blanche Louise Flanagan, b Dec. 7, 1910; d at birth.

1921

40 Rose Tanner Hackworth=40 Hugh L. Wadell
Daughter of Elijah Alonzo and
And Frances J. Smith Hackworth.

Progeny: None
1916

41 Harry Smith Hackworth=41 Mary Lawrence Agee
Son of Elijah Alonzo and
Frances J. Hackworth.

Progeny: One Child
42	I	Harry Agee Hackworth, b May 10, 1922.
43		William Armstrong Aldredge Conner was born 1823; son of 44 Thomas Conner; a native of Virginia.

1850

11 Emily Alzira Smith=43 William A.A. Conner
Daughter of John and Maria Smith and
Great-granddaughter of Hon. John Adair.

Progeny: Ten Children

44	I	Mary Adelin Conner, b July 21, 1851.
45	II	John Adair Conner, b June 1, 1853; d Nov. 1854.
46	III	Thomas Williard Conner, b Feb. 11, 1855; died Aug. 14, 1877.
47	IV	Joseph Aldredge Conner, b Sept. 15, 1858.
48	V	Charles William Conner, b Sept. 12, 1860.
49	VI	Eliza Brownlow Conner, b April 13, 1863; d June 21, 1875.
50	VII	Harry Smith Conner, b Dec. 11, 1865.
51	VIII	Edward Everett Conner, b Nov. 13, 1868.
52	IX	Frederic Jewel Conner, b May 28, 1872.
53	X	George Gilbert Conner, b Nov. 1875; d March, 1876.

1875

44 Mary Adeline Conner=**44** Samuel Marshall Cooper
Son of James Jackson Cooper.

Progeny: Five Children

55	I	Stella Irene Cooper, b Oct. 7, 1876.
56	II	Claud Cuthbert Cooper, b Oct. 8, 1878.
57	III	Karl Stewart Cooper, b Nov. 18, 1880.
58	IV	Nellie Cooper
59	V	Wilbur Cooper (twins), b Aug. 12, 1883.

1906

56 Claud Cuthbert Cooper=**56** Dora Humes

Son of Samuel M. and Mary A. Conner Cooper

Born Feb. 26, **1884.** Daughter of **60** Thomas W. and Mary Sexton Humes and grandniece of Thos. W. Humes, former president of the University of Tennessee.

Progeny: Three Children

61	I	Margaret Catherine Cooper, b June 19, 1907.
62	II	Samuel Marshall Cooper, Jr., b Dec. 10, 1912.
63	III	Mary Nelle Cooper, b Feb. 19, 1915.

1922

57 Karl Stewart Cooper=**57** Bertha Cupp, b June 25, 1897

Son of Sam M. and M.A. Conner Cooper

Daughter of Maynart and Christine Cupp of Claibon Co., Tenn.

Progeny

64	I	John Harrison Cooper, b May 2, 1923.

1914

59 Wilber Curtis Cooper=**59** Hazel Marie Shonts

Son of Samuel Marshall and M.A. Cooper

Born April 1, **1889.** Daughter of **65** William S and Ida Carkhuff

Shonts, who were Pennsylvania People who came south on their wedding day.

Progeny: Two Children

66 I Neel Shonts Cooper, b March 15, 1917.
67 II Helen Virginia Cooper, b Dec. 13, 1920.

1887

47 Joseph Aldredge Conner=Kete Lucinda Anderson 47

Son of Wm. A.A. Conner and E. A. Smith Conner

Born Jan. 4, 1856. Daughter of Claibourn and Mary Caldwell Anderson, And great-granddaughter of Isaac Anderson, Founder of Maryville College. She died in 1914.

Progeny: Two Children

68 I Mary Emily Conner, b Feb. 4, 1889.
69 II Margaret Conner, b March 1, 1894.

1888

48 Charles William Conner=Margaret Catherine Caldwell 48

Son of Wm. A. Conner and E. A. Smith Conner

Born Oct. 22, **1863**. Daughter of John and 70 Nancy J.A. Caldwell And great-granddaughter of the Founder of Marysville College.

Progeny: Two Children

71 I John William Conner, b Dec. 25, 1888.
72 II Annette Jane Conner, b Dec. 29, 1890.

1914

71 John William Conner=Jessie Ann Wilson 71

Son of Wm. A.A. Conner and E.A. Smith Conner.

b Feb. 6, 1889; daughter of 73 Capt. Joseph Wilson of Knoxville.

Progeny

74 I Charles Wilson, Conner, b Aug. 11, 1916.
75 II John William Conner, Jr., b Sept. 17, 1920.

72 Annette Jane Conner=72 Charles N. Britt

Daughter of Charles w. Conner and M.C. Caldwell Conner.

Progeny: None

1904

50 Harry Smith Conner=Hattie Elizabeth Yarnell 50

Son of Wm. A.A. and E.A. Smith Conner

Daughter of Jas. M. and 76 Elizabeth C. Yarnell, b Oct. 23, 1874.

Progeny: None

1905

51 Edward Everet Conner=Eva Mae Bishop **51**

Son of Wm. A.A. and E.A. Smith Conner

b Sept. 1, 1889; daughter of John Mc. Bishop and Margaret M.W. Bishop.

Progeny: One Son

77   I Percy Bishop Conner, b April 8, 1910.

1908

52 Frederic Jewel Conner=52 Nina Carrie Hammer

Son of Wm. A.A. Conner and E.A.S. Conner.

b July 24, 1882; daughter of Doctor Thomas B. Hammer and Sarah J.C. Hammer.

Progeny: Two Children

78   I   Thomas William Conner, b Sept. 6, 1910.
79   II Emily Jane Conner, b Jan. 7, 1913.

Descendants of Sarah Maria Smith

1859

12 Sarah Maria Smith=12 Benjamin Franklin Sanders
Daughter of John and Maria Smith.

Progeny

80   I   Hattie A. Sanders, b June 6, 1860.
81   II   William E. Sanders, b Dec. 16, 1862. (Single)
82   III   John Wiley Sanders, b April 19, 1865.
83   IV   Eugene L. Sanders, b Feb. 21, 1867. (Single)
84   V   Florence Sanders, b March 4, 1869; d June 15, 1871.
85 and 85 V and VI   Della and George Sanders (twins), b May 18, 1872.
87   VII   Samuel Sanders, b July 24, 1874.

1887

80 Hattie A. Sanders=80 Sam E. Hill
Daughter of B.F. and S.R. Sanders.

Progeny

87   I   Reba Sanders Hill, b July 25, 1888
88   II   Ralph Morrell Hill, b Oct. 7, 1894.

1920

87 Reba Sanders Hill=87 St. John Reynolds

1921

82 John Wiley Sanders=82 Della Allison

Progeny

89   I   Allison Cecil Sanders, b Sept. 2, 1902.

1905

85 Della Sanders=**85** John Mathis
Daughter of B.F. and Sarah
Maria Sanders.

Progeny

90	I	Reba Barbara Mathis, b Feb. 2, 1906.
91	II	Sarah Christian Mathis, b Oct. 30, 1911.

87 Sam Sanders=**87** Lucy Matthews
Son of B.F. and Sarah Maria Sanders.

Progeny: None

1872

92 Maria Sapphire Smith=**92** Andrew C. Simpson
Born 1845; died 1906

Progeny: Four Children

93	I	Harriet Amelia Simpson, b April 21, 1878.
94	II	Alice Idelle Simpson, b Feb. 14, 1880.
95	III	Edward Bachman Simpson, b Oct 10, 1882.
96	IV	Howard Heron Simpson, b Oct. 29, 1886.

1905

93 Harriet Amelia Simpson=**93** Arthur S. McCampbell
Daughter of Andrew C. and Maria
S. Smith Simpson.

Progeny: Two Children

97	I	Clarence S. McCampbell, b Nov. 30, 1905.
98	II	Kathleen Idell McCampbell, b July 10, 1909.

1914

94 Alice Idell Simpson=**94** Ray E. Freet
Daughter of A.C. and M.S. Simpson.

Progeny: None

1908

95 Edward Bachman Simpson=**95** Clara Stephenson
Son of A.C. and M.S. Simpson.

Progeny

100.	I	Edward B. Simpson, Jr., b March 2, 1915.

1844

8 Israel Owen Smith=**8** Lucy Grimmit Smith
Son of John and Maria A.
Christian Smith.

Progeny: Seven Children

101.	I	Maria Sapphira Smith, b Aug. 16, 1845.

102. and 103 II and III   Judson and Homer Smith, twins, b Oct. 19, 1846.
104. IV   Charlotte A. Smith, b Oct. 9, 1849.
105. V   Sarah L. Smith, b July 29, 1851.
106. VI   Lucy Ann Smith, b March 22, 1853; d Aug. 22, 1877.
107. VII Mahala Prudence Smith, b Feb. 2, 1855, d.
108. VIII Emma Isabella Smith, b May 24, 1857.

1876
106. Lucy Ann Smith=106 Matthew Rogers
Sixth child of Israel O. and
Lucy G. Smith.

Progeny: One Son
109. I   Arthur Haden Rogers, b March 25, 1877.

1871
103. Homer Smith=103 Julia Ann Harris
Third Child of Israel O. and   born July 3, 1840.
Julia Ann Harris Smith.

Progeny: Five Children
110. I   Hattie Louise Smith, b July 24, 1873.
111. II   Charles Owen Smith, b Oct. 9, 1975.
112. III William Judson Smith, b Feb. 4, 1878.
113. IV   Alice Coffin Smith, b Aug. 6, 1880.
114. V   Jennie Smith, b Dec. 11, 1883.

1903
110. Hattie Louise Smith=110 Alonzo Webb
First child of Homer and Julia
Ann Harris Smith.

Progeny: None

1906
111. Charles Owen Smith=111 Lou Ella Lankford
Progeny: None

190. 9
112. William Judson Smith=112 Clara Hearn
Son of Homer Smith and   She Died.
Julia A. Harris Smith.

Progeny: None
112. William Judson Smith, married 2d, 112 Florence Smith
Progeny:
115.   Beattie Smith, b about 1919.

1871
103. Judson A. Smith=103 Hester Ann Baker

Born 1846.   Of Athens, Tenn.
                    Progeny: Four Children
    117.   I   Mattie Lula Smith, b July 5, 1876.
    118.   II   Alvin Nicholas, b Aug. 26, 1877.
    119.   III Lucy Delilah Smith, b Nov. 27, 1879.
    120.   IV   Flora May Smith, b July 13, 1881.
                            1894
    117. Mattie Lula Smith=117 John George Walton
    Daughter of Judson A. and
    Hester Ann Smith.
                      Progeny: None
Mattie died in Augusta, Ga., July 25, 1912, and was buried there.
                            1913
    118. Alvin Nicholas Smith=118 Hazel Stewart
Daughter of Judson A. and   of Saranac, New York.
Hester Ann Smith.
                      Progeny: None
    They reside in Knoxville.
                            1906
    119. Lucie Delilah Smith=110 Eugene E. Caldwell
    Daughter of Judson A. and
    Hester A. Smith.
    They live in Knoxville.
                         Progeny
    122.   I   Margaret Elizabeth Smith, b March 2, 1914.
                            1909
    120. Flora May Smith=120 Edwin Morrow
    Daughter of Judson A. and
    Hester A. Smith.
                   Progeny: Two Daughters
    123.   I   Martha Ann Morrow, b March 31, 1910.
    124.   II   Lucie Eugenia Morrow, b Ot. 14, 1911.
    They live in New York.
                            1870
    105. Sarah Larmar Smith=105 Augustus Gustavus Buffat
    Daughter of Isreal O. and
    Lucy Grimmit Smith.
                   Progeny: Eleven Children
    126.   I   Chrissie Buffat.
    127.   II   Daisy Buffat.

128. III   Emile Buffat.
129. IV   Francis Israel Buffat.
130. V   Gustavus Buffat.
131. VI   Anna Bell Buffat, dead.
132. VII   Blanche Buffat.
133. VIII   Emma Buffat.
134. IX   Lula Buffat.
135. X   George Buffat.
136. XI   Lydia Buffat.

126. Chrissie Buffat=126 Julian Larpin
Of Switzerland. He died,
leaving
A daughter named 137 Julian.

Chrissie then married 139 George Davies of Knoxville.

Progeny: Six Children

140. I   Guss Davies.
141. II   Benjamin Davies.
142. III   Elizabeth Davies.
143. IV   Margaret Davies.
144. V   Dan Davies.
145. VI   One dead.

146. Julian Larpin-147 J.J. Welch of Chattanooga
No children

148. Daisy Buffat=148 C.B. Pattillo of Spring Place
No Children

128. Emile Buffat=128 Ella Wright
Of Beaver Cree, Arizona

Now live at Tucson, Arizona.

Progeny: One Girl, Two Boys

150. I   Hellen Gladys Buffat, m 150 Jim Reid of California. No children.
151. II   Monford Buffat.
152. III   Gene Buffat.

129. Francis Israel Buffat=129 Ella Taylor
Of Concord, Tenn.

No children

130. Gustavus Buffat=130 Grace Keener
Of Chattanooga, Tenn.

Progeny: Five Children

153. I   Ruth Buffat.
154. II   Mildred Buffat.
155. III   Mary Charlotte Buffat.

156. IV Gussie Buffat.
157. V Raymond Buffat.
132. Blanche Buffat, seventh child of A.G. and Sarah L. Buffat

132. (1st marriage) Blanche Buffat=158 Marian Driscoll
Of Knoxville
One Daughter
159. Beatrice Driscoll.
(They were then divorced.)

132. (2d marriage) Blanche Buffat=160 Francis Vandergriff
Of Knoxville, died

132. (3d marriage) Blanche Buffat=Charlie Crowder
Of Knoxville, he died.

159. Beatrice=159 M. Gallaher of Byington, Tenn.
One Daughter
161. Margaret Gallaher.

133. Emma Buffat=133 J.H. Moyers
Daughter of A.G. and of Morriston, Tenn.
Sarah L. Buffat.
Progeny: Two Boys, One Girl
163. I Floyd Ernest Moyers.
164. II Lucile Moyers.
165. III Theodore Moyers.

134. Lula Buffat=134 George Frederick Frye
Of Chattanooga
Progeny: None
135. George Buffat is single.

136. Lydia Buffat=136 Carl Smith of Knoxville
Progeny: One Girl
166. I Sara Elizabeth Smith.

1867

14 James Harvey Smith=14 Margaret Ann Anderson
Son of John and Maria Christian Smith.
Progeny: Four Children
167. I Lucinda Adalin Smith, b Jan. 28, 1868.
168. II Mary Christian Smith, b Dec. 6, 1869.
169. III Sallie Douglas Smith, b June 16, 1872.
170. IV Fannie Gertrude Smith, b Aug. 21, 1876.

1898

167. Lucinda Adaline Smith=167 George William Broome
Daughter of James Harvey and
Margaret A. Smith.

Progeny: Three Children
172. I William Smith Broome, b Sept. 15, 1900.
173. II Harvey Benjamin Broome, b July 15, 1902.
174. III Margaret Elizabeth Broome, b April 28, 1907.

1914

170. Fannie Gertrude Smith=170 Twiman W. Coile
Daughter of James Harvey and
Margaret A. Smith.

Harvey Benjamin Broome was born in Knoxville, Tenn., July 15, 1902.

His mother, before her marriage, was Miss Adaline Smith, a daughter of James Harvey Smith, who is one of the oldest living descendants of John Adair.

His father, George William Broome, was born in England, and came to this country in 1872.

In his very young days Harvey was rather weakly, but by the kind, persistent work of his physician, coupled with righteous living, he has overcome the handicap and is now a strong, healthy young man.

He entered the Knoxville city schools as soon as he was old enough, passing through high school with honors. In his Senior year he was made business manager of the Voice, which is issued annually at the close of the school year. He graduated in June, 1919, from the city schools, and the following September was admitted to the University of Tennessee. By continued hard work and close application to his studies he made good, graduating with honor in the class of 1923. While in University he was active in many lines, doing work with the Literary Society, Young Men's Christian Association and the Athletic Association. He was chosen as editor and was called upon to produce the University annual, which is known as the Volunteer. In this position he showed marked ability and a capacity for much hard work.

He made up his mind some years ago to enter the legal profession and is now preparing himself for that work. The school years of 1922 and 1923 at the University were spent in the Law School, and the following September he entered Harvard University to continue his studies. One year has been spent there, and he hopes to put in two more years.

1893

108. Emma Isabella Smith=108 George R. Jackson
Eighth and youngest daughter of
Israel O. and Lucy Grimmit Smith.

Progeny

175. I George R. Jackson, b May 29, 1894.

On June 21, 1917, he enlisted for training in the World War. After spending the required time in the training camp, he served with the A.E.F. from May 26, 1918, to March 23, 1919. He was in the following battles, engagements, skirmishes and expeditions:

Aug. 27 to Sept. 11, 1918: Defense of the Toul Sector.
Sept. 12 to 14, 1918: Mihiel Offensive.
Sept 12 to 14, 1912: Meuse-Argonne Offensive.
Sept. 26 to Oct. 8, 1918: Defense of Woevre Sector.
Oct. 11 to Nov. 7, 1918: Offense of Woevre Sector.
Nov. 11, 1918, the Armistice was signed.

He belonged to Battery C, 114th Field Artillery.

He was honorably discharged from the military service of the United States at Fort Oglethorpe, Ga., April 7, 1919.

Mr. Jackson is now employed by the U.S. Steel and Iron Construction Co. at Lynch, Ky.

He is still single. His mother lives at 715 Walnut St., Knoxville, Tenn.

HONORABLE JOHN ADAIR OF KNOXVILLE

John Adair, so far as available materials indicates, was born in the Providence of Ulster, in the north of Ireland, either in the year 1731 or 1732. Practically nothing is known of his life in Ireland, but two books, one in the possession of James Harvey Smith, and the other belonging to Harvey Benjamin Broome (both descendants of John Adair), bearing Adair's signature and certain dates, show that at some time in his life he lived in Belfast. One date, the date of the purchase of the books in Belfast, was 1766; the next date is 1776, and clearly points to the fact that he was in America at the time, so he must have come to this country.

As a matter of personal Interest, one of these books is a law book, and the other is a dictionary. We may deduce from this that he must have been rather a scholarly man and, perhaps, above the average pioneer in his educational attainments. Moreover, the public offices he held in Tennessee later in his life show the same thing.

The next definite date we have is that of 1779. In that year he was appointed "Entry Taker" for Sullivan County, N.C., now a part of Tennessee. The population of that section (the Knoxville District) were mostly settlers who had spent all their money to pay for their new homes, so the people had but little money. Mr. Adair was a friend and associate of Col. Isaac Shelby and Col. Sevier when they were organizing their expedition against the

British forces under Col. Furgusson at Kings Mountain (located on the line of North Carolina and South Carolina south of Knoxville).

Colonels Shelby and Sevier needed money with which to equip their troops, but no funds were in hand or in prospect. These patriotic officers tried to borrow the money on their own account, but it was not to be had. Colonels Shelby and Sevier then turned to the Land Agent, as he had nearly all the money of the country, for a loan of the public money in his hands. The name of this Land Agent was John Adair. His reply to Colonels Shelby and Sevier, who wanted the money to meet a public exigency, is worthy a patriot. It should and did immortalize John Adair. Said he: "I have no authority in law to make that disposition of this money. It belongs to the impoverished treasury of North Carolina, and I dare not appropriate a cent of it to any purpose; but if our country is overrun by the British our liberties are gone. Let the money go, too. Take it. If the enemy by its use, is driven from the country, I can trust that country to justify and vindicate my conduct, so take it."

The money was taken and expended for ammunition and necessary equipment. The loan amounted to $12,735, and Shelby and Sevier pledged themselves to see it refunded, or the act of the Entry Taker legalized, which they did, and the history of North Carolina shows it.

Colonels Shelby and Sevier, with their expeditionary force, marched through the defiles of North Carolina, and reached Kings Mountain in time to take part in this decisive battle between the Americans and the British. The Americans were victorious, and utterly routed the British, making one of the turning points in favor of the Americans in the War of the Revolution. This great battle of Kings Mountain took place early in October, 1781. General Furgusson was slain, and Lord Cornwallis, who was commander-in-chief of the British forces, and was encamped in Eastern North Carolina and Virginia, was so discouraged that he moved his army onto Eastern Virginia, and surrendered to Gen. Washington at Yorktown, thus ending the war.

In 1788 John was Commissioner for purchasing supplies for the Cumberland Guard, which acted as an escort for travelers through the wilderness to the Cumberland Plateau.

In 1794, when Blount College was established, John Adair became one of the trustees. This college is now the University of Tennessee.

In 1796 John Adair was a member of the Constitutional Convention which made the first Constitution for Tennessee. He was a Presidential Elector for the Hamilton District in 1796 and in 1800. Adair and Gen. James White were contemporaries and friends. The latter founded Knoxville in

1792, and Adair was one of the Commissioners.

John Adair was a trustee of Hampden-Sidney Academy, and an Elder in the First Presbyterian Church organized in Tennessee.

The Legislature of North Carolina granted Adair a section of land four and one-half miles north of Knoxville for his services. This was in 1791. He built himself a house, something like a blockhouse. Part of his land is still owned by a branch of the family. The city of Knoxville has grown and taken it in, and it is called Adair Station. The little creek running through it is called Adair Creek.

John Adair was a member of the first County Court of Knox County, Tenn., which met June 16, 1792.

Finally, John Adair died on Feb. 24, 1827, age 95 years. Following is a copy of his death notice from the Knoxville Register of March 28, 1827:

> DIED—On Feb. 24, 1827, at this residence in this County, John Adair, Esq., at the advanced age of ninety-five years. He was among the early settlers in this County, a man of enterprise and respectability, for many years an Elder in the Presbyterian Church; unblemished in his deportment with the world and continued to the end to evince in the integrity if his heart and sincerity of his profession."

His wife's name is not certainly known, but Mother Louisa Smith, the oldest known living descendant of John Adair, says "to the best of her knowledge, Mrs. Adair's name was Ellen Crawford."

No date is given of their marriage. The number of their children is not known.

Until quite recently it was thought that Adair's only child was a daughter, Mary, who married Robert Christian, son of Gilbert Christian, of Sullivan County, and it was thought that Mary and Robert Christian had a lone child, a daughter, Maria, who married John Smith, but now it appears that the Christians had other children besides Maria Smith.

According to Historian Calvin M. McClung (now dead), John Adair, Sr., had a son named John Adair, Jr., who applied for a pension from Wayne County, Ky., aged 78 years, the 24th day of September, 1832. He was born in Ireland in the County of Antrim, 1754. His father, with him and the family, came to America, and landed in Baltimore, the year he cannot state, but it was when he was a youth not quite 18 years of age. His father lived in Maryland upwards of a year. He moved to Pennsylvania and stayed there a year. When the War of the Revolution commenced, he was living in Sullivan County, N.C. (coming there about 1772), and lived there until 1791, when he moved to Knox County, Tenn. He lived in Tennessee for 14 years. Then moved to

Wayne County, Ky., 28 years of age, where he has since lived. He lived in Sullivan County, N.C., where he entered the service of the United States as a private volunteer. He states that it was usual in that part of the country where he lived for men to volunteer in small companies without any commissioned officer. He states the captain or supreme officer who commenced in their expedition was named McCampbell."

"This John Adair goes on to state that his father, John Adair, was drafted, and he went out in his place in 1780. His pension was granted."

John Adair, Sr., made a "Will," and willed everything to his wife, and made no mention of any of his children.

Several other Adairs, relatives of John Adair, Sr., came out from Ireland later, and settled in and around Knoxville. They must have lived near the Washington Church, as they are buried in that churchyard. Hon. John Adair had one brother, David, who lived here, and is probable that James Adair was also a brother. David Adair's "Will," September, 1821, speaks of his brother John, his two oldest sons, David and Alexander, and son John and grandson Robert Adair. He makes his two oldest sons and his brother John executors of his will, which is signed by John, and Robert Meek. This James Adair had several land grants in which he mentions the line running along his brother, John Adair's, line.

These Adairs were great in ownership of land. The records show thousands of acres belonging to them, and the Honorable John Adair, the subject of this sketch, was the largest individual landholder.

The following paragraph illustrates the intense patriotism of the populace at this period:

"Here," said Mrs. Sevier, pointing to her son, not yet sixteen years old; "here, Mr. Sevier, is another one of our boys that wants to go with his father and brother to the war, but we have no horse for him, and, poor fellow, it is a great distance to walk." (This shows the patriotism of the populace.)

The Americans were victorious at the battle of Kings Mountain, in fact, they practically annihilated the British army under the command of Col. Ferguson and is discouraged Lord Cornwallis and demoralized the whole British force, so that they pushed on east and surrendered at Yorktown and ended the war. Kings Mountain was the turning point and, therefore, an important battle of the Revolutionary War.

In 1788 John Adair was commissioner for purchasing supplies for the Cumberland Guard, which acted as escort for travelers through the wilderness to the Cumberland Plateau.

In 1794, after Blount College had been established, he was elected one of its trustees. In 1796 Adair was a member of the Constitutional Convention which made the first Constitution of Tennessee. He was one of the Elders of the first Presbyterian Church established in Tennessee. He was a Presidential Elector for the Hamilton District in 1796 and 1800.

The North Carolina Legislature granted him a section of land four and one-half miles north of the center of the city of Knoxville. It is now in the city of Knoxville and called Adair Station. A little creek runs through the place called Adair Creek. He built him a house something on the order of a block house. Adair and Gen. James White were contemporaries and friends. The latter founded Knoxville in 1792, and Adair was one of the Commissioners.

So far as known, John Adair had only one child, a daughter named Mary Adair. She married Robert Christian, whose father was a citizen of Sullivan County.

Robert and Mary Christian had one child; a daughter named Maria Christian.

John Adair died in 1827, aged above ninety years. He and his wife are buried on a knoll on their old homestead.

LINE E

CHAPTER XLIV:

GENERAL DAVIESS LAFAYETTE ADAIR
His Ancestors and Descendants

1 Joseph Adair was born in Ireland about 1760. Our knowledge of his lineage and youth is very meager. The first we hear of him he had landed in Pennsylvania; the next we hear of him he is in Ohio, at Aberdeen, some distance above Cincinnati by the river. He married 2 Miss Chiles.

1 Joseph Adair=2 Miss Chiles
Progeny: Four Children

3	I	Isaac Adair.
4	II	Alexander Adair.
5	III	Abner Adair.
6	IV	Mary Adair, who married a Mr. Moore at Aberdeen, Ohio.

The family all moved to Kentucky.

4 Alexander Adair married and settled in Green County, Ky., and his descendants are still at Greensburg.

5 Abner Adair married and went to Kansas City, where they had two sons.

3 Isaac Adair studied medicine, settled at Elizabethtown, Ky., and married. He was a surgeon and second to Governor Adair in his field of honor meet with General Andrew Jackson, 1816.

3 Doctor Isaac Adair=7 Miss Millian Edwards
Progeny: Two Children

| | I | Daviess Lafayette Adair. |
| 9 | II | Mary Adair. |

Mary Adair=10 Mr. Riddle

They settled in St. Joseph, Mo.

Progeny: Three Children

11	I	Will Riddle, a druggist in Helena, Mont.
12	II	Haden Riddle.
13	III	Belle Riddle, m a 14 Mr. Smith, and lives in Oshkosh, Wis.

1849
8 Daviess Lafayette Adair=15 Sarah Ann Sterett

Son of Doctor Isaac Adair.

Progeny: Eight Children

| 16 | I | Millian Adair, d in childhood. |

17	II	Eliza Adair.
18	III	William Sterett Adair, of Dallas
19	IV	John Sterett Adair.
20	V	Mary Adair, m Ed Johnson; lives in Vermillion, Kans. Progeny: None.
21	VI	Dood Jefferson Adair.
22	VII	Isaac Chiles Adair.
23	VIII	Joseph Adair, d in childhood.

18 William Sterett Adair=**24** Mae Swinton Figh

Is an editorial writer on the Dallas Daily

News and magazine writer of note.

Progeny: Two Sons

25	I	John R. Adair, a comedian and violinist with the Keith Circuit of the theaters in the East.
27	II	D.L. Adair, Jr., is a mechanical and electrical engineer.

1916

27 D.L. Adair, Jr.=**18** Vera Gary

Progeny: Three Children

29	I	Margareet Adair.
30	II	David Adair.
31	III	William Sterett Adair, Jr.

1891

22 Isaac Chiles Adair=**32** Louise McAdams

Seventh Child of Gen. D.L. Adair

Progeny: One Child

33   I   Marion Adair, b Aug. 8, 1892.

(First marriage) **33** Miss Marion Adair=**34** James Hastings Snoden

1909

Granddaughter of Gen. D.L. Adair.   A Many times millionaire oil operator of New York.

1923

(Second marriage) **33** Marion Adair=**35** Walter Sherman Davidson

Progeny: Three Snowden Children

36	I	Marion Snoden.
37	II	Janet Snoden.
38	III	James Snoden, Jr.

19 John Sterett Adair, a lawyer, banker and Politician. He is the fourth child of Gen. D.L. Adair.

1882
19 John Sterett Adair=39 Cora Brown
Progeny: One Daughter
40   I   Brownie Adair.

1912
40 Miss Brownie Adair=41 Henry Calhoun Gans
Daughter of John S. Adair.
Progeny: Two Children
42   I   Mary Laurrier Gans.
43   II   Henry Calhoun Gans, Jr.

21 Miss Dood Jefferson Adair is a single daughter of General D.L. Adair. Postmaster at Hawesville for 14 years; she is a politician, often attends conventions in the capacity of delegate. She toured Kentucky in the interest of Roosevelt in 1912 and for Harding in 1920.

17 Miss Eliza Adair, the General's second daughter is a lawyer, but does not practice. She is noted for superior intelligence.

Having finished school at Elizabethtown, Davies LaFayette Adair went to Hawesville, Ky., in 1839, where he studied law and civil engineering under his half-brother, James E. Stone, who was clerk of the county and circuit courts. At the age of 21 he entered largely into the practice of civil engineering in Hancock and adjoining counties. His plots and maps were so correct that they are still the guides of land surveyors. He owned and edited the first newspaper published in that part of the State, the Pick and Plow. He conducted the defense in the celebrated murder trial of Moses and Robert Kelly, who were hanged at Hawesville in 1853, and afterward wrote a history of the crime, which in book form went through two large, illustrated editions.

He was the earliest florist, horticulturist, fine stock raiser and beekeeper in Western Kentucky. His volumes on Bee Culture gained for him a national reputation, were translated into several foreign languages, and are to this day authority on the subject. His article on the Queen Bee is regarded as a masterpiece of literature. No improvement has ever been made in his sectional beehive, which he patented in 1867, and his meliput, a machine for extracting honey from the comb by centrifugal force, patented about the same time, is in use by beekeepers all over the world. All his life he was a contributor to scientific and historical magazines. He was authority on the geology and botany of Western Kentucky and was recognized as such by Prof. Shaler and Asa Gray. He was known locally as a mechanical genius, a mathematical prodigy, and was famed for a memory that never failed him even in the minutest details.

When the war with Mexico started, he enlisted in the Fourth Kentucky infantry, and was appointed quartermaster sergeant under Colonel John S. Williams, but was honorably discharged before the end of the war on account of wounds sustained while in the line of duty. The following extract from a letter he wrote from Camp Owsley, near Vera Cruz, Nov. 22, 1847, will show what he thought of the war:

"The trip has thus far been a source of great pleasure, amusement and information. I am doubly anxious to proceed into the interior. I had some idea of seeking glory while out here, but such an idea is out of the question now. It is the general belief that there will be no more fighting; and even if there should be, there is, in my judgement, very little to be gained by whipping such people as there. When I entered Vera Cruz and saw the people, I blushed with shame at the thought of warring against them. They are small, weakly, half made-up being, much better calculated to excite compassion than to stir the martial spirit."

Davies Lafayette Adair was married to Sarah Ann Sterett at Hawesville, Dec. 21, 1849. Eight children were born to them: W.S. Adair of Dallas, Texas; John S. Adair, Havana, Cuba; Isaac Chiles Adair, deceased; Joseph Adair, deceased; Millie Adair, deceased; Mrs. Edward Johnson, Kansas City; and Misses Eliza and Dood Adair, Hawesville, Ky. The grandchildren are: D.L. Adair, electrical and mechanical engineer, Dallas, Texas; John Rufus Adair, comedian and musician, on the vauderville stage; Mrs. Brownie Adair Gans, Louisville, Ky., and Mrs. Marian Adair Davidson, Constantinople, Turkey, and New York. The great-grandchildren are Marian, Janet and James H. Snowden, New York; Mary Quarrier Gans and Henry Callhoun Gans of Louisville, Ky., and Margaret, David L. and William S. Adair of Dallas, Texas.

LINE F

CHAPTER XLV

SIR JAMES ADAIR, BART
AND SOME OF HIS DESCENDANTS IN AMERICA

1 Sir James Adair, Bart, of Scotch parentage, was born in Ballynahinch, County Down, Ireland, in 1724. He married Anne, daughter of James, Earl of Cleland. She was born in 1727 on her father's estate near Belfast, Ireland.

1748
1 Sir James Adair, Bart=**2** Anne, daughter of James, Earl of Cleland
Progeny: Five Children

4	I	William Adair.
5	II	Robert Adair.
6	III	John Adair
	IV	Lavinia Adair.
	V	Elizabeth Adair.

7 Sir William Adair, Bart, was born in Ballynahinch, Ireland, 1752. He married 8 Esther Smilie, who was born in Galloway County, Scotland, in 1755. They came to America in 1778 and settled in the southern part of Westmoreland County, Pa., where they remained until their death, and are buried there.

7 Sir William Adair=Esther Smilie
Progeny: Six Children

9	I	Elizabeth Adair, m Andrew Frazier and came to American in 1801; settled in Philadelphia, later moving to Brown County, Ohio. Her son, 10 James, was a missionary to Syria.
11	II	Anne Adair, m Mr. Black and remained in Ireland.
13	IV	John Adair, who lived in Union Township, Fayette County, Pa.
14	V	James Cleland Adair, who remained in Ireland until his education was finished, came to American in 1803. He married 16 Belinda Jones of Hagarstown, Md.
15	VI	Patrick Adair, m 17 Ann Anderson, moved to Wayne County, Ohio.

18 James Cleland Adair was born in Ballynahinch, County Down, Ireland, Feb. 29, 1786. Remained there until his education was completed in 1803. He then came to his father's in Westmoreland County, Pa. He moved to Uniontown, Fayette County, Pa., where he taught a preparatory school. In

1835 he moved with his family to Jackson County, Ohio. In 1854 they moved to Jay County, Ind., where he lived the remainder of his life, and his and his wife were buried there.

1809
18 James Cleland Adair=16 Belinda Jones of Hagarstown, Md.
Progeny: Nine Children

19	I	Anne Adair, b Oct. 10, 1810, m James Golden.
20	II	William Patrick Adair, b June 5, 1812, m 33 Aurilla Prentiss.
21	III	Lavenia Adair, b Aug. 31, 1814, m 34 Thos. Frazier
22	IV	John Jones Adair, b July 9, 1816; m 35 Mary Ann Kreeps.
23	V	Mary Jane Adair, b Dec. 27, 1818.
24	VI	Robert Smilie Adair, b April 2, 1821; m 36 Lucy Whitcome.
25	VII	Eliza B. Adair, b Oct. 1, 1823; m 37 Chas. McClure.
26	VIII	James Guthrie Adair, b Aug. 11, 1820; m 28 Sarah Hutson.
27	IX	Belinda Adair, d young and unmarried.

30 John A.M. Adair is the youngest son of 26 James Guthrie Adair, and grandson of James Cleland Adair. He was a former Congressman from the Portland District of Indiana. He ranked high as a congressman and was chairman of the Committee on Expenditures in the War Department.

23 Mary Jane Adair was born in Fayette County, Pa., Dec. 27, 1818; moved with her father to Jackson County, Ohio, in 1835. In 1837 she was married to 29 David Poor. In 1849 they came to Jay County, Ind., where they lived on a farm two miles north of Portland, Ind.

1837
23 Mary Jane Adair=37 David Poor
Progeny: Four Children

38	I	James Adair Poor, b in Jackson Co., Ohio, Aug. 31, 1837; d Jan. 2, 1885.
39	II	Cynthia Belinda Poor, b in Jackson Co., Ohio, 1842; m 42 J.A. Harvey.
40	III	Hugh Gample Poor, b in Jackson Co., Ohio, Nov. 30, 1844.
41	IV	Helen Mar Poor, b Jan. 5, 1859, in Jay Co., Ind.; m 43 George W. Hall.

41 Helen Mar Poor married 44 G.W. Hall, a prominent lawyer in Portland, Ind. Residence 1160 West Walnut St.

1884
41 Helen Mar Poor=44 George W. Hall
Progeny: Two Children

45	I	Donald Adair Hall, b Aug. 3, 1885; m 47 Vadia Holmes, Oct. 30, 1909.

46   II   Jean Johnston Hall, b Oct. 14, 1892; m 48 Francis D. Stokes, March 4, 1910.

45 Donald Adair Hall, born 1885; attended De Pauws University at Greencastle, Ind., and Cornell University at Ithica, N.Y. Married 47 Vadia Holmes in Portland, Oct. 30, 1909. For a number of years Mr. Hall was private secretary to Congressman Adair. He is now engaged in manufacturing business. Residence, 503 West Walnut St., Portland, Ind.

1909
45 Donald Adair Hall=47 Vadia Holmes
Progeny: Two Children

50   I   Helen Holmes Hall, b Aug. 30, 1910.
51   II   Lee George Hall, b Aug. 16, 1915.

46 Jean Johnston Hall was born Oct. 14, 1892. Attended Mary Baldwin Seminary at Staunton, Va. Married 48 Francis D. Stokes. Residence, 500 Prospect Ave., N.E. Grand Rapids, Mich.

1910
46 Jean Johnston Hall-48 Francis D. Stokes
Progeny: Two Children

53   I   Maybell Dudley Stokes, b July 29, 1910.
54   II   Jean Hall Stokes, b Dex. 16, 1912.

38 James Adair Poor=55 Sarah Amanda Milligan
Son of Mary Jane and David Poor

Progeny
56   David Homer Poor, and others.

46 David Homer Poor=57 Lydia Alwilda Smith
Son of James Adair Poor and
Sarah Amanda Milligan Poor.

Progeny:
58   Mary Ann Poor of Porland, Ind.

LINE G

CHAPTER XLVI

GEORGE BANCROFT ADAIR OF SEATTLE

GEORGE BANCROFT ADAIR, son of 1 Henry and Mary (Van Tuyl) Adair, was born in Romulus, Seneca County, N.Y., July 13, 1847. He spent the earlier period of his boyhood in the vicinity of Senecca Falls, receiving part of his schooling there. Removing to Syracuse at an early age (13 years), he apprenticed himself, as was the custom, in the hardware business. Soon he had made such successful progress in business life that he decided to take up and finish his education, which he did by completing a four years' course in Ames College, now known as the University of Syracuse.

After leaving this institution, seeking broader opportunity for advancement in commercial life, he entered the employ of a large hardware concern in Elmira, N.Y., where he remained until 1868. At that time, his health being none too rugged, he decided that a change of climate might prove beneficial to him. In keeping with his decision, he arranged to join his father, who was at that time developing a large ranch in California, to the eastward of San Francisco. Taking his mother with him, he made the trip by way of the Isthmus of Panama, crossing the Isthmus on the old railroad in use at that time.

Shortly after joining his father, not being able to accommodate himself to the life, after his training along mercantile lines, he took a position teaching the school of that district. He did not continue long at this, however, for before many months had passed the management of Hooker & Co., a large wholesale hardware and supply house in San Franciso, had sought him out and arranged for him to take over one of their departments and manage it. He remained with this concern until 1872, when he associated himself with Pillsbury & Co., same city, large hardware jobbers and brokers, as a silent partner. This concern afterward became Pillsbury, Hussey, Adair & Co., well known in San Francisco business circles. The partnership, however, was dissolved through unfavorable circumstances, and in 1876 Mr. Adair removed to Napa, California, where he entered partnership with A.G. Clark & Co., a large hardware concern.

Critical illness overtaking him here, made it necessary that he give up all business activity for a period, hence this business was disposed of. During the latter part of 1878, having meantime returned to San Francisco, he associated himself with James E. Gordon & Co., a jobbing and importing house in the hardware line. In 1883, very important business matters arising in Seattle, Wash., it was found that immediate personal representation was most necessary, and Mr. Adair went to Seattle on that mission, not only has connected with his own company's interests, but as special representative of the San Francisco Board of Trade, on that and various other matters.

It was during this visit that he foresaw some of the great opportunities for the development of Seattle and the Northwest country. Deciding to remain in Seattle, he organized the Gordon Hardware Co., a concern which rapidly grew to be the largest concern of its character in the entire Northwest, prospering and growing with the city and its environment. He remained with this concern as its manager and treasurer until 1893.

The president of this concern having been deceased for some little period, and the other relationships being of a character not in harmony with his ideas, he withdrew from the company, entering business for himself as special representative of the lines of some of his former old connections. This business prospered, and in 1895 his son, George H., entered partnership with him, which relationship continued, with slight changes, until July 8, 1918, at the time of his death.

Aside from being very prominent in business associations along the entire coast, he was most active in civic affairs and matters of general welfare to his community. In his San Francisco life he was always prominent in business associations and trade organizations, being especially strongly identified with the San Franciso Board of Trade for a long period of years. As soon as he had definitely determined to remain in Seattle, he, in 1884, was instrumental in organizing the Seattle Board of Trade, of which he was president until its merger with the Seattle Chamber of Commerce after the Seattle fire.

This Board of Trade was a power for good and advancement in the early days of the city, accomplishing much which had vitally to do with the permanent growth and prosperity of Seattle and the Puget Sound country. Probably its most signal achievement was its victory in compelling the Northern Pacific Railroad to recognize Seattle as a terminal point and connect her with the rest of the country by rail. It was a bitter fight with millions of money behind Tacoma and the railroad interests but this plucky little body of men won the day.

He never had political aspirations of any character, his nearest political office being that of honorary aide to Governor Watson C. Squire during his term as Governor of Washington. He did, however, take a most active and determined part in all political affairs, especially when there was any question of good government at stake. He was an active member of Seattle's first Charter Commission, sitting in that body for forty days.

With fraternal organizations he had very little to do, claiming to have too little time for attention to them and his other duties. He mingled somewhat socially and in social organizations. He was a member of the Seattle Chamber of Commerce—one of its oldest members—and a charter member of the Arctic Club, an organization in which he took much pleasure.

The earlier years of his life he was an official and most active member of the Methodist Episcopal Church. This affiliation was dropped some years before his decease, and he became a supporter of the Presbyterian Church and a very warm adherent of Rev. W.A. Major, pastor of this church.

As to his family life, he was married Aug. 10, 1871, to Martha Elizabeth Jones, daughter of Seneca and Elizabeth Jones, early pioneers of San Francisco, prominent in church and social life there. This union was of exceptional happiness, and into it were born 9 George Henry, 10 Edna Elizabeth, 13 Georgia May, 14 Florence Lesle, 11 Winifred, and 12 Ruby Jean, all of whom survive with the exception of 10 Edna Elizabeth, who died in early childhood.

His personality was extremely strong, yet pleasingly magnetic, these qualities being most strongly exemplified in his home ties; the remarkable evidence of this being patent in that none of the children—nor grandchildren, of which there are four—has ever removed from the near vicinity and influence of the home which he established and held together with his love and presence—and now holds with memories. G.H.A.

Feb. 6, 1923.

CHAPTER XLVII:
HINGS FOR FUTURE INVESTIGATION

List of records of proof of military services in the War of the Revolution. These records were made right after the war but copied lately for this work. We publish this list for the convenience of persons who desire evidence of eligibility for membership in patriotic societies, such as the D.A.R. and Sons of the Revolution.

It must be remembered that South Carolina paid its own soldiers soon after the revolutionary war.

State of South Carolina:
To Alexander Adair £ Shillings Pence
Charleston Army settlement   88   00   0
Received settlement.

State of South Carolina:
To Benjamin Adair   £   12   2   10
For horse lost in 1779.

State of South Carolina:
To Isaac Adair
His account of military duty as private in Charleston Army
£   192-   10-   0
£   27-   10-   0

Received payment from the Treasury, June 14, 1785.
State of South Carolina: September 7, 1783.
Received of James Adair, Sr., 200 lbs. of flour for the use of widows and distressed families of Colonel Casy's Regiment.
JOSEPH ADAIR, SSR., Co. D Commissary.

State of South Carolina:
To James Adair.   Duty per Col. Anderson's Regiment.
To military duty before and since the reduction of Charleston.
£ 566 -- --
£ 60 17 1 ½

178. 0 State of South Carolina to Jas. Adair:
To services done as wagon master for Col. James Williams' Regiment on duty from 29 day of March, 1780, to 20 May, both days included, being 52 days.
£   169-   0-   0
£   24-   2-   10 ¼
Settled.

State of South Carolina:
    Jas. Adair, Jr., 200 lbs. flour   £   1-   17-   6
Paid for recovery of horses lost at Augusta
    In May, 1779   £   7-   6-   6¼

                       £   9-   4-   1¼

State of South Carolina: To Jas. Adair; his acct. for 120 days of military duty in Gen. Marion's Brigade in 1781, also for gun.
    Charges for duty   1/6   £   9-   0-   0
    Charges for gun impressed   £   1-   3-   4
    Deduct loss on duty   8-   7

                       £   9-   14-   9

Sept., 1784.
Vouched by Hugh Harry, Lt. Col, Commanding.
    (Mr. Salley, secretary of the South Carolina Historical Commission, said this was not a Laurens County Adair, and that he has his autograph on record as "Adare.")

State of South Carolina: To John Adair
    His account for military duty as private since the reduction of
Charleston   Sterling   £   60-   0-   0
                       £   8-   11-   5

Received satisfaction, June 14, 1785.
    (Orders and Indents on file.)
State of South Carolina: To John Adair
    His account for sundries for military use amounts to
                       £   268-   14-   3/4.
                       Received satisfaction.

State of South Carolina: To Jospeh Adair, Sr.
    His account of number of days duty as Commissary, for provisions, forage, hire of wagon and team & so forth for militia account in 1781.
         Sterling   £   673-   19-   9
                  £   96-   5-   8

A Commissary Pay Bill of Joseph Adair, Sr., Commissary, commencing 20 of Aug., 1781. ? in March, 1782, both days included.
    Full itemized expense list is on record and has been photographed by Lyles Studio of Columbia, and is certified by Levi Casey, Colonel.

State of South Carolina: To William Adair
    June 18, 1780—To 60 days as adjutant   £   38-   11-   5
    Feb. 12, 1781—To 30 days as adjutant
    Less   £   9-   12-   11

    Amount due   £   28-   18-   6

(Sworn to by Lt. Col. Casy.)
State of South Carolina: To William Adair

Sept. 19, 1781—Received of William Adair 1070 lbs. flour, 5 ½ bushels of wheat, 5 bushels of corn, for the use of widows and distressed families in Col. Casey's Regiment.

Sworn to by Col. Casey. Per Joseph Adair, Sr., Commissary Co. D.

Sarah Adair has an account of salt and wagon furnished the Militia on record.

There are numerous wills on file at Lauren Court House during the XIX century that will be interesting in the study of special lines of descent, and there has been a fast amount of trading in land by the Adairs, all of which will interest a special investigator of any particular lines.

Pennsylvania has furnished ten Adair soldiers in the American Army during the War of the Revolution, which are available, published in the Military Annals of the Revolution for that State.

The posterity of the Pennsylvania Adairs have greatly scattered to the states to the westward since the revolution; therefore are difficult to trace.

GEORGE ADE

George Ade, author and journalist, born at Keland, Newton Co., Ind., Feb. 9, 1866, was the son of John and Adaline Bush Ade, and his grandparents of the maternal side were Adairs.

He was graduated at the Purdue University, Lafayette, Ind. He attained his B.S. degree in 1887. Afterward became a reporter and telegraph editor on Lafayette Evening Call. From there he went in 1891 to Chicago, where he was employed as reporter on the morning issue of the Chicago daily News, now known as the Chicago Record. He is still engaged in general and special work on the staff of the Record.

Mr. Ade is widely known as the author of many humorous sketches which have appeared in newspapers and which have afterward been rewritten and published in book form.

The common-sense, as well as the fun contained in these volumes, appeal to a very large public and quickly brought their author into favorable notice. In a picturesque dialect he writes of everyday life, which he sees from an individual point of view and renderers with a delightful freshness of observation.

Some of his published works are "Artie" (1896), Pinck Marsh (1897), "Doc. Home" (1898), "Fables in Slang" (1899) and "More Fables" in 1900.

Mr. Ade lives on Hazelden Farm, Brook, Indiana.

The following two lineage tables without dates were furnished by Mrs. Josie Bell Gaston of Montgomery, Alabama. Having no dates, we place them on a special page.

James Moore=Eliza Neufville
William Adair=Mary Moore
Mary Adair=John Nixon, 1st Husband
Mary Adair=David McCalla, 2d Husband
John Hemphill=Mary Nixon
Joseph Lucius Gaston=Margaret Hemphill
Joseph Lucius Gaston, Jr.=Josie Butna Bell
George W. Gage=Jani Gaston

Jani and Lucius Gaston were the only children of Lucius Gaston, and Margaret Hemphill.

James Moore=Eliza Neufville
William Adair=Mary Moore
David McCalla=Mary Adair
James Moore McCalla=Butna Hemphill
John P. Bell=Isabella Hemphill Caldwell
Mason A. Posey=Jani Marlin Bell
Joseph Lucius Gaston=Josie Butna Bell

Jani and Josie Bell were the only children of John and Isabella Bell.

THE MISSISSIPPI ADAIRS

JOHN ADAIR, was born, reared, educated and married in the north of Ireland.

They migrated to America about 1765 and settled in South Carolina. He became a soldier in the American Army, Gen. Francis Marion's Brigade. John Adair came to his death at the hands of the Tories while on a furlow home from the Army of Independence.

It appears that at that time the Tories were making up a company of young men to join the British forces, and they could not agree who should be Captain of the new Company, and it was agreed that the first man to kill a loyal American soldier should be Captain. So, a squad sought to kill John Adair whom they knew was at his home at the time. So, they proceeded to his cabin and let him know their business, where-upon John closed the cabin door and having two guns handy proceeded to fire at the Tories, while Ruth, his wife, loaded the guns. He succeeded in killing seven of the invaders before his ammunition was exhausted. He tried then to make his escape through a back door, but before he got far was shot down and killed. The outlaws then proceeded to burn down the cabin, leaving the mother and three little children to the mercy of the wild beasts which then infested the country, which was somewhere in one of the Carolinas. His wife then built a pen of common rails and covered it the best she could and placed her offspring therein to ward off the wolves until she could make her way to the neighbors six miles away for help. There is no record that Ruth, the widow of John Adair, ever married again, but managed to rear her children as best she could.

For proof of military service rendered the American Revolution in South Carolina by John Adair, father of the Mississippi branch. See page 299. The other John Adair mentioned on that page was a son of Joseph Adair, Jr.

*****

John Adair=Ruth Greer

Was the American soldier She was Scotch. murdered by Tories near the close of the Revolution.

Progeny: 3 children, all small when their father was murdered.
  I Isaac, b. 1778, d. 1871, age 93.
  II Jacob, posterity unknown to his brother and sister.
  III * Jane, * m. Mr. Reid.

Isaac Adair Mary= Walker Crenshaw

Son of John Adair, the American
soldier who was cruelly murdered
by Tories, as above recited.

Progeny: 13 children, 4 daughters and 9 sons.

I Ruth m. Frank A. Allen, eight children, Marsalis H., John R., Mary, Sallie, James Polk, Isaac N., Thomas and Ruth.

II Daniel Adair, m. Stacy Russell, nine children, John, William, Marion, Sallie, Mary Sam, James, Daniel and Belle.

III Johnathan, died young.

IV Weyman, died young.

IV Pleasant Walker, m. Marthia Ann Herring, six children, Issabelle, Susan Ann, Lee Roy, Fannie, Marthia and Willie.

V Pleasant Walker, m. Marthia Ann Herring, six children, Issabelle, Susan Ann, Lee Roy, Fannie, Marthia and Willie.

VI Granger Adair, m. Mary Parker, four children, William, Mollie, Lula and Walter.

VII Francis Marion Adair, m. Sarah Ann Thompson, one child, Mollie.

VIII Mary Adair, m. William Moore first and then Robert Martin, there were five Moore children, Monroe, Alfred, Rachel, Sallie, and William, and four Martin children, but names forgotten.

IX Issabelle, died young.

X Susan Adair m. Argyle Heslip, several children, names not known.

XI James C. Adair m. Kisiah Herring, six children, Thomas, Mollie, Denman, moved away to Texas; Mark, died young, Banner died young, married, but no children. Kissiah m. Frank Shaw, several children; Drewetta m. James Bell, several children; Ped W., married and resides in New York city, one child; Absolem Isaac Adair m. Miss Stafford, four children; Norman m. Annie Thompson, no children; Lula Adair m. Mr. Haynes, one child; Clemie not married, and John Lee Adair, not married, saw service in France during the World War; and remained on the Rhine with the Army of Occupation several months after the Armistice.

XII William H. Adair was a Captain in the war between the States.

XIII Thomas Nepolion Adair, was a physician and Colonel in Confederate Army and wounded five times.

*****

Ruth Adair=Frank A. Allen

Progeny: 8 children, 5 sons and 3 daughters.

I Marsalis H. (called Art) spent two years of his young manhood in California, near Sacramento; served through-out the Civil War as Lieutenant, served two terms in Mississippi Legislature, died age 82, 3 children, John R., Anna, and Marsalis H., Jr.

II John R. Allen served throughout the Civil War as Captain, moved to Arkansas directly after the War and became Sheriff for several years of Little River County, and was in good circumstance when he died, age 79 years.

III Mary Allen m. Robert Walpole, a writer of some distinction, and an Editor, both dead, children reside in Florida. IV Sallie Allen m. Wash Irvine a large merchant, three children, Allen, Lula Allen Irvine, m. Rasmus Flowers, several children.

V William Allen served throughout Civil War, severely wounded, m. Miss Flowers and reared several children.

VI James Polk Allen, served one year in Civil War, died soon after.

VII Isaac N. Allen, became a merchant, but died when a young man.

VIII Thomas Allen, died soon after growing to manhood.

IX Ruth Allen, died in young womanhood.

*****

Captain William H. Adair=Miss Elisabeth Frances Ross
Progeny: 3 children, 2 sons, 1 daughter.

I Lory Lawless Adair, was a lawyer, and died in Arkansas. in 1880.

II Urilda Alice, m. Joe T. Crewshaw, a distant relative.
Three living children, Lory, Frank and Joe.

III Charles Pinkney Adair, b. 1858, 12 miles south of Sacramento, Calif. To where the family had migrated and settled in 1847, but returned to Mississippi in 1860. Charles Pinkney Adair educated himself for a lawyer, but only practiced his chosen profession a few years before drifting into the editorial work of newspaperdom, in which avocation he was regarded as successful. He quit the editorial work in 1904 and engaged in farming, building, buying, renting and owning farm and city property. He was mayor of his hometown, Indianola, Miss., for three terms and represented Sunflower County in the Mississippi Legislature in 1908-10. He is an elder in the Presbyterian Church, a 32d degree Mason and a Knight Templar, and has been for 25 years local correspondent of Memphis and New Orleans papers.

Charles Pinkney Adair=Julia Eldridge Colmerg
Progeny, none. Present address, Indianola.

*****

Col. Thomas Nepolion Adair=Elizabeth Frances Adair·
widow of his deceased brother William H. after his death at Vicksburg

I William Thomas Adair. He married Pauline Valentine to whom no children are born. William Thomas is quite an extensive planter in the Yazoo, Miss., delta, cultivating about 2000 acres of that fertile land, all his own. Present address, Doddsville.

*****

More complete biographical material as to Charles Noble, Page 124, No. 424.

Charles Noble, fourth child of Ann Catharine Pleasants and Rev. Mason Noble. Born in New York City, December 3, 1847. Rev. Charles Noble was a great grandson of Governor Adair.

Educated at Rittenhouse Academy, Washington, D. C. Williams College, Mass., class of 1866. Union Theological Seminary, New York, 1871.

Two semesters at University of Berlin, 1872-3. Other special studies at Harvard University and six months at Oxford University, England.

Married: (1) Alice Thomas, Norwich, Conn., Jan. 21, 1874. She died May 12, 1879. (2) Mary Stedman Carlisle, Norwich, Conn., June 16, 1886.

Pastor, successively of Congregational churches at Franklin, N. Y., Woodbridge, N. J., and Charles City, Iowa. Professor of English at Grinnell College, Iowa, 1893-1919. Since that Emeritus. Residing in Washington since 1920.

Published "Studies in American Literature," MacMillan, N. Y. "The Story of English Speech," Badger, Boston. "Grinnell Vespers: The Abundant Life," Torch Press, Cedar Rapids, Iowa.

LINEAGE OF MARY MOORE ADAIR
Wife of William Adair, and mother of Governor Adair.

We have had numerous calls for this lineage; and the following copy of it is furnished by a great granddaughter of Governor Adair, to wit: Mrs. M. H. Affleck of Brenham, Texas. The father of Mrs. Mary Moore Adair was James Moore, Jr., Governor of South Carolina in 1719, and the wife mother was Eliza Neufville. The grandfather was James Moore, Sr., Governor of South Carolina in 1700; whose wife was Lady Berringer, a stepdaughter of Sir John Yeamans. The line is traced on back through Lady Margaret Foster and Lieut. Berringer, who came to America, S. C., from Barbados in 1663. And the celebrated Irish conspirator against Cromwell.

ACKNOWLEDGMENT

The Adair History and Genealogy has been published and in the hands of its readers for nearly two years, and the Editor has received unstinted praise from scores of readers, for which he hereby tenders his sincere thanks.

This book will perpetuate the names and good deeds of those members who have been stilled by death; and it should be a source of pride and invaluable information to their progeny.

To my dear wife, Virginia Hare Adair, whose counsel and cooperation have helped to make the book a success, this volume is respectfully dedicated as a loving remembrance from her husband.

www.ingramcontent.com/pod-product-compliance
Lightning Source LLC
Chambersburg PA
CBHW071812160426
43209CB00032B/1938/J